Also in the Variorum Collected Studies Series

JOHN MONFASANI
Language and Learning in Renaissance Italy: Selected Articles

JOHN MONFASANI
Byzantine Scholars in Renaissance Italy: Cardinal Bessarion and Other Emigrés

D. S. CHAMBERS
Individuals and Institutions in Renaissance Italy

D. S. CHAMBERS
Renaissance Cardinals and their Worldly Problems

PAUL F. GRENDLER
Books and Schools in the Italian Renaissance

RICHARD SHERR
Music and Musicians in Renaissance Rome and Other Courts

VINCENT ILARDI
Studies in Italian Renaissance Diplomatic History

EDWARD P. MAHONEY
Two Aristotelians of the Italian Renaissance: Nicoletto Vemia and Agostino Nifo

JOHN E. LAW
Venice and the Veneto in the Early Renaissance

RICHARD A. GOLDTHWAITE
Banks, Palaces and Entrepreneurs in Renaissance Florence

J. B. TRAPP
Essays in the Renaissance and the Classical Tradition

DAVID ABULAFIA
Italy, Sicily and the Mediterranean, 1100–1400

G. A. LOUD
Conquerors and Churchmen in Norman Italy

ROGER LING
Stuccowork and Painting in Roman Italy

VARIORUM COLLECTED STUDIES SERIES

Courts and Courtiers in Renaissance Northern Italy

Stephen Kolsky

Courts and Courtiers in Renaissance Northern Italy

Routledge
Taylor & Francis Group
LONDON AND NEW YORK

First published 2003 by Ashgate Publishing

2 Park Square, Milton Park, Abingdon, Oxfordshire OX14 4RN
711 Third Avenue, New York, NY 10017

Routledge is an imprint of the Taylor & Francis Group, an informa business

First issued in paperback 2018

ISBN 978-0-86078-929-1 (hbk)
ISBN 978-1-138-37552-9 (pbk)

British Library Cataloguing-in-Publication Data
Kolsky, Stephen
Courts and Courtiers in Renaissance Northern Italy. –
(Variorum Collected Studies Series: CS779)
1. Castiglione, Baldassare, 1478–1529. Libro del cortegiano 2. Courts and Courtiers 3. Courtesy – Italy, Northern – History – 16th Century 4. Italian Literature – 16th Century – History and Criticism 5. Literature and Society – Italy, Northern – History – 16th Century 6. Courtesy Books – Italy, Northern – History – 16th Century 7. Courts and Courtiers in Literature 8. Courtesy in Literature 9. Italy, Northern – Civilization – 16th Century 10. Italy, Northern – Social Life and Customs – 16th Century. I. Title
395'. 0945'09031

US Library of Congress Cataloging-in-Publication Data
Kolsky, Stephen.
Courts and Courtiers in Renaissance Northern Italy / Stephen Kolsky.
p. cm. – (Variorum Collected Studies Series: CS779).
Includes bibliographical references and index.
1. Castiglione, Baldassarre, conte, 1478–1529. Libro del cortegiano 2.Courts and Courtiers – Italy. 3. Renaissance – Italy. 4. Courts and Courtiers – Early Works to 1800. 5. Courtesy – Early Works to 1800. I. Title. II. Collected Studies: CS779.

BJ1604.K65 2003
945'.06–dc22 2003057863

Transferred to Digital Printing in 2013

VARIORUM COLLECTED STUDIES SERIES CS779

CONTENTS

This volume contains xx + 328 pages

For my wife Helen

and son Daniel

In gratitude for

their unfailing love and support

INTRODUCTION

Baldassar Castiglione's *Book of the Courtier*, published in 1528, transcended its narrow focus on the court of Urbino to become essential reading throughout Renaissance Europe. It was quickly translated into the major European languages.[1] The work can be regarded as an authentic Renaissance bestseller on a par with Ariosto's *Orlando furioso* (published in its definitive edition in 1532).[2] The *Book of the Courtier* had its intellectual roots in the early sixteenth-century courts of northern and central Italy. Its composition follows the peripeteia of Castiglione's own career that saw him move from court to court (Mantua–Urbino–Mantua–Rome–Madrid). The author's life experiences are transformed into a text which emphasises the type of values and skills that would have currency in any kind of court society. This process of 'generalization' can be seen at work in the final draft of the *Book of the Courtier*, in the writer's elimination of numerous references to the leading actors of the northern Italian courts. Castiglione refocused the text so that its axis was no longer 'local', but more broadly international.

The minor courts that figured so prominently in earlier drafts play a much reduced role in Castiglione's 'new' text, responding to changing political conditions in Europe. In this renewed vision, the writer privileges the role of Isabella I of Spain (1451–1504), as founder of international Spanish power that would reach its apogee under Emperor Charles V (1500–1558). As a consequence, the 'other' Isabella, Isabella d'Este (1474–1539), is rather overshadowed in the final version. This considered disengagement from the 'petty' concerns of Italian court life in order to concentrate on wider implications enabled the *Book of the Courtier* to be read as relevant to all courts, whatever their geographical position.

The present collection of articles has a threefold purpose. The first is to analyse the text of the *Book of the Courtier*, subjecting it to a variety of critical approaches that highlight its changing attitudes to the role and functions of a courtier (Part 1 below). These approaches emphasise

---

[1]See Peter Burke, *The Fortunes of The Courtier: The European Reception of Castiglione's 'Cortegiano'* (Cambridge: Polity Press, 1995), pp. 55–80, 158–62.

[2]For the editorial success of Ariosto's poem see Daniel Javitch, *Proclaiming a Classic: The Canonization of Orlando furioso* (Princeton, N.J.: Princeton University Press, 1991).

Castiglione's historical context and elucidate his reactions to the European political situation in the first quarter of the sixteenth century. Secondly, this collection presents several case studies that demonstrate courtiers' efforts to enter and adapt to the power systems of the northern Italian courts. The studies argue that texts created in the courtly environment in turn contributed to contemporary concepts of court and courtier (Part 2). The third objective of this collection is to analyse the roles of women at court and the ways in which these were theorised by men (Part 3).

The themes that emerge in the three parts of this collection were central to the discourses that developed in the late fifteenth and early sixteenth centuries to justify the courtiers' privileged existence, and the 'new' modes of conduct in the northern Italian courts. Castiglione's *Book of the Courtier* not only recaps contemporary ideas about court life and behaviour, but in its final version re-views them in the light of the writer's increasingly cosmopolitan and 'internationalist' aspirations. Overall, it is one of the purposes of this book to recuperate some of those people and texts that Castiglione left behind, when he literally cancelled their names from his final drafts.

A figure that touches almost all of the courtiers treated in this collection of articles is that of Isabella d'Este. Her arrival on the cultural and political scene is marked by her marriage in 1490 to Francesco Gonzaga, Marquis of Mantua (1466–1519).[3] Isabella d'Este was the daughter of Ercole I, Duke of Ferrara (1431–1505): she formed part of the system of dynastic alliances that saw her elder sister, Beatrice (1475–1497), married to Ludovico Sforza (1451or 1452–1508), ruler of Milan, and her half-sister Lucrezia d'Este (d. 1516) espoused to Annibale Bentivoglio (1469–1540). Isabella d'Este's sister-in-law was Elisabetta Gonzaga (1471–1526), wife of Guidobaldo Montefeltro, Duke of Urbino (1472–1508), who presides over the dialogues of the *Book of the Courtier*.

Such close affiliations also included the courtiers themselves, who sometimes served in more than one court during the course of their career: Castiglione worked at different times for both the Gonzaga and the Montefeltro. Although each court presents its own set of cultural characteristics, all were bound together in a complex web of social and cultural relations. The strongest nexus that emerges from these studies is the dynamic inter-play between Mantua and Ferrara. Marriage alliances often

[3]For a brief biographical sketch of Isabella d'Este see Roberta Iotti, 'Isabella d'Este' in *Isabella d'Este. La primadonna del Rinascimento*, a cura di Daniela Bini (Modena: Il Bulino and Mantua: Artiglio, 2001), pp. 9–19.

sought to strengthen relations between smaller city-states that were increasingly threatened by the much more powerful nation-states such as France and Spain. The French entry into the Italian peninsula in 1494 upset the precarious balance of power between the Italian states. To survive in this new situation, states like Mantua and Ferrara depended on their diplomatic prowess rather than military strength. It is notable that both Castiglione and the Mantuan courtier Mario Equicola (1470–1525) placed military skills low on their list of priorities; both were extremely uncomfortable on or near a battlefield, and did their utmost to avoid it, also preferring to rely on skills in diplomacy.[4] All the figures discussed in this collection were confronted with the constant threat of loss of power and perhaps annihilation. As a result, a strong sense of emasculation and anxiety about the courtier's relations with power emerges in the writings and life experiences that are examined in the first two parts of this collection.

The *Book of the Courtier* does not stand above the vicissitudes of the courts nor of the personal *iter* of Castiglione himself. The dialectic between the powerful and the powerless becomes a focus of his writing and of his career as a diplomat (I). Specifically, his text negotiates the intemperances of political power by moving the field of combat to the private rooms of the Duchess of Urbino. At the same time, numerous manuscript redactions of the *Book of the Courtier* trace the diverse ways in which Castiglione attempted to engage with the wider realities of the court system; the changing perspectives that can be read in the manuscripts register the author's commitment to redefining the courtier as the zenith of culture. His success can be gauged not only by the innumerable translations, adaptations, and re-elaborations of the text, but also by the lasting imprint it left on Western civilisation.[5]

Thus Castiglione re-wrote some of the fundamental tenets of contemporary court culture whilst maintaining his profound attachment to its values and achievements. The *Book of the Courtier* mapped out the boundaries of good and acceptable behaviour. Yet unlike the majority of medieval and Renaissance manuals on conduct, it did not provide completely clear-cut, itemized rules and regulations. The work itself plants the seeds of inconclusivity. Its general, even ambiguous formulations left room for contrasting interpretations; indeed, certain indications in the text were

[4]See John R. Hale, 'Castiglione's Military Career', *Italian Studies*, 36 (1981), pp. 41–57.

[5]See Norbert Elias, *The History of Manners*, Volume 1 of *The Civilizing Process*, trans. Edmund Jephcott (New York: Pantheon, 1982).

increasingly read as instructions for the practice of courtly subterfuge and deception.[6]

The ultimate lack of precision is further emphasised by Castiglione's use of a non-Socratic dialogic form, along the lines of the polyphonies in Boccaccio's *Decameron.* This form in particular exposes the *Courtier* - both the text and the person - to conflicting discourses. For example, it appears that after Book III the debate on women has been 'settled'. In the final version, Giuliano de' Medici (1479–1516) has put forward seemingly decisive arguments in defence of women, 'defeating' the anti-woman faction. However, such a victory proves illusory: at the very end of the *Book of the Courtier*, Francesco Maria della Rovere (1490–1538), future Duke of Urbino and employer of Castiglione, insists that the debate ('la lite') needs to be decided in a more formal, legalistic manner. And although Francesco della Rovere desires an unambiguous settlement of the question, resolution is continually deferred; the desire for finality is expressed by the future leader but is not delivered. This brief example illustrates the way in which a kind of 'uncertainty principle' pervades the *Book of the Courtier*. Articles III, V and VI in this collection closely examine ambiguities in Castiglione's text, respecting them without flattening them out. The study on women (II) appears with these articles in Part 1 because it shares an interest in the *Book of the Courtier*'s ambiguous messages.

Perhaps the most debated issue concerning the *Book of the Courtier* is the significance and relevance of Book IV to the rest of the work. There has been a recent tendency to understate or close the gap between the first three books and the fourth, which was a late addition. The debate is important because in Book IV the role of the courtier changes almost beyond recognition: the pleasure-loving 'parasite' with only distant aspirations to seriousness becomes no less than the architect of princely policy. No doubt Castiglione envisaged a smooth transition from Book III to Book IV, evidenced by his laborious revisions. However the fit remains imperfect.

The articles on Mario Equicola (VII, VIII, IX) map out an alternative career path to that taken by Castiglione. From 1508 onwards, Equicola was always employed by the Gonzaga of Mantua, although by different members of the family.[7] Equicola's focus was on career advancement and, at first sight,

---

[6]See J.R. Woodhouse, *From Castiglione to Chesterfield: The Decline in the Courtier's Manual. An Inaugural Lecture Delivered Before the University of Oxford on 25 October 1990 in the Presence of His Excellency the President of Italy* (Oxford: Clarendon Press; New York: Oxford University Press, 1991).

[7]For Equicola's biography see Stephen Kolsky, *Mario Equicola. The Real Courtier* (Geneva: Droz, 1991).

he appears to personify the courtier of the first three books of Castiglione's *opus*, seeming consumed by the practices of court life, including the rites of *amore*. On numerous occasions Equicola served as Isabella d'Este's personal envoy in the period 1508–1519, but his main responsibility was to further the *Marchesana*'s personal politics: Isabella d'Este was normally most concerned to protect the family interests of the Gonzaga and the Estensi. By contrast, Castiglione was involved in diplomacy at a 'higher', more formal level as ambassador of princes.

Equicola's informal service indicates that a woman like Isabella d'Este needed to use her own resources if she wished to influence the course of political events. Following the logic of the *Book of the Courtier*, Equicola's personal and humanistic charms enabled him to become close to Isabella d'Este so that he could play an essential role in her personal politics. It does not appear that he influenced policy; rather he contented himself with being a willing tool in the *Marchesana*'s hands. From her point of view, one of Equicola's most attractive qualities was his intimacy with the Ferrarese court scene and in particular with her brother Alfonso d'Este (1476–1534), Duke of Ferrara after her father's death in 1505. Isabella d'Este's political strategy was based on the concept of the dynastic survival of the ruling houses of Mantua and Ferrara.

Such concepts came under increasing scrutiny from Castiglione in those years which saw the dramatic remodelling of the *Book of the Courtier*. The process of re-thinking came about because of Castiglione's contact with the papal court of Leo X (1475–1521). In some respects, the papacy may have acted as another Italian court, but it had pretensions to leadership, and a determination to subordinate other Italian states, especially the minor northern Italian states. Given the developing conflict between France and Spain for European hegemony, the papacy had a crucial role to play on the international stage. From this perspective, a Mantua or a Ferrara was but a pawn in a much larger game; such a city's loss of independence was inevitable. It became increasingly clear to Castiglione that the most important decisions were made far away from those northern Italian courts which suffered their effects. He appears to have understood that the days of the independent court were numbered and that its survival could be ensured only by a politics that allowed the court to enter a 'great' power's sphere of influence. This new international reality was true for Venice, and especially Milan, the once natural poles of attraction for protective alliances amongst the Italian states. In the early sixteenth century neither Venice nor Milan were powerful enough to create bulwarks against threats of subjugation from outside the Italian peninsula. Although it was not altogether new, this changed situation revealed the terrible vulnerability of a state like Mantua. Even the papacy proved powerless to influence the emerging domination of Spain. Castiglione saw that an understanding between Charles V and the Pope represented the only chance for an Italian settlement.

The articles in the second part of this collection throw light on the intellectual terrain that nurtured Castiglione's theoretical concerns. The *Book of the Courtier* is intimately connected with the 'system' of the Renaissance northern Italian courts, even if Castiglione re-moulds and ultimately reduces the courts' specificity. Equicola is almost symbolic of the tendencies of court culture in the early sixteenth century: he represents its 'excesses', rejected by Castiglione, and its seductive qualities, some of which are captured in the *Book of the Courtier*.

Indeed, Equicola is a useful point of comparison, indicating how far Castiglione had moved from his Mantuan colleague. For as evidenced by their theoretical writings, there are fundamental differences between Castiglione and Equicola, although the latter's earlier concept of the courtier was to influence Castiglione. Equicola embedded his courtier in a general theory of love that bears little resemblance to Castiglione's final flourish of Neoplatonism in Book IV of the *Book of the Courtier*. Equicola's concept of love was based on the senses, and in spite of his efforts to construct a more spiritual ending in the final book of the *Libro de natura de amore*, he all too easily falls back on a materialist version of love.[8] For Equicola, love is the perfect metaphor for the courtier and his situation at court. This metaphor carries the sense of power and powerlessness; it registers the necessity to share social space with other bodies. Altogether the lover carries a heavy load of signification in Equicola's *Libro de natura de amore* since he becomes an allegory of the situation in which both individuals and states found themselves after 1494. The shock of being suddenly unable to shape one's own destiny is condensed into this figure of the lover. The lover's dependence on others and the suspended nature of his task to win over the lady both contribute to a sense of impotence, to a sense that all control over one's future has been relinquished.

Equicola assumes a complex attitude towards the possibilities of the lover's agency. In painstaking detail he describes the natural phenomena that seem to determine human actions, yet he maintains a humanistic belief in

[8]Published in 1525, Equicola's *Libro de natura de amore* had a history similar to that of the *Book of the Courtier*, insofar as the only surviving manuscript of Equicola's *magnum opus* can be dated to the period 1508–1511; with some linguistic corrections, possibly as late as 1516. See *La redazione manoscritta del 'Libro de natura de amore' di Mario Equicola*, a cura di Laura Ricci (Rome: Bulzoni, 1999), pp. 27–8.

reason's ability to subdue nature.[9] Equicola's lover seeks to escape nature's fixity and create his own signs. Nevertheless, while 'Odio' is always threatening to submerge this lover-cum-courtier, any open hostility is anathema to Equicola—the *amante* has neither the social prestige nor the power to resist overt attack. As an allegory for the embattled Italian states, he cannot make enemies. And like the Renaissance diplomat, the writer requires strategies to avoid open confrontation and help him achieve his goals. This is the foundational moment for the courtierly behaviour that Castiglione will proceed to develop. If Equicola provides the cultural script, then Castiglione in the Urbino dialogues enacts the performance of courtliness.

Equicola is clear about the aims and strategies of his lover-courtier, whose single goal is the attainment of a precise object of desire, the woman. Even so, the author is aware that the same strategies might easily be transferred to other aspects of court life: the lover in the *Libro de natura de amore* displays those talents and skills towards the beloved that Castiglione's courtier will use for more overtly political ends. In his work, Equicola adapts classical norms from Cicero, Quintilian, and others that place conversation at the centre of the lover-courtier's activities.[10] This supplies the main point of departure for Castiglione's reflections on the courtier. It has not gone unnoticed that the *Book of the Courtier* is formulated around conversations, enacted dialogues that attempt to influence listeners whilst avoiding serious dissension.

Both Equicola and Castiglione survived at court and realised certain ambitions better than many of their contemporaries. Lelio Manfredi (XI) is a telling example of a courtier who failed in his attempts to gain preferment. Although a prolific producer of literary 'goods' that were in demand at the courts of Ferrara and Mantua, he was unable to gain a permanent foothold at either of these courts. He received some help from Isabella d'Este, but not sufficient to keep him from the poverty that dogged his last years. Manfredi was unsuccessful because he does not appear to have been able to offer a full

[9]One can note two crucial comments in the manuscript of the *Libro de natura de amore*: 'et che facilmente ogni inclinatione nostra naturale si po con ragione in megliore redure' and 'Il savio domina alle stelle, et che questo sia vero et che multo possa in ogni actione la prudentia si experimenta' (*La redazione manoscritta*, p. 459; p. 461).

[10]'La terca è sapere moderatamente conversare con li homini, li loro studii disponere, le voluntà tirare, le opere excitare et movere per nostri commodi per che, benché multo possa in le humane cose la fortuna, benivolentia è necessaria ad farne deventare excelsi. Constrengono li homini ad amarne, con la fama et opinione di constantia fede et mansuetudine, senza simulatione' (*La redazione manoscritta*, p. 473).

range of services. 'Rivals' like Castiglione and Equicola could carry out delicate diplomatic tasks and were also sought after as 'entertaining' courtiers. The process of 'natural selection' at court rooted out those men whose conversation and versatility were insufficiently developed for the rulers' tastes. Manfredi's failure to secure long-term patronage contrasts markedly with the case of the court poet Serafino Aquilano (1466–1500), who was represented by Vincenzo Calmeta (c.1460–1508) as the zenith of late fifteenth-century court culture (X). Calmeta dignified Aquilano with a biography, placing the poet on almost equal standing with the canonical poets of the Italian tradition (Dante and Petrarch). This was the first time that a contemporary vernacular poet had been thus distinguished. The biography amounted to recognition that the courts were making a unique contribution to cultural renewal in Renaissance Italy. But like the *Book of the Courtier*, the *Life of Serafino Aquilano* was also a commemoration of something irretrievably lost. The fall of Milan first to the French and then to the Spanish emphasised that in Italy court culture as an expression of certain freedoms was on the verge of extinction.

Calmeta makes it clear that Serafino Aquilano's major patrons and audience were women. Aquilano would perform mainly for his female clients. The role of women at court has received much attention in recent years, with studies focussing on the representation of women in court texts, and on the activities of women at court. To paraphrase the words of Cesare Gonzaga (1475–1512) in the *Book of the Courtier*, to conceive of a court without women would be unthinkable. Discussion of women's role in society permeated the writings of men who were involved in the northern Italian courts. It was a theme appropriate to many genres, from specific treatises to romance epics: Ariosto's epic poem *Orlando furioso* complicates and develops various discourses on women (XV). Even a writer like Sabadino degli Arienti (c.1445–1510), who appears closer in spirit to the 'republican' traditions of his native Bologna, confirms the important role that court women played in patronage. His *Gynevera de le clare donne* insists on conservative values such as chastity, whilst also acknowledging that women have acquired greater autonomy in the court environment (XVI).

The life of Isabella d'Este testifies to an increased autonomy for certain women; her interests were proteiform and her agency could not be easily hindered. Isabella d'Este is one of the threads that draws this collection together—not only was she known to all the courtiers studied here, but she exerted a heavy influence on a number of them. She is a key reference point for the elaboration of court culture, her activities challenging its traditional modes of female behaviour. Her role in the development of Renaissance northern Italian court culture cannot be underestimated. It is true that her patronage of the arts has attracted some criticism. Yet Isabella d'Este was working against stereotypes that fixed women as objects of the male gaze. The emphasis on Isabella d'Este is justified here because of her energetic quest for a self-image that emphasised her agency in pursuits too often associated solely with men (XII, XIII).

This book contends that the evolution of the courtier in theory and practice owes a great deal to the 'minor' courts of northern Italy. Castiglione's *Book of the Courtier* itself gains in depth when examined through the lens of these courts, as much for what is rejected as for what is eventually maintained in the final version. The 'minor' courtiers whose names are either eliminated from Castiglione's printed text or who never reappear in the various manuscript redactions present a fascinating array of responses to the court situation. They indicate ways in which powerlessness could be recast as a position of strength. During a period of intense social and political crisis, intellectuals at court developed a conception of behaviour which was to form the basis of proper conduct both in and outside court society. The legacy of the courts remains with us even today. The courtiers studied here shaped forms of consciousness that would be elaborated throughout the early modern and modern periods.

STEPHEN KOLSKY

The University of Melbourne
March 2003

ACKNOWLEDGEMENTS

In the course of some twenty years of studying the courts of Renaissance northern Italy one incurs numerous debts. The University of Melbourne has fully supported my efforts in Renaissance research. I especially thank Alison Patrick, who as Head of the Italian Department for a short, but formative time, enthusiastically encouraged me in my research. Over the years the Faculty of Arts has aided my research with vital funding. More recently Small Grants from the Australian Research Council (1991, 1994) have greatly assisted the process of research.

I gratefully acknowledge the following institutions, journals and publishers for permission to reproduce the articles included in this volume: Istituto Nazionale di Studi sul Rinascimento and Leo S. Olschki Editore, Florence (I); Irish Academic Press, Dublin, and Frank Cass & Co Ltd (II); Society for Renaissance Studies and Oxford University Press (III); Society for Italian Studies (IV, XII); *Italica* and the American Association of Teachers of Italian (V, X); *Forum Italicum*, Center for Italian Studies, SUNY at Stony Brook, NY (VI); Pubblicazioni dell'Università Cattolica del Sacro Cuore, Milano (VII); *The Italianist* and the departments of Italian Studies, University of Reading and University College, Dublin (VIII); *Critica Letteraria* (IX); Il Bulino edizioni d'arte (XI); The Warburg Institute (XIII); *Spunti e Ricerche* and the Italian Studies Program, La Trobe University (XIV); *Romance Notes*, Department of Romance Languages, The University of North Carolina, Chapel Hill, NC (XV); Berg Publishers, Oxford (XVI). John Smedley of Ashgate has been most generous with practical support and advice throughout the process of preparing this volume.

I have over many years received support and encouragement from many people. At The University of Melbourne, Ian Robertson has supplied intellectual stimulation, camaraderie, and wine. For the development of my ideas and research on Renaissance northern Italian courts I am particularly indebted to Mantuan specialists Clifford Brown, David Chambers, Anna Maria Lorenzoni and William Prizer. I am also grateful to John Gatt-Rutter for his friendship and to the late Peter Armour for his unstinting support. Special thanks to Cynthia Troup for her patient editorial work and the painstaking production of the index. Finally, I want to express my sincere thanks to Helen and Daniel who made every effort to take me away from my research into other realms.

STEPHEN KOLSKY

Carlton, March 2003

PUBLISHER'S NOTE

The articles in this volume, as in all others in the Variorum Collected Studies Series, have not been given a new, continuous pagination. In order to avoid confusion, and to facilitate their use where these same studies have been referred to elsewhere, the original pagination has been maintained wherever possible.

Each article has been given a Roman number in order of appearance, as listed in the Contents. This number is repeated on each page and is quoted in the index entries.

I

BEFORE THE NUNCIATURE: CASTIGLIONE IN FACT AND FICTION

To separate Castiglione's literary production from his career as a courtier and diplomat is to lose a crucial dimension of his biography. Such a view does not mean to suggest that the critic should simplistically assume that Castiglione's literary works are faithful autobiographical documents. It will be argued in this article that they represent his response to a precise set of historical circumstances. Castiglione's fictions, to be understood, need to be read in the context of his own political and personal choices. Thus, if the historian finds Castiglione's versions of events inaccurate such a defect ought not to be attributed to his lack of knowledge but to a determined attempt to rewrite history, indeed to mythologize it.[1]

Castiglione was employed as a professional mediator for the greater part of his adult life. Such experiences were not lost on Castiglione the writer.[2] They might involve subjecting the manuscript of the *Libro del cortegiano* to the scrutiny of Pietro Bembo [3] or casting his most famous work in dialogic form in order to allow the interplay of contrasting opinions. The *Libro del cortegiano* lends authority to the rules of diplomatic behaviour – the author is absent on perhaps

---

[1] See, for example, the introduction to B. Castiglione - G. Della Casa, *Opere*, a cura di G. Prezzolini, Milan 1937, and M. Rossi, *Baldesar Castiglione, la sua personalità, la sua prosa*, Bari 1946. I wish to thank Dr. Cecil Clough for his encouragement and useful advice in the early stages of the preparation of this article.

[2] For Castiglione's biography consult J. Cartwright, *Baldassare Castiglione, the Perfect Courtier. His Life and Letters (1478-1529)*, 2 vols, London 1908; V. Cian, *Un illustre nunzio pontificio del Rinascimento. Baldassar Castiglione*, Città del Vaticano 1951; C. Mutini, *Castiglione, Baldassarre*, in *Dizionario Biografico degli Italiani*, XXII, Rome 1979, pp. 53-58.

[3] See B. Castiglione, *Le Lettere*, a cura di G. La Rocca, I, *1497-marzo 1521*, Milan 1978 [henceforth *Lettere*], pp. 383-384, 543. For Bembo's rôle in the *Cortegiano* see G. Arbizzoni, *L'ordine e la persuasione. Pietro Bembo personaggio nel « Cortegiano »*, Urbino 1983, and the provocative study by T. Cachey, *In and out of the margins of a Renaissance controversy: Castiglione in the second « Asolani » (1530)*, « Rivista di Letteratura Italiana », 3, 1985, pp. 253-262.

what he considered his most cherished mission, the ceremonial admission of the Duke of Urbino, represented by Castiglione, into the Order of the Garter.[4] As a consequence, the authorial voice appears less imperious and more ambiguous. By emphasizing the « alliance » between Urbino and England Castiglione was drawing attention to the possibilities that diplomacy offered to the city-state, enabling it to form ties with far greater powers.[5] Urbino, through the « invisible » work of its diplomats was in a position to maintain its autonomy and increase its prestige. Implicitly, war with its destructive directness, was to be avoided at all costs. The hidden history of Guidubaldo Montefeltro's failure as a « condottiere » and the recent expulsion of the ruling family from Urbino only served to confirm the essential role of diplomacy.[6] The diplomat's absence signals that the work to ensure the survival of the state has not ceased.

The *Libro del cortegiano* discreetly alludes to the end of the Montefeltro dynasty. The Duke of Urbino is absent from the discussions through ill-health, his spouse is already referred to as a widow; she is childless.[7] The sole remaining strategy for survival was adoption which, in practical terms, meant the end of the Montefeltro name. Castiglione refrains from alerting the reader too overtly to the imminent demise of the regime and prefers to suggest continuity. Julius II's passage through Urbino on his return from the capture of Bologna indicates the manner in which the writer succeeds in *not* highlighting a troublesome event: « con l'aiuto de' Franzesi ridutto Bologna alla obedienzia della sede apostolica » (*Il Cortegiano*, p. 88). One can note that the right of the pope to subjugate Bologna is not questioned and is made to seem a natural fact of history. The logic of the situation dictates that Urbino be next in line for annexation, as the text subtly suggests, but once again, it will be a peaceful transition.

The arrival of the next ruler of Urbino, Francesco Maria della Rovere, is

---

[4] For which see CARTWRIGHT, *Baldassare Castiglione*, cit., I, pp. 179-187; J. DENNISTOUN, *Memoirs of the Dukes of Urbino*, London-New York 1909, II, pp. 462-470 and E. ASHMOLE, *The Institution, Laws and Ceremonies of the Most Noble Order of the Garter*, 2 vols, London, Nathaniel Brooke 1672, Fol.

[5] See C. H. CLOUGH, *The relations between the English and Urbino courts, 1478-1508*, in *The Duchy of Urbino in the Renaissance*, item XI, London 1981 and ID., *Review of Baldassar Castiglione*, « *Le Lettere* », « Modern Language Notes », 97, 1982, pp. 192-208 [pp. 204-205].

[6] For Guidubaldo da Montefeltro consult G. FRANCESCHINI, *I Montefeltro*, Varese 1970, pp. 545-570. See also A. K. ISAACS, *Condottieri, stati e territori nell'Italia centrale*, in *Federico di Montefeltro. Lo stato le arti la cultura*, I, *Lo stato*, Rome 1986, pp. 23-60 and M. L. MARIOTTI MASI, *Elisabetta Gonzaga duchessa d'Urbino nello splendore e negli intrighi del Rinascimento*, Milan 1983.

[7] « Non posso pur tacere una parola della signora Duchessa nostra, la quale, essendo vivuta quindeci anni in compagnia del marito come vidua ... » (B. CASTIGLIONE, *Il libro del Cortegiano con una scelta delle opere minori*, a cura di B. MAIER, Turin 1964, p. 407 [henceforth *Il Cortegiano*]).

marked by a sense of mystery, if not bewilderment. Without knowing who it is everyone is attracted by the approaching noise. The text stresses that his arrival is an interruption, the introduction of disorder which will have to be rapidly absorbed by the assembled company if chaos is not to ensue (« un *gran* calpestare di piedi con strepito di parlar *alto* », *Il Cortegiano*, p. 181 [my emphasis]). The Prefect of Rome makes his appearance in a blaze of light, perhaps to suggest that death and darkness will be overcome for a while by the future Duke. He stands « alla porta della stanza » (*Il Cortegiano*, p. 181), ready to complete the necessary rites of passage. If everyone stands up once it is realized who it is, Francesco Maria himself restores order to the situation by recognizing that his power is for the future. He will be merely a listener who is there to learn the art of government and courtly conduct. The outsider must be transmuted into an insider so as to erase any feeling of unease: « si pose ancor esso a seder nel cerchio con alcuni de' suoi gentilomini » (*Il Cortegiano*, p. 182). His integration into the circle only takes place at the very end of the first book (chap. LIV) – his arrival had been noted in chapter VI. In the meantime a number of essential topics have been discussed by the group, such as the fundamental importance of arms to the courtier and the need to have a certain culture, including a linguistic one. There might be a slight irony intended here by Castiglione who was perhaps implying that Francesco Maria never learnt to be a terribly successful « condottiere » and was rather uncultured! Furthermore, it is suggested that without the pope whom he has accompanied a part of the journey back to Rome, he is just an ordinary member of the gathering.

Castiglione fully realized the potency of an alliance between the pope and his protegé. In fact, his first duty undertaken in Guidubaldo's service was to take part in the military operations aimed at dismantling the last remnants of Cesare Borgia's state and returning such territories to the authority of the pope.[8] The pattern would be repeated to Urbino's detriment when Leo X installed Lorenzo de' Medici as the new ruler of Urbino. It was probably one of the reasons why Castiglione was later so enthusiastic about Federico Gonzaga accepting the rank of Captain-General of the Church. His ultimate disillusionment with such a narrow model may have convinced him of the absolute need to think on a larger scale – European horizons instead of limited Italian ones. However, that would be a gradual process and at this stage Castiglione could probably see only advantages. Such knowledge undoubtedly contributed to his decision to leave the service of Francesco Gonzaga in June 1504 and take up employment with Guidubaldo Montefeltro. The Consistory's formal confirmation of Francesco Maria as the Duke's successor took place on 10 May 1504. Guidubaldo's subsequent appointment as Captain-General of the Church offered sure con-

[8] See J. R. HALE, *Castiglione's military career*, « Italian Studies », 36, 1981, pp. 41-57 [45-46].

firmation of Castiglione's political logic.[9] It would seem that Castiglione's career path was determined by a desire to be close to the powerful, using whatever means at his disposal to enter into particular spheres of influence. Rome was the focal point of his ambitions. It was a universal power which seemed to transcend the boundaries of petty Italian politics: « Roma pur va continuando di essere quasi del mondo, ché seben non ha forza d'arme, pur mantien dominio sopra molte nazioni ».[10]

Castiglione's famous utterance on the deep impression made on him by the « Urbs », « Gran cosa è Roma », suggests the relentlessness of his ambitions which could be satisfied only on a universal scale. Like numerous other Italian intellectuals of the period Castiglione was well aware of the peninsula's military weakness, including the papacy which intermittently took to the battlefield. His experience as a diplomat would have made him aware that the most crucial battles were fought in the anterooms of princes or their audience-chambers. An actual war represented defeat for a person like Castiglione, especially in view of the peninsula's lack of military status.[11]

Immediately following his eulogy of Rome Castiglione enters into a discussion of « condottieri » so that he can praise Federico Montefeltro whose capabilities in war were never questioned.[12] The mention of the Duke of Urbino automatically casts judgement on his son and the present generation of « condottieri ». It was probably one of the reasons why Castiglione eliminated the passage from the final version. The military history of Italy from Guidubaldo Montefeltro to the Sack of Rome could only provide more evidence of decline and incapacity. Urbino, after Federico, could not defend itself. His son was captured in battle, expelled from his state and reduced to impotence and

---

[9] Cf. Clough, *Review* cit., together with the *Additions and corrections* to the latter piece in the volume *The Duchy of Urbino*, cit., J. D. Falvo, *Urbino and the apotheosis of power*, « Modern Languages Notes », 101, 1986, pp. 114-146, proposes the alternative view that Castiglione was the wronged party. It is surely an exaggeration to state that the courtier « had given the best years of his life » (p. 138) to Francesco Gonzaga when he had only been in his service less than five years? Falvo does not mention that Castiglione abandoned the Marquis at a particularly sensitive moment so that the latter's anger is entirely comprehensible. It is necessary to read Castiglione's letters in the knowledge that he was a diplomat and would not often express himself directly. In this context see the comments of D. Javitch, *Poetry and Courtliness in Renaissance England*, Princeton 1978, particularly pp. 19-49 and J. R. Woodhouse, *Baldesar Castiglione. A Reassessment of « The Courtier »*, Edinburgh 1978, pp. 61-62.

[10] *La seconda redazione del « Cortegiano » di Baldassarre Castiglione*, edizione critica per cura di G. Ghinassi, Florence 1968, p. 78. See, by the same writer, *Fasi dell'elaborazione del « Cortegiano »*, « Studi di Filologia Italiana », 25, 1967, pp. 155-196 [176-181].

[11] Cf. C. Dionisotti, Review of V. Cian, *Un illustre nunzio pontificio*, « Giornale Storico della Letteratura Italiana », 129, 1952, pp. 31-57.

[12] *La seconda redazione*, cit., p. 78.

immobility. In turn, his adopted son, Francesco Maria della Rovere, was also expelled from Urbino and his military expeditions, particularly those in the service of the papacy, were noted for their lack of determination to achieve success.[13] In these circumstances, in particular the decline of the papacy to a third-rate power in military terms, unable to lead effectively the other Italian states or to subjugate them, it is not surprising that Castiglione looked beyond Italy to satisfy his ambitions. His profession was also precisely the one for which there was a great demand.[14]

It may be useful here to analyse in broad terms the ways in which diplomacy had become essential to the Italian states in their dealings with one another and foreign powers. In a sense, the Italian states could be divided between those who employed other states and those who were employed by the former. The smaller states could offer the larger ones such as Florence, Venice, Milan and papal Rome, soldiers and military expertise.[15] These « condottieri »-princes had need of skilled negotiators to maximize any possible advantage they might have over their more powerful neighbours. The negotiators had to be clever jugglers, taking into account the susceptibilities of their employers on matters that affected their honour and, equally important, their purses, since honour could easily be measured by financial gain. Once a contract had been successfully negotiated this was not the end of the story, for the « condottiere » often had to prod his employer for payment, thus necessitating a continuous diplomatic presence.[16]

With this breakdown in the traditional framework of negotiation, it became imperative for the envoy to be someone who could be relied upon to assess quickly changing situations in order to report back to the prince in the most accurate way possible, using his understanding of human affairs to its fullest extent. Hence, humanist diplomats found a practical outlet for their skills.[17]

---

[13] A readable account of the reigns of both these Dukes is provided by Dennistoun. For Guidubaldo see *op. cit.*, I, pp. 295-424 and for Francesco Maria, II, pp. 313-456, III, pp. 3-125. After Francesco Maria's expulsion from Urbino, the Duke managed, even before Lorenzo de' Medici's death, to recover some of his state and hold on to it until 1521. In 1522 Pope Hadrian VI officially reinstated Francesco Maria as Duke of Urbino.

[14] Cf. J. Guidi, *L'Espagne dans la vie et dans l'oeuvre de Baldassare Castiglione: de l'équilibre franco-hispanique au choix impérial*, in *Présence et influence de l'Espagne dans la culture italienne de la Renaissance*, ed. A. Rochon, Paris 1978, pp. 113-202.

[15] Cf. M. Mallett, *Mercenaries and their Masters*, London 1974.

[16] This is the situation in which Castiglione found himself after Federico Gonzaga was appointed Captain-General of the Church. He had to stay in Rome to solicit payment for the Marquis and to defend his military actions. Cf. Cartwright, *The Perfect Courtier*, cit., II, p. 119.

[17] Cf. M. L. Doglio, *Ambasciatore e principe. L'« Institutio Legati » di Ermolao Barbaro*, in *Miscellanea di studi in onore di Vittore Branca*, III, 1: *Umanesimo e Rinascimento a*

But this alone was not enough. If diplomacy in the peninsula can be described as a continuous process of bargaining, the diplomat-salesman also had to be knowledgeable about the product he was selling, therefore some kind of military background would have been useful. If Castiglione's mother, together with Isabella d'Este, placed so much emphasis on a humanistic training, it was not forgotten by Francesco Gonzaga that Baldassarre's father, Cristoforo, was primarily a military man.[18] The latter's death, in the same years as the fall of Ludovico il Moro, must have contributed to his son's impatience with military life, as both events ended all hopes for stability and a leisured existence.[19] War shattered Castiglione's notions of self-sufficiency since it meant first-hand contact with the decidedly uncomfortable world of fighting and absence from the court. The tent, in sharp contrast to the solid walls of the palace at Urbino, becomes a symbol of the physical hardships and anxieties of war; its flimsy structure and extreme mobility aptly sum up Castiglione's sense of stress and his aspirations.

In this context, Castiglione's excitement at the prospect of being given the fief of Ginestretto by Francesco Maria della Rovere assumes added significance: « Le particularità de Genestreto sono che l'è posto in una colina de le più belle che se possino trovare ... e lì intorno le più belle possessioni che se possi imaginare, da piacere e da utile. E perché la M.V. pò comprhendere quanto io mi contentasse havere qualche facultà for di là, per potere una volta stare in casa che fosse mia ... perché in effetto al mondo non è altro che un poco de honore, benché ogni cosa è fumo » (*Lettere*, p. 329). A fief of this kind, far from representing a closer dependence on his lord, seems to imply for Castiglione a sense of freedom and independence. The fief would represent somewhere stable where he would no longer have to perform in the presence of superiors.

The fief also represents for Castiglione the concrete expression of success. The slippery world of diplomacy based on falsehoods and half-truths, promises not often kept, may have made him feel that reality was an illusory concept. Marks of appreciation, whether they be the chain given him in England or the fief granted by Francesco Maria (« per infiniti respetti ho hauto piacer assai di questo castello », *Lettere*, p. 329) are clearly the aim of Castiglione's efforts in diplomacy. They are the reason for which he allowed himself to suffer the sometimes humiliating treatment by his political masters.

Firenze e Venezia, Florence 1983, pp. 297-310. In his review of E. Barbaro, *De Officio Legati, De Coelibatu*, a cura di V. Branca, Florence 1969, P. Floriani draws parallels between *De Officio Legati* and Castiglione's *Cortegiano* (« Giornale Storico della Letteratura Italiana », 147, 1970, pp. 449-452).

[18] See G. Rodella, *Tradizione diplomatica e 'cortigiana' nella famiglia Castiglioni*, in *Baldassarre Castiglione. V centenario della nascita 1478-1978*, Viadana 1978, pp. 13-42.

[19] See Cartwright, *The Perfect Courtier*, cit., I, pp. 15-24.

Right from the start of his career he was being trained as a professional diplomat. Francesco Gonzaga, Marquis of Mantua, realized that war was fought not only on the battlefield, but also in the courts of one's allies and enemies. That was why Francesco Gonzaga employed him at a local level as a « commissario » in Castiglione, a town not far from Mantua. It was meant to provide the future diplomat with invaluable experience in administration.[20] But the Marquis also insisted on a more traditional role: he was expected to go to war with his lord. Castiglione's first real test as a soldier came in the campaign of 1503 in southern Italy. Francesco Gonzaga had been put in charge of the French troops, whom he was unable to control, and certain of the inevitability of defeat had retired to Mantua. At such a desperate moment in the Marquis' fortunes Castiglione decided to leave his service. His motives are not altogether clear. But certainly, ambitions for himself and his brother Girolamo, played a crucial part in his decision. The excuses he made to Francesco Gonzaga in a letter of 4 October 1503 seem rather puerile: « le strate sonno tanto mal secure » and the scarcity of good horses (perhaps the Marquis was ironically reminding Castiglione of his poor excuse when he offered the envoy an old nag to give the King of England as a gift!).[21]

Castiglione was obviously unimpressed by the Marquis' martial skills, a shadow of his former self if compared to his 'performance' at the battle of Fornovo. The courtier may have intuited that the Marquis had made a wrong political choice and wished to dissociate himself from its possible disastrous consequences. His extended stay in Rome was possibly a way of lessening any personal damage that may have been caused by the Neapolitan campaign. He perhaps had more faith in his « tanti amici » (*Lettere*, p. 18) in Rome than the Marquis' influence or ability to improve his career prospects. The presence of Cesare Gonzaga at Urbino may have also been an encouragement to him. Although the latter was apparently employed as a soldier, he was able to make use of his skills as a diplomat and writer. The court of Urbino might have appeared to Castiglione to be simply more congenial.

In his letter of 10 June 1504 to Francesco Gonzaga Castiglione placed the responsibility for his change of employer on Guidubaldo Montefeltro: « Heri hebi littera dal Sig.r Duca d'Urbino, ne la quale Sua S. *me ricerca* ch'io voglia, essendo di contento de la Ex.tia V., andar a li servitij suoi, *promettendo farmi bon trattamento* » (My italics; *Lettere*, p. 20).

Castiglione could not afford to antagonize the Marquis any more than he already had by even faintly suggesting that he himself had anything to do with the move. It is not, however, to be denied that the Duke of Urbino had his own motives for employing Castiglione. It does not seem a wild hypothesis to claim

---

20 See CIAN, *Un illustre nunzio pontificio*, cit., pp. 18-22.

21 *Lettere*, pp. 18-19. See n. 9 for bibliographical references.

that the Duke was intent on lending his court a cosmopolitan character by employing men from various parts of the peninsula who all have the highest credentials. Castiglione emphasizes this point both in the *Tirsi* and the *Cortegiano*. He principally mentions those courtiers who were not of Urbinate origins and indeed were recent arrivals at court.[22] The gathering together of so many courtiers from such disparate parts could be interpreted as a conscious strategy on Guidubaldo's part to bolster the prestige of his regime after the conquest of Urbino by Cesare Borgia.

It was the aftermath of this cataclysmic event that provided Castiglione with his first task in the service of Guidubaldo Montefeltro. The latter was in charge of a campaign, to restore papal rule to various towns in the Romagna. The courtier's rôle in this military exercise reads like a scene from a comic opera, the high-point of which is reached when a mule injured his foot.[23] Military life was definitely not to his liking: « questa maledeta impresa de questa Roca ce ne ha desfatti » (*Lettere*, p. 23). Yet he was preparaed to put up with it in the short term because he foresaw long-term benefits: « Un dì spero pur che saremo richi, ma dubito staremo un poco assai » (*Lettere*, p. 33).

In spite of the breakdown in relations with the Marquis of Mantua Castiglione was generally happy at his new situation, not even the suffering caused by the misbehaviour of his mule could make him regret his move from Mantua to Urbino: « et avegna ch'io sia lontano da la patria e da tante persone ch'io amo assai, pur mi contento e patisco voluntieri li sinistri, per haver l'animo quieto come ho » (*Lettere*, p. 24). Castiglione had, in more ways than one, abdicated his responsibilities. He could no longer be involved in the day-to-day running of his estates. This onerous burden he left to his mother who was not at all convinced of the correctness of his choice. In a letter to her son, written in 1513, she recognized that Castiglione's absence had given her power which otherwise she would not have enjoyed: « me hay lassata patrona e cum grandissima libertà de governar la roba tua como ho voluto ». Yet, she still reproaches him for what amounts to the dereliction of his duties: « ma molto più cara mi seria la presentia tua che questa libertà ».[24] The courtier did not really need his mother's admonition as can be seen by the defensive tone of many of his letters

---

[22] See *Tirsi*, stanzas 39-45, in *Il libro del Cortegiano*, ed. cit., pp. 565-568. For further critical commentary consult J. Guidi, *Thyrsis ou la cour transfigurée*, in *Ville et campagne dans la littérature italienne de la Renaissance*, II: *Le courtisan travesti*, Paris 1977, pp. 141-186 [pp. 173-177]; C. Varese, *L'« Aminta »: corte e letteratura dal Sannazaro e dal Bembo al Castiglione allo Speroni e al Tasso*, « Schifanoia », 3, 1987, pp. 17-27 [p. 20]. See also Falvo, *op. cit.*, pp. 133-146 and C. Dionisotti, *Regioni e letteratura*, in *Storia d'Italia*, V: *I Documenti*, 2, Turin 1973, pp. 1375-1395 [p. 1389].

[23] See Hale, *Castiglione's military career*, cit., pp. 45-46.

[24] Quoted in V. Cian, *Nel mondo di Baldassarre Castiglione. Documenti illustrati*, « Archivio Storico Lombardo », n.s., 7, 1942, pp. 3-97, [p. 93].

to her. He often tried to justify his apparently excessive expenditure in order to demonstrate to his mother that he was not leading a dissolute life far from home: « E veramente al parer mio non mi lasso transportare a li apetiti, e son certo che, se la M.V. ha inteso la carestia che questo anno è stata in Roma, e le spese che non se sono potute fugire, non li parerà stranio ch'io habia fatto debito cento e quaranta duccati; e son certo che s'io fosse stato a casa, pur mi seria anchor stato forza spendere qualche cosa. Lassarimo questa parte » (*Lettere*, p. 78).

Although Aloisa Castiglione performed to perfection the rôle of a woman as defined in the *Libro del cortegiano* her son seemed to wish to exclude her from important areas of his life.[25] There must have been strong feelings of guilt on his part. In his letters home, Castiglione operated a kind of censorship; he referred as little as possible to political events and figures with the excuse that they would not have interested her (*Lettere*, pp. 30, 51).

The grandeur of Rome, the power of the Roman Curia (that exclusive men's club), together with the hope of obtaining a benefice for his brother Girolamo, served to impress upon Castiglione the difference between the closed nature of Mantuan society and the openness of Curial circles. His mother could only see disadvantages in her son's move: it had gained him the enmity of his feudal lord which put strains on the dynastic ties between the Montefeltro and the Gonzaga.

Realizing Baldassarre's need for powerful allies, Aloisa was relentless in her search for a suitable bride. Castiglione saw the matter more crudely: for him the taking of a wife meant receiving a large sum of money as a dowry (« mercantia »).[26] Certainly, he was well aware of the problem that his slighting of Francesco Gonzaga had brought in its wake. The Marquis appears to have made a point of teaching Castiglione a lesson, of demonstrating to his employer the disadvantages of using someone held in low esteem by himself. Consequently, Castiglione's ego suffered from these rebuffs. A case in point is his abortive mission to Mantua in December 1505. In order to prevent his master and himself from being publicly shamed, Castiglione pretended to proceed from Ferrara to Mantua as if nothing were amiss, but when he was two miles out of Ferrara he went to a friend's house to hide (*Lettere*, pp. 80-81). Because of Castiglione,

---

[25] See the following passage from Book III, chap. 5 of the *Cortegiano*: « l'esser bona e discreta, il saper governar le facultà del marito e la casa sua e i figlioli quando è maritata, e tutte quelle parti che si richieggono ad una bona madre di famiglia » (pp. 342-343).

[26] See *Lettere*, p. 265. The standard account of Castiglione's search for a bride is V. Cian, *Candidature nuziali di Baldassarre Castiglione*, Venice 1892. Cf. J. Guidi, *De l'amour courtois à l'amour sacré: la condition de la femme dans l'oeuvre de B. Castiglione*, in *Images de la femme dans la littérature italienne de la Renaissance. Préjugés misogynes et aspirations nouvelles*, Paris 1980, pp. 9-80 [p. 16].

Francesco Gonzaga was willing to sacrifice good relations with Urbino; an indication of just how far his feudal sensibility had been offended. The Marquis of Mantua was a powerless witness to the destruction of the social system which had seemed solid enough until the French invasion of 1494. Therefore, Castiglione's defection was a further blow to the Marquis' self-esteem and sense of honour. In this particular case, the Marquis could demonstrate his power since the object of his anger was not a king of France but one of his own subjects, even if he was the representative of the Duke of Urbino. At this moment Castiglione felt all the precariousness of his position: « perché non venendo, so certo che nascerà gran sdegno in core al S.r Duca, e non vorei che questo venisse, e *maxime* per causa mia » (*Lettere*, p. 81). This was not the only incident between Castiglione and the Marquis.

The courtier's dictum of « chi non se arisca, non guadagna » does not seem to have paid off since the Marquis was capable of jeopardizing Girolamo Castiglione's chances of a career in the Church, Baldassarre's chief goal in the years immediately preceding his brother's death (*Lettere*, p. 62). The furtherance of Girolamo's career would have been a good indication of Castiglione's influence. Perhaps his brother died just that too soon. However, a couple of months after the incident noted above, Giovanni Gonzaga, Francesco's brother, explained why he could not employ Girolamo: « per non mostrar al patrone de voler favorire quelli che lui non ha tropo cari, *maxime* essendo accaduto questo mio caso pochi dì fa » (*Lettere*, p. 85). Giovanni had only been approached because Francesco's other brother, Sigismondo, now a cardinal, had also refused to compromise himself (*Lettere*, p. 894). Francesco Gonzaga missed no opportunity to humiliate his former servant. Asked for a horse that could be presented to the King of England, the Marquis offered one that was blind and lame.[27] Nonetheless, Castiglione managed to carry out this mission which represented the high point of his service under Guidubaldo Montefeltro. Castiglione himself saw his mission to England as representing a concrete mark of favour on the part of the Duke and, at the same time, offering the opportunity of extending his own network of friends and benefactors.[28] The Duke's use of Castiglione as a proxy and perhaps as an ambassador, implied that he had enough confidence in his new courtier to allow him to act in his name. To emphasize his intimacy with the Duke, Castiglione wrote in the *Epistola ad Henricum VII*: « ego enim qui semper illi assidebam, nec unquam digito longius aberam », suggestive of the courtier's insistence on remaining close to the sources of power (*Lettere*, p. 181). However, by the time of Guidubaldo's death, the material advantages of Ca-

---

[27] *Lettere*, pp. 96-97; Cartwright, *The Perfect Courtier*, cit., I, pp. 170-175.

[28] *Lettere*, p. 58. Castiglione hoped to make the journey to England in the company of Silvestro Gigli, Bishop of Worcester and English ambassador at the papal court, « et è amicissimo mio quanto si pò » (*Lettere*, p. 60).

stiglione's move to Urbino were difficult to gauge; neither the ambitions he had for his brother nor his own had been achieved.

Castiglione must have retained a certain degree of optimism about the possibilities that his connection with Guidubaldo Montefeltro and his court might afford him. It cannot be mere coincidence that the period 1504-1508 was particularly productive in terms of literary output. A start was made on what was to transform slowly into the *Libro del cortegiano*. The Latin eclogue *Alcon*, the pastoral drama *Tirsi* and the *Epistola ad Henricum VII* form the ideological centre of Castiglione's writings involving his absence from Mantua. The *Alcon* and the *Tirsi* constitute two separate, yet associated moments of death and regeneration. The character of Iolas (Castiglione) is common to both works:

> « flebant pastores; ante omnes carus Iolas
> tristia perfundens lacrimis manantibus ora,
> crudeles superos, crudeliaque astra vocabat »
>
> (*Alcon*, ll. 5-7).[29]

Iolas is overwhelmed by the sense of his own powerlessness. Tears of grief are his destiny in both pieces. One will find a similar situation in the *Epistola* when Guidubaldo dies before fulfilling his early promise: « in ipsa floridior[e] aetate e medio tolleretur » (*Lettere*, p. 164). Likewise, Alçon is taken « sub flore iuventae » (l. 1). The elegy concentrates on Iolas' grief which, as in *Tirsi*, is expressed in solitude, in order to emphasize his impotence before destiny:

> « tantum inter silvas, aut solo in litore secum
> perditus, et serae oblitus decedere nocti »
>
> (*Alcon*, ll. 21-22)

The first half of the poem is in the form of a tirade against the injustice of the Fates. We do not find here the stoic resignation of Guidubaldo faced with the inevitability of death; there is no sense of Christian consolation (something that would be learnt later):

> « tunc lacrimae incassum, tunc inrita vota, precesque
> funduntur. Fert vota Notus, lacrimasque, precesque »
>
> (*Alcon*, ll. 65-66).

Castiglione briefly sketches the ideal of an intellectual community. It acts as a buffer against the harsh realities of life and will achieve artistic consummation in the *Cortegiano*.[30] The poem in the second half lays stress on the sense of dis-

---

[29] *Alcon* is to be found in I. D. McFarlane, *Renaissance Latin Poetry*, Manchester 1980, pp. 196-205 (with English translation).

[30]
> « non ego te posthac pastorum astante corona
> victorem aspiciam volucri certare sagitta,

I

placement and alienation felt by Iolas. The poet analyses the sentiment of distance and the impossibility of coming together. The cause of such distance is discreetly alluded to:

« heu male me ira deum patriis abduxit ab oris! »
(*Alcon*, l. 83).

Politics never fails to intrude, even in pastoral settings. The reference to the Marquis of Mantua is intended to make the separation of Alcon and Iolas yet more poignant. The gods are no other than Castiglione's political masters who pass the grim sentence of exile on those who displease them. Hence, the pastoral form becomes the representation of a place where justice can reign and where shepherds can rediscover the spirit of community. The pastoral scene in the *Alcon* is not, however, Urbino but the Roman countryside, particularly the banks of the Aniene, a tributary of the Tiber. It is near these rivers that the impossible reunion between Alcon and Iolas is imagined taking place. *Tirsi* is set in the one spot where such intellectual bonds can, according to Castiglione, actually be realized. The ideal is the same in both works:

« sic tandem optato laeti sermone fruemur,
aerumnasque graves, olim et transacta vicissim
damna referre simul, rursusque audire iuvabit »
(*Alcon*, ll. 112-114).

The past viewed as something painful is vanquished by the present which takes the form of *sermo*. The past is treated similarly in *Tirsi*.

The obvious political statement about Urbino needs little elucidation except to stress its Neoplatonic origins. The profundity of Castiglione's debt to Poliziano's *Stanze per la giostra* has to be fully recognized.[31] It is not solely a question of the *Tirsi* borrowing structural and textual elements. Ideologically the works are very close, to the extent that the mythical worlds they create are ruled over by a deity, identified in the *Stanze* as Venus. Equally important, love and the politics of power are interwoven in order to show that there is a cosmic harmony which is reflected on earth in the person of the good ruler. The *Tirsi*, perhaps

aut iaculo, aut dura socios superare palaestra » (ll. 68-70).

The intellectual closeness of Castiglione and his dead friend is evoked a couple of lines later:

« non tua vicinos mulcebit fistula montes,
docta nec umbrosae resonabunt carmina valles » (ll. 73-74).

[31] The *Stanze per la giostra* are often mentioned in connection with *Tirsi*, though usually in a rather restrictive manner. Cf., for example, Guidi, *Thyrsis*, cit., p. 159 and Falvo, *Urbino*, cit., p. 135. It may not be too outrageous to suggest that the *Cortegiano*'s delicate balance between ' reality ' and ' myth ' owes something to his reading of the *Stanze*.

more conventionally, attaches the Neoplatonic philosophy to Christian notions of « pastori » and « santa legge ». In addition, the image of the sun as centre of the celestial harmonies and the ruler as its equivalent in terms of human institutions is not new to Neoplatonic thought.[32] Castiglione further elaborates this theme with constant reference to music. To emphasize this point, near the conclusion of the eclogue, the shepherds form a chorus and on hearing it, Tirsi exclaims:

> « Tanta dolcezza è nel mio cor discesa,
> Dameta, udendo l'armonia di questi,
> ch'io sento da un desir l'anima presa
> che mi rallegra il core e i sensi mesti »
> (*Tirsi*, stanza 53, pp. 570-571).

The image of song appears throughout the *Tirsi*. It is particularly noticeable when Castiglione picks out some of the more illustrious courtiers at Urbino. One quality receives pride of place in the short « rassegna »: their ability to compose poetry or its equivalent, namely, the playing of a musical instrument.[33] On one level it is a celebration of the intellectual achievements of the court of Urbino. On another, the connection between love and poetry allows Castiglione to enhance even further the theme of Urbino as the place where cosmic harmony reigns. The crucial significance with which poetry and music are endowed becomes still more evident if we consider that Poliziano's *Stanze* are constructed around the idea that history, in order to be palatable, should be mythicized. Poliziano alludes to this process in the poem:

> « ... e già la Gloria
> scendea giù folgorando ardente vampo:
> con essa Poesia, con essa Istoria
> volavon tutte accese del suo lampo »
> (*Stanze*, II, stanza 32, ll. 1-4).

---

[32] See Guidi, *Thyrsis*, cit., pp. 179-180 and A. Brown, *Platonism in fifteenth-century Florence and its contribution to early modern political thought*, « Journal of Modern History », 58, 1986, pp. 383-413. The *Epistola ad Henricum VII* offers further usage of the sun-symbol in reference to Guidubaldo da Montefeltro and to Henry VII himself. The latter is referred to in the following manner: « ut quemadmodum solis lumen sidera obumbrat » (*Lettere*, pp. 178-179). And the former's death is expressed in terms of loss of light: « sic nobis tenebrosi et sine sole dies iere » (*Lettere*, p. 193). Elisabetta Gonzaga's decision to shut herself away in a darkened room also reflects the symbolism of the loss of a leader: « in tenebris deget: clausisque fenestris invisum solis arcet lumen. Nullam prorsus atro cubiculo lucem admittit » (*Lettere*, pp. 196-197). Castiglione's personal comments to his mother use the same imagery: « Io sono ritornato ad Urbino: ne le lachrime, e ne le tenebre » (*Lettere*, p. 152).

[33] See *Tirsi*, st. 40, l. 8; st. 41, l. 8; st. 42, ll. 3-6; st. 43, l. 7; st. 44, l. 6.

Encomiastic poetry need not ignore history but it does have to 'purify' it of unpleasant reminders of reality. The same process is in evidence in the *Epistola ad Henricum VII* and in the *Cortegiano*. The former work marks the end of the actual reign of Guidubaldo Montefeltro and his dynasty and the beginning of a long rewriting of his history and that of his court. The *Epistola* is the text that lies behind the *Cortegiano*; its absence may be a recognition that something ended with the Duke's death but, certainly, court activities could continue and the courtiers themselves seek other means of advancement.

The epistle does not hesitate to beatify the dead Duke – it almost seems a document to support his canonization. The Christian stoicism of his last days is the first indication of his nobility and superhuman qualities « quaedam igitur perscribere constitui, quae licet admirabilia, nullam tamen nobis admirationem attulere » (*Lettere*, p. 163). Castiglione links, in this way, history and myth or « Poesia » and « Istoria ». Guidubaldo himself is a model courtier. In other words, the prince is really an exalted *courtier* who is distinguished by birth. One can list the qualities attributed to Guidubaldo Montefeltro and see that they share striking resemblances with the social skills and other attributes of the courtier presented in the *Cortegiano*. The Duke of Urbino demonstrated an equal interest in arms and letters (« alter Pollux », p. 166). Physically he was the embodiment of his court before the onset of illness: « totum denique corpus adeo concinne compositum » (p. 166). He took part in jousts and ball-games (« cuius erat scientissimus », p. 166). He was also a humanist prince: « In adolescentia assiduae lectionis fuisse traditur » (p. 175). His style of discourse and conversation is permeated by « gratia » (p. 177). Moreover, he was adept at the linguistic games of court society: « privatim facetissimus dicteriis totus scaturiens, comis ac facilis, non tamen ut quisquam serio aut ioco unquam ab eo, vel adhuc puero, fatuum aut inane verbum audierit » (p. 177). As a prince, Castiglione regards him as being endowed with all the necessary virtues. Guidubaldo Montefeltro's words, from his death-bed, anticipate the advice found in Book IV of the *Cortegiano*: « Quaedam insuper de clementia iustitiaque erga populos mandavit: quomodo se omnibus gratum amabilemque exhiberet » (p. 188).

Thus, Guidubaldo is put forward as an « exemplum » of the perfect Christian prince who is also the first courtier of his court. Blame for non-fulfilment of expectation falls on Destiny; Castiglione represents the Duke as a victim who is himself faultless. The account of Guidubaldo's military exploits makes interesting reading. Castiglione writes with consummate tact that « multas summa cum gloria pugnas pugnavit, Pisasque in Florentinorum ditionem *pene* redegit » (My emphasis; p. 182). And again when Guidubaldo is employed by the pope to defeat the Orsini: « Ille autem ea expeditione Ursinorum res adeo labefactavit, adeo contrivit, ut *pene* funditus deleverit » (My emphasis, p. 183). The *pene* here differs from the first example in that Castiglione is reconstructing history to a greater degree. History tells another story: defeat at the hands of the Orsini, capture and then ransom. Hardly a glorious moment in Guidubaldo's military career. Castiglione cannot allow the stain of defeat to spoil these pages of glorification. Writing is employed to eradicate the past, to convert history into propaganda.

It might be effective if, as in this case, the recipient is far away from the peninsula and possibly not aware of all the complex details of recent history. The nobility and grandeur of the subject also reflected on the writer of the *Epistola*. Castiglione was someone who communicated with kings – an intermediary who told of their desires to others. This was not the first letter he had written to the King: « ut quod olim ad Te scribendi mihi iucundissimum era argumentum » (p. 162). As Joseph D. Falvo points out, « the *Epistola* presents itself as an ' economic ' exchange governed by the principle of utility ».[34] The text is yet another example of Castiglione's instrumentalizing literature for reasons of personal politics.

The *Epistola* indirectly hints at the possibility that Castiglione's ambitions were far from satisfied. Guidubaldo did not have the means and the courtier was unsure about the future with the new Duke Francesco Maria della Rovere. Henry VII might have been viewed as a source of patronage. Nevertheless, in the end, Castiglione himself did not have much choice in the matter: « De l'esser mio: credo pur ch'io resterò col S.r Duca novo, con la medema conditione, perché Sua Ex.tia mostra molto vedermi voluntiera, et anchor la S.tà del Nostro Sig.re pare che desidera che M. Cesare et io restiamo. Fra tanto non cesserò de far il mio debito verso la S.ra Duchessa e S.r Duca » (*Lettere*, p. 152). The intimacy of the relationship between the new Duke and the pope must certainly have raised his expectations, especially since the latter indicated that he should remain in Urbino. Another reason for his staying was the affection he had for Elisabetta Gonzaga, Guidubaldo's widow. Her confidence in his abilities was demonstrated by the fact she used him on at least one delicate mission during the « interregnum ».[35]

At first nothing seems to have changed in Castiglione's personal position under the new Duke: we find him still complaining about the same problems, particularly his financial difficulties.[36] He was once more thrust onto the battlefield due to the Duke of Urbino's involvement in Julius II's plans for the

---

[34] *Urbino and the apotheosis of power*, cit., p. 127.

[35] Evidence of Castiglione's affection and admiration for Elisabetta can be found in numerous parts of the *Cortegiano* and in the poem *De Elizabetha Gonzaga canente* (cf. Cian, *Un illustre nunzio pontificio*, cit., pp. 217-219). In a letter of 11 April 1508 Castiglione wrote « la povera Sig.ra Duchessa, la quale io ho deliberato servir fin tanto che la veggia assettata a qualche modo: Dio ce aiuti » (*Lettere*, p. 151). See also *Lettere*, pp. 152, 939.

[36] For example, *Lettere*, p. 216. See also G. Gorni, *Il rovescio del « Cortegiano » o le lettere del Castiglione*, « Paragone. Letteratura », 30, 1979, pp. 63-75.

expansion of the papal states, first at the expense of Venice, followed by Ferrara. Illness and misfortune dogged Castiglione's attempts to become a competent fighting man.[37] The campaign against Ferrara was the one fraught with the most difficulties, since Francesco Maria had not the slightest intention of taking Ferrara, much to the pope's anger. In this the Duke had probably been influenced by Elisabetta and Eleonora Gonzaga. Without a doubt, Isabella d'Este's presence is to be seen in the measures taken to protect her brother and prevent the further erosion of the city-state system.

Deception became the hallmark of Castiglione's activity in these years. He was used by the Duke of Urbino to try and allay the pope's suspicions about the lack of success in taking Ferrara. The battles Castiglione fought were not on the battlefield but in the audience-chamber. His efforts to keep the peace between uncle and nephew did not meet with the greatest success. When he went to congratulate the pope on the capture of Mirandola, he received the brunt of Julius II's abuse directed against Francesco Maria. The Venetian ambassador who recounts this incident referred to Castiglione as the Duke's « primario ».[38] This would seem to indicate that Castiglione was extremely busy on the diplomatic side, employed by the Duke as his « frontline man » in the intricate subterfuges needed to maintain his insecure position.

As the Duke's most trusted ambassador and the personal instrument of his politics, Castiglione found himself in increasingly difficult situations. He was asked to justify what had already happened rather than prevent the deed occurring in the first place. The murder of cardinal Alidosi by Francesco Maria (not the first instance of the Duke's violent temperament), required that Castiglione be sent to Rome to justify it.[39] Whatever Castiglione's personal feelings of disgust at Francesco Maria's act of treachery, the courtier was in no position to raise any objections. Indeed, if he did, that would have marked the end of his special relationship with the prince. Castiglione's particular value lay in his ability to perform rather morally questionable actions for his master. The reward of a feudal estate (Novilara was granted to Castiglione in September 1513), was the result of this morally dubious behaviour (*Lettere*, pp. 791-793). To make matters worse, Castiglione was sent on a secret mission to the King of France, something which amounted to an act of high treason against the pope on the part of the Duke of Urbino.[40] To his mother he said not a word about the nature

---

[37] Hale, *Castiglione's military career*, cit., pp. 47-49.

[38] M. Sanudo, *I Diarii*, X, col. 773. Cf. Cartwright, *The Perfect Courtier*, cit., I, pp. 288-289.

[39] Cartwright, *The Perfect Courtier*, cit., I, pp. 224-229, 296-300.

[40] See *Lettere*, p. 1045; Guidi, *L'Espagne*, cit., pp. 125-126. Cf. V. Cian, *Il perfetto cavaliere e il perfetto politico della Rinascita: Baldassarre Castiglione e Francesco Guicciardini*, in *Francesco Guicciardini nel IV centenario della morte (1540-1940)*, Florence 1940,

or even the place of his mission, perhaps only partially because of security reasons: « Creddo che la M.V. habbia inteso a questi dì ch'io ero absente da Urbino: il che è stato per alcune mie occurrentie, che seria lungo a scrivere » (*Lettere*, p. 312).

This silence can be interpreted as an expression of Castiglione's shame and sense of dishonour. If Castiglione did not dare to raise his voice at the time, he was certainly scathing of some unnamed princes in the *Cortegiano*. He criticizes their politics of magnificence which serves only to exhaust their treasuries and at the end of the day offers only an illusion of power: « E questi (princìpi) sono, al parer mio, come i colossi che l'anno passato fur fatti a Roma il dì della festa di piazza d'Agone, che di fori mostravano similitudine di grandi omini e cavalli triunfanti e dentro erano pieni di stoppa e di strazzi » (*Il Cortegiano*, p. 454). They have lost all sense of reality and their moral sensibilities are in tatters. Because these princes consider themselves gods, they also feel that they do not need advice from their courtiers. The intellectual side of the courtier's role has been reduced to a minimum. Faced with the power politics of greater forces, the Italian princes had to exploit every possible advantage: « Ma piacesse a Dio che i prìncipi de questi nostri tempi accompagnassero i peccati loro con tante virtù, con quante accompagnavano quegli antichi » (*Il Cortegiano*, p. 455). Changes will only be achieved by following the Ancients as an ideal model. Looking back to the past and looking forward to the future reveal Castiglione's profound dissatisfaction with the present.

With the advent of Pope Leo X, Francesco Maria della Rovere lost the privileged position he had enjoyed under Julius II. The Duke of Urbino was now seen as an intruder who had to make way for members of the new papal family. As Leo X's intentions became clearer, Francesco Maria's position as Duke of Urbino was clearly threatened. Once more, Castiglione was required to defend an impossible situation as he had done under the previous pope. He was first of all sent as the Duke's representative at the funeral of Julius II and accompanied his lord to the coronation ceremony of Leo X. The following month (May 1513) Castiglione returned to Rome to deal with more urgent business.[41] His first task was to keep the Duke informed about the military situation since he had been kept on in his capacity as Captain-General of the Church (*Lettere*, pp. 348-349).

Information is particularly scant for this vital period before the expulsion of Francesco Maria from his duchy, even though Castiglione spent long periods

---

pp. 49-95, who describes this episode as « in un certo senso e dal punto di vista morale, il brutto rovescio di quella medaglia che splende delle glorie del nostro Rinascimento » (p. 77).

[41] CARTWRIGHT, *The Perfect Courtier*, cit., I, pp. 345, 349-351, but see also *Lettere*, p. 1074.

in Rome (*Lettere*, p. 1074). Secrecy must have been the order of the day, which is why so few letters remain addressed to the Duke; other means of communication were certainly improvised. Cristoforo Tirabosco becomes prominent in Castiglione's correspondence during these years. He seems to have been an important link between Urbino and Mantua, writing on his master's behalf to his mother and other persons in his native city (*Lettere*, pp. 351-368). Castiglione used Tirabosco as an intermediary in business matters (for example, loans). That only five letters to his mother survive for the period 1513-1516 would seem to indicate either a complete breakdown of direct communication or an alternative means of correspondence. One has the impression that Castiglione has gone out of his way not to appear in direct contact with his mother. Aloisa Castiglione, as a relative of Isabella d'Este, would have been in a good position to act in the role of intermediary, especially since the « Marchesana » took such a serious interest in her dynastic responsibilities. Now that they seemed to be particularly threatened, her activity would have increased. It should be remembered that Isabella's daughter, Eleonora, was Duchess of Urbino. As a consequence, Castiglione found that he had regained a foothold in Mantua, although a somewhat shaky one.

Whatever diplomatic manoeuvre Castiglione and the Duke tried, it was bound to fail with the pope's determination to make a Medici ruler of Urbino. The sense of utter powerlessness and overwhelming inevitability of the events of 1516 led Castiglione to seek refuge in Mantua. After a desperate attempt to save his duchy, Francesco Maria also made his way to the same city. Hence, Castiglione did not cut himself off totally from the Duke at this stage nor did the Duke completely disown his ambassador, at least not yet. He was still useful in a limited fashion (*Lettere*, pp. 376-379).

At Mantua Castiglione could never regain the confidence of Francesco Gonzaga. The Marquis did attend his wedding but, apart from this, there was no other mark of recognition. As far as Francesco was concerned, Castiglione was still in the service of his son-in-law.[42] The management of his estates, the composition of the *Cortegiano*, the consolations provided by Isabella d'Este's circle and the occasional letter on behalf of Francesco Maria were all the pleasures or duties allowed him until the death of the Marquis in 1519.[43]

Immediately upon his accession, Federico Gonzaga saw the advantages to be gained by employing Castiglione as his ambassador to Rome. The Marquis' mother no doubt supported the idea, if she did not actually suggest it herself.

---

[42] Castiglione did not, in fact, officially leave the Duke of Urbino's service until July 1521, that is precisely the moment of the proclamation of Federico Gonzaga as Captain-General of the Church (cf. CARTWRIGHT, *The Perfect Courtier*, cit., II, pp. 116-117).

[43] *Lettere*, pp. 376-389; M. BANDELLO, *Tutte le opere*, I, novella 21, pt. 2, Milan 1952.

At this time, Isabella was in charge in Mantua: « A Madamma Illustrissima se riferisce il tutto e senza sua saputa et consenso non si move foglia ».[44]

Isabella realized that Castiglione was well suited to her needs, namely, the protection of her brother Alfonso d'Este against papal expansion, the restoration of Francesco Maria della Rovere to Urbino and the establishment of good relations between her son and the pope. There was also other official business to attend to in Rome and Florence: condolences on the part of the new Marquis for the death of Lorenzo de' Medici, ruler of Urbino. These naturally led to the question of Francesco Maria and Mantua's relationship with the papacy (the second of these matters only on a general level).[45] Although the death of Lorenzo de' Medici left the Captain-Generalcy of the Church vacant, there would have been no desire on Isabella's part to obtain it for her son because of the possibility that Federico might have to fight against her brother Alfonso. For the Gonzaga it was essential not to earn the wrath of the Pontiff by harbouring an outlaw of the Church in Mantua; there would have been strong memories of the bitter dispute between Isabella and Julius II over giving shelter to the exiled Bentivoglio.[46] In spite of all the dangers and problems, Castiglione was principally involved in attempting to persuade the pope to allow Francesco Maria to return to his state as Duke (*Lettere*, pp. 397, 400-401).

It seems that Francesco Maria did not have much faith in Castiglione's ability to persuade the pope to allow him to return to his territories. Or, to state the problem in other terms, it was clear that the pope was determined not to give up any acquisition that would strengthen the papacy, especially now that it had Florence under its control and was still seeking to subjugate Ferrara. Francesco Maria knew that the only way to win back Urbino during the pope's lifetime was to seek an alliance with a state strong enough to keep the papacy weak and ineffectual in Italian politics. This Francesco Maria succeeded in doing. Under such conditions, Castiglione was no more than a puppet. With his master acting behind his back and Leo X expecting such behaviour, the diplomat found himself unable to influence the course of events: « Io con certe altre parole, pur in questa medema sententia, mi partì tutto di mala voglia, parendomi quasi essere in priggione ... Pensi V. Ex.tia ch'io sto in su la croce, e parmi esser martirizato » (*Lettere*, p. 502). Instead of being the manipulator of events, as sometimes has been suggested, Castiglione was

---

[44] Archivio di Stato di Modena, Archivio Segreto Estense, Cancelleria Ambasciatori: Mantova, busta 2, 21 March 1519, Mario Equicola to Alfonso d'Este.

[45] *Lettere*, pp. 390-393. Throughout 1519 Castiglione kept in close contact with the ex-Duke of Urbino, as can be seen from the letters addressed to him. However, the situation radically changes in 1520 for which year there are no surviving letters to the Duke who has been forced to leave Mantua under papal pressure (Cartwright, *The Perfect Courtier*, cit., II, p. 115).

[46] Dionisotti, Review of Cian, cit., pp. 53-54; Guidi, *L'Espagne*, cit., p. 174.

their victim. Without the threat of real power to support his claim, the diplomat was trapped in a game, the outcome of which he could not influence. Nothing that Castiglione could say would have been able to alter the pope's determination to maintain and even extend the papal state. To Castiglione's remark on the need to foster « quelle poche force che sono in Italia » (*Lettere*, p. 488), in particular Francesco Maria – otherwise the papacy's very power will be seen to have been built on sand – the pope replied: « ' Noi non dormeno, e pensamo a questo più che non credete. E forsi ne conciaremo più di una '. E credo che volesse dir di Ferrara » (*Lettere*, p. 489). The above quote is a concise way of explaining his intention of subjugating certain Italian states and bringing others into the orbit of the papacy.

Castiglione did not consider himself to be in the confidence of the pope. He lamented the lack of « uno bono amico de autoritate, come Medici » because « io non ho quel credito » (*Lettera*, p. 489). In fact, Leo X was noted for his secrecy; the death of his cousin, the Cardinal de' Rossi, represented the loss of his most trusted confidant: « cum el quale unico se sborava in tutte le cose sue famigliare più confidentemente cha *cum* alcun altro » (*Lettere*, p. 468).

Giulio de' Medici now achieved even greater prominence in the pope's affairs because of the demise of the cardinal. Castiglione was painfully aware of his limitations which were brought home to him by his inability to persuade (for want of more effective means) the pope to restore Francesco Maria to Urbino. Leo X did not need a Castiglione to tell him what to do; he understood himself what his objectives were. Even though Castiglione knew what *he* had to do on behalf of his lord, the former Duke of Urbino, he refused to act and take responsibility for actions which had not been countenanced by his masters in Mantua. Hence, the reason for his innumerable complaints about not having received any letters. This situation repeated itself on his second mission to Rome and became almost impossible for him when he was papal nuncio in Spain.[47] The constant delays in receiving letters did not give Castiglione the opportunity to work on his own initiative, as one might have perhaps expected. Instead he remained, in his own words, « sospeso » and « pieno di fastidio » (*Lettere*, pp. 420, 470). However, Castiglione had a genius for pushing ahead with a course of action that had been determined along its general lines by his superiors. He was never short of ideas or the necessary perseverance to help his case (*Lettere*, p. 449). For Castiglione this remained the essence of his task during his employment by Federico Gonzaga.

---

[47] For example, *Lettere*, p. 450; L. von Pastor, *The History of the Popes*, IX, London 1950, pp. 352-356. See also G. La Rocca, *Una tradizione finora inavvertita di autocensura editoriale su un testo politico del Cinquecento*, in *Guerre stati e città. Mantova e l'Italia padana dal secolo XIII al XIX*. Atti delle Giornate di Studio in omaggio ad Adele Bellù, Mantova 12-13 dicembre 1986, a cura di C. M. Belfanti *et al.*, Mantua 1988, pp. 345-374 [pp. 359-368].

Castiglione left Rome to return to Mantua in November 1519 without having achieved any of his principal objectives. However, two papal bulls addressed to Federico (the pope did not want to enter into direct contact with Francesco Maria), claim that further negotiations were possible and that Castiglione fulfilled the rôle of go-between most satisfactorily (*Lettere*, pp. 832-833). The ambassador returned to Rome in July 1520, some seven months later. This time he worked exclusively for the Marquis of Mantua. For the year 1520 no letters written by Castiglione to Francesco Maria survive. It is quite clear that the diplomat had changed allegiance in the realization that the pope did not intend to restore the ex-Duke and that Federico had a chance of supplanting him (remembering that the Duke was a former Captain-General of the Church). Also, Federico Gonzaga had a state; not a minor matter when so many Italian princes had lost theirs. If one wishes to speak about Castiglione's betrayal of the Duke, it can be said to have taken place then.

By the time Castiglione returned to Rome, relations between Mantua and the papacy had steadily deteriorated. There had been causes for tension on Castiglione's previous visit but now the situation had worsened. The quarrels between the pope and the Gonzaga were numerous. Leo X refused to ratify the concession of the bishopric of Mantua to Ercole by his brother Sigismondo. He was further worried by the possibility that Annibale Bentivoglio (expelled from Bologna by the previous pope) was planning to return to his state with the help of an alliance with the Gonzaga since Pirro Gonzaga hoped to marry Camilla Bentivoglio. Other problems concerning Tolomeo and Alessandro Spagnuoli, as well as the pope's prohibition of public armed combats in Mantua (permission for which had been granted by the Marquis), all added fuel to the fire.[48] The situation had deteriorated to such an extent that Federico accepted the advice of some friendly cardinals: « Havendo noi inteso da messer Pandolpho della Mirandula il parere de quelli reverendissimi Cardinali [Fieschi and de Grassis] di mandare lì lo magnifico messer Baldessare. Laudando il consiglio amorevole et prudente di loro reverendissime signorie havemo dimandato a dimandarlo che l'era fori del paese. Et presto sarà qui et lo inviaremo subito a Nostro Signore ».[49]

A question the historian needs to ask at this point is whether all these disputes were a matter of pure chance or whether one can detect a pattern behind them.

---

[48] Mario Equicola, in his *Chronica di Mantua*, Mantua? 1521?, 4°, claims that the major cause of the dispute was Sigismondo Gonzaga's resignation of the bishopric of Mantua in favour of his brother Ercole: « fu altrimente che non se estimava resposta, querelevase del Signor Marchese de cose falsissime in tucto vane da maledicentia di maligni sente » (f. CC2*r*). See also *Lettere*, p. 1216 and *Mantova, la storia*, Verona 1961, II, pp. 269, 321-322.

[49] Archivio di Stato di Mantova, Archivio Gonzaga, b. 2963, Libro II, Mantua, 5 June 1520, Federico Gonzaga to Angelo Germanello.

It would seem that the pope was placing Mantua in a difficult position, almost besieging it. Up until Castiglione's mission to Rome, Mantua was treated as a hostile power by the papacy. Any move that smacked of dynastic politics was attacked by the pope. It appears as if Leo X were trying to prevent the reformation of a cohesive alliance of Italian states bound by dynastic ties, by actively seeking to take a firmer hold on the surviving northern Italian states. In the particular case of Mantua, this policy effectively meant a personal attack on Isabella d'Este and her politics since it was she who attached so much importance to the idea of family bonds providing the best and strongest form of political union. She still held this view in spite of the fact that the system was falling apart under pressure from greater powers. Isabella, above all, wanted the promotion of her son Ercole to the cardinalate, the destruction of her mortal enemy Tolomeo Spagnuoli, the strengthening of dynastic bonds, particularly with her brother's state of Ferrara which was constantly under threat from successive popes.[50]

In these circumstances, then, Castiglione made his way to Rome. It has been the almost unanimous opinion of historians that it was Castiglione who persuaded the pope to appoint Federico Gonzaga Captain-General of the Church. Consequently, this diplomat is considered to have been acting according to general political principles to which even the interests of his masters were subordinated. The appointment is seen as Castiglione's achievement; an achievement which will give him an important place in the events that were reshaping Italian history. No longer is Castiglione an instrument in the hands of his masters; the roles are reversed because he has now become the manipulator.[51] The manner in which this episode is interpreted has general consequences for Castiglione's biography. The appointment of Federico Gonzaga was the one major success of his career, indeed, the high-point of his diplomacy in Italy. If it can be demonstrated that Castiglione was as much a victim here as in his other missions (though this time in the opposite sense), it would mean that the image of him as an all-powerful and truly influential figure would suffer a hard blow. It could then be said that at no time in his career was Castiglione able to exert

---

[50] Dionisotti, Review of Cian, cit., p. 53; *Mantova, la storia*, cit., p. 269. On Spagnoli, see S. Davari, *Della famiglia Spagnolo*, Mantua 1873 and E. Bolisani, *Tolomeo Spagnoli, segretario alla corte dei Gonzaga, filologo ed umanista*, « Atti dell'Istituto veneto di scienze, lettere ed arti », 118, 1959-1960, pp. 11-51.

[51] Dionisotti, Review of Cian, cit., p. 53; G. La Rocca, *Il contributo di Baldassar Castiglione alla formazione della politica estera gonzaghesca negli ultimi anni del papato di Leone X: 1519-1521*, in *Mantova e i Gonzaga nella civiltà del Rinascimento*. Atti del convegno, Milan 1978; Id., *Il Castiglione diplomatico e politico* (*profilo ermeneutico*), in *Convegno di studio su Baldassarre Castiglione nel quinto centenario della nascita*, Mantua 1980, pp. 61-80. As far as I know, only L. Mazzoldi, *Mantova, la storia*, cit., has suggested, without going into any details, that the Pope may have been behind these manoeuvres (II, p. 270).

influence as a maker of policies, as opposed to the executor of other people's schemes. In the case of Castiglione there should be little difficulty in discerning the boundaries between the diplomat's competence and that of the ruler. It is true that Castiglione *does* make suggestions and give advice to the young Marquis, usually within the framework of an already decided policy, but this has to be distinguished from actually directing policy. Federico Gonzaga, as we shall see, had his own reasons for accepting the appointment.

Castiglione himself confessed that the thought of Federico being appointed Captain-General had not even entered his mind at the start of his mission: « E pensi che quando io venni a Roma, non se parlava de capitaniato, ma di rimovere una mala oppinione che havea Nostro S.re di V. Ex.tia, et di tutta Casa sua: la quale non solamente è rimossa, ma terminerà (se piace a Dio) in quello ch'io hormai tante volte ho scritto » (*Lettere*, p. 740). This was what Castiglione thought would be the central question of his mission: the re-establishment of good relations with the papacy. In his discussions with Giulio de' Medici all the emphasis was on the points of tension with the pope: « Et dilatatomi in farli intendere quanto despiacere quella haveva, presentendo che N. S.re era mal satisfacto di lei, e come la mi mandava per iustificarsi, non che d'ogni sua actione ma pur d'ogni pensiero » (*Lettere*, p. 548). Giulio de' Medici does not seem to have informed Castiglione of the pope's intention, that is, if even he knew about it. So, when Castiglione had his audience, he launched into a detailed defence of the Marquis: « Per quanto fu in poter mio, me sforzai de iustificare Vostra Ex. delle imputationi che quella haveva inteso esserli datte apresso S. S.tità » (*Lettere*, p. 553). After heated discussion of the accusations Leo X, like a master magician, performed his last and best trick: « ' Et haranno (the Gonzaga) da noi più che non sapranno dimandare '. E qui me fece una grande offerta ... » (*Lettere*, p. 554).

The offer came as a great surprise to Castiglione as to everyone else. Castiglione quickly grasped its significance and urged the immediate acceptance of it by the Marquis. However, his experience as a diplomat convinced him that the pope had other political surprises up his sleeve: « A me pareria che V. Ex.tia ringratiasse sommamente Nostro S.re de la offerta, e *mostrasse* desiderarne l'effetto sommamente, e restringesse la cosa presto, a fine che se potesse conoscere ove la tende: perché io estimo che la habbia qualche cosa de nascoso » (My emphasis; *Lettere*, p. 557).

The historian must next ask how far Castiglione should take the responsibility for persuading Federico to accept the offer. Would Federico have needed much persuasion? In the first place, the post was advertised in such a way so as to appeal to the sensibilities of the young prince. Castiglione reported that Leo X « li farebbe dare una grossa condotta e sicura da un gran principe », something that was close to Federico's heart (*Lettere*, p. 556). The promise of future gain, especially Ercole Gonzaga's advancement in the Church, had to be weighed against the veiled threats if the Marquis refused. Even Isabella would have seen some of the advantages of such an alliance. For her it meant the possibility of perhaps exerting some control over the pope's anti-Ferrarese policies in the person of her son. But her son saw the appointment in a different light: it represented a chance of becoming his own man, freed from the interference of his mother. As Captain-General of the Church he could exercise an authority in the state which would help to eclipse his mother's. Thus, Castiglione, who in any case was absent from Mantua, did not really need to press a case for accepting. For Federico it would have been enough to know that his father had never been appointed to such an exalted position and that the son was about to prove himself superior. Throughout the negotiations, Federico was not very pleased about the length of service to be stipulated in the « condotta » – he did not want a reduction in the time he would be bound to the pope. Instead, he desired an *increase*, completely against Castiglione's advice.[52] Federico did not intend to make a pretence of accepting the Captain-Generalcy, as first suggested by Castiglione. As soon as the Marquis arrived on the battlefield, he showed a great deal of faith in his title as is shown by his refusal to accept the superiority of Prospero Colonna in matters of strategy and tactics. He held himself to be the supreme commander: « Et come è sta' certe parole tra il Signor Prospero et dito Marchese per causa di la Concordia dove el Signor Marchese ha posto un suo segno, et dito Signor Prospero ne voleva meter uno suo; siché nel suo campo par sia discordia ne li capi ».[53]

Castiglione's reward for the successful negotiation of the Captain-Generalcy was the offer, made by the Marquis, of being put in charge of fifty men-at-arms. This seems to suggest that Federico was not interested in creating a specialist-class of courtier but was concerned to call his servant back to his feudal duty. Perhaps there was also an element of worry at the possibility of Castiglione staying too long in Rome and passing into papal service. Even though Castiglione wielded enough influence with the Marquis to prevent his removal from Rome after the completion of his task, nevertheless he was required to appear at various points in Federico's military campaigns.[54]

For the most part, Castiglione spent his time in Rome in a state of almost complete anguish. Before the Captain-Generalcy was officially announced, he had spent his energies in trying to urge the pope to publish the appointment at the earliest possible date. But the pope did not act until he was totally assured

---

[52] The only copy of the « condotta » that Castiglione sent to Federico on 27 August, 1520, stipulated a period of two years plus a possible extra year (*Lettere*, pp. 580, 583). Federico replied: « et però supplicareti a quella che la se degni ordinare che il tempo del fermo habbi ad essere tre anni et il quarto a beneplacito » (Archivio di Stato di Mantova, AG, b. 2193, « minute di cancelleria », 31 August 1520, f. 63*v*).

[53] SANUDO, *I Diarii*, XXXI, col. 168.

[54] CARTWRIGHT, *The Perfect Courtier*, cit., II, p. 197.

of his alliances; something that was outside Castiglione's control. The death of Leo X in 1521 represented a moment of deep crisis for the Gonzaga who were now exposed to the wrath of their enemies. Castiglione felt particularly disheartened: « Mi pareva pure che ogni bene che nasceva da questa radice fosse pur stato coltivato e mosso in qualche parte dalle opere mie ».[55] Here, Castiglione emphasizes the important part he had in stimulating the pope to act in favour of the Gonzaga; this statement is qualified by the « in qualche parte » and should be seen to refer to his work as a tireless representative of the Marquis. In a bid to retain his post in Rome and cultivate an equally intimate relationship with another pope, Castiglione acts as his own publicity agent, stressing the essential nature of his work which could not have been done by anyone else.

There is no doubt that life became truly difficult for Castiglione during the period before Hadrian VI came to Rome in 1522. Federico Gonzaga was still fighting the French even without the financial support of the College of Cardinals. In these circumstances the political divisions of this body were almost fatal. But, after overcoming many obstacles, he was able to obtain some money for his master.[56] As well as being marked out as a supporter of the Imperial cause, which he could not have avoided through the military situation of the Marquis, Castiglione helped to dismember the Papal states at a critical moment. He pleaded for the return of the Duke of Urbino to his state on various occasions perhaps because he understood the fatal weakness of a papal state that had not developed the ability to survive without the presence of a particular pope. In 1523 he accompanied Isabella d'Este on a visit to Venice where he asked the Republic to appoint Francesco Maria Captain-General.[57] It could have been that Castiglione was disappointed by the meagre reward he received from Federico for his efforts, so he attempted a rapprochement with Francesco Maria through Isabella who had, by now, been excluded from the government of Mantua.[58] Giulio de'

---

[55] E. Bianco di San Secondo, *Baldassarre Castiglione nella vita e negli scritti*, Verona 1941, p. 130.

[56] *Ibid.*, pp. 142-148.

[57] Cartwright, *The Perfect Courtier*, cit., II, pp. 192-193.

[58] The appointment of Federico Gonzaga as Captain-General meant that Isabella lost her controlling influence over her son, particularly since the Marquis was enamoured of the other Isabella, Isabella Boschetti. The Pope had placed her in an impossible position, as she explained to her much-worried brother Alfonso d'Este: « et perochè se dubitasse che N. S.re havesse qualche cosa latente in queste offerte del Capitaniato, tuttavia non se potette refutare per essere cosa tanto honorevole et lui tanto grande homo et noi non molto favoriti da Francesi, donde seria stata la total roina nostra ad non monstrar desiderarla ». Her reasons for accepting the offer were not exactly the same as those put forward by Castiglione. She was very much aware of Mantua's vulnerability if it were to remain dependent on untrustworthy allies. In her view, to have her son as Captain-General of the Church was to possess a powerful tool against papal designs on Ferrara. Isabella was always seeking the aggrandizement of her son.

Medici would not have been unaware of Castiglione's activities in this respect and this, combined with knowledge of his Imperial sympathies, no doubt contributed to his being appointed papal nuncio to Spain.[59] Castiglione's earnest character, the reputation of being a supporter of Charles V and his tirelessness in chasing his goal (for Giulio he might have been considered a rather uncomfortable nuisance), were all factors in Clement VII's choice of Castiglione as someone who had enough credibility to convince the Emperor of the seriousness of the pope's intentions.

If one were searching for the characteristics of Castiglione's diplomacy in the period of his service in the Italian peninsula, one of his particular traits is his perseverance, in itself an indication of the weakness of his position and that of his employers. He needed to work so hard because most events happened without reference to himself or his masters. His was a trade of impotence, an unending and unfruitful quest to influence the decisions of the powerful. His personal situation was characterized by the animosity of the princes who had employed him and whose service he had left. The ruler's idea of a servant did not conform to Castiglione's own vision. The feeling that a ruler could do what he wished with a servant of the stature of Castiglione went against the latter's sense of his personal worth: he saw himself no longer as a mere reflection but as a person in his own right, someone who could be distinguished from his employer.

In the *Cortegiano*, Federico Fregoso confirms the right of the courtier to leave his employer if the latter is considered to be « malo ». This is not merely a moral judgement; it implies a judgement of a ruler's capacities of governing his state (*Il Cortegiano*, pp. 224-225). The courtier is seen as the instrument for the renewal of the Italian peninsula. Indeed, the courtier must do everything in his power to increase his prestige, even the manner in which he received rewards from his patron is considered important in building up a reputation (*Il Cortegiano*, pp. 220-221). Once such a reputation had been acquired it was possible for a courtier to obtain new employment. Hence Federico Fregoso's insistence that the courtier should not perform tasks that will be seen as reprehensible:

Once Federico had obtained the Captain-Generalcy she saw no reason why Ercole should not be made a cardinal: « sì che perseverate pur gagliardamente in negociare questa pratica finché l'habbiate tratta al desiato et aspettato fine con quella bona mano et felicità che haveste in *perficere* quella del Capitaniato del S.r Marchese che se hanno a conoscere li meriti vostri in questa come in quella » (Archivio di Stato di Mantova, Archivio Gonzaga, busta 2997, Mantua, 3 December 1521, Isabella d'Este to Castiglione; my italics).

[59] von Pastor, *The History of the Popes*, cit., IX, pp. 349-356. As « nuncio », Castiglione had very limited powers of negotiation. In fact, in 1525 Cardinal Salviati was sent to Spain as papal legate with much wider powers than Castiglione possessed (p. 280). See also D. E. Queller, *The Office of Ambassador in the Middle Ages*, Princeton 1967, pp. 3-17.

« Ma sete obligato a non farlo, e per voi stesso, e per non esser ministro della vergogna del signor vostro » (*Il Cortegiano*, p. 226). The act of disobeying one's lord is not recommended in the *Cortegiano*, especially as far as changing his instructions is concerned. The most essential quality of the courtier is that he be adaptable, as fluid as the changing political circumstances of the Italian states: « Laudo ben che sopra tutto abbia rispetto alla natura di quel signore a cui serve e secondo quella si governi » (*Il Cortegiano*, p. 228).

On the other hand, Castiglione did take it on himself to advise his « signore » on occasion, particularly in the case of Federico Gonzaga. He advised the Marquis to accept the offer of the Captain-Generalcy. Whether his advice was decisive in swaying the Marquis is open to doubt, as I have suggested earlier. When Castiglione went to Spain it was as if he had no employer, so distant was he from Italy and from the uncertainties of Clement VII. Here was his chance to act decisively on a level that could effect not only Italy but the whole of Europe. But, as on his missions to Italy, the same problems arise, this time in a more acute form, such as the lack of instructions from the papal court and the feeling that he is acting in a vacuum. This higher level of political action in Spain corresponds, in a sense, with the higher goal of the courtier in the *Cortegiano*; that of directing the prince on to the « camin della virtù » (*Il Cortegiano*, p. 451). For Castiglione, both were equally illusory.

II

Women through Men's Eyes: the Third Book of *Il Cortegiano*

A dramatic happening towards the end of the second book of *Il libro del cortegiano* seems out of place in the midst of the gallant conversations that characterize the tone of the work. On Elisabetta Gonzaga's signal a band of women rise up to punish their sexist opponent:

> Allora una gran parte di quelle donne ben per averle la signora Duchessa fatto così cenno, si levarono in piedi e ridendo tutte corsero verso il signor Gasparo, come per dargli delle busse, e farne come le Baccanti d'Orfeo, tuttavia dicendo: "Ora vedrete, se ci curiamo che di noi si dica male".[1]

The disorder is only apparent; the serious nature of the act is undermined at the very moment of its inception ("e ridendo tutte"). It is rather a good-natured theoretical statement which playfully underlines the women's exasperation and impotence without there being the risk of a more serious confrontation. The situation is thus defused. The repetition of "come" serves to reinforce this point: the blows are fictitious, Gasparo-Orfeo will not be torn to pieces. The entertainment value of the set-piece ("tra per le risa"; II, xcvii; 252) functions in order to deflate the ironical criticism of Gasparo Pallavicino.[2] Furthermore Emilia Pia rebukes him in a way that moves the focus of attention away from the incident. Her reply points to the third book as the place where finally discourse will ally itself with the female cause and vanquish "così acerbo nemico nostro" (II, xcvii; 253). It should be remarked that Emilia Pia's language maintains the war/violence metaphor. She extends the metaphor to include the idea of a joust fought with words: "ma noi metteremo in campo un cavalier piú fresco, che combatterà con voi, acciò che l'error vostro non sia così lungamente impunito." (II, xcvii; 252-53) A civilized rite replaces and sublimates the non-linguistic act of the previous chapter. We hear echoes of the battle of the sexes but with the definite expectation that Emilia Pia cannot lose the debate (if such it is!).[3] It has been observed that the failure of the female interlocutors to speak in their own voice casts doubt on the extent of

Castiglione's adherence to "feminist" or more accurately, proto-feminist politics. Whether one can talk about sixteenth-century feminism or about feminism in works written by men is a matter for debate.[4] It would be better to examine the strategy by means of which Castiglione the author imposes silence on the women in the *Cortegiano*. Such a strategy is rich in ideological implications for Castiglione since it involves self-censorship emanating from the *regina*.[5] It is therefore an action that results from the women themselves at the behest of their leader:

> ma la signora Duchessa sùbito disse: 'Poiché madonna Emilia non vole affaticarsi in trovar gioco alcuno, sarebbe pur ragione che l'altre donne partecipassino di questa commodità, ed esse ancor fussino esente di tal fatica per questa sera, essendoci massimamente tanti omini, che non è pericolo che manchin giochi.' (I, vii; 27)

Elisabetta Gonzaga demonstrates an eager alacrity in interrupting Costanza Fregoso without warning or consultation (the adverb "sùbito" suggests the speed with which she cuts in and the force of her intervention is caught by Castiglione taking the point of view of Costanza "la qual già s'apparechiava a dire"). In this way, the rigid hierarchy of the women becomes clear, even to the point of the Duchess's disregard for her newly-appointed "locotente" (I, vi; 26). Elisabetta's order is immediately obeyed and without question: "'Così faremo', rispose la signora Emilia; ed imponendo silenzio a madonna Costanza . . .". (I, vii; 27) The principal of authority, delegated or otherwise, is thus enunciated. The women are obedient to the leader of their sex and consequently no blame can be attached to the men. The choice appears unimpeachable as it is unwarranted. However, it does owe something to a ghetto-mentality: the women form a (silent) minority in the *Cortegiano*: "ché *quasi* sempre il numero degli omini era *molto* maggiore" (I, vi; 25, my emphasis). The "quasi" does nothing to dispel the idea that the court is a place dominated by men; again the use of an adverb, "molto" makes this abundantly clear. The husband may be absent but the Duchess seems to be acting under the shadow of his authority; her relationship with Emilia Pia can be compared to hers with the Duke. The male voice predominates in this society. Defences of women were written by men. If there is a positive advance it must be that women are allowed more space; although enclosed, they can manoeuvre more freely. Their rôle becomes that of being arbiters of the male courtiers. In the most subtle of interpretations that acknowledges the supremacy of the indirect, one might argue that a reversal of rôles has taken place. The women challenge the men, keep them in order and generally forbid them to speak out of turn. This kind of interpretation would be seductive for those who see Castiglione as a proto-feminist. One of the points this contribution will examine will be how effective are the interruptions of the women and how far they can be considered a subtle form of control over the men.

1. *Joking about Women*

The discussion about women had been set off by heated debate on Boccaccio's treatment of them in two stories from the *Decameron*. The wider context was the general topic of jokes. Not that this should be seen as denigrating women, not treating them seriously, but the connection between women and joking already delineates the social space available to women at court.[6] Their principal function is to entertain or be entertained. And the second book of the *Cortegiano* provides the rhetorical handbook for such an enterprise. Courtly behaviour depends upon a superficial sense of the jocular and the ability to socialize: "la qual cosa ["foggia dell'intertenersi con omini e con donne"] a me par di molta importanzia, considerato che 'l più del tempo in ciò si dispensa nelle corti" (II, xxxi; 165). The court is equated with conversation and hence the pressing need for this to be regulated in a kind of grammar.[7] It will be an essential part of the strategy of the *Cortegiano* to separate the first three books bound together by the ethic of the joke from the last book, the language of which is based on a different grammar that attempts to broaden the horizons of court society by speaking in a new voice. The grammar of jokes provides the rules for acceptable usage. Since women form an integral part of the court, their particular situation needs to be taken into consideration. For Castiglione it is a moral question which concerns the ethical sensibilities of women: "Alcuna volta, pensando per quello esser arguti e faceti, in presenzia d`onorate donne e spesso a quelle medesime, si mettono a dir sporchissime e disoneste parole." (II, xxxvi; 173-74) Castiglione's attempts to clean up the image of the courts involve an operation which is both innovative and retrograde. If women are to come out in the full view of this society, traditional values associated with them, "onestà" in particular, receive strong male confirmation.[8] The writer condemns actual practice in order to present the possibility of the court's becoming a more ordered and less sacrilegious place ("sporchissime" indicates the libertine qualities connected with the court and the effort needed to censure "bad" language).

It is perhaps Castiglione's view of moral behaviour that influences the form of joking. Francesco Maria Della Rovere, the future Duke of Urbino, who holds out the hope for change and for a more pleasant court, notes the kind of atmosphere that is engendered by the "parlar piacevole", namely "per indurre riso e festa con gentil modo" (II, xlii; 182). Jollity is the keynote of court life. Historically speaking, it seems a refuge from menacing political forces, an attempt to construct a self-contained world. Francesco Maria was brutally deposed by Lorenzo de' Medici in 1516 which was not much to laugh at.

The new direction given to the discussion is imposed from above. The new subject-matter will take up the rest of the second book, so the future Duke's intervention has a profound influence on the course of the discussion.[9] Neither the Duchess nor her lieutenant speak at this crucial juncture; they only intervene in what might be considered a technical matter: who should be chosen to speak? Emilia Pia takes charge and imperiously selects Bernardo Bibbiena: "e 'l carico del parlar delle facezie daremo a messer Bernardo Bibiena" (II, xliv; 185). Inclined to participate in courtly pastimes rather than analyse them, Bibbiena proceeds to crack an in-joke the meaning of which is clear only to the incestuous court society ("a tutti era notissima", II, xliv; 186) However, Emilia Pia is not satisfied with her student's work:

> Cessato il riso, disse la signora Emilia: 'Lasciate voi adesso il farci ridere con l'operar le facezie ed a noi insegnate come l'abbiamo ad usare e donde si cavino, e tutto quello che sopra questa materia voi conoscete. E per non perder più tempo cominciate omai.' (II, xlv; 186)

The use of three imperatives indeed show a strict schoolmistress. The instructions serve as markers to indicate the direction Bibbiena's discourse will take. But, in spite of her precise and seemingly watertight commands he still prevaricates. This time the rest of the circle protest more efficaciously: "Quivi sùbito risposero molti non essere ancora, né a gran pezza, l'ora consueta di dar fine al ragionare" (II, xlv; 186). Only the majority are able to sway him and compel him to proceed. So it can be stated that Emilia Pia's injunction was not as forceful as it first appeared to be; she needed support from the others, the undefined "molti".

Once Bibbiena commences his discussion he gives examples which come dangerously close to attacking women. He plays on the ambiguity of women in court society in order to produce a category of joking (II, xlvii; 190). However, it is Gasparo Pallavicino's insistence on female immorality that sets the debate on course for the more general discussion on women.[10] Bibbiena lays down an overriding principle that will serve in all cases: "e sopra tutto aver rispetto e riverenzia, così in questo come in tutte l'altre cose, alle donne, e massimamente dove intervenga offesa della onestà." (II, lxxxix; 245) Women are to have special status and privileges in the court. In a sense, the males must protect them because of their adherence to the traditional doctrine of "onestà". This is the cost of women's socialization: chastity acts as a general control of their behaviour, defining and limiting their actions. Bibbiena openly acknowledges this fact ("noi stessi, avemo fatto una legge . . . " (II, xc; 246). No attempt is made to change it; rather, it must be accepted and everyone's behaviour modified by such considerations: "dico che dovemo morderle in altro ed astenerci da questo." (II, xc; 246).

In this context Boccaccio's presentation of female behaviour is to be condemned. In particular, the story of Ricciardo Minutolo institutes a relationship based on illegality and deceit as being more satisfying than marriage.[11] Catella's joyful acceptance of Ricciardo can be read in courtly terms as a challenge to one of the basic structures of any society through a recognition of woman as a sexual being constrained by the male order of things. Castiglione stresses the value of a 'nobil core' (II, xciv; 250) as opposed to the corrupt practices of Boccaccian society. The writer is distancing himself from that world, claiming a moral superiority for the Urbino court. In spite of superficial similarities Castiglione makes it clear that on the fundamental question of women he reads Boccaccio negatively. The medieval author seems to be an unacceptable source for the high-minded court society that Castiglione is proposing. Indirectly, he is also suggesting that Boccaccio's language must be deemed inadequate for the purposes of court life, as the content of the stories undoubtedly is.[12]

At the end of the second book the next evening's discussion is fixed. It is important to note here the limitations of Giuliano de' Medici's brief. Chosen as the women's champion, he will be prepared to formulate "una donna di palazzo" (II, xcviii; 254) who will possess, according to the Duchess's instructions, every perfection: "così si formi una donna di palazzo con tutte le perfezioni, come hanno formato questi signori il perfetto cortegiano". (II, xcix; 255) Yet Giuliano had already made it clear that perfection was gender-differentiated:

> [un tanto ingenioso e tanto eloquente] formasse una donna di palazzo con tutte le perfezioni *appartenenti a donna*, così come essi hanno formato il cortegiano con le perfezioni appartenenti ad omo. (II, xcviii; 254, my emphasis)

There already appears an implicit hierarchy of male and female activities which will become explicit in the third book. Even the title of *donna di palazzo* given to the court lady denotes her space; the term "cortegiana" has obviously disparaging overtones (Emilia Pia is afraid that one of Pallavicino's allies "ci formi una cortegiana che non sappia far altro che la cucina e filare" (II, xcix; 255). And Frigio tiresomely asserts that "ben è questo il suo proprio officio".) Thus, from the start, the woman-courtier is restricted to the palace whereas her male counterpart has no such limitation – the battlefield is the place where he is expected to perform most often. Only on one occasion is an equivalent term used, referring to men: "omini di palazzo" (I, xvi; 43).

2. *The Prehistory of the Third Book of the "Cortegiano"*

The work needed to produce the section on women was serious and far from being taken lightly by Castiglione. As has already been noted by Ghinassi, the *Cortegiano* probably began life as a treatise on women.[13] As such the early stages of the work are distinguished more for their concern with learning—information of a general nature on famous women past and present — than with a militant stance on the position of women. In a letter to a humanist, identified as Paolo Canal, Castiglione seems more interested in acquiring knowledge about as many famous women as possible, "che fossero state clare in qual si voglia cosa".[14] He does not appear to be aware of contemporary treatises on women which made ample use of this kind of material; or if he was aware of them, he preferred, probably because of humanist scruples, to go directly to the original sources: "basterami sapere li auctori, per poter cum min<or> faticha vostra satisfarmi".

Evidence of Castiglione's use of such information can be found in a Latin fragment which has closer links with the subsequent development of the *Cortegiano*. Castiglione was undoubtedly alerted to Plutarch from whom he faithfully transcribed all the women mentioned by the Greek writer. Some of the *exempla* would of course reappear in the various redactions of the *Cortegiano*.[15] Yet, it is quite clear that Castiglione had already ventured beyond a mere catalogue of notable women. For in the same fragment we find brief notes that are certainly Neoplatonic in inspiration. They are connected with the preceding lists of female names in that Castiglione has made women the basis of Neoplatonic love:

> Nam amor est desiderium fruendi pulchrum, et generandi in pulchro; et pulchritudo magis peculiaris mulieribus quam hominibus. Et, quia tendit ad finem suum, amor erga mulieres laudabilis, erga mares vituperabilis. (La Rocca, p. 367)

He has disregarded in one crucial aspect the original Platonic and later Ficinian definitions of love which had previously not included women explicitly. Indeed, he excludes homosexual love central to Plato and his followers. Women are henceforth at the centre of Castiglione's universe which by this move becomes courtly, less philosophical. There follows a philosophical dialogue that bears a strong resemblance to parts of the third book of the *Cortegiano*, most of the arguments being taken up again. These rough notes that consist mainly of lists of *exempla* are interspersed with a more evolved notion of how his future dialogue will develop. The culminating point of these notes is the four lines in the vernacular which constitute something of a shock in the context of the erudite Latin formulations (La Rocca, p.371). The shock is also one of recognition on the part of the reader of the *Cortegiano*. The lines seem to refer to the last pages of the *Cortegiano* perhaps more precisely to its *Seconda Redazione*. It may be argued that from its inception Castiglione was tempted by a large scale series of dialogues that might possibly be written in the vernacular, treating of women and love. It would make sense for him to write his notes in Latin because of the nature of his source materials. And it would be normal, if the fragments were written in the period 1506-8, to write a philosophical dialogue in Latin. In addition, a number of treatises on the position of women were written in Latin in order to lend their subject some respectability in humanists' eyes.[16] What is surprising is the extent to which the broad outlines of Castiglione's treatment of women are already mapped out (Castiglione may have originally been thinking of two separate works on women, both set in a court ambience). Nonetheless, the vernacular fragments bear out the hypothesis that Castiglione by this time had a shrewd idea of the direction of the third book of the *Seconda Redazione*. Connected with these fragments and linked to a decision to write in the vernacular is the so-called *Lettera al Frisio in difesa delle donne*, which may represent an intermediate stage, later entirely enveloped in the *Cortegiano*.[17]

It has become a commonplace of Castiglione criticism to associate the early drafts of his work with contemporary treatises on women, without much detailed comparative analysis. Perhaps the most important work in this respect is Mario Equicola's *De Mulieribus* or *Perigynaecon* since it represents one of the most forceful expressions by a male courtier of the possibilities open to court women. Equicola's work is in many ways typical of the genre. It consists of three obligatory sections that have the purpose of liberating women from the misogynist prejudices that threaten their entry and co-existence with men at court. (1) A philosophical introduction which is clothed in scholastic argumentation to demonstrate the equality of men and women. (2) *Exempla* of famous women from the past where all kinds of sources are utilized. (3) The encomiastic element in which women either known to or contemporary with the writer are mentioned. It will be seen that this programme forms the basis for the discussions in the third book of the *Cortegiano*.[18] The erudition that leaves its mark on the *Perigynaecon* may have influenced Castiglione's *Seconda Redazione* in particular.

Equicola does not hesitate to refer to writers of the Neoplatonic corpus though the nexus between divine love and women is left undone. Plato is frequently mentioned in turns of expression like "monstrat Plato" or in more direct references to his thought on particular matters such as the immortal soul. Equicola displays his learning, using a strategy that intends to demonstrate the status *certain* women enjoyed in classical antiquity:

> Gloriant Socratici Diotima et Aspasia. Superbit Academia dum Iascheniam Mantineam, Axiocheam Philasiam quae virili utebantur veste Platonis discipulas extollit et laudat. (f.a8r)

Equicola's lists do not appear to be entirely devoted to names of women. He perceives historical and social variations and pursues a comparative method which points the way to change:

> In Galletia, in extremo Hispaniae littore, feminas, non mares a agrorum culturas administrant. Apud Aegyptios feminae negociantur, componantur et institoris operis vacant. Apud Gallos, Thraces et Scythas virorum mulierumque communis est utilitas. (f.a8r)

Both Equicola and Castiglione tend to distance themselves from the Boccaccian tradition by having a more sympathetic and historical viewpoint. Equicola, in particular, was well aware of the opportunities the court provided for women with the requisite backgrounds. The domestic labour of women at home was for him the equivalent to life-imprisonment, whereas the palace provided a freer, less restricted space.[19] The three contemporary women whom Equicola chooses to mention all have Mantuan/Ferrarese court connections.[20] Isabella d'Este is at the apex with Margherita and Cornelia Cantelmo as her "ladies-in-waiting". The latter is not described with any personal warmth. She is present as a type close to what Castiglione will later call *donna di palazzo* in stark contrast to the *donna di casa*. She is described in terms of courtly expectations for women:

> Corneliam Cantelmam tuam tibi affinitate iunctam quis satis laudet? Cuis ut taceam suavissimae vocis leporem et formosissimi vultus decentiam quam mira gestuum dignitas convenustat. Sermo nunquam inanis, grata semper urbanitas, temperata severitas, maximum in verbis pondus et sine superstitione religio, cui non sunt admirationi? (f.b3r)

Both for Castiglione and Equicola, conversing at court is the most important occupation for a *donna di palazzo.* Indeed, Equicola himself almost coins the term: "ad quas exequendas ita ut fieri solet in magnis domibus et ipsa regia"(f.b3v). I would therefore argue that Equicola is more "advanced" than other contemporary writers on women and that Castiglione's theories were probably stimulated by his readings of the *Perigynaecon.* The similarities do not end here. For both writers will include in the *Cortegiano* and *Libro de natura de amore* respectively a discussion of women in relation to Neoplatonic love. Equicola and Castiglione seem concerned to employ Neoplatonism in the court environment so as to ennoble vulgar pastimes.[21]

It may be useful here to look briefly at another treatise of the same period in order to gauge the intellectual distance that separates Equicola and Castiglione from the more mundane writers on women. A suitable example is that of Bernardino Cacciante Aletrinate whose treatise *Il libretto apologetico delle donne* was dedicated to Elisabetta Gonzaga, in itself a good indication of the cultural interests of the Urbino court that link it (through the Gonzaga dynasty) to literary phenomena of Mantua and Ferrara.[22] Elisabetta was on reasonably close terms with Isabella d'Este so that one may be justified in speaking of cultural exchange precipitated by Isabella's "programme" of literary self-aggrandisement.

Cacciante's formula is to use large numbers of *exempla* without a real theoretical framework. Although the *exempla* are grouped around certain themes such as friendship, justice and so forth there is no distinct ideology present — the *exempla* could have just as easily been men. The themes may indicate that women are capable of adhering to male virtues but that is the extent of his commitment to the "female cause". His "Alli calumniatori de le donne" (pp. 185-86) does not contain proper arguments, rather assertions of a not very profound nature. However, he does confess that the work is not the best example of his intellectual potential: "Non havemo in questa tale operetta tutto el nostro ingegno adoperato; non molto tempo consumato. Due mesi soli tra componere e scriverela ce sono corsi." (pp. 185-86) He argues that if he had spent more time then, he would have been able "non solo con exempii, ma con verissime et efficacissime ragioni, provando in niuna cosa le donne devere essere posposte a gli homini" (p. 186). A work of this kind allows the writer to get it off the conveyor-belt without much thought. Therefore, Castiglione was only following fashion up to a point: he was developing an intellectual strategy that used pre-existing materials, in this case, the demand for books on famous women. The weight of *exempla* bore down heavily upon

Castiglione and it is only with the *vulgata* that he learns to manage them successfully.

3. *Towards the "Vulgata": Revisions and Alterations*

It is well known that Castiglione initiated substantial changes to the *Seconda Redazione*, resulting in a quite different final version. As far as Book III is concerned, these changes are far- reaching. In the first place, the material of the earlier version is divided into two books with the result that the women have a "separate space". It may offer a more dignified appraisal of their situation, but at the same time it distances these discussions from those on government. This fundamental alteration of itself required further alterations to the structure of the new Book III. One of the most striking is the closing section of the *Seconda Redazione* becomes the beginning of the new book on women. Thus, the section on the femininity of the *donna di palazzo* (*SR*, pp.319-21, chapter cxxv) provides the starting-point for discussion in the *vulgata* whereas previously it only reached a dead-end and could not be taken further through lack of time (III, iv; 264-65). In the *vulgata* Castiglione shows a surer hand in his representation of the "donna di palazzo". Before, she seemed almost an afterthought and the writer may have repented his too close dependence on the general treatises on women. On the whole, Castiglione quite regularly shifts sections or chapters in order to make the revised book more coherent and logically constructed. The *Seconda Redazione* had offered instances both of confusion and forced connections; for example, there is a tenuous link set up between divorce, considered ugly, and the following discourse on beauty (*SR*, p.288, chapter xciv). The *vulgata*, on the other hand, follows a logical course from chastity to love.

Another important set of changes occur with the interlocutors. Some disappear altogether while others undergo important modification.

(i) *Giuliano de' Medici vs. Camillo Paleotti*

Camillo Paleotti lends a particular tone to the *Seconda Redazione*.[23] He is of a scholarly bent, a university professor, who gives to the masses of *exempla* and argumentation a lifeless quality. The third book of the *Seconda Redazione* in this respect is extremely academic without the sense of more pressing urgency that can be discerned in the *vulgata*. This may be one of the reasons why he was replaced by Giuliano de' Medici. The substitution put someone in the text who was known as a courtier, if not a prince, someone very much *in* court society. Giuliano was also a poet writing lyrics which were close to the heart of courtly pleasures.[24] Politically, the change represented Castiglione's partial allegiance to the Medici power — he served Clement VII (Giulio de' Medici) as ambassador to Spain. The third book might serve as homage to a courtly member of the dominant Italian family in the peninsula. Paleotti had been employed by the University of Bologna but then had become Bernardo Bibbiena's secretary. This may have finally swayed Castiglione to eliminate him from the last redaction. As secretary, his erudition served the designs of the powerful Bibbiena; it was a subaltern position. Thus, in reality, Paleotti was not in a position to effect change. However, he was on good terms with some of the interlocutors and considered an integral part of that society: in a letter to Jacomo Calandra, then castellan at Mantua, Paleotti writes that in Rome "messer Pietro Bembo, el qualle è in casa di Monsignor l'arcivescovo di Salerno (Federico Fregoso) dove sono anchora io" have often spoken about Calandra. From the same letter it transpires that Paleotti knew "[il] magnifico messer Ptolomeo" [Spagnoli; Francesco Gonzaga's secretary] and the "gentillissimo messer Antonio Thebaldeo".[25] So Paleotti was not unknown in court circles and seems to have been respected for his learning. From the little we know about Paleotti, it is clear that his erudite interests did not extend much beyond writing academic commentaries on Latin authors. It was the kind of work expected of a university teacher and fosters the impression of someone who tended to separate his culture from his social activities.[26] It is no small part due to Paleotti that the section on women in the *Seconda Redazione* remains a bookish exposition of what for him would appear to be a topic of merely academic interest. With Giuliano the same section becomes a display of courtly virtuosity meant to impress the female members of his audience.

(ii) *Emilia Pia and the Duchess of Urbino*

Critics have noted in general terms the reduced authority that Emilia Pia has in the *vulgata* in comparison to the *Seconda Redazione*.[27] Furthermore, Castiglione has toned down her aggressive barbs at the male attackers. A good example occurs in Book II, just after the Bacchae episode, where Castiglione simply drops a more forceful statement made by Emilia Pia:

> e quando con ragione sarete convinto, come spero, noi vi condennaremo a quella pena che ci parrà bastante a fare che siate exempio che niun altro mai più ardisca parlare di tal modo contra le donne (*SR*, p.179; chapter xciii).

The earlier version contains an explicit indication of a tension between reasoning (and hence persuasion) and a taste for punishment with the balance tipping towards exemplary sentencing. This notion perhaps goes against the more gentle, softer rhetoric of the *vulgata*, distancing itself from medieval "court" games. Such a remark would not stand well with a general attitude of reconciliation between men and women.[28]

We find the same process taking place in the third book of the *Cortegiano*. In this instance again some lines of Emilia Pia's are deleted:

> Alor la signora madonna Emilia: 'Voi' disse 'ce vorresti provocar tanto che vi facessimo qualche iniuria per aver causa di dolervi di noi e di fugire questa battaglia, nella quale vi conoscete dovere restare perditore; ma non ve virrà fatto' (*SR*, p.187).

Her stern reply to Ottaviano Fregoso, not without its irony, answers his assertions concerning the illegality of the situation, its essential unfairness, making references to a "tribunale" and "li iudici". Thus, there has been a systematic elimination by Castiglione of any suggestion of putting men on trial, of dividing the court into two armed camps. In the *vulgata* Castiglione seems to have no longer felt the need to borrow so heavily from other forms of interaction (law-courts, battlefield). The court was now more autonomous in his thought and could provide its own types of formal (re-)presentation.[29]

One could multiply the number of examples that involve Emilia Pia in judicial or military imagery in the *Seconda Redazione*. A particularly telling one occurs at the cross-roads that separates the third book of the *Seconda Redazione* from that of the *vulgata*, namely, the reversal of the subject-matter (government before women) and its division into two books. In this episode one can note a sharp differentiation between Emilia Pia and the Duchess. The latter is seen to favour men's topics, relegating discussion on women to second place. She is represented as being more interested in hearing an arch-enemy of women speak on the male courtier:

> Invero io vogio pure che noi veggiamo se l'ingegno vostro[Ottaviano Fregoso's] è tanto che sappia ancor aggionger qualche cose alle già dette sopra el cortegiano, ché me ne farò maraviglia. (*SR*, p.188)

Although her comments contain a clearly-directed barb at Ottaviano's supposed competence they do not have the same cutting-edge as Emilia Pia's.[30] Indeed, her "locotenente" claims to see through male strategies much more easily than the Duchess. Emilia Pia's reply has the tone of a rebuke; a situational conflict is a distinct possibility:

> Non vi accorgete voi, Signora, che questa è una fallacia del signor Ottaviano, el quale pensa con questo modo sotterfugger la battaglia con messer Camillo, conoscendosi dover restar perditore et averne forsi il castigo conveniente al peccato che ha fatto? (*SR*, pp.188-89).

The elimination of this "exchange" was not only due to the change in the order of the subject-matter. It introduces a too large gulf between Emilia Pia and the Duchess and the male opponents. An element of discord, of uneven levels of female consciousness is presented in the *Seconda Redazione*, absent in the *vulgata*. A few lines later, open conflict between the two female protagonists seems imminent:

> Rispose la signora Duchessa: 'Per non lassare le cose imperfette direte del corteggiano'. 'Imperfette seranno' disse madonna Emilia 'se la causa delle donne se mette in silenzio, essendosi già tanto parlato a carico loro' (*SR*, p.189).

The Duchess is rebuked by Emilia Pia for not allowing women any space in the courtly discourse. Even if the former will take up by right the rôle of judge in the *querelle* ("serò iudice di questa lite", *SR*, p.189) the modern reader will probably not have much confidence in her impartiality, given that she is acting in the rôle of a supportive "wife" to the men. The Duchess of the *Seconda Redazione* attempts to appear as *the* mediator, as someone fair to both sides. She should be a model of the golden mean, unexcitable, unlike Emilia Pia, yet just. She will not allow Ottaviano Fregoso's discourse to be interrupted: "ché in questo ragionamento avete detto tanto bene che 'l male detto delle donne prima ragionevolmente se vi può perdonare" (*SR*, p.231). The Duchess is noble enough to pardon, Emilia Pia can only punish. Yet, the superiority of male knowledge, unrestricted in its purview, tends to make the meagre attempts of the women to be self-assertive all the more tenuous. It may be that Castiglione realized the contradictions in his portrayals and wished to rewrite the *Cortegiano* without the sense of war and antagonism that marks the *Seconda Redazione* so heavily, but leaving intact the general lines of opposition between women and the same male detractors.

In general terms Emilia Pia's rôle is much reduced and that of the Duchess increased in the *vulgata*. No longer does Emilia Pia control the dialogue in the direction of the equality/superiority of women, the Duchess has become for the most part the ideological point of reference. If there are new additions for Emilia Pia, these can be rather bland words of encouragement for the speakers with only a minute trace of a spirited attacker of men:

> Allor la signora Emilia, 'non defraudate,' disse, 'le donne di quelle vere laudi che loro sono debite; e ricordatevi che se'l signor Gasparo ed ancor forse il signor Ottaviano vi odono con fastidio, noi e tutti quest'altri signori ve udiamo con piacere' (III, xxxii; 299-300).

A subtle change has taken place; Emilia is no longer isolated, she is in fact playing precisely the same part as the Duchess of Urbino. Although there are her habitual ironic remarks directed at Gasparo and Ottaviano, they are not terribly biting and often disguise a request for information.[31] At times comments made by Emilia Pia are deleted in the *vulgata* and replaced by new instructions formulated by the Duchess (III, iv; 264). In one case, right at the beginning of the discussions in Book III Castiglione added an encomiastic passage, put in the mouth of Giuliano de' Medici: "ma della regina non mi bisogneria andar troppo lontano e solamente basteriami imaginar le divine condizioni d'una Signora ch'io conosco" (III, iv; 264). Power relations combined with a greater conservatism help to formalize the structures in the final version of the *Cortegiano*.

Both the female interlocutors suffer slightly when they are not named but only alluded to amongst famous contemporary Italian women in the *vulgata* as they had been in the *Seconda Redazione*. The space allotted to them is hence reduced as is their external reputation:

> e se li menti della signora Duchessa nostra e della signora madonna Emilia non fossero tanti che dubbio non ci è né pericolo de adulazione, io non ne parlerei in lor presenzia. (*SR*, p.256)

And this is what Castiglione has done. And again, in keeping with the general reduction of references to notable Italian women, particularly those in positions of power, an earlier reference to our two women is eliminated in the *vulgata*. Paleotti had paid a courtly compliment to them in the same way as before: "E poich'io non posso parlare né della signora Duchessa qui presente né della signora madonna Emilia . . ." (*SR*, p.258). There is in the *vulgata* a Castiglione less convinced about the international situation of the Urbino court and its rulers. The *Seconda Redazione* reads more comfortingly commonplace: "Rispose messer Cammillo: Io non dirò, perché in ogni modo di quello ch`io taccio circa questo tutto il mondo parla" (*SR*, p.256).

When there is a crucial change in the subject-matter in Book III one can take note of a perhaps surprising prominence of Emilia Pia. The discussion of the *donna di palazzo per se* is deemed completed. However, a doubt is raised concerning the omission of a vital part of her education in a male-dominated court "insegnar alle donne lo amare" (III, lx; 340). This is a subject brought up by the men, but in the *vulgata* the Duchess is introduced as a regulatory element (she was absent in the *Seconda Redazione*). Roberto da Bari also makes an appearance here (III, lx; 340), perhaps only so that he can be put in his place by the Duchess of Urbino ("ma la signora Duchessa gli diede il torto"). It is, however, Emilia Pia who holds the stage, practically unaltered from the *Seconda Redazione*. In the earlier redaction Emilia Pia had actually chosen the Unico Aretino to speak on love whereas in the *vulgata* he has already spoken without being designated and is simply ordered to continue (III, lxi, 341 as in *SR*, p.296). In both redactions Emilia Pia is allowed to discourse for an entire chapter (albeit a short one).

A female speaker may broach this aspect of the question of love because it directly involves women in interaction with men (Bembo will treat the philosophical issues raised by Neoplatonic love). Emilia Pia and the Unico Aretino cán lay the ground-rules for proper behaviour between the sexes. It is interesting to note how Castiglione shifts position on this matter. The *Seconda Redazione* had shown an uncertain attitude towards love between men and women. Bernardo Accolti, the Unico Aretino, had first of all asserted that love could not really be taught: "Però estimo superfluo lo insegnare quello che le stelle, la fortuna o Dio sforzano l'omo a fare" (*SR*, p.296). Such doubts concerning the efficacy of teaching love are completely dissolved by the time Castiglione is writing the *vulgata* where he states: "Ben è conveniente. . . insegnar alle donne lo amare" (III, lx; 340). The court is placed beyond celestial interference at this point to become a place where knowledge is essential in the struggle for success. Women are viewed as a possible source of this practical wisdom. They are thus installed at the centre of the discourse: "Ma invero bisogna impararlo dalle donne, le quali *meglio che altri* sanno ciò che desidrano e quello che ha da fare lo amante per compiacerle." (*SR*, p.296; my emphasis) In the *vulgata* less emphasis is given to the Unico Aretino's assertion which is linked syntactically with comments on women's excentricities ("credo che bisogni impararlo dalle medesime donne" [III, lxi; 341], rendering the whole statement less serious. Emilia Pia's lesson on how men should ingratiate themselves with women is brief and is cut short by an interruption from Bernardo Bibbiena. Soon the discussion on the practice of love returns squarely to the men who re-focus the discourse on male behaviour and dominance. Emilia has become superfluous since love is considered a man's game of conquest of woman. Emilia can express herself principally in ways that emphasize her reliance on experience rather than abstract knowledge. In the *vulgata* her more fearsome forays against some of the male interlocutors are either toned down or eliminated to make her appear more playful and more worthy. Now she acts as a counsellor for men who wish to love women.

The close of the third book in the *vulgata* and the finale of the *Seconda Redazione* betray the changed emphasis that I have already noted. It is worthwhile examining in some detail the expurgated section which, although it conferred a sense of closure on the earlier redaction, did not open up the court to the influence of metaphysical speculation. It remained grounded, in the *Seconda Redazione*, in the concept of the courtly game (the shadow of true justice). The *vulgata* retains a minute fraction of the adversorial tactics of the *Seconda Redazione* signalled by Emilia Pia:

> Rise la signora Emilia e rivolta alla signora Duchessa, 'Eccovi,' disse, 'Signora, che i nostri avversari cominciano a rompersi e dissentir l'un dall'altro.' 'Non mi date questo nome,' rispose il signor Ottaviano, 'perch'io non son vostro avversario' (III, lxxvi; 358).

This exchange is not enough to dissuade Emilia Pia who a few lines later reiterates her claim, using the same construction as here to create this impression of energy always associated with her: "'Eccovi,' disse la signora Emilia, 'che pur siete nostro avversario.'" (III, lxxvi; 359). Thus, the reappearance of "armed camps" is confirmed by Emilia Pia in the use of the adjective "nostro", picking up Ottaviano Fregoso's "vostro". However, she does not seem to get the best of the encounter. Ottaviano insinuates that "questa contenzione" (no longer a legal battle) induced exaggeration on both sides: "e 'l signor Magnifico e messer Cesare a laudarle [women] forse un poco piú che 'l debito" (III, lxxvi; 358-59). Here, Ottaviano no longer poses as an outrageous offender of women. He errs on the side of caution ("forse un poco piú") unlike his previous extravagant claims. He seems to be making a serious point about the ways in which this form of literary debate operates, forcing positions and making reconciliation less probable. The material of the third book is thus rendered suspect and doubts are raised about its adequacy for the task. Interestingly enough, Emilia Pia does not answer this criticism. She chooses to direct her attention to the second criticism concerning the length of the debate on women which precluded more discussion of the courtier. Here, Ottaviano, in his usual vein, is being openly provocative and it seems easy for his female antagonist to rebuke him: "né voi, credo, né altri potrebbe aggiungervi piú cosa alcuna; ma per la invidia che avete all'onor delle donne" (III, lxxvi; 359). If her statement had appeared in the *Seconda Redazione* then it would have been more than acceptable since the work ended shortly after. Now, in the *vulgata*, Ottaviano's bluff is called (both by Emilia and more encouragingly by the Duchess) and the result is the extension of the material into a fourth book. Emilia Pia's antagonistic attitude ends up by reducing her credibility; her argument falls flat confronted with Ottaviano's superior male knowledge. Indeed, the Duchess's final remarks do not allow much status to the preceeding conversation even if one accords a touch of irony to her words (III, lxxvii; 359). She does not laugh while speaking, a normal indication of irony in the text. Furthermore, she speaks of "quella verità" which Ottaviano will reveal; this will not be belied by the contents of the fourth book.

In the *Seconda Redazione* the situation was somewhat different. The court of love structure receives further emphasis from Emilia Pia whose impatience leads her to alter the course of the discussions (*SR*, p. 321) in a forceful manner coherent with her representation in the *Seconda Redazione*. The interruption shows her determination to pursue the mechanical processes of the game:

> et ora vi è tempo di dire tante cose, perché ancora bisogna dar la sentenza de la lite tra il signor Ottaviano e messer Camillo, e forsi tante sorti de punizione se daranno a chi ha errato, che serà forza mettervi gran tempo (*SR*, p.321).

Her proposal heightens the rhetorical and unreal qualities of the game because the punishments will be fictional and not "real" sentences.[32] The removal of this concept focuses on the discursive, serious aspects of the question. The inter-changes are rougher in the *Seconda Redazione* and the hierarchy of power not so clearly delineated - between the two women, at least:

> 'In pena?' disse il signor Gasparro 'adonque voi avete già data la sentenza cosí senza processo; raccordative che alla signora Duchessa sta el iudicare e non a voi: però lasciate che essa parli'. Rispose madonna Emilia: 'La signora Duchessa mi substituisce a questo officio' (*SR*, p.321).

There are no doubts about who is in control. Elisabetta Gonzaga's usual stance of playing the merciful goddess is directly *challenged* by Emilia Pia: "Non fate già questo errore, signora, ché non è ragionevole che la clemenzia sia tanta che asmorzi in tutto la iustizia" (*SR*, p.322). It is nothing less than an open attack on the Duchess's style of justice, rationality and ability to control the situation. However, the Duchess remains unmoved except on one point:

> date almeno una buona punizione al signor Ottaviano, il quale è stato el principale et el piú accerbo inimico nostro de tutti gli altri, et ha mosso l'animo di questi dui [Frisio and Pallavicino] et induttigli ad errare (*SR*, p.323).

In the spirit of the game, she accepts Emilia Pia's imperious proposal but with a proviso that a vote be taken! (*SR*, p.323) Not only amongst the women, but also the men. A democratic procedure of this kind is akin to the discussion on divorce in so far as certain freedoms are permitted to the courtiers and is eliminated in the *vulgata.* The two redactions offer two contrasting views of authority which required elucidation on Castiglione's part in the revised third book. In Emilia Pia's case her rôle is reduced and "tamed", whereas the Duchess receives a slightly higher profile. It should be stated that both women only occasionally interrupt the flow of male talk and in *numerical* terms do not constitute a high percentage of the discourse and only have a relative influence on its direction.

(iii) *Women in the third book of the "Cortegiano"*

It is obvious that women do not speak at great length in the *Cortegiano.* Even taking into account the Duchess's and Emilia Pia's interruptions and comments, it does not add up to much. However, Castiglione has adopted a strategy which allows him to shift the decisional power for this choice to the Duchess herself. As we have seen, within the narrative it is her command that prevents women from speaking. At the end of the first book, with speech denied them, the Duchess confirms the ladies in stereotyped female activities: "impose la signora Duchessa a madonna Margherita e madonna Costanza Fregoso che danzassero" (I, lvi; 113; *SR*, p.75). These are the only two women to be separated from the group and in the *vulgata* their functions are greatly reduced. The control of the female leaders of the discussion is much firmer. Margherita Gonzaga had managed to contravene the *order* and say her piece about her proposed game in the earlier version (*SR*, pp.17-18). In the *vulgata* all references to this episode are eliminated. Indeed Margherita loses out to Costanza Fregoso in the printed text, whereas in the manuscripts she had been the person named and in general her slender role is made even more slender.[33] It could be part of a coldness towards the Gonzaga that might be most easily expressed in this manner without touching the major characters. Or that Castiglione was concentrating little into one person.

(iv) *Other Interlocutors*: *Ottaviano Fregoso.*

His role is made more prominent in the printed version of the *Cortegiano.* In the *Seconda Redazione* a unique incident happens that causes him to be absent. He is called away by one of the Duke's servants. The reason for his departure is intentionally kept secret by Castiglione. Neither the interlocutors nor the readers are allowed to hear ("gli parlò secretamente", *SR*, p.233). It is something quite urgent since the Duke's messenger arrived "in fretta" (*SR*, p.232) and Ottaviano leaves without hesitation ("esso subito levatosi in piedi", *SR*, p.233). Ottaviano's departure has a number of consequences for the *Seconda Redazione*. First Frisio is called upon to take his place: "a me bisogna andare al signor Duca; però lasso el ragionamento al Frisio" (*SR*, p.233). And secondly, the Duke's business is more pressing than taking part in court discussions. It puts these conversations low on the Duke's priorities. Furthermore, Ottaviano, the arch-enemy of women, is Guidobaldo's *confidente*, suggesting that *real* power not only excludes women but actively oppresses them.

Castiglione's elimination of this episode avoids a series of rather pointless discussions concerning who will lead the attack against women. Some of these disputes border on the infantile and peevish:

> Allora messer Cammillo: 'Signor Ottaviano' disse 'voi entrate nella parte del Frisio; ma io vi protesto che non voglio rispondere piú che ad uno'. Disse el Frisio, quasi adirato: 'Signor Ottaviano, lassate dir a me; voi andate dicendo tutto quello che volevo dir io contra le donne' (*SR*, p.229).

Even though the passage just quoted shows discord in the anti-female camp, it does not improve any of the three interlocutors' image. Frisio, in particular, is almost at breaking point, having discarded the rule of the Golden Mean. He rudely interrupts Ottaviano Fregoso's discourse on the hopes that the "young" Federico Gonzaga brings with him: "Or non piú . . . ma date oggimai luogo agli altri di parlare" (*SR*, p.230). The Duchess has to forcefully bring him to order. Her rebuke is omitted in the final version but Frisio's remark is allowed to stand in part.[34] In each redaction the same basic remark has different consequences. In the *vulgata* it is virtually ignored whereas in the earlier redaction it leads to yet more preparatory skirmishes on the question of women.

Perhaps one of the most noticeable changes concerning the allocation of parts is the partial redemption of Ottaviano Fregoso in the *vulgata*. There is a significant shift in Ottaviano's characterization brought about by reducing his prominence in the third book. If he is labelled by Bernardo Bibbena as "troppo acerbo inimico delle donne" in the *Seconda Redazione* (p.174), in the *vulgata* he has been won over by the pro-female arguments and wishes to be the architect of a reconciliation (III, li; 410). There had been, it is true, some attempt made to protect Ottaviano in the *Seconda Redazione* by having Frisio take his place:

> mettetime in luoco vostro a dir mal delle donne contra messer Camillo ché me ne muoro di voglia, e forsi le resvigliarò io un poco piú gagliardamente che non faresti voi (*SR*, p.189).

There is the hint here that Ottaviano would have been more restrained than the unbridled Frisio. A reason for this may have been the fact that Ottaviano is Castiglione's choice to speak on the good government of the prince so that his attitude to women might be seen to detract a little from his authority on the former subject and again forces the connection between misogyny and power. Hence, his disappearance before the debate gets into full swing. However, he is frequently invoked by the anti-female lobby as "capo della coniura" (*SR*, p.279) and Emilia Pia wishes to mete out punishment to him especially (*SR*, p.323). There is a certain ambiguity hovering over this figure which is only partially dissipated in the *vulgata.* He becomes a more honourable courtier, with a touch of irony, he refuses the title of enemy of women, thus lending quite a different tonality to that of the *Seconda Redazione.*[35]

4. *Getting the Conversation Started*

The new opening of the final version of Book III, necessitated by the removal of its former *proemio* to Book IV purposely sets out to create a mythification of Urbino, linking the foundation of the Olympic games by Hercules to the games played at court. However, it cannot be accidental that the reference to "play" is made at the beginning of the book devoted to women. This suspicion gains in credence with the implied definition of games as an activity that does not require total commitment ("*l'altre* operazion virtuose, ov'eran gli animi intenti e *totalmente* dediti" [III, i; 259-60, my emphasis]). "Valore" ("virtuose", "valorose") can only be connected with action in the real world whereas the universe of the *Cortegiano* is constituted by words — "eloquenzia" in opposition to "valore".[36] The third book offers in its central section ample opportunity for a display of eloquent discourse. In this context, the discussion on women cannot go beyond rhetorical brilliance because of the deliberate dislocation of the *donna di palazzo* from the historical process. It is not surprising then that the *exempla* gathered together by Castiglione seem to show more interest in *regine* than in the category he is describing.

The initial skirmish before the discussion on women actually eventuates is far briefer in the *vulgata* than in the *Seconda Redazione*, even discounting the "digression" on the government of the prince. The assertion that Federico Fregoso has more interesting things to say about the formation of the courtier in order to delay proceedings is first of all put into the mouth of the antagonistic Ottaviano, then in that of Giuliano himself in the final version. So instead of an ironic attack on the merit of women as a subject, Giuliano is made to display an ambiguous modesty, a courtly courtesy. Indeed, in his first speech he is unsure of himself, calling on the women to help him out:

> ma se queste donne, che pur lo san fare, non m'aiutano ad acconciarla, io dubito che non solamente il signor Gasparo e 'l Frigio, ma tutti quest'altri signori aranno giusta causa di dirne male (III, ii; 261).

This call to participate asks to be read as a sign of weakness. And the tenuous nature of the innovative subject-matter, no longer "donne" but "'l formar questa donna di palazzo" (III, iii; 262), is underlined by Giuliano's next foray: "e certo molto minor fatica mi saria formar una signora che meritasse esser regina del mondo, che una perfetta cortegiana, perché di questa non so io da chi pigliarne lo esempio" (III, iv; 264).[37] The terminological uncertainty, that is, the rarely used "cortegiana" with its unfortunate nuances, points to Giuliano's difficulties as he sees them. It might strike the reader as strange that he cannot find contemporary examples of the *donna di palazzo*. If Elisabetta Gonzaga so easily fits into the category of *regina*, why cannot this also be possible for Emilia Pia to do likewise for the "cortegiana"? There is the impression that Castiglione is concerned with creating a non-historical model rather than allowing his text to praise women who have less than regal status. It may be an indication of the work's ambition to pour praise upon rulers first and foremost. This position implies a rejection of the contemporary reality of the lady-in-waiting. Isabella d'Este's *dames d'honneur*, for example, were notorious for their lax morals.[38] Something of this is present in Giuliano's prefatory remarks:

> Seguitò il Magnifico: 'Io adunque, Signora, acciò che si vegga che i comandamenti vostri possono indurmi a provar di far quello ancora ch'io non so fare, dirò di questa donna eccellente come io la vorrei; e formata ch'io l'averò a modo mio, non potendo poi averne altra, terrolla come mia a guisa di Pigmalione.' (III, iv; 264)[39]

All help from *other* sources is denied even if there is a claim of ignorance concerning the *donna di palazzo*. Giuliano's narcissistic attitude is made obvious by the repetitions of "io" and "mio" which point up the male source of the court lady. She will be an innovative creation, even with respect to the *Seconda Redazione* which did not name "questa donna eccellente" as the *donna di palazzo*. The reference to Pygmalion is enlightening in this context. Although meant half-jokingly, it does throw light on the development of the *donna di palazzo*. According to Ovid, Pygmalion was a misanthrope because he viewed with disgust the first prostitutes. In this account Pygmalion seeks refuge from the world of real women and he creates his dream through the intercession of a favourable Venus.[40] In the fourth book of the *Cortegiano* Bembo utters a prayer to love (IV, lxx, 451-52) which might be considered in general terms as a plea for the transformation of court society.

5. *The Court Lady*

Women at court are considered essential to the well-being of the men there, particularly in the field of love and pleasure. They should act as a stimulus to the male courtiers. The limits of the lady at court are clearly identified from the start. Whereas for the courtier "piacere" is an impetus to greater things, for the woman it is the goal and end of her comportment. The newly arranged material (III, iv-xiii; 264-76) has the purpose of rendering the proposal of a "donna di palazzo" more plausible and more attuned to the conditions of court society than a generalized discourse on women would have been.

The raison d'être of the "donna di palazzo" is briefly mentioned, not by Giuliano but by the *regina*, Elisabetta Gonzaga ("chi possa degnamente servirla", III, iv; 264) and then promptly forgotten. Unlike the courtier for whom service to the prince is paramount, the "cortegiana" has other more socially vital tasks. Passive attributes are more important for her, notably beauty, which indirectly points to the Neoplatonic solution for women outlined in Book IV ("perché in vero molto manca a quella donna a cui manca la bellezza", III, iv; 265 — the "molto" will be transformed into an absolute to conform to the thrust of Neoplatonic philosophy). In fact, the attributes that the courtier and *donna di palazzo* have in common are for the former relatively minor except for two exceptions: "la nobilità, il fuggire l'affettazione" (III, iv; 265). The first confirms the exclusive nature of Castiglione's concept of the court both in regard to the male courtier and the lady-in-waiting. The other qualities, supposedly held in the same esteem by the courtier, produce a placid female figure whose main aim is not to attract unwanted criticisms ("che di sé si dica male", III, iv; 265 — she will not be able to attack her opponents, unlike Elisabetta Gonzaga at the end of Book II). A sense of modesty should pervade all her behaviour: she should be, among other things, "prudente" and "non contenziosa". The qualities that distinguish the male courtier above all, the notions of *sprezzatura* and *disinvoltura* have no place here. They would assume a woman too intent on hiding her aspirations of upward mobility. The principal activity of the courtier is mentioned in penultimate position without special emphasis between the adjective "inetta" and the last item on the list, the need for women to do suitable "esercizi" (the adverb "aggraziatamente" echoes the "aggraziata" of a few lines earlier): "sapersi guadagnar e conservar la grazia della sua signora e *de tutti gli altri* " (III, iv; 265, my emphasis). Thus, the lady whom the *donna di palazzo* serves is placed on the same level as any other *male* at court, in this way, differentiating her functions from those of the courtier's. She must be pleasant to everyone. That is why her gender is made so distinct: nouns and adjectives that denote softness, fragility, lack of will are essential to Castiglione's definition.

By contrast, the courtier conveys dynamism, determination and solidity. What is expected of the new *donna di palazzo* is brought out in a reworked and much extended section of the *Seconda Redazione* (pp. 320-21). The facetious assertion of the Unico Aretino concerning how women fought naked with men is not passed over without comment as in the previous version: "Rise messer Federico e soggionse: 'Questo non si usa piú; però le cose già dette bastano ancor per questo'"(*SR* , p.320). The *vulgata* sets up a situation that dismisses contemporary practice. Rather surprisingly it is Cesare Gonzaga, the advocate of woman as a stimulus to love at court, to speak: "Ed io a' mei dí ho veduto donne giocare alla palla, maneggiar l'arme, cavalcare, andar a caccia e far quasi tutti gli esercizi che possa fare un cavaliero" (III, vii; 270). Cesare Gonzaga appears to be subscribing to the "myth" of the Renaissance virago seen as something positive and not just a confusion of genders. It is obvious that his remark condemns itself since it breaks the cardinal rule of the rigid definitions of rôle functions. Furthermore, it is presented as an historical observation ("a' mei dí") which is immediately picked up and refuted by "il Magnifico":

> Poich'io posso formar questa donna a modo mio, non solamente non voglio ch'ella usi questi esercizi virili cosí robusti ed asperi, ma voglio che quegli ancora che son convenienti a donna faccia con riguardo, e con quella molle delicatura che avemo detto convenirsele (III, viii; 270).

The *donna di palazzo* is not formulated in a vacuum but as a reaction, in this instance, to certain women who overstep the boundaries created by male definitions of gender. Castiglione is closing the circle, restricting female activities. The slightest hint that women become different or default from these prescriptions is met with stern resistance by Giuliano. Applying a Renaissance commonplace to women as far as playing a musical instrument is concerned, he states:

> Imaginatevi come disgraziata cosa saria veder una donna sonare tamburri, piffari o trombe, o altri instrumenti; e questo perché la loro asprezza nasconde e leva quella soave mansuetudine che tanto adorna ogni atto che faccia la donna (III, viii; 271).

The text had already established the correctness of a woman playing an instrument despite Gasparo Pallavicino's insistence to the contrary (I, xlvii; 99).[41] He had insinuated that music was an activity which broke with the stereotyped image. Music is suitable: "forse ancor ad alcuni che hanno similitudine d'omini, ma non a quelli che veramente sono [donne]" (I, xlvii; 99). Canossa only refutes this line of argument indirectly by reviewing the noble history of music (I, xlvii; 99-101), thus leaving some space for ambiguity. It will be closed only with the precise directions on how to avoid the accusations of Pallavicino in Book III.

Castiglione wishes to draw a clear distinction between *his donna di palazzo* and other women. In the first place, he will not discuss in this connection the more profound virtues of action that she is supposed to share with the courtier. This decision has the effect of foregrounding the lady's social graces and her rôle as a high-society hostess. In the second place, her rôle in the home as mother is minimized. If this can be considered in one way as liberation from traditional duties, it can also be viewed as a further reduction in the lady's powers: her essential function will not be as manager of property, like Castiglione's mother, where she could exert *real* influence in crucial matters. Instead, she must entertain men:

> dico che a quella che vive in corte parmi convenirsi *sopra ogni altra cosa* una certa affabilità piacevole, per la quale sappia gentilmente intertenere *ogni sorte d'omo* con ragionamenti grati ed onesti, ed accommodati al tempo e loco ed alla qualità di quella persona con cui parlerà (III, v; 266, my emphases).

The *donna di palazzo* will need to renounce her home and yield to the hierarchies of the court. Service to the *Signora* takes second place to entertaining *all* the men of the court (in a modest way). The emphasis is on discourse to remove any suspicion that the *donna* is a courtesan and the court an amoral place. The emphasis on *onestà* institutes a system of checks on female behaviour with the threat of punishment.[42] Whatever the reactions court women may have to risqué material these may be used against them as Castiglione eloquently demonstrates (III, v; 267). Once a woman is positively evaluated and fits into the male-constructed system she will win the general approval of the male courtiers. However, such an analysis is too straightforward and, indeed, too obvious in a text which adopts a confrontational schema creating areas of uncertain interpretation for the reader. One is asked to read these admonitions bearing Bibbiena's confession in mind: "noi stessi avemo fatta una legge . . ." (II, xc; 246). Although in a different book of the *Cortegiano*, it serves to underline the self-awareness of the laws promulgated in the third book. Even if their essential injustice is recognized, nothing is changed. Perhaps it is worse because the possibility of change has been refuted. Any resemblance to latter-day feminism seems to be on the superficial level rather than on a more profound level. Moreover, women do not receive a fair trial, they are hanged solely by the "mala opinione" (III, v; 267) of men. True knowledge which will be the ultimate goal of the male courtier is excluded *a priori* from his treatment of women.

On the superficial level, there is the positive account of the woman's own knowledge which according to an earlier formulation (III, v; 266) should be directed towards the art of entertaining (III, vi; 268).[43] It is revised in an abstract sense: "per esser virtuosa ed acciò che queste virtù la faccian tale, che meriti esser onorata e che ogni sua operazion sia di quelle composta" (III, ix; 272). It would appear that the court lady may be able to offer something beyond *divertissement* and that knowledge equal to that of the courtier could be the instrument to ensure her liberty and equal place in the hierarchy of the court. Yet, we shall see that her knowledge is far from complete. In fact, she needs to acquire some knowledge, principally, of military matters, solely for the benefit of men: "per saper laudare ed apprezzar i cavalieri più e meno, secondo i meriti" (III, ix; 272). There is the implication however that the women will be in a position to judge the men but whether this will have any consequence is left unsaid. Thus, knowledge, which has the power to transform the world, as can be seen from Book IV, remains as a vague potential for women who still depend on male values and assent ("che meriti esser onorata") in this society.

By a logical progression the argument leads to a crucial question about the relationship of the *donna di palazzo* to the source of power: "[Maravigliomi pur. . .] che non vogliate [addressing Giuliano de' Medici] ancor che esse governino le città e faccian le leggi e conducano gli eserciti; e gli omini si stiano in cucina o a filare" (III, x; 272). Pallavicino's assertion is not intended to be taken seriously from the start as the "stage-direction" "disse allora ridendo" makes clear and Giuliano de' Medici's reply is made in the same spirit "pur ridendo". The former's remark begins logically enough, but by the time we reach the semi-colon it has degenerated into pure mockery. He refuses to give credence to any notion of social equality. By this means, using exaggeration, Castiglione can avoid a too serious discussion of a problematic issue. The reply again posits potential as its basic ideology: "forse che questo ancora non sarebbe male" (III, x; 273). The expression of hesitation "forse") over the suitability of women for public life still leaves intact its future actuation. But Giuliano's following statements throw the whole matter into confusion. He first of all makes an important distinction: "Ma io non ho lor dati questi offici, perché formo una donna di palazzo, non una regina" (III, x; 27. There is no reference to the possibility of differing levels of power suitable for the lesser nobility. And if Giuliano's reply seems clear cut then the list of *exempla* is too favourable to the *regina*. All of Book III wavers between discussion of women in general, the *donna di palazzo* and the woman as ruler. The debate is thus cut short. The reader is given no indication at this point of how Castiglione will justify the courtier's political rôle which should have been truncated in a similar fashion, "cortegiano-re". This problem will be alluded to in Book IV. The solution is not to diminish the courtier's position vis-à-vis the ruler, rather to exalt it until comparison with Plato and Aristotle becomes readily acceptable. In order to allow this metamorphosis of the courtier into a philosopher-minister some political influence is given to the lady-in-waiting by Ottaviano Fregoso, an opponent of Giuliano: "Ché già non saria proibito alla donna ancora instituir la sua signora e tender con essa a quel fine della cortegiania, ch'io ho detto convenirsi al cortegian col suo principe" (IV, xlv; 417-18). Fregoso accompanies his concession with laughter ("rise") which tends to lessen its credibility. Unlike the courtier the *donna di palazzo* is not actively encouraged to pursue influence over the ruler nor is it seen as the culmination of her skills. Rather it is a grudging comment; "ché già non saria proibito" does not exactly urge women on this path. Furthermore, in the Italian states, power for the most part was concentrated in the hands of the prince so there are varying degrees of power at stake.[44]

After this no more is said of the political aspirations of the *donna*. In Book III Giuliano decisively changes the course of the conversation by shifting it towards philosophical discourse from which discussions the women will be definitely excluded.

6. *A Scholastic Defence of Women*

Chapters xi-xviii form a unit with the theme of a philosophical discussion of the (in)equality of women in general. The text moves away from a particular category of women to a general discussion from which the equality of all women can be inferred. It consists of a number of exchanges between Pallavicino and "il Magnifico". The former challenges the assertions of equality made by the latter who in turn refutes Pallavicino's arguments. Some doubts are expressed by Giuliano concerning the aptness of a defence based on scholastic philosophy and language:

"benché non si convenga forse ora entrar in queste suttilità" (III, xii; 274-75). Castiglione is putting into dialogue form what had become the rather arid material for defences of women written in the same period, such as the one composed by Agostino Strozza.[45] Although a necessary part of the task to establish the credentials of the generality of women, he saw that it was a tedious exercise out of place in relation to the court-setting he was creating. But the main body of this section remains unchanged from the *Seconda Redazione*. Emilia Pia's interruption of the proceedings does not produce instant results such is the desire to complete the argumentation so as not to be less than scrupulous with regard to the other treatises on the subject. Emilia Pia's injunction "parlate di modo che siate inteso" (III, xvii; 280) represents a challenge to male-dominated learning.

This section is dwarfed by the extensive range of *exempla,* used later, concerning women which entirely meets the approval of the female members of the group. Even though the women are excluded from this knowledge as they were from the universities that propagated it the text does not allow male philosophy to predominate in this form. The court woman follows another set of rhetorical rules which are being broken by the philosophical discourses. Women are told not to bore men "con l'esser troppo prolissa, non gli generar fastidio" (III, vi; 268). Moreover, "i ragionamenti soi saranno copiosi e pieni di prudenzia, onestà e piacevolezza" (p. 269). The principal defect of this group of chapters is obviously the lack of "piacevolezza" so this could explain in part the amount of space devoted to novella-length *exempla*. The third book demonstrates different types of discourse and how these relate to the social status of court women. Even in this so-called philosophy section Giuliano points forward to the more congenial section of *exempla* ("Se considerarete poi l'istorie antiche . . .", III, xiii; 276). History records a time past in which women were equal to men in all respects ("e fatto tutto quello che s'abbian fatto gli omini"). Philosophy seems to play a more restrictive rôle since it seeks an interpretation of natural events which will be universally applicable and against which historical aberrations can be measured. The universal model for men and women is the family with its carefully constructed rôles based on philosophical principles:

> per quella debole fievolezza le donne son menanimose, per la medesima sono ancor poi più caute; però le madri nutriscono i figlioli, i padri gli ammaestrano e con la fortezza acquistano di fori quello, che esse con la sedulità conservano in casa, che non è minor laude (III, xiii; 276).

Even if the third book favours historical examples of famous women, a conservative doctrine (men "di fori" and women "in casa") cannot be entirely avoided. Yet, the two live in a dialectical tension because "gli effetti della natura" can be improved by historical examples of progress. This section is presented as a tiresome but necessary part of the rehabilitation of women in general and the *donna di palazzo* in particular. However, before the array of *exempla* can be fully introduced (III, xix; 282-83 represents a preliminary skirmish: Eve opposed to the Virgin Mary) there is another interruption or digression.

7. "*Ippocriti maledetti* "

To include a chapter on the irreligious behaviour of the *frati* seems strange to say the least, given the precise subject-matter of the third book. It must have been of sufficient urgency to Castiglione to override fears of papal displeasure. His untempered wrath, not against the Church as a whole but only a minor part of it, finds its outlet in a piece of rhetorically heightened prose, a *vituperatio*, that bears more than a passing resemblance to diatribes made by Machiavelli on the corruption of the Church. The ostensible excuse for this chapter is to be found in the preceding one (III, xix) where there is a vague reference to female Christian martyrs, which supports Giuliano's contention that women are equally capable of religious sentiment. And this vein is continued in the chapter on the *frati* where the contrast between them and cloistered nuns could not have been made sharper. The *frate* is viewed as an anti-courtier to which Castiglione's "cortegiano" might be the remedy. All that the courtier must not do, the *frate* does:

> spesso tutti i lor pensieri volgono a contaminare il casto animo di qualche donna; spesso a seminare odii tra fratelli, a governar stati, estollere l'uno e deprimer l'altro, far decapitare, incarcerare e proscrivere omini, esser ministri delle scelerità e quasi depositari delle rubbarie che fanno molti prìncipi (III, xx; 284).

It seems that no deed is too infamous for which the *frati* can be blamed. They are a convenient target to strike in that they are usurpers of power (Castiglione's) and are considered a major element of the predicament of the Italian states. They have turned the meaning of religion upside down and have created chaos in the principal institutions of the states.

Again Emilia Pia has to interrupt the discourse in the name of "buon senso": "'Tanto piacer,' disse, 'avete di dir mal de' frati, che for d'ogni proposito siete entrato in questo ragionamento'" (III, xx; 28). Certainly Emilia Pia hits the mark, talking of "piacer", the rhetorical decisiveness of his shafts. In spite of this critique the attack on the *frati* stands as a digression that is too thinly connected with the material of the third book. It may be an indication of Castiglione's attitude to the discussions on women that he thought he could best insert here the diatribe against the *frati*. Emilia Pia puts the dialogues back on course by threatening to leave and hence break up the game: "'ch'io per me estimo grave peccato l'ascoltarvi e però io, per non ascoltarvi levarommi di qui'" (III, xx; 285). Emilia Pia is used in the text to bring some semblance of orthodoxy and put a stop to the disorder.

8. "*Laudi delle donne*"

The text thus returns to its rational ordering and continues the discourse, began in chapter xix, for no less than twenty-eight chapters (until xliv): "ma tornando alle laudi delle donne" (III, xxi; 285).[46] This dense group of chapters represents the evidence for a re-evaluation of women's place in society. It was always an essential part of any self-respecting treatise on women. And Castiglione re-works *exempla* that could be found in numerous other contemporary texts principally because of their common origins, namely Plutarch or Boccaccio. Indeed, the *exempla* seem to have remained fixed since the time he wrote to Paolo Canale asking for assistance.[47] There are changes in the contemporary women whom he cites but the rest are affected by minor alterations only.[48] The *exempla* are articulated around two principal themes. The first, more general one, covers chapters xxi-xxxvii and the second, on female chastity, chapters xxxvii-xlix. The first series has as its basic principle the illustration of woman as the helpmate of men; her excellence is considered only in so far as it benefited men. However, Castiglione narrows down the range even further—for the women who are mentioned are all expressly related to the men they help by family-ties:

> dico che 'l signor Gasparo non mi troverà omo alcun singulare, ch'io non vi trovi la moglie, o figliola o sorella di merito eguale e talor superiore; oltra che molte son state causa d'infiniti beni ai loro omini e talor hanno corretto di molti loro errori (III, xxi; 285-86).

In respect to the *Seconda Redazione* one finds the acknowledgement (absent in the earlier version) that on occasion women might be superior. But in general Castiglione has slightly toned down his belief in the beneficient effect of women on men. The "spesso" of the *Seconda Redazione* is replaced by the more restrained "talor" ("e spesso sonoli state causa di beni et onori et giovevoli assai"). The limitation that perhaps changes the manner in which the reader is asked to interpret essentially the same classical *exempla* is the introduction, in the *vulgata*, of family ties. The *Seconda Redazione* stressed the universal value of female action while discreetly alluding to restrictions imposed by the family-structure: "et esse con la virtù hanno corretto et emendato li difetti delli uomini" and a little later "che siano degne di equal laude con li suoi o padri o fratelli o attinenti, o che siano state alli uomini cagion di bene alcuno, o abbino corretto li loro difetti, penso che restareste impedito" (*SR*, p.245). In rewriting these passages one might discern a desire for clarity, to remove ambiguities, but in so doing the women are being pushed back into their families. Castiglione repeats in the first case the possessive adjective as if afraid of not making his point clear: "oltra che molte son state causa d'infiniti beni *ai loro* omini e talor hanno corretto di *molti loro* errori" (III, xxi; 285-86, my emphasis). The second example is rewritten using the same criteria:

> e certo s'io vi addimandassi quali siano, o siano state queste gran donne tanto degne di laude, quanto gli omini grandi ai quali son state moglie, sorelle, o figliole, o che siano *loro* state causa di bene alcuno, o quelle che abbiano corretto i *loro* errori, penso che restareste impedito (III, xxi; 286, my emphasis).

In order to offset both this change of direction and the apparently seamless *exempla* that follow Castiglione inserts a rather vague statement in which he mentions that his "donna di palazzo" would share many of the qualities of the women in the *exempla* :

> atteso che sempre sono state al mondo, ed ora ancor sono, donne cosí vicine alla donna di palazzo che ho formata io, come omini vicini all'omo che hanno formato questi signori (III, xxi; 286).

However, this assertion only complicates matters further. Having relegated domestic concerns to second place with the introduction of the *donna* to the court environment ("circa il governo della casa, dei figlioli e della famiglia [il che però voi non volete che sia la sua prima professione]" III, vii; 269) the family is re-instated as the mechanism by which female achievement is judged. In this way, attachment to values of the family is not only not broken but reinforced. The court is not an absolute value which can destroy traditional rôles: it may put them aside for a while but essentially serves to enhance female stereotypes. The innovative features of the earlier chapters are severely curtailed by the traditionalism of the *exempla*.

The examples themselves have been tidied up and in the case of the pre-modern ones re-arranged, though only moderately, in order to make them more coherent. And this cohesion is achieved here by following the categories that Castiglione set up in the introduction to this section. For example, Roman women are characterized by their relationships to *their* famous men: "vi contarei a questo proposito la istoria d'Ottavia, moglie di Marc'Antonio e sorella d'Augusto" (III, xxii; 286). The example of "quella Alessandra, moglie pur d'Alessandro re de' Giudei" (III,xxii; 287) serves to demonstrate the political strategy of a woman so that *her* sons may rule in peace. The Plutarchan account of Camma illustrates a wife's devotion to the grave, an almost total abnegation of personality even if it has the effect of destroying a tyrant: "e sopra l'altre cose con tutto il core amava suo marito" (III, xxvi; 291). A persuasive interpretation would put marital bonds before political idealism. The text therefore offers a reductionist account of female action with it nearly always being "causa di bene agli loro omini" (III, xxxi; 298-99). So, the leitmotif formulated from chapter xxi is regularly displayed in this section.

If the pre-modern *exempla* were almost commonplace and did not radically change from one version to another, the same cannot be said for the examples of contemporary women. This section underwent much rethinking before the *vulgata*, as has already been noted by scholars. There is a noticeable diminution in the number of Italian women, a widening of horizons at the expense of a "local" focus.[49] This sometimes entails the limitations of details the significance of which would only be available to a relatively restricted audience and certain women's reputations may not have been international and may have begun to fade with time. In the *vulgata* "questa nobilissima casa di Montefeltro" (III, xxxiv; 302) is placed on a par with other Italian dynasties without any special distinction perhaps because Castiglione now wanted to distance himself from the Urbino experience whereas in the *Seconda Redazione* we found: "come quella madonna Batista, moglie del signor Galeazo Malatesta, alla quale scrive cosí onoratamente Leonardo Aretino" (*SR*, pp.255-56). The same chapter also omits encomiastic references to the Duchess and Emilia Pia in its hurry "per uscir di Italia" and reach an extended chapter on Queen Isabella of Spain.[50] Not only political episodes of major *Italian* significance are deleted: "l'autorità e presenzia di madonna Margarita si concluda a Cambrai" (*SR*, p.257) becomes "la quale con somma prudenzia e giustizia insino a qui ha governato e tuttora governa il stato suo" (III, xxxiv; 303). The seal of internecine strife, the league of Cambrai against Venice, is exchanged for the image of the woman ruler. Isabella herself becomes the supreme example of a *regina* (III, xxxv; 303). Her portrait anticipates that of the perfect prince in Book IV. All his virtues are hers and not easily obtainable by historical princes: "che forse a' tempi nostri pochi prìncipi hanno avuto ardire non che di imitarla, ma pur d'averle invidia" (III, xxxv; 304). She sets an example for men but not as a woman. It seems that Castiglione is attracted by the idea of power, of a monarchy that knows how to treat its ministers. He makes special mention of Isabella's judgement of character: "il maraviglioso giudicio ch'ella ebbe in conoscere ed elegere i ministri atti a quelli offici nei quali intendeva d'adoperargli" (III, xxxv; 304). In addition, Isabella had the power to advance the careers of capable ministers: "a' nostri tempi quasi tutti gli omini grandi di Spagna e famosi in qualsivoglia cosa, sono stati creati dalla regina Isabella" (III, xxxv; 305). The verb *creare* is important here since it is an indication of the queen's power that in the face of the local nobility she could select her own men. Such an ability was important for someone like Castiglione who, at the end of his life, was becoming involved in the court of Charles V. And in general it represented the possibility of advantageous mobility.

Queen Isabella stands apart from the other contemporary *exempla* because in terms of space an entire chapter is devoted to her without mention being made of other women. Implicit comparison is made between her power based on the nation-state and the lack of power inherent in the Italian states. The terms of the comparison are unequal and innate worth cannot bridge the gap: "Ritornando adunque in Italia, dico che ancor qui non ci mancano eccellentissime signore" (III, xxxvi; 305). Yet the politics of the Italian situation is made clear enough. Either these Italian princesses suffered the anguish of exile ("nelle procelle di fortuna ha mostrata la virtù e 'l valor suo", III, xxxvi; 306) or their states did not do their virtues justice:

> essa [Eleonora d'Aragona] non solamente era degna figliola di Re, ma che meritava esser regina di molto maggior stato che non aveano posseduto tutti i suoi antecessori (III, xxxvi; 306).

This panorama of Italian princesses is also a description of the sad state of the peninsula.[51] It is not by chance that in these pages "fortuna" is the word used to define loss of state and other misfortunes (III, xxxvi; 306-307). There is a definite lack of confidence in Italian institutions to withstand foreign threats in contrast to Isabella's massive *virtù*.

It cannot have escaped the attentive reader that Castiglione is breaking his own rules. Instead of speaking about the *donna di palazzo* he prefers the *regina.* The courtier manages to maintain his presence even in Book IV because he has direct access to political power and may influence history. If the fourth book does discuss the prince at some length he will always be advised by the courtier. The *donna di palazzo* does not have the same political outlets and so Castiglione's interest is inevitably drawn towards those women who exercise power. It is interesting to note that women who could be safely called *donne di palazzo* were dropped from the *vulgata*. Even with such an illustrious personality as Isabella d'Este there is no trace of enthusiasm or personal devotion, possibly due to her secondary role in politics in the 1520s. In the *Seconda Redazione* she was the "specchio di costumi singularissimi e di supprema belleza". In the *vulgata* this is replaced by: "alle eccellentissime virtù della quale ingiuria si faria parlando così sobriamente, come saria forza in questo loco a chi pur volesse parlarne" (III, xxxvi; 306). The full force of this alteration only becomes apparent once it is realized that the same expression was used to describe another, lesser personage in the *Seconda Redazione*, deleted from the final version (too minor a figure?): "Non si può tacere la Duchessa di Francavilla, benché forse ingiuria se gli fa parlando così sobriamente di tante sue rare et excellentissime condizioni" (*SR*, p.257). This is not the only time Castiglione resorts to this device of "silencing" details which are no longer of any consequence (III, xxxvi; 307); it is also a good indication of his non-commitment to the Italian state institutions. In this light, it is not surprising that there is no further reference to women who might be described as *donne di palazzo*. Margherita Sanseverina, Veronica Gambara, Graziosa Pia, Margherita Cantelmo all disappear. The poetess, Veronica Gambara, is subsumed in a general statement that does not allow prominence or individuality to any particular woman: "Potrei dirvi d'alcune eccellentissime in lettere, in musica, in pittura, in scultura; ma non voglio andarmi più rivolgendo tra questi esempi, che a voi tutti sono notissimi" (III, xxxvi; 307). This statement serves principally to lessen the reputation of these women by not naming anyone. Margherita Cantelmo had a place of honour in Equicola's treatise, yet she too is of little political consequence and her name Cantelmo recalls the undoing of one of the greatest baronial families in the Kingdom of Naples. Moreover the Cantelmi were one of a number of noble and royal families forced to flee the Kingdom and mentioned in the *Seconda Redazione* (Antonia del Balzo, sister of the former Queen of Naples, lived at Gazzuolo, near Mantua). These names were a reminder of the turmoil that struck Italy after the French invasion of 1494.[52]

9. *Public and Private*

The mention of Cleopatra and Semiramis (III, xxxvi; 307) puts Giuliano de' Medici onto a different tack. No longer is it a question of what women have done for men in the public sphere. In a sense, it is what men have done to women or rather the regulatory controls that are imposed on their behaviour. More space is devoted to discussion and some of the *exempla* themselves are manipulated in a dialectic of opposition. The changed topic of discourse is marked by Giuliano's assertion "voi volete pur, Frigio, uscire de' termini" (III, xxxvii; 308) and then in chapter xl by a change of speaker. Cesare Gonzaga replaces Giuliano de' Medici (in the *Seconda Redazione* Camillo Paleotti had merely continued), perhaps in order to emphasize the variation in the subject-matter. This section consists of a series of exchanges that concern sexuality and its practice at court, leading logically on to the relations between the sexes (discussion of love). But before freely-entered relationships are discussed, the pressures on women are revealed and coherently defended. The text first takes a sympathetic line on chastity, again stressing the double-standards of men:

> Ma se volete dir il vero, voi ancor conoscete che noi di nostra autorità ci avemo vendicato una licenzia, per la quale volemo che i medesimi peccati in noi siano leggerissimi e talor meritino laude, e nelle donne non possano a bastanza esser castigati se non con una vituperosa morte, o almen perpetua infamia (III, xxxviii; 309).

The terms of reference are clear: the authority of men over women is not put in doubt, only its wrongful excesses. Sexuality is furthermore a public and political matter. The term *autorità*, with its connotations of governance, makes it abundantly evident. There is no challenge whatsoever to the fundamental presuppositions of chastity and political order. However, in the *vulgata* Castiglione is not so open about his views as he was in the *Seconda Redazione*:

> Pur da poi che così siamo assueti, non contradico a questo né tengo già che nelle donne non sia grave peccato e che la onestate non si debba conservare a guisa d'una gemma preziosa (*SR*, p.261).

Custom, that is, male traditions of power, dictates the state of play and is such a force in society that Castiglione does not dare to challenge it. However, the romanticization of chastity is lost in the *vulgata* partly through a greater awareness of political realities. Those who criticize women most, for their lack of morals, are often themselves the most culpable:

> governano le republiche con quella severità catoniana nel viso, che promette tutta la integrità del mondo; e sempre allegano il sesso feminile esser incontinentissimo; né mai essi d'altro si dolgon più, che del mancar loro il vigor naturale per poter satisfare ai loro abominevoli desidèri (III, xl; 312).

Their "abominevoli desidèri" had been carefully listed in the *Seconda Redazione*, exposing to view the seamy side of court life ("e cercano ogni modo e via di esser femmine, comprando con danari gli amanti, con li quali così strane sorti di libidine usano che non solamente dirle, ma pur imaginarle mi par vergogna", *SR*, p.262). Castiglione is more restrained and subtle in the final version than in the earlier one, yet the idea remains the same. Those who hold power must possess the requisite moral qualities and not debase or prostitute themselves; traditional gender-rôles must be respected. Women are shown to offer a better example in some cases. However, their sexual mores are a direct result of the social (male) structures: "la più parte di quelle che son custodite con troppo stretta guardia, o battute dai mariti o padri, sono men pudiche che quelle che hanno qualche libertà" (III, xli; 313). Cesare Gonzaga is advocating a relaxation in the severity of the system without relinquishing male domination: women will still have to be "custodite" (warders - prisoners?) and "qualche libertà" still maintains male supervision.

Society is seen in terms of conflict and violence (against women). Women, in the *exempla*, are victims, even if heroic ones, since chastity and death are closely linked.[53] Society seems unable to offer women justice or protection and to achieve that would imply making a clean sweep of existing social structures. So, instead, Castiglione sets out to make his women more worldly and hence more aware of the inequalities of the system which leads to female oppression ("la qual, *vinta* dalle *false* lusinghe, dalle lacrime finte, dai preghi continui, dai lamenti, dalle *arti*, *insidie* e *periuri*, s'ha lassato indurre ad amar troppo; poi senza riservo, s'è data incautamente in *preda* a così maligno spirto?" III, xlii; 314, my emphases). Court society has become a battleground in which the males not only fight for domination amongst themselves but extend their need for conquest to women. Language becomes a useful tool in ensuring that women at court are kept within well-defined boundaries. This at times goes too far and the powerlessness of the women was illustrated by the mock attack, already discussed, in Book II.

The misuse of language is attacked by Castiglione: "par loro che il dir male e trovare invenzioni, acciò che di qualche nobil donna per lo vulgo si levino fabule vituperose, sia una sorte di cortegiania." (III, xlii; 313) The *Seconda Redazione* had been more audaciously specific and covered a greater number of people: "Ma oggidì a molti pare che 'l dir male delle donne sia una sorte di cortegiania" (*SR*, p.263) Castiglione's *exempla* serve to rectify the situation by proposing "fabule" that tell true/positive stories about women.

The "fabule" have essential elements in common: the heroic stance of women confronted by over-powering men, chastity being the equivalent of death, the women as victims ("la meschina, vinta dal crudelissimo affanno . . .", III, xliii; 316). It is ironic that these "fabule" which intend to offer examples of chastity reveal much more about the violent nature of contemporary society and the uncommitted response of the cultured élite. In the *Seconda Redazione*, on hearing of the suicide by drowning of a "contadinella", all Bembo can say is: "'Invero' disse 's'io sapessi il nome di questa così nobil contadinella, gli farei uno epitafio'" (*SR*, p.271).[54] One of the reasons for the deletion of these lines could have been the realization that a literary response reduced the episode to a courtly game. However, the inclusion of this episode was a conscious attempt at writing women's history, giving them a place denied to them by the mainstream of male writers: "queste sono le miraculose continenzie che di se stessi scrivono gli omini, accusando per incontinenti le donne, nelle quali ogni dì si veggono infiniti segni di continenzia" (III, xlvi; 320). Although some effort is made to review female history, nonetheless it is put forward from the point of view of the male-regulated order. The text arouses sympathy for the "meschine", while at the same time confirming those values that brought about the tragic situation in the first place.

The reliance on narrative examples at the expense of rational argumentation reaches its peak in this section on *onestà*. Even Frisio is sufficiently convinced to produce *exempla* of his own, something he had been opposed to up to this point. He had opposed the presentation of women in this way which more or less would have prevented him (and Pallavicino) from interrupting the flow of the conversation because of the unified nature of narrative and the means by which a story was told:

> 'Questo mi par,' disse, 'il principio d'una qualche lunga fabula.' Allora il Magnifico Iuliano, voltatosi ridendo a Madonna Margherita, 'Eccovi,' disse, 'che 'l Frigio non mi lascia parlare' (III, xxiv; 290).

It comes as something of a surprise that Frisio will resort to the same methodology to which he is objecting here. It is a measure of the conciliatory tone of the last version that Frisio uses the form of communication that has been designated "female".

Narrative in the central part of Book III resembles the definition given in Book II of a particular type of "facezia" which "s'estende nel ragionar lungo e continuato" and these narratives require to be expressed "con tanto bona grazia e così piacevolmente" (II, xliii; 183). The term used to categorize these "facezie" is "festiva narrazione", not without significance for the third book where "ridere" attends a large proportion of the basic statements about women. The *exempla*, then, would be part of the pleasurable activity of listening to tales which so pleased court society. They may be seen as correctives to *novelle* by Bandello, and Boccaccio in particular, which at times were unflattering to women.[55] This kind of discourse is explicitly linked to women and entails representation and perhaps *catharsis* so that real change may be avoided.

10. *For a Chaste Love*

The preceding group of chapters on chastity constitute the ideological centre of the following section on love at court, colouring its presentation to a large degree. It seems to be regarded as the peak of pleasurable activity and is the equivalent for the woman of counselling the prince. It is accepted as such by all the interlocutors and any pretence at producing an oppositional current is dropped. At this point in the *Cortegiano* it is not love that is being discussed, but rather lovers; the practical performance that lays the basis for the more abstract musings of Book IV. These later meta-social musings are born of a vision of conflict between men and women. Using this premise, social harmony is unattainable and must be sublimated in Bembo's ecstatic state of *raptus*. The imagery employed to translate love into terms of social organization is once again that of war, "battaglie d'amore" (III,l;.325). It might be thought that Castiglione was merely following poetic convention. Yet, the imagery is sustained throughout the section, permeating language and behaviour. Once again, the court lady is considered defenceless, in grave need of protection. It is the aim of chapters l-lxxv forming the last section of Book III, to provide essential advice. In the competitive court society favours are not only desired from the ruler but also from the court ladies ("grazia"). And so it is not surprising that the same ethos of appearances and deception of the earlier books becomes a matter of some importance. A lady ("quella combattuta giovane", III, l; 325) is always under attack from "i stimuli degli amanti, le arti che usano, i lacci che tendono sono tanti e così continui" (III, l; 325). Indeed, with the whole of society ranged against her, its patriarchal system seemingly invincible and the possibility of radical social change not really contemplated, the court lady does not appear to have much of a chance: "Or pensate come da tante reti possano esser sicure queste semplici colombe, da così dolce esca invitate" (III, l; 326).

In such unpromising circumstances Castiglione offers a reading-lesson ostensibly to the lady but indirectly to the men as well (who would now be in an even better position to take advantage of these innocent creatures whose previously outlined attributes do not seem to count for much). The reading lesson posits the connection women-love-court in such a way as to re-assert the centrality of the female presence at court. Love represents possible reconciliation of men and women; at its best love resembles Poliziano's view of it as an ennobling force for the good of men. Having its roots in medieval traditions of chivalry and its stilnovistic transcriptions, women have a necessary place in rendering the court more noble and less debauched. Although the strongest impression we have of women is that of spectators: "nel combattere sapeano essere dalle lor donne mirati . . ." (III, li; 328) there is the notion that through love the court acquires greater dignity and hence respect. It is only in the last section of Book III that the reader can understand the full significance of "intertenere": "estimo io però che più che alcuna altra cosa le bisogni saper quello che appartiene ai ragionamenti d'amore" (III, liii; 331). This will be her "principal professione" in contrast to the more active courtier. The basic subject-matter proceeds from this premise: "Però vorrei sapere come debba questa donna circa tal proposito intertenersi discretamente e come rispondere a chi l'ama veramente e come a chi ne fa dimostrazion falsa" (III, liii; 331). The lesson consists in distinguishing true and false, based on the notion that men are normally false ("quelli che simulan d'amare e quelli che amano veramente", III, liv; 332). The *donna di palazzo* needs to learn how to read correctly every "segno d'amore" with which she is presented (III, lvii; 336). Each individual "segno" forms part of a system, male-constructed, which is now deconstructed from within because the interlocutors are revealing the key to the code. In this way a new male-constructed code is erected which will enable the woman to "read" men. The code of conduct that follows on from this is both cynical and worldly. In order to maintain chastity as the ruling element of female behaviour Castiglione introduces a bi-partite division into his concept of *donna di palazzo* ; the "maritate" and "le non maritate" (III, lvii; 336). Male values penetrate even further. For they rule female bodies so that only the soul is free in the case of married women ("voglio che ella niuna altra cosa allo amante conceda accetto che l'animo", III, lvi; 335). There seems to be a hint here of Capellanus's *amor purus*. And as far as unmarried women are concerned, "'Se la mia donna di palazzo,' rispose il signor Magnifico, 'non sarà maritata, avendo d'amare voglio che ella ami uno col quale possa maritarsi'" (III, lvii: 336, and see also III, lvi; 334).

The text is puritanical in its theorization of pleasure between the sexes. A freer attitude might imply looser social hierarchy with less emphasis on the nobility. Clearly, illegitimate children would not be a problem in these circumstances. It is also stressed that love should only be between those who might be in a position to marry, thus, avoiding the possibility of class mobility. Patriarchal and family bonds are never too far from the text's surface, even if it offers (very briefly) the alternative view of a freer arrangement. Federico Fregoso underlines the monastic rigidity of the new order: "mi par molto austera, e penso che l'abbiate imparata da qualche predicator" (III, lvi; 334-35). The text presses home its conservatism on this matter with few concessions which involve only the true lover, that is, the one who is presumably going to marry her. It has become more conservative with Castiglione entering minor orders and the service of the Church ("predicator" may have a touch of self-irony).[56]

Another aspect of the text's increasing conservatism is the treatment of divorce. It is treated in sharply contrasting ways in the *Seconda Redazione* as compared to the *vulgata*. It is not altogether eliminated in the later version but radically transformed. The most obvious feature of the later text is the rapidity with which the possibility of divorce is denied instead of the passionate, humanistic plea for divorce ("se a queste tali fosse licito fare il divorzio", III, lvi; 335). Camillo Paleotti only put an end to the discussion after Ludovico Canossa had had his say: "Non parliamo or di questa parte, che non si può exequire; ché invero forse saria utile el poter fare el divorzio con quegli modi che si converriano" (*SR*, p.287). Thus, the possibility of divorce is left open and perhaps even encouraged as a last resort for women oppressed within the institution of marriage. The final version appears to us to be rather cynical and careful to avoid discourse which may threaten the social structures. Castiglione eschews the more emotive language of the *Seconda Redazione* in its description of the horrors of an unhappy marriage. In the former version we find: "allor sono quelli dui infelici marito e moglie sepolti vivi in eterna miseria et in peggior stato che se fossero ne l'inferno" (*SR*, p.286), later replaced by "quelle infelici anime, legate crudelmente nella indissolubil catena insino alla morte" (III, lvi; 335). From the one version to the other the tone of anguished suffering has more or less disappeared, subsumed in the single adverb "crudelmente" and the more concrete "marito e moglie" becomes the abstract and less socially concrete "anime". However, the oppressive nature of marriage as an institution ("alle quali [le maritate] i mariti senza causa portano grandissimo odio e le offendono gravemente", III, lvi; 335) forms the basis in the final version of a different strategy.

One could perhaps state that the factors of social causation are more clearly indicated in the *vulgata*, namely the patriarchal nature of society: "alcune sono dai padri maritate *per forza* a vecchi, infermi, schifi e stomacosi, che le fan vivere in continua miseria" (III, lvi; 335, my emphasis). With statements such as these one would have thought that divorce was not only acceptable but necessary. The practice of marriagebroking and its financial implications seem to ask for a revision of the marriage-process, something that would require an even more radical re-evaluation of social structures. Castiglione does not offer alternatives nor does he now permit the possibility of divorce. His new solution is to link up "intertenere" ("ragionamenti d'amore") with these oppressive social conditions. In other words, the *donna di palazzo* may take a lover but only as long as physical contact is not involved (considerations of legitimacy undoubtedly play a part here). Love-affairs then act as a safety-valve, almost an escape from the oppression of married life for some of the ladies at court. Castiglione's emphasis on extra precautions makes sense in this context because he wishes to upset the *status quo* as little as possible. The social conditions of some women may be appalling and they are denounced as such by Castiglione, yet his solutions verge on the unethical because he is unclear about the way in which even minimal change can be brought about (divorce is unacceptable to the Church of which he was a member and could mean severe social dislocation).

It could be argued, therefore, that the lessons imparted to the *donna di palazzo* all have the principal aim of preventing social disturbance. The Unico Aretino will be the teacher of the practical aspects of love at court (III, lx; 340). These will be based on the principles enunciated, albeit indirectly, by Giuliano de' Medici. A number of key words are sufficient to guide the reader and instruct him/her in the ways of correct behaviour. Adjectives such as "austera" and "prudente" set the moral tone and, especially with the second adjective, limit the nature of the love-affair, stressing the need to be "discreto"; "discrezione" represents a crucial concept: not interfering too openly with the extant networks of relationships. "Inganni" pose a constant threat to a court lady's integrity. Male power is seen to deceive unprotected and innocent women and this is one of the leitmotifs of this section of the book. These themes are continued by the Unico Aretino and Castiglione has ensured that he loses no opportunity to emphasize it. For example, although chapter lxiii of the *vulgata* is substantially the equivalent of chapter CIII of the *Seconda Redazione* we notice a significant addition: "ma el vostro tanto dolervi di lei è testimonio che volete quello che essa non vole." (*SR*, p.297; compare with: "ma il vostro tanto dolervi di lei denota qualche inganno, come ho detto, o veramente fa testimonio che voi volete quello che essa non vole" (III, lxiii; 343). Everyone's behaviour is suspect and should condition one's response to it. Language, more than anything else, is considered suspect. There may be an implicit acknowledgement that it is the tool of male domination and so is untrustworthy. There may also be a link between this mistrust and the bacchic "frenzy" led by Elisabetta Gonzaga with which this essay opened: body-language as the only authentic language for women, one that can be made her own: "ché veramente talor più affetto d'amor si conosce in un suspiro, in un rispetto, in un timore, che in mille parole" (III, lxvi; 345).

It is no accident that this assertion is followed by a substantial passage on the rôle of the eyes in love. Although it is impossible to ignore the longevity of this tradition, from the *dolce stil novo* to Neoplatonism, it does not seem out of place to emphasize in this context the non-linguistic nature of this love, its bodily rather than intellectual presence, its effective silence: "perché spesso con maggior efficacia mostran [gli occhi] quello che dentro vi è di passione che la lingua propria o lettere o altri messi" (III, lxvi; 346). Love is not completely out of the control of the intellect, otherwise it would become anarchic and hence dangerous. It must be controlled ("si governa cautamente", III, lxvi; 347); otherwise passion, similar to *pazzia*, will cause disorder. Hence, women are still excluded from language, presented to them as alien, and are positively encouraged not to use it. Their language is not made up of words. The other principal element of the lesson is that "troppo dura cosa è un amor publico" (III, lxvi; 347). Secrecy is the order of the day: "Però se 'l nostro cortegian volesse usar del mio consiglio, io lo confortarei a tener secreti gli amori suoi" (III, lxvii; 348). This attitude springs partially from a concern with the woman's *onestà*. It also means that love is not an official part of the court structures — it will always have something illicit about it. Castiglione appears to be making the point, directed at contemporary court society, that the loves between courtiers and ladies-in-waiting were not the final goal of the court. And indeed, women like Isabella d'Este's notorious ladies-in-waiting were better forgotten or passed over in silence. Thus, Castiglione's discussion on the practice of love is aimed at reducing its prominence and troublesome aspects. Not only must it be well regulated (taught and not left to the natural play of forces) but these rules should lead to love's self-effacement. Secrecy constitutes the subject-matter of no less than six chapters. At one point Gasparo Pallavicino forcibly brings back the discussion to this question: "sete debitor de insegnarli a tener secreti gli amori suoi" (III, lxxii; 353). It should be noted that the focus of Book III has subtly shifted back to the men and their preoccupations which prepares the way for the male-centred discourses of Book IV. Women's needs are no longer first and foremost because the courtier has to create the right impression in order to pursue his vaster ambitions. So, the judgement of the others is a vital force in moulding behaviour ("creduti e giudicati da tutto 'l mondo", III, lxxv; 357).

11. *Women Through Men's Eyes*

Elisabetta Gonzaga's command to Ottaviano Fregoso sounds ironic if understood with respect to the work as a whole: "Poiché non ci costa altro che parole, dichiarateci per vostra fé tutto quello che v'occorreria in animo . . ." (IV, xxx; 399). Words for the men in the conversations come easy, whereas for the women they hardly come at all. They are not silent: they form a chorus of assent or dissent as the occasion requires. They are not spoken about *in absentia* which makes the dialogues all the more convincing since Castiglione has artfully had them approve limitations imposed on them.

In these circumstances, the fact that Castiglione offers the two sides of the "querelle des femmes" in the one text is of particular significance. It creates the illusion that the "querelle" is no longer a valid measure of female inequality, that all difficulties have been resolved. At times the third book of the *Cortegiano* resembles a scholastic treatise: one point of view is put forward, then challenged, finally most of the doubts concerning the first statement are dissipated with the result that it is allowed to stand. Thus, the text uses to some extent at least a well-established male system of thought to lend credence to its utterances.

There can be little doubt that Castiglione was following fashion in including the section on women, yet, at the same time, it was an admission of the privileged rôle women could play at court and perhaps not elsewhere. The annotations on women, however, do provide some foundations for a limited reappraisal of the position of women in general. But this is not really Castiglione's concern; the tri-partite structure of the book culminates in woman's principal activity at court: love.

The third book presents a paradoxically conservative vision of the court lady. On the one hand, she is liberated from the crushing reality of the everyday; family bonds appear loosened, she has an education and can mix relatively freely in society. On the other hand, family ties do loom large; deeds are done for the family and there is an ineluctable search for a suitable lover to marry. Even if patriarchal society is pointed out as the persecutor of women, only the slightest indication is given of solutions. That the men should not abuse their power is the slender response of the text and it is not pushed home with any force.

In the end it is hard to define the exact nature of Castiglione's presentation of the *donna di palazzo*. Certainly, there was some innovation although we should not succumb to the temptation of overestimating it.

NOTES

1. All references to *Il libro del Cortegiano* will be abbreviated as follows: book number, chapter number; page number. The edition I have used is Baldassar Castiglione, *Il libro del Cortegiano*, Introduzione di Amedeo Quondam, Note di Nicola Longo, Milan, Garzanti, 1981. The passage quoted here is from II, xcvi; 252. I wish to thank Dr. Denise Ryan for her assistance and helpful advice in the preparation of this essay and Miss Doris Fletcher for her useful comments on this contribution.

2. Pallavicino contrasts "forza" (referring to the women) and "ragionamento" (III, xcvii; 252) which is clearly ironic in that it is the men who possess the power, not the women, both physically and related to discourse. The episode is discussed by Marina Zancan, "La donna e il cerchio nel *Cortegiano* di B. Castiglione. Le funzioni del femminile nell'immagine di corte" in *Nel cerchio della luna. Figure di donne in alcuni testi del XVI secolo*, edited by the same, Venice, Marsilio, 1983, pp.13-56. This contribution as a whole is written in the mould of studies published under the aegis of the *Centro Europa delle Corti*. It shows the influence of the kind of critical discourse promulgated by Amedeo Quondam (an example of which is his introduction to the Garzanti edition of the *Cortegiano*). As such it emphasizes the production of discourse, the significance of the "parola" (general influence of Saussure). However, Zancan's reading represents the most serious attempt so far to grapple with the text's complexities. Her analysis of the Bacchic rites notes the contrast between male discourse and the women's "parole del corpo". What she fails to note is the comic aspects of the scene (careful stage-directions as well as the humorous quip of the Duchess). The tone of the passage is crucial to its understanding and one reaches only a partial evaluation of it through a content-oriented analysis.

3. See Joan Kelly, "Did women have a Renaissance?" in *Women, History and Theory. The Essays of Joan Kelly*, Chicago U.P., 1984, pp.19-50; and, in the same volume, "Early feminist theory and the 'Querelle des Femmes'", particularly pp.74-5. I. Maclean, *The Renaissance Notion of Woman*, Cambridge U.P., 1980, notes that Castiglione "reproduce[s] synthetic views of woman which concord with the intellectual outlook of their day" (p.5).

4. José Guidi asks at the beginning of his "De l'amour courtois à l'amour sacré: la condition de la femme dans l'oeuvre de B. Castiglione" in *Images de la femme dans la littérature italienne de la Renaissance*, Paris: Université de la Sorbonne Nouvelle, Centre de Recherche sur la Renaissance Italienne, 1980, pp.9-80, a pertinent question: "Est-on fondé pour autant à parler d'un féminisme structurel de l'ouvrage, et du milieu de cour qui s'y trouve représenté. . .?" (pp.9-10) The author's response is definitely negative, particularly because the female interlocutors play such an innocuous role: "Elles n'interviennent dans la conversation qu'incidemment, et sans modifier en aucune sorte le cours du raisonnement" (p.35). This point of view may be too sweeping to be totally acceptable. Indeed, Guidi's method of relating the various redactions of the *Cortegiano* to the historical circumstances of Castiglione's life is sometimes heavy-handed and tends to over-shadow the work of textual exegesis.

The opposite view is taken by J.R. Woodhouse, *Baldesar Castiglione. A Reassessment of the "Courtier"*, Edinburgh U.P., 1978. Giuliano de' Medici is called a "reasonable feminist" (p.109); certain chapters are said to "exalt the position of women" (p.128). It might be interesting to compare these two conflicting male views with two other contributions by women made under the auspices of the *Centro Europa delle Corti*. One by G. Saccaro Battisti, "La donna, le donne nel *Cortegiano*" in *La corte e il "Cortegiano"*, Vol.1, *La scena del testo*, a cura di C. Ossola, Rome, Bulzoni, 1980, pp.219-49, emphasizes, like Guidi, the silence of the women but feels that the defence of women by men is lacking in conviction ("vi è quindi, nel modo in cui vien condotto il discorso generale sulla donna, un certo grado di oziosità", p.229). However, the critic is more intent on showing how women from all levels of society are presented in the *Cortegiano*; an element that she perhaps exaggerates and misinterprets (Cf. the criticisms of M. Zancan, *Nel cerchio*, p.21, n.21). Adriana Chemello, "Donna di palazzo, moglie, cortigiana: ruoli e funzioni sociali della donna in alcuni trattati del Cinquecento" in *La corte e il "Cortegiano "*, vol. 2, *Un modello europeo*, a cura di A. Prosperi, Rome, Bulzoni, 1980, pp.113-32, promises a feminist reading of the text and she certainly does cover some aspects of it that are susceptible to this kind of interpretation.

5. The point is briefly made by G. Saccaro Battisti, pp. 224-25 but without relating it to the broader question of textual strategies. The imposition of silence on the women is presented in the *Cortegiano* as something positive, a "commodità", not a denial of privileges, thus making it more palatable.

6. I cannot agree with D.A. Trafton, "Structure and meaning in *The Courtier*", *English Literary Renaissance*, 72 (1971), pp. 283-97. He states that the section on jokes does not "aim at anything more than the passing amusement of the drawing room" (p.290). This formulation is too reductionist in so complicated a text. Jokes help to standardize and hence keep at a distance inter-personal relationships and they constitute a body of "knowledge" that can often only be fully understood by those inside court society. For a detailed analysis of this section consult J. Guidi, "*Festive narrazioni, motti* et *burle (beffe)*. L'art des facéties dans *Le Courtisan*" in *Formes et significations de la 'beffa' dans la littérature italienne de la Renaissance*, (Deuxième Série), études réunies par A. Rochon, Paris, Université de la Sorbonne Nouvelle, Centre de Recherche sur la Renaissance Italienne, 1975, pp. 171-210.

7. I should point out that I am using "grammar" in a literal sense: a series of rules that allows certain kinds of linguistic behaviour and prohibits others. Quondam, in his introduction to the *Cortegiano* uses "grammatica" in a much wider sense, as an equivalent to "dominante tipologia culturale" or "codice totale" (p.XLI).

8. Cf. A. Chemello, "Donna di palazzo" where the ideological importance of "continentia" is stressed: "l'uomo imporrà il suo controllo repressivo facendo obbligo alla donna di esercitare la 'continentia'" (p.122). Chemello states that the one reason for this is protection of noble lineages. However, I would argue that Castiglione was attempting to create a more moral court, answering implicit criticisms of it as a worthwhile institution.

9. The future Duke is thus seen idealistically as the embodiment of an elegant and sophisticated culture which he will guarantee for his court in the form of a series of rules. His request to be taught ("insegnarci", II, xlii; 182) shows a willingness for court behaviour to be improved and regulated.

10. For a brief discussion see D.A. Trafton, "Structure and meaning", p.291, where the connection between women and joking is seen solely "to provide a transition to the subject of the third book" and "to reintroduce a note of moral seriousness to the discussions" (had it not always been there in the attempt made to "clean up" joking?).

11. G. Boccaccio, *Il Decameron*, Giornata Terza, novella sesta.

12. On Castiglione's linguistic theories see M. Pozzi, "Il pensiero linguistico di B. Castiglione", *Giornale Storico della Letteratura Italiana* (henceforth *GSLI*), 156 (1979), pp. 179-202.

13. See G. Ghinassi, "Fasi dell'elaborazione del *Cortegiano*", *Studi di Filologia Italiana*, 25-26 (1967-68), pp. 155-96, but in particular, pp.173-74.

14. Castiglione's letter is to be found in B. Castiglione, *Lettere inedite e rare*, edited by G. Gorni, Milan-Naples, Ricciardi, 1969, pp.109-10. The identification of the addressee was made by G. Ghinassi, "Postille sull'elaborazione del *Cortegiano*," *Studi e problemi di critica testuale*, 3 (1971) 171-8; 172-3.

15. The fragment has been edited by G. La Rocca, "Un taccuino autografo per il *Cortegiano*", *Italia Medievale e Umanistica*, 23 (1980), pp. 341-73.

16. One that was undoubtedly known to Castiglione was Mario Equicola's *De Mulieribus* or *Perigynaecon* (probably published in 1501 in Ferrara). That Castiglione held the work in high esteem at around the time of the composition of what is now known as the *Seconda Redazione* (henceforth *SR*, edited by G. Ghinassi, Florence, Sansoni, 1968) is shown by a reference to Equicola. This reference was deleted to cover up the extent of his debt or to accentuate the different qualities of his own contribution to the subject (*SR*, p.181).

17. For the *Lettera* see G. Ghinassi, "Fasi dell'elaborazione", pp.189-96.

18. It is interesting to note that Equicola rewrites the *Perigynaecon* and incorporates its position into the much more grandiose *Libro de natura de amore*, Venice, Lorenzo Lorio da Portes, 1525, 4°. The link between women and Neoplatonism is firmed up, much in the same way as it will be by Castiglione in the *vulgata*, thus raising the question of Equicola's possible influence on Castiglione, given the respective dates and manuscript traditions of the two works. See I. Rocchi, "Per una nuova cronologia e valutazione del *Libro de natura de amore*", *GSLI*, 153 (1976), pp. 566-85. I would argue that it is not merely a question of coincidence, mutual influence aside, but a profound urge in the two writers to provide the court and its activities with philosophical justifications.

19. See J.R. Woodhouse, pp.115-16.

20. Further discussion of Equicola's treatise can be found in S.D. Kolsky, *Mario Equicola. A Biographical Reappraisal*, Ph. D. thesis, University of London, 1981, pp.66-73 (to be published in a revised version by Droz, Geneva).

21. See note 18. Both works contain similar warnings to women about the deceptions of men, partly due to a common source in Ovid and partly due to a shared concern about the morality of court life with an implicit sense of pessimism about the capacity for change in men:

Qual mai amante si trovò che molto piú in parole, in sembianti, in apparentia non se demonstrasse amare che in effecto non amava? In desiderio fengemo ardere che in voluntà a pena ne rescaldamo... Et mille altre persuasioni con lequali, o donne, dal vostro proprio elemento che è pudicitia et honestà, como del pesce l'acqua, tentano trarvi a loro appetiti (*Libro*, fs. 228r-228v).

The animalistic imagery serves to emphasize the instinctual level of behaviour prevalent in court society; "appetiti" should be seen in opposition to reason/reasonable behaviour. The women themselves are advised by Equicola to behave in accordance with court canons: "Attendasi secundo il tempo et loco con dolci ragionamenti et *degni de corte* nobili intertenere. Humanità sopra tutto da voi ricerco" (*Libro*, f.229r, my emphasis) The similarities with Castiglione are obvious. However, Equicola is open about the reasons for a strict supervision of behaviour, namely, a higher vision of the court. He treads a difficult path between what critics might have called "promiscuous" behaviour on the part of women and the Christian view of chastity. For a fuller discussion of Equicola's treatment of women and chastity, see S. Kolsky, "'The good servant': Mario Equicola. Court and courtier in early sixteenth-century Italy", *The Italianist*, 6 (1986), pp. 34-60, but in particular pp. 51-4.

22. The work is edited by M. Martini, *Bernardino Cacciante Aletrinate. Contributo alla storia dell' umanesimo*, Sora, Centro di Studi Sorani "Vincenzo Patriarca", 1982.

23. For Paleotti see P. Floriani, *I gentiluomini letterati. Studi sul dibattito culturale nel primo Cinquecento*, Naples, Liguori, 1981. Chapter III, "I personaggi del *Cortegiano* " (pp.50-67) reviews a number of the interlocutors and the changes they underwent, including Paleotti (pp.56-58). For a full analysis of the revisions consult G. Ghinassi, "Fasi dell'elaborazione", *passim.*

24. The critical edition of his poetry is Giuliano de' Medici, Duca di Nemours, *Poesie*, a cura e con uno studio di G. Fatini, Florence, Le Monnier, 1939.

25. Archivio di Stato, Mantua, Archivio Gonzaga, busta 860, Rome, 20 August 1512, Paleotti to Calandra.

26. V. Cian provides essential data on Paleotti in his edition of *Il Cortegiano*, Florence, Sansoni, 1947 (commentary on II, lxii, line 26; pp.234-35). One can also usefully consult *Notizie degli scrittori bolognesi raccolte da Giovanni Fantuzzi*, vol. 6, Bologna, San Tommaso D'Aquino, 1788, pp. 235-36. Other important information is conveyed by Camillo's brother, Alessandro, in a letter to Castiglione:

Molto magnifico Conte maggior mio honorando,
Per il reverendo et magnifico signore messer Ludovico da Bagno ho receuto la lettera di Vostra Signoria de dí xxii dil passato, a me tanto grata quanto dire si possa, et ho inteso

Il desiderio suo che serebbe de vedere qualchi comentarii della bona memoria di messer Camillo[a] o altri soi anotamenti sopra Plinio et altri autori. Alla quale respondendo dico che il prefatto messer Camillo non scrivea cosa ordinata né tra li scritti soi trovo cosa da mandare in mane a homo di grande litteratura et de exacto giudicio come è Vostra Signoria. Pure per satisfarli li mando certi fragmenti li quali non hano né principio né fine et pure anchora certi anotamenti sopra Plinio scrite in su certi soi memoriali, le quale cose se serano a proposito di Vostra Signoria l'haverò molto grato. Quando che anchora non fussero al proposito suo pregola me li remandi per ciò che pure per essere state cose di quello fratello ch'io tanto amava, assai me sono care.

Vedrò de rehavere certi anotamenti sopra a Ausonio gallo, Ovidio in Ibim che erano assai boni, et se Vostra Signoria haverà caro gli le mandi. Le darò al reverendo et magnifico signore messer Augustino da Gonzaga che gli le mandi. Et s'altro è ch'io possa Vostra Signoria me comandi perché a me é summo piacere fare cosa che li sia grata. Et la ringratio per infinite volte che spesso adimandi di me et tenghi verde la memoria della Casa Paleota tutta sua et a Vostra Signoria di core me racomando, pregandola che saluti il Calandra per parte mia et bene valeat etcetera. Di Bologna alli iii di maggio MDXXIII.

Di Vostra Signoria come
menor fratello et servitore.
Alessandro Paleoto.

(a) *ho* deleted in text.
(Biblioteca Apostolica Vaticana, Vat. Lat. 8211, f. 488r)

The letter hints at Alessandro Paleotti's embarrassment at the paucity of Camillo's literary testament. In spite of Alessandro's efforts and Castiglione's interest it does not appear anything came of this exercise. Camillo is revealed through this letter as a chaotic commentator who was perhaps capable of brilliant work but did not very often reach the peak of his potential. This state of affairs would have confirmed Castiglione in his decision to remove Paleotti from his privileged rôle in the third book.

Apart from his work as a commentator Paleotti did try his hand at Latin poetry. What seems to be the presentatin copy of his *Silva* is to be found in the British Library (Ad. Ms. 30,067) dedicated to Henry VIII: "Ad invictissimum Henricum dei gratia regem Angliae et Franciae ac Dominum Hyberniae Camilli Paleoti Bononiensis Sylva cui titulus Amor" (f. lv). A copy of the same poem is included in a Mantuan miscellany (British Library, Harley Ms. 3462: "Camilli Paliotti Bononiensis Silva ad Serenissimum, Regem Anglie de Ovidio poeta" (fs. 91r-97r).

In Book II there remain a number of references to Camillo and his brother Annibale, in the section on jokes (II, lxii; 209 and II, lxxv; 223 and for Annibale II, lviii; 203). It would seem that the Paleotti were not so insignificant nor so alienated from court society as to be completely eliminated. Indeed, Annibale is considered very much part of court society in that he is referred to as "il nostro messer Annibal Paleotto".

27. See, for example, J. Guidi, "De l'amour courtois", pp.35-6, 55.

28. Bernardo Bibbiena sets the ideological framework for the discussion on women which in the *vulgata* is firmer and less beset by contradictions: "Gran guadagno in vero fariano

le donne se potessero riconciliarsi con dui suoi tanto gran nemici, quanto siete voi [Ottaviano Fregoso] e 'l signor Gasparo." (II, xcii; 247)

29. It may also be argued that Castiglione wished to be less dependent on medieval *forms* of discussion, such as the courts of love, in order to emphasize the innovations he was bringing to the subject. For all that, certain parts of the *Cortegiano* remind one of scholastic debate; although formally scorned, it seems present in the endless rounds of propositions, counter-propositions or doubts and an eventual synthesis.

30. Cf. M. Zancan, *Nel cerchio*, pp.23-5.

31. One of these remarks seems to indicate a fiery Emilia Pia, ready to do battle with her old adversaries: "Quivi risero tutti gli omini e donne; e la signora Emilia, pur ridendo, 'Veramente', disse, 'signor Gasparo, se vi pensate un poco meglio, credo che trovarete ancor qualche altro bello esempio di continenzia simile a questo'" (III, xlvi; 319). Her irony is obvious enough but it is the context of her statement that is more revealing. The group is considered a unity brought together by their laughter at Cesare Gonzaga's witty remarks. Castiglione wishes to emphasize that Emilia Pia belongs to the group ethos even if the structure of the sentence isolates her, only to bring her back to the others ("pur ridendo"). Thus, her remarks serve to heighten the sense of entertainment as well as extinguish any deep-rooted animosities.

32. G. Ghinassi, "Fasi dell'elaborazione", calls this scene "la lunga commedia del processo intentato contro i calunniatori delle donne" (p.173). It is true that Emilia Pia's behaviour might be termed grotesque by some, too single-minded to be convincing in the leisurely group of courtiers.

33. On the rare occasions when these other women speak, it is usually in the form of a request for information or more details from the men. Margherita Gonzaga is involved in a number of exchanges which are characterized by her desire for more narratives on women. Such a request appears practically unaltered from the *Seconda Redazione* in the *vulgata*: "Parmi che voi narriate troppo brevemente queste opere virtuose fatte da donne" (III, xxiii; 289). And, as in the earlier redaction, Camillo now Giuliano, makes a point of singling out Margherita as the person most interested in these narratives: "e voi, madonna Margherita, mettete cura di tenerlo a memoria" (III, xxv; 291). Margherita Gonzaga had asked at least two questions in the *Seconda Redazione* (pp.290, 329); these and other remarks are most often just simply eliminated by Castiglione in the final version.

34. Frisio is made more civilized and less impolite by committing himself to a pro-Italian stance: "Allor il Frigio, 'Or non piú,' disse, 'pregaremo Dio di vedere adempita questa vostra speranza'" (IV, xlii; 415). In this way, Frisio is no longer a barbarous and senseless detractor of women and hence becomes more dignified.

35. Ottaviano acts as the peace-maker, urging moderation to prevail: "e veramente avete torto ed oramai dovreste esser mitigato" (addressing Frisio and Pallavicino, III, lxxvi; 358). He goes on to clarify his position asserting that "io non sono vostro avversario" and that *his* courtier would be neither a misogynist nor pro-women as described in the third

book: "né in altra cosa lo mutarei, se non in farlo un poco piú amico delle donne che non è il signor Gaspar, ma forse non tanto quanto è alcuno di questi altri signori." (III, lxxvii; 359) This statement represents the enactment of the philosophy of reconciliation alluded to earlier. Even the expression of doubt "forse" lessens the force of what could have been more controversial criticism.

36. For some discussion of this notion, see M. Zancan, *Nel cerchio*, pp.21-7 and C. Ossola, "*Il libro del cortegiano.* Ragionamenti ed expeditioni", *Lettere Italiane*, 31 (1979), pp. 517-33. However, my argument's conclusions differ substantially from these two critics.

37. Ottaviano mentions solely "il parlare di donne" (*SR*, p.188) without being more specific and in the course of the chapter the theme is seen as the general one of "donne". Some of this attitude remains in the printed text when Frisio, taking over Ottaviano's discourse of the *Seconda Redazione*, retains the universal "il parlar di donne" (III, iii; 263). In spite of the inconsistency Castiglione in the opening section is focusing on his creation, the *donna di palazzo*.

38. A noteworthy example of one of Isabella's ladies-in-waiting who became implicated in her mistress's sexual politics is documented by R. Castagna in *Un viceré per Eleonora Brognina alla corte di Isabella d'Este Gonzaga*, Mantua, Moretti, 1982. It might be argued that Castiglione perceived this outrageous sexual behaviour in terms of a lack of nobility. And for this reason he sets up nobility as the basic property of the *donna di palazzo*, as well as for the courtier. But it should not be deduced from this that there were not noble *donne di palazzo*. Margherita Cantelmo, married to a Neapolitan baron, was closely connected with Isabella but she is eliminated in the *vulgata*. For an over-view of the *donzelle* see my "Images of Isabella d'Este", *Italian Studies*, 39 (1984), pp. 47-62; p.61.

39. A partial explanation of the passage is to be found in M. Zancan, *Nel cerchio*, pp.43-4.

40. Ovid, *Metamorphoses*, X, 243-97. Pygmalion is represented as the consumate artist by Ovid: "ars adeo latet arte sua" (l. 252) who is able through his "ars" to make the ideal real. He needs the assistance of Venus to breathe life into the statue which will be untouched and pure, in stark contrast to the first prostitutes described by Ovid: "utque pudor cessit sanguisque induruit oris, / in rigidum parvo silicem discrimine versae "(X, 241-42).

41. See S. Kolsky, "Images", p.53 and I. Fenlon, *Music and Patronage in Sixteenth-Century Mantua*, Cambridge U.P., 1981, pp.15-22.

42. See G. Saccaro Battisti, "La donna, le donne", pp.229-31, who notes that the *donna di palazzo* only has an illusory freedom with respect to women of other social classes. It is discourse, created by male courtiers, which has terrifying power over women's actions. Castiglione clearly identifies the problem but his position of insisting on nobility and the consequent conservative notions of morality do not make him an advocate for radical

change. Indeed, his response on the question of love is for the woman to remain silent and keep everything secret so that she will not be talked about.

43. Cf. M. Zancan, *Nel cerchio*, pp.46-8.

44. It cannot be denied that some women were able to take control of political affairs, though normally in the absence of their husbands. Such was the case of Elisabetta Gonzaga who ruled Urbino in the interregnum created by the death of her husband Guidobaldo in 1508. It is well known that Isabella d'Este ruled Mantua during her husband's imprisonment by the Venetians (see S. Kolsky, "Images", pp.55-7).

45. See C. Fahy, "Three early Renaissance treatises on women", *Italian Studies*, 31 (1956), pp. 31-55; J. R. Woodhouse, *Baldesar Castiglione*, pp.116, 122; S.D. Kolsky, *Mario Equicola*, pp. 67-70; I. Mclean, *The Renaissance Notion of Women*, pp.28-37.

46. I will explain later how this extensive group of chapters can be sub-divided into two major sections: (1) the *exempla* (2) chastity (with appropriate *exempla*).

47. See G. Ghinassi, "Postille", pp.172-73; P.A. Stadter, *Plutarch's Historical Methods: An Analysis of the "Mulierum Virtutes"*, Harvard U.P., 1965. Bernardino Cacciante's sources are listed by M. Martini in the foot-notes to his edition of the *Libretto apologetico delle donne*.

48. In general, Castiglione has re-grouped the *exempla* according to principles of chronological continuity, that is, ancient examples followed by modern ones. Certain examples in the *Seconda Redazione* are moved from the end of the third book nearer the beginning in the *vulgata*, so as to make the whole more coherent (for example the chapter on Camma, xc in the *Seconda Redazione* becomes xxvi in the final version). The same examples, therefore, are grouped together in sub-sections. Chapter xxviii of the revised text uses examples from *SR*, lxiii, but carefully arranged under the heading of wives helping their husbands — the foundation of Rome, the Sabine women, and so on.

49. G. Ghinassi, "Fasi dell'elaborazione", p.181.

50. For discussion of these changes see J. Guidi, "L'Espagne dans la vie et dans l'oeuvre de Baldassare Castiglione" in *Présence et influence de l'Espagne dans la culture italienne*, Paris, Université de la Sorbonne Nouvelle, Centre de Recherche sur la Renaissance Italienne, 1978, in particular, pp.184-90.

51. D.A. Trafton, "Politics and the praise of women: political doctrine in the *Courtier* 's Third Book" in *Castiglione. The Ideal and the Real in Renaissance Culture*, edited by R.W. Hanning and D. Rosand, Yale U.P., 1983, pp.29-44, considers that Castiglione asserts "their [women's] essential equality with men" (p.33) and that the examples are politicized. Altogether, it is not an illuminating contribution, given the work of Guidi, but it does encourage a closer look at the ideology of the *exempla* chosen by Castiglione.

52. Not only are the names referred to deleted (*SR*, lxix becomes chapter xxxvi), but general statements concerning the worthiness of some of these women are either curtailed

or eliminated altogether: "e se comparar le vorrete con li suoi padri e mariti e fratelli, vedrete che esse hanno molto piú parte nella nobilità delle lor famiglie per il proprio valor suo che per le riccheze o per causa delli uomini" (*SR*, p.257). The framework of familial relations is not used in this instance as an oppressive measure. On the contrary, these women are seen to be greater than the institutions which manipulate them.

53. The Duchess of Urbino herself is considered a living *exemplum* of chastity related to death: "essendo vivuta quindeci anni in compagnia del marito come vidua" (III, xlix; 324). She refuses to be disloyal to her ailing husband and hence she is a figure of heroic proportions that validates the other *exempla* on *onestà*.

54. In the *Seconda Redazione* a further detail had been added, later deleted: "ornata d'un bellissimo sepolcro e d'infiniti epigrammi" (*SR*, p.272) perhaps to lessen the emphasis on the girl's death as a literary event.

55. Bandello neatly summarized the tensions in court intellectual life on the question of chastity in the dedication to his *novella* on Lucretia (Parte II, novella xxi). He represents Equicola as part of the libertine trend of court society, "e Mario diceva che ella era stata pazza ad ammazzarsi" (*Tutte le opere di Matteo Bandello*, edited by F. Flora, Milan: Mondadori, 1952, vol.1, p.843). In response Castiglione recounts the story of Lucretia, indicative of his position of death being preferable to sexual dishonour. Bandello claims that the *novella* is Castiglione's own work and indeed it could have easily been one of the *exempla* of the third book: "E che cosa può esser in una femina di salvo, come ella ha perduta la pudicizia?" (pp.849-50)

56. For Castiglione's biography, consult V. Cian, *Un illustre nunzio pontificio del Rinascimento. Baldassar Castiglione*, Città del Vaticano: Biblioteca Apostolica Vaticana, 1951 and S. Kolsky, "Castiglione's biography: The courtier and the Italian princes", *Spunti e ricerche*, 1 (1985), pp. 1-34.

III

Making and breaking the rules: Castiglione's Cortegiano

The opening pages of the *Cortegiano* contain a statement concerning the author's perception of the genre and scope of his work:

> In these books we shall not follow any strict order, or list a series [regula] of precepts [precetti distinti], as is the normal practice in teaching. Instead, following many writers of the ancient world, and reviving a pleasant memory, we shall recount some discussions which once took place among men who were singularly qualified in these matters.[1]

Castiglione is making the point that as a writer dealing with matters pedagogical he was faced with a choice between two literary genres: the first a book of rules concerning the rights and wrongs of comportment, and the second the humanist dialogue modelled on classical example. The latter choice represents the possibility of allowing space for artistic creativity in a treatise on behaviour: the verb 'seguire' (even in its negative condition) suggests a mechanical regurgitation of a systemic code highlighted by its logicality and universal applicability ('precetti distinti'), whereas 'recitaremo' proposes a far wider range of nuanced meanings. 'Recitare' (according to the *Vocabolario della Crusca*) has a primary meaning of 'telling, narrating'.[2] It also has the meaning of acting a role, playing a part – concepts close to the themes of the *Cortegiano* because of the text's emphasis on knowing artifice. It is clear that the writer is consciously arguing against a dry exposition of rules as the optimum way of effecting behavioural changes, or even

[1] I, i. 40 (references are to book, chapter, and page). All translations are from B. Castiglione, *The Book of the Courtier*, trans. G. Bull (Harmondsworth, 1976). Occasional modifications have been made to the translations to improve clarity.

'Noi in questi libri non seguiremo un certo ordine o regula di precetti distinti, che 'l più delle volte nell'insegnare qualsivoglia cosa usar si sòle; ma alla foggia di molti antichi, rinovando una grata memoria, recitaremo alcuni ragionamenti, i quali già passarono tra omini singularissimi a tale proposito.' All references to the Italian text of the *Cortegiano* will be to the edition of B. Maier, *Il libro del cortegiano con una scelta delle opere minori di Baldesar Castiglione* (2nd edn, Turin, 1964), here, 80–1. Cf. V. Cox, *The Renaissance Dialogue: Literary Dialogue in its Social and Political Contexts, Castiglione to Galileo* (Cambridge, 1992), 48, 54.

[2] *Vocabolario degli Accademici della Crusca* (Venice, 1612; reprinted Florence, 1974), 690: 'raccontare, narrare'.

of describing such precepts. He thus imposes a narratorial order on the material, placing a premium on the art of telling a story; perhaps even to the detriment of a clear, precise exposition of the rules themselves. Castiglione's account requires a specific human presence – the 'exceptional men'[3] who bear the burden of the discussions. Although the actors take on the exuberance of exemplarity, the conversations themselves were limited to a precise time and place, unlike the litany of rules which normally speaks to a future state of affairs or to an enhanced present.

Regulae have as their most important goals the reduction of diverse behaviours to a single set of rules; the codification of hierarchy within a given organization; the setting of precise boundaries. Castiglione shifts the focus elsewhere. His stated aim is to meld together elements of the distant literary past (the ancient dialogue) with those of the closer historical past (the interlocutors).[4] At the same time he introduces a further set of values in contrast to the time-serving *regulae* which construct a strictly hierarchical court society: 'reviving a pleasant memory'. The present participle makes explicit the link between present and past, while the verb itself is suggestive of various levels of renewal. The text, in a programmatic way, renews the forms of ancient dialogue in accordance with humanist cultural ideals and contemporaneously imbues them with an experiential reference: personal recollection. This does not mean that the *Cortegiano* should be read as autobiography. Far from it.[5] Although Castiglione's rules are contextualized in time and place, their usefulness is not limited to any one particular court – on the contrary, they can be said to aspire to universal coverage. For him rules are not prescriptions which explicate every movement of a person, but guidelines to open out the possibilities of action. And such possibilities are enveloped by the concept of pleasure which insinuates itself into the multiple layers of the text.[6] Castiglione attempts to move both within and beyond utilitarian considerations, exploring the polysemic possibilities of literary creation; producing an 'open work'.[7] Closure implies finitude, a cutting short of one's ambitions, and hence is a concept to be avoided.

The passage with which we began also illustrates Castiglione's methodology. It is a rewriting of a statement made by Cicero near the opening of his

[3] The superlative 'singularissimi' is to be noted because it assigns the male interlocutors to a special category of human beings, endowing them with a privileged status which separates them from ordinary men. See N. Ordine, 'Il dialogo cinquecentesco italiano tra diegesi e mimesi', *Studi e Problemi di Critica Testuale*, 37 (1988), 162–6.

[4] See W. A. Rebhorn, 'The enduring word: language, time and history in *Il libro del cortegiano*', in R. W. Hanning and D. Rosand (eds), *Castiglione: The Ideal and the Real in Renaissance Culture* (New Haven, 1983), 69–90; Rebhorn argues vigorously for the historical dimension of the text, but his conclusion points to 'the paradoxical status of *Il cortegiano* . . . caught up in history and effectively timeless' (p. 89). Thus, Rebhorn really mystifies the past–present relationship in the dialogue. See the comments on this essay by G. Mazzacurati, *Il rinascimento dei moderni* (Bologna, 1985), 156–7 n. 6.

[5] B. Maier asserts in his 'Baldesar Castiglione', in *Letteratura italiana: I minori* (Milan, 1961), II, 891–925, that the 'motivo dominante' of the work is 'autobiografico-rievocativo' (p. 902).

[6] For a brief analysis of the concept see S. D. Kolsky, 'Theorizing pleasure in the Renaissance', *Spunti e Ricerche*, 4–5 (1988–9), 33–49: 39–41.

[7] Cf. Cox, *The Renaissance Dialogue*, 58–9, 84–8, 106.

De oratore. The use of similar terminology alerts the reader to this fundamental source which permeates the *Cortegiano*.[8] The Renaissance writer also alludes indirectly to the critical issue of conversation as the basic tool for social interaction in the dialogues and at court in general. The *De oratore* recognizes that its interlocutors are especially distinguished by their eloquence.[9] An almost hidden connection between past and present can be teased out because the term generally used for an ambassador in the Quattrocento was *oratore*. A Renaissance diplomat normally functioned in court circles and had to employ extensive negotiating skills, often in difficult circumstances.[10] Such a link emphasizes the way in which the text subtly mediates ancient and contemporary cultural and political knowledge.

The basic dialogic structure is indicative of the importance of classical sources for the *Cortegiano*.[11] In fact the text vaunts its knowledge of classical culture and seeks its own validation from the privileged position of ancient civilization in the humanist canon. The discourse of the *Cortegiano* creates the impression that no other tradition matters.[12] Castiglione asserts that the models for his courtier are to be found in the texts of Plato, Xenophon, and Cicero.[13] What is more, his immense debt to Aristotle is apparent from a close reading of the text.[14] Indeed, the two greatest ancient philosophers, Aristotle and Plato, are appropriated by the text as archetypal courtiers in order to suggest that philosophy is not independent of nor separable from the court environment. Such a position also strongly suggests that Castiglione was prepared to go to extreme lengths in order to create the most illustrious parentage possible for the courtier-philosopher.[15] Therefore, it might appear that Castiglione has consulted only classical sources and that there

[8] *De oratore*, I, vi. 23. The characterization of rule-books as consisting of 'un certo ordine o regula di precetti distinti' renders the Ciceronian 'quemdam ordinem praeceptorum'. From this one can see that Castiglione has introduced the term 'regula', the significance of which becomes clear if it is seen as an oblique reference to ecclesiastical rules. On the relationship between the *Cortegiano* and *De oratore* see, J. Guidi, 'Reformulations de l'idéologie aristocratique au XVIe siècle: les différentes rédactions et la fortune du *Courtisan*', in *Réécritures I: Commentaires, parodies, variations dans la littérature italienne de la Renaissance*, CRRI 11 (Paris, 1983), 124–5; A. Michel, 'L'Influence du dialogue ciceronien sur la tradition philosophique et littéraire', in M. T. Jones-Davies (ed.), *Le Dialogue au temps de la Renaissance* (Paris, 1984), 9–24; A. F. Kinney, *Continental Humanist Poetics: Studies in Erasmus, Castiglione, Marguerite de Navarre, Rabelais, and Cervantes* (Amherst, 1989), 97, 120–55; E. Soletti, *Parole ghiacciate, parole liquefatte: Il secondo libro del 'Cortegiano'* (Alessandria, 1990), 39–67; Cox, *The Renaissance Dialogue*, 14–16.

[9] Cicero calls them 'men who were the most eloquent of our nation' (*De oratore*, trans. E. W. Sutton (London and Cambridge, Mass., 1967), I. vi. 23 and 19.

[10] See J. R. Woodhouse, *Baldesar Castiglione: A Reassessment of 'The Courtier'* (Edinburgh, 1978), 55, 59–62.

[11] See L. Valmaggi, 'Per le fonti del *Cortegiano*', *Giornale Storico della Letteratura Italiana*, 14 (1889), 72–93.

[12] See P. Burke, 'The Renaissance dialogue', *Renaissance Studies*, 3 (1989), 10.

[13] Dedication, III, 35–6.

[14] See A. D. Menut, 'Castiglione and the Nicomachean ethics', *PMLA* 58 (1943), 309–21; Kinney, *Continental Humanist Poetics*, 97, 100–1, 114–15, 125–7.

[15] See S. Kolsky, ' "The good servant": Mario Equicola. Court and courtier in early sixteenth-century Italy', *The Italianist*, 6 (1986), 44–6.

are no further intertexts present in his dialogues. However, as the *Cortegiano* itself tells us, it is concealing its polysemic possibilities and, paradoxically, at the same time provides the reader with literary and linguistic clues.[16]

The *Cortegiano* is not unrelated to the literary concerns of the Renaissance. It has not gone unnoticed that Boccaccio's *Decameron* constitutes a notable subtext in the hierarchy of sources that inform the dialogues.[17] There are obvious similarities (and differences) between the settings of the two works. However, one common feature, which is fundamental to both texts, is their dialogic nature. Both the *Cortegiano* and the *cornice* of the *Decameron* in particular take the form of conversations embedded in narrative that have the dual purpose of *divertissement* and education. Exegesis is rendered complex in both texts by the diverse voices that disturb straightforward interpretation – authority is not always readily apparent. They both present contradictory discourses which are often not reconciled and lead to critical uncertainty. Readers are left to work things out for themselves. Both texts, in their different ways, reject the treatise form as being too restrictive, authoritarian, and hence too unsubtle to represent the multi-dimensional realities with which their fictions engage.[18] They both present a series of statements and counter-statements out of which the reader attempts to synthesize a workable version of the 'truth'.

There were other, narrower, reasons for the presence of the *Decameron* in the *Cortegiano*. The revival of Boccaccio as a linguistic/literary model by Bembo in his dialogues, the *Asolani* (1505) and the *Prose della volgar lingua* (1525), is not incidental to the *Cortegiano*'s strategy of creating itself as an authoritative model which might challenge Bembo's linguistic theory concerning the supremacy of Tuscan, while retaining Boccaccio as a symbol of the new writing.[19]

It is true that the *Cortegiano* can be regarded as a series of mini-treatises that deal with those issues that were of greatest interest in the court environment (arms *v.* letters, rules of public comportment, women, love, etc.), but the dialogue form ensures that the impression is given that meaning is created by the reader instead of being presented as a God-given pronouncement of the author. The individual topics discussed in the *Cortegiano* have manifold links with the copious treatise production of the Renaissance. Often the same arguments are found in both.[20] Topics in vogue were adapted to the particular exigencies of the court. One can think here of Neoplatonic love as an example of the way in which Castiglione was not only aware of the

[16] I, xxvi. 67.

[17] See below and Cox, *The Renaissance Dialogue*, 15–16.

[18] Cf. E. Saccone, 'The portrait of the courtier in Castiglione', *Italica*, 64 (1987), 4, 8.

[19] See P. Burke, *The Fortunes of the Courtier: The European Reception of Castiglione's 'Cortegiano'* (Cambridge, 1995), 21–2.

[20] Cian's commentary in his edition of *Il libro del cortegiano* (Florence, 1947) provides abundant material on possible sources in this area. It is impossible, given the constraints of space, to provide more than a general indication of the processes involved in Castiglione's manipulation of the treatise genre.

current trends in intellectual debate, but was prepared to adapt some of the tenets of Renaissance theorists, such as Ficino and Diacceto, to the needs of the court.[21]

The foregoing discussion does not by any means exhaust the types of intertext available and used in the *Cortegiano*. Although the work appears to be the epitome of Renaissance culture, both in its presentation of a highly cultivated literary genre and its adhesion to classical form, recent scholarship has emphasized that the *Cortegiano* has other, unexpected, connections with the medieval period, and indeed was part of traditions that were particularly vital in the Middle Ages. C. Stephen Jaeger has forcefully argued that the figure of the courtier was not an invention of the Renaissance, but was deeply rooted in the practice and theory of the early Middle Ages. Moreover, the imperial bishops of the eleventh and twelfth centuries were, in this interpretation, the precursors of Castiglione's courtier.[22]

It has recently been argued that lay treatises of the Renaissance on comportment were closely related to monastic and clerical writings which prescribed the rules for the proper behaviour of monks and other ecclesiastics, particularly novices.[23] In this interpretation, contrary to Norbert Elias's theory of the development of civilized behaviour, codes of comportment are not seen as the product of the courts, but as the adoption by the courts of ideas on normative behaviour which emanated from the monasteries and other church institutions.[24] The connection between religious life, court, and wider civil society is certainly an attractive and alluring idea, especially as control of the body ('disciplina') is a conspicuous feature of clerical and lay disquisitions on behaviour alike. While the *Cortegiano* carefully maps out its own territory, it also reappropriates aspects of the medieval process of training novices with the aim of incorporating these insights into a new Renaissance synthesis. The key words that Castiglione makes a show of refusing in the passage that opened this paper are 'regula' and 'ordine'; words which convey the idea of regularity and linearity, and emit resonances which are complex and far-reaching. Both words are suggestive of the monastic system of defining human behaviour, and as such, on a conscious level, appear to be rejected by the text. Castiglione

[21] Cf. S. Kolsky, "The good servant", 53–4.

[22] See C. S. Jaeger, *The Origins of Courtliness: Civilizing Trends and the Formation of Courtly Ideals* 939–1210 (Philadelphia, 1985), 108–10, 259–62. Cf. Burke, *The Fortunes of the Courtier*, 12–15.

[23] Fundamental to this revised perspective on the relationship between medieval ecclesiastical and Renaissance lay treatises on comportment is the essay by D. Romagnoli, 'Cortesia nella città: un modello complesso. Note sull'etica medievale delle buone maniere', in *idem* (ed.), *La città e la corte: Buone e cattive maniere tra Medioevo ed Età Moderna* (Milan, 1991), 21–70. Another important essay which appeared at the same time makes similar points, although it does not specifically analyse the *Cortegiano*: D. Knox, '*Disciplina*: the monastic and clerical origins of European civility', in J. Monfasani and R. G. Musto (eds), *Renaissance Society and Culture: Essays in Honor of Eugene F. Rice, Jr* (New York, 1991), 107–35.

[24] See Knox, '*Disciplina*', 113–14, and J.-C. Schmitt, *Il gesto nel medioevo*, trans. C. Milanesi (Rome and Bari, 1990), 154–78.

seems to be referring to the sort of foundation document exemplified by the Benedictine Rule (one of the most influential documents used to regulate monastic behaviour) in order to register his 'disapproval' and break with a certain tradition of regulation. In this context the adhesion to rules in the body of the text appears to override Castiglione's opening statement, or at least to render it problematic.

One such example can be seen in Federico Fregoso's categorical statement: 'Then in everything he does or says I should like our courtier to follow certain universal rules' (II, vii. 115). From this it would seem that all aspects of a courtier's behaviour at court should be controlled by regulation. However, these do not appear to be rules which govern precise moments or individual situations, but deep structures from which more specific rules may possibly be generated. In this sense Castiglione is interested in making his courtier universally acceptable – hence the number of textual references to the courtier being newly arrived or changing court. Each court had its own specific practices and individual differences which the writer is trying to transcend in order to create a common ground that would allow his prototype to move easily between courts. This would increase the courtier's adaptability, and put into action the ideal of a universal secular 'church'.

The second book of the *Cortegiano* puts the skills of the courtier outlined in the first into practice. Federico Fregoso is chosen as the official spokesman in the ensuing discussion of how the courtier should behave in the public glare of the court, using all the advantages granted him by Lodovico da Canossa in the first book. Not unexpectedly, Federico Fregoso needs to suggest the parameters of acceptable behaviour for the model courtier and in so doing proposes 'certain universal rules'. Federico's view of regulation is challenged by Morello da Ortona,[25] an elderly courtier who seems to possess little credibility throughout the *Cortegiano*. In the final book he opposes Bembo's Neoplatonizing vision of love and in the process makes a spectacle of himself by urging the desirability of old men as lovers.[26] Morello represents the old school of courtiership and consequently becomes a figure of fun: he has failed to adapt to changing circumstances and cannot come to terms with the ageing of his body. Therefore, he is considered the incarnation of an earlier and rejected style of court behaviour.[27] It is perhaps for this reason that scholars have neglected his exchange with Federico Fregoso, an exchange which, although treated in an ironic and ambiguous manner, is central to the ideological foundations of the *Cortegiano*.

[25] Morello da Ortona's name is always preceded by 'il signor', indicating a certain respect but not without a touch of irony. For biographical details consult the 'Dizionarietto biografico', in V. Cian (ed.), *Il libro del Cortegiano* (Florence, 1947), 523–4. See also P. Floriani, *I gentiluomini letterati* (Naples, 1981), 66.

[26] See esp. *Cortegiano*, IV, LI, and LV–LVI.

[27] Morello da Ortona is upbraided for his outrageous behaviour on a number of occasions, usually related to the fact that he is trying to appear young in spite of his advanced years (see, in particular, II, xiv. 122–3). He is the butt of rather cruel jokes which reveal the downside of the 'new' court society. The court, in its efforts at renewal, cannot easily accept the presence of 'old-style' courtiers.

Morello's first objection is that he has not learnt anything from Federico's disquisition ('It seems to me that these rules of yours teach us very little', II, viii. 115). Secondly, he points out the derivation of some of the regulatory discourse: 'I do remember having heard them some time or other from the friars at confession, and I believe they called them "the circumstances" '. Thus, the repressed other of ecclesiastical inquiry and discipline literature is brought to the surface by the slightly ridiculous Morello. Though not indicated directly, a methodology similar to the one that provided a systematic framework for the confessional underlies the concept of clerical rules. The text is discreetly and indirectly pointing the reader towards the possibility that such rules may not be so alien to the ethos of the *Cortegiano*. Federico Fregoso rises to the challenge by demonstrating that his 'regule' do indeed teach proper behaviour. As a response to Morello's original remark, he pointedly employs the expression 'sotto la nostra regula' ('in accordance with our rule'), implicitly claiming a space for the rules of court behaviour. And when he has finished the first part of his reply, he asks, repeating the same terminology: 'Now don't you think, signor Morello, that our rules are able to teach something?' (II, ix. 116). The emphasis on 'our' is intended to differentiate court rules from ecclesiastical ones. The *exemplum* that Federico presents in order to illustrate the concept of 'the circumstances' is particularly courtly in that it offers to the reader the spectacle of a soldier whose only thoughts are of fighting, even when a refined lady of the court tries to dance with him. It is an instance of the adaptation of clerical rules of behaviour to a court situation. The presence of a woman was obviously alien to the monastery, but the underlying principles are the same, that is, the necessity to adapt one's behaviour to the particular circumstances in which one finds oneself: 'These are the kind of mistakes made by those who have no regard for those "circumstances" you say the friars told you about' (II, ix. 117). Federico, it would appear, fully accepts the principle of the 'circumstances' as a valid means of regulating behaviour. His problem lies in its ecclesiastical origins. His statement implies an effort to secularize the term, to rend it from its traditional usage. Federico returns to the theme in his discussion of everyday conversation, where he once again disparagingly mentions the origins of this type of regulation: 'And for my part I know no other rules to give on this subject, except perhaps the ones we have already heard from signor Morello, which he learned at confession as a child' (II, xvii. 124).[28]

What is surprising is that nine chapters later Federico Fregoso appears to agree that his rules are the very same as those used in confessional manuals. The passing reference to Morello's age, stressing his advanced years, can be

[28] For a detailed discussion of a medieval treatment of conversational rules see C. Casagrande, 'Le regole del parlare e del tacere: la disciplina in locutione di Ugo di San Vittore', *Fondazione Giangiacomo Feltrinelli: Quaderni*, 23 (1983), 127–47; C. Casagrande and S. Vecchio, *I peccati della lingua: Disciplina ed etica della parola nella cultura medievale* (Rome, 1987), 73–102; D. W. Robertson, Jr., 'A note on the classical origin of "circumstances" in the medieval confessional', *Studies in Philology*, 43 (1946), 6–14.

considered another ironic jab at the elderly courtier; a way of detracting from the correctness of his observation, implying that his account might no longer be reliable. The mention of his age might also be considered an oblique reference to the introduction of Book II, where it is stated as a general principle that old men generally have a greater attachment to the past than to the present, which they continually criticize. Within the dynamics of the *Cortegiano* Federico Fregoso's remarks are ironic. They are an obvious way to short-circuit discussion and release the speaker from the onerous duty of describing the perfect courtier. At the same time, Federico Fregoso is casting doubt on the efficacy of those rules derived from religious practices to describe *totally* the behaviour of the courtier. This is underlined by the fact that the speaker is forced to continue, and indeed he takes up the topic of conversations with the prince. Federico Fregoso might adhere to clerical rules of conversation which emphasized the necessity of taking into account the rank of the interlocutor and other such factors, but he decisively introduces the notion of personal judgement, an indispensable element in Castiglione's remoulding of the rules.[29]

The dispute over 'circumstances' is also part of a polemic in the *Cortegiano* against certain aspects of ecclesiastical influence in court society. The fact that Morello refers to the 'frati', can only increase Federico's antipathy, bearing in mind the diatribe against them in Book III, chapter xx, where their behaviour is seen to be the equivalent of the most untrustworthy and deceptive imaginable, the natural consequence of their rules without faith in God. They are considered to be usurping the roles and functions of the professional courtier. In this way Castiglione demonstrates an ambiguous relationship to medieval ecclesiastical literature, reluctant to acknowledge any influence it might have had on his dialogue. It is as if he is embarrassed by this heritage – indeed, as a writer with humanistic leanings it might have been expected that he would not refer to it at all. Yet Castiglione felt compelled to allude to this crucial source for his methodology, albeit indirectly, although he implicitly suggests that he has superseded such an outdated technique and that by adapting it to the needs of the court he has irrevocably altered it. The episode shows his awareness of the type of analysis used by the clergy in order to regulate behaviour and, even if it is impossible to identify exactly which treatises Castiglione may have read, on the basis of the above episode it can be stated that he was familiar with confessional literature and, as an extension of those techniques, discipline literature. Alternatively, it could be argued that this is one way of bringing court and church together, grounding the one, more fragile, institution in the vaster and more assured structures of the other.

[29] 'Therefore whoever has to accommodate his behaviour to dealings with a considerable number of people must be guided by his own judgement and, recognizing the differences between one man and another, must change his style and method from day to day, according to the nature of those with whom he wants to converse' (II, xvi. 124). Federico Fregoso had previously stated that converstional rules were the hardest to formulate because of the many different situations in which conversation took place. Judgement is beginning to supplement discretion as a key factor in formulating contingent behaviour.

The rest of this essay will be concerned with an examination of one of the most influential of these medieval training guides – *De institutione novitiorum liber*, attributed to Hugh of St Victor, possibly written in the first quarter of the twelfth century.[30] This text became particularly influential in the later Middle Ages.[31] The purpose of my analysis is to draw out the possible connections between this text (considered a model of its genre, covering all the major areas in which self-control was required in a religious setting, appropriate in this instance for canons regular) and the *Cortegiano*. If it is not certain that Castiglione actually knew this particular text, there is a strong case to be made that he was aware of the genre, as indirectly indicated by the Federico Fregoso–Morello da Ortona encounter in the *Cortegiano*. Furthermore, *De institutione novitiorum liber* details those areas which were of particular concern to the *Cortegiano*, which hints at a direct line of transmission between the two texts, although there is no external evidence to support this hypothesis.

The discourse of *De institutione novitiorum liber* focuses on the relationship between behaviour and the aim of devoting oneself to God by becoming a canon. Crucial here is the link between everyday interactions, within and outside the sacred space of the cloisters, and the necessity of making behaviour conform to certain patterns acceptable to the goals of a godly community. Thus, the *prologus* provides the ideological vantage-point from which behaviour is to be judged. The particular rules make sense only when considered from the point of view of ends. 'Disciplina virtutis' is the essential strategy by which the soul may attain beatitude.[32] The concept of 'disciplina' effectively draws together the idea of bodily control and ideal Christian behaviour. Control over one's body (the latter conceived as a social and religious semiotic) is perceived as the basis for an ordered Christian society.[33] The discipline of the body falls under four main headings in Hugh of St Victor's treatise: dress, gesture, speech/conversation, and eating.[34]

To begin with, I wish to examine the points of contact between the *Cortegiano* and clerical codes of behaviour, using Hugh's treatise to illustrate this system of thought. The most obvious similarities can be found in the treatment of the ways in which the novice/courtier relates to the external world. The greater part of Hugh's treatise is concerned with 'appearance' on the social stage of the cloisters. However, for Hugh there is a compelling

[30] See Romagnoli, 'Cortesia nella città', 38–48; C. S. Jaeger, *The Envy of Angels: Cathedral Schools and Social Ideals in Medieval Europe, 950–1200* (Philadelphia, 1994), 254–68. The text of *De institutione novitiorum liber* is to be found in J.-P. Migne (ed.), *Patrologiae Cursus Completus: Series Latina*, vol. CLXXVI (hereafter *PL*). For the manuscript tradition of this work consult R. Goy, *Die Überlieferung der Werke Hugos von St. Viktor: Ein Beitrag zur Kommunikationsgeschichte des Mittelalters* (Stuttgart, 1976), 340–67.

[31] See Knox, '*Disciplina*', 113–15; Jaeger, *The Envy of Angels*, 257.

[32] 'Ad beatitudinem autem nemo venire potest nisi per virtutem, et virtus non alio modo veraciter apprehenditur, nisi disciplina virtutis non negligenter custodiatur. Usus enim disciplinae ad virtutem animum dirigit, virtus autem ad beatitudinem perducit' (*PL*, col. 925A-B).

[33] See Burke, *The Fortunes of the Courtier*, 12–13.

[34] *PL*, col. 935D.

connection between the soul and the body: 'correct' external behaviour reveals an orderly soul. Both Castiglione and Hugh are fully aware of the necessity of presenting a good appearance, although for Castiglione its relationship with the 'inner spirit' is sometimes obscure, whereas for the medieval writer 'intus' and 'foris' are inextricably linked to emphasize the religious life of the canon. At the base of all behaviour for Hugh is the concept of 'disciplina', that is, bodily control related to gesture and speech in particular, but also to dress and eating. For Hugh, discipline is also the art of appearances, though these are more readily connected to inner imperatives than in Castiglione; of bodily harmony leading to a better existence.[35]

Hugh's definition of 'disciplina' does include elements that were to become central in Castiglione's system. In a sense Castiglione's 'grazia', which is one of those terms that tends to defy definition and strict rule-bound behaviour, is moving to replace an overt dependence on clear-cut basic rules, perhaps building on sparse indications in *De institutione novitiorum liber.*[36] Hugh puts forward a view of movement pertinent to the novice: 'Men's gestures must be gracious in every act without being effeminate.'[37] Hugh goes on to use a variation of this term in his discussion on speech; he tells his audience, referred to as 'fratres', that 'his way of talking must be humble so that his speech finds favour with his listeners'.[38] He advises the novice to exercise care in his every action in order to produce acceptable behaviour, and to create the impression of total physical harmony through the suppression of disordered desires.[39]

The emphasis of *De institutione novitiorum liber* falls on knowing how to apply the rules of behaviour in relation to people, time, and place. Hence, the importance of 'discretio'. Although Hugh's 'discretio' has much in common with Castiglione's 'discrezione', it is not an exact match.[40] For the medieval treatise is mathematically exact about the frame within which the novice

[35] 'Disciplina est conversatio bona et honesta, cui parum est mala non facere, sed studet etiam in iis quae bene agit per cuncta irreprehensibilis apparere. Item disciplina est membrorum omnium motus ordinatus, et dispositio decens in omni habitu et actione' (*PL*, col. 935A–B).

[36] See E. Saccone, '*Grazia, Sprezzatura, Affettazione in the Courtier*', in R. W. Hanning and D. Rosand (eds), *Castiglione: The Ideal and the Real in Renaissance Culture* (New Haven, 1983), 51–3.

[37] 'Gestus hominis in omni actu esse debet gratiosus sine mollitie' (*PL*, col. 943C). The discussion aroused by Bibbiena's 'grazia' (although limited at this point to the courtier's face) in the *Cortegiano* resembles this basic concept of Hugh's: 'we can see that your appearance is very agreeable [gratissimo] and pleasing to all, even if your features are not very delicate, though then again you manage to appear both manly and graceful [grazioso]' (I, xix. 60–1).

[38] 'humilis debet esse gestus loquentis, ut apud auditores gratiam sermo eius inveniat' (*PL*, col. 943B).

[39] The body becomes the site of a political annexation in that the 'concordia' of its members – the role and function of each one – is compared to the body politic; a further indication of the immense value Hugh places on hierarchy, and on every thing and every individual having an assigned place in this universe: 'Est enim quasi quaedam respublica corpus humanum, in quo singulis membris sua officia distributa sunt. Dum ergo unum membrum alterius membri officium inordinate sibi vindicat, quid aliud quam concordiam universitatis perturbat?' (*PL*, col. 943A).

[40] Cf. R. Klein, '*Giudizio et gusto* dans la théorie de l'art au Cinquecento', *Rinascimento*, 1 (1961), 107–13. Both the courtier and the canon share other behavioural characteristics – they both need to be cautious and prudent in their dealings with society (*PL*, col. 934B, and *Cortegiano*, II, vii).

operates. In fact Hugh nominates different subdivisions of 'discretio': 'temporum', 'personarum', 'actionum', and 'loquendi', all of which relate precisely to that aspect of behaviour which is being discussed.[41] The text enumerates the types of people and the kinds of impermissible behaviour so that the reader clearly understands the parameters of the society within which the novice must function. Castiglione will use the term 'discrezione' in a similar way to Hugh, that is, to signify the correct application of the concept of 'the circumstances'.[42] However, the Renaissance writer seems to suggest that a mere mechanical application of rules to particular circumstances will not always be enough at court. Therefore, discretion suggests a *modus operandi* which does not upset the delicate balance of the court, almost becoming the equivalent of good judgement in a more general sense.[43] Like Hugh, Castiglione places considerable emphasis on discretion; it is frequently referred to as an essential part of the courtier's *savoir-faire.* The rules have to be adapted to individual circumstances and discretion is one of the tools used in order to facilitate that process.[44] Hugh does found a 'scientia vere discretionis', which largely consists of a series of individual elements focusing on a particular aspect of behaviour. Hugh states categorically at the beginning of the treatise that 'disciplina' and 'discretio' are inseparable, that is, self-control for religious purposes cannot be viewed apart from its social context. Occasionally these are amalgamated into a mode of behaviour which was later developed in Castiglione's analysis;[45] 'discretio' will not suffice for the courtier, who will also have to make other kinds of evaluation at court. There is an overwhelming sense of hierarchy which permeates *De institutione novitiorum liber.* This is not altogether lacking in the *Cortegiano,* but is played down because, whatever the courtier's rank or social status, but especially if he is noble, it is crucial for him to be able to cut through the class-bound society of the court and reach the ruler, almost to be his equal. It is this unsettling sense of social movement or even its mere possibility that releases the courtier from a hierarchical vision of the court. And indeed, all his skills are intended as a means to bypass the fixity of meaning that Hugh of St Victor wishes to be apparent from the external appearance and gestures of his ideal novice.

In this scheme of things the topic of dress assumes significance and is treated both by the *Cortegiano* and *De institutione novitiorum liber.* Hugh states that dress must reflect the station and purpose of the novice and therefore should not be used as an excuse to display wealth or refinement.[46]

[41] *PL,* cols 928D, 941C, 946A.

[42] See, for example, II, vii, xiii, and xviii.

[43] See II, xli.

[44] 'But in any case, everything should be tempered by discretion; for it is just not possible to imagine all the circumstances possible, *and if the courtier is a good judge of himself* he will adapt himself to the occasion . . .' (II, xiii. 121; my emphasis).

[45] See *PL,* col. 930D.

[46] *Ibid.,* cols 937D–938A. An element that resembles Castiglione's 'sprezzatura' is also present in the section on clothes 'plus neglecte quam accurate composita vel adaptata amare'.

Clothes are an external expression of the cleric's purpose, a sign of his humility (*PL*, col. 936A). Castiglione also recognizes the semiotic power of dress. Both writers utilize a similar pattern of negative examples to illustrate how clothes can separate a person from his professional group by sending out the wrong signals about his social aspirations.[47] Both writers agree that black or a dark colour is best suited for their ideal creations, thus bringing the courtier into the domain of ecclesiastical taste.[48] Castiglione has assimilated some of the fundamental concepts that constitute the basis of behaviour in *De institutione novitiorum liber* or in cognate texts. However, Castiglione is at pains to emphasize particularly the concept that rules do not, and cannot, cover all eventualities – hence the reappearance of 'consuetudine' at this point in the *Cortegiano*: 'To be sure, I would not know how to lay down any hard and fast rules [regula determinata] about dress, save that one should adapt oneself to the custom [consuetudine] of the majority' (II, xxvi. 134). Thus it can be seen that Castiglione wished to ensure that the courtier conformed to the dress code of his social group, since his performance would be judged with reference to other courtiers.[49]

Clothes, of course, are the perfect example of the complex relations between the outer and inner man, and it is here that the sixteenth-century writer complicates the more open-and-shut discourse of Hugh St Victor; he does not exactly challenge it, but indicates the necessity for a subtle re-evaluation of such views. Gaspare Pallavicino ironically makes a point about the need for greater skill in judgement that goes far beyond mechanical rules, with reference to a well-known proverb that may have a subtle irony in our context. He claims that 'parole' and 'opere' are more important than clothes in reaching any judgement about a person: 'and there is good reason for the proverb which says that the habit does not make the monk' (II, xxviii. 136). However, Federico Fregoso does not agree with him, insisting that one can tell something about a courtier from his clothes, even if one is not always correct, culminating in his concluding declaration that in general 'these habits and manners', including clothes but not restricted to them, 'are in great part what men are known by' (II, xxviii. 137). One can note the ambiguous position taken by the writer on this crucial point. In particular, the dovetailing of inner and outer man still prevails *in great part*, but the text does not present it as a completely certain fact. Clothes are one of the indices which allow the courtier to make *judgements* about his fellow courtiers. They represent one element in a complex calculation which will allow the courtier to make a correct assessment. He may sometimes be wrong. The rule is there and can generally be applied. It is not a question of 'discrezione', but of judgement. In the space of this one brief chapter (chapter xxviii) the word 'giudicio'

[47] *Ibid.*, col. 937A, and *Cortegiano*, II, xxvii. 136.

[48] *PL*, col. 936A, and *Cortegiano*, II, xxvii. 135.

[49] Castiglione does introduce another aspect to the dress code which is absent from Hugh, that is, the nationalistic element. Here, dress becomes a political semiotic whereby style of dress is read as a statement of political domination or subjugation.

is employed three times, together with the verb ('giudicar') and a plural form ('giudìci resoluti'). It is not just a matter of fitting in with a series of pre-existing rules, but of the courtier trying to understand the tactics of others, that is, of the political use or non-use of the rules, in order to maintain or gain his position of superiority: 'and yet all these external things *often* provide information [dà notizia] about what is within' (II, xxviii. 137; my emphasis). The phrase 'dà notizia' is highly suggestive of the necessity of having information that the courtier can use in order to exploit interpersonal relations to the fullest. Yet such information is not foolproof. That is where judgement comes in. From this example it may be seen that not only is the ethos of the courtier different from that of the canon, but that the court is a place of greater uncertainty where judgements are less reliable.

Castiglione perhaps comes closest to Hugh of St Victor in the matter of talk, even if, as we have already seen, he is ambiguous about the origins of his guidelines on conversation. After the skirmish with Morello, it seems suprising that Castiglione should so obviously make use of Hugh's schema. The latter is concerned with the ways in which conversation is affected by the 'qualitas personarum', in particular their 'conditionem ac statum' (*PL*, col. 944B) from the point of view of whether the person to whom they are speaking is a cleric or not. The *Cortegiano* adapts such a position in order to apply it to the court situation, precisely grounding it in the 'circumstantiae'. Instead of the 'superiores' we find the prince, ultimate goal of the courtier's attentions. In this respect, the courtier is urged to be 'modest and reserved, observing always, and especially in public, the reverence and respect which should mark the attitude of a servant towards his master' (II, xviii. 222).[50] In making conversation with the prince the courtier has to be aware of the 'ubi dicatur' (*PL*, col. 943D) and the subsequent changes required in the subject-matter. Thus, when the prince is in his private quarters the courtier should not talk business, since it is a time in which the ruler will want to relax. Consequently, the courtier must learn to 'become another person [dee vestirsi un'altra persona], defer serious matters to another time and place, and engage in conversation which will be pleasing and agreeable to his master' (II, xix. 126).[51] There could be no clearer application of the principle enunciated in the *De institutione novitiorum liber*. The second book of

[50] The similarities with Hugo are striking: 'Superioribus obedientiam, timorem, obsequium et venerationem debemus exhibere' (*PL*, col. 929B). He goes on to state that the canon must carry out any work for a 'superior' 'cum omni humilitate et reverentia'. Differences appear because of the rigidity that Hugo implies in social divisions: 'Illorum conversatio supra nos est, quam venerari quidem et admirari possunt, imitari autem non valemus' (*PL*, col. 929D). The sense of difference between the courtier and the prince, so clear at the beginning of the text, becomes somewhat blurred towards the end, whereas in Hugo there is no likelihood of any relaxation of social barriers and distinctions. There is also the possibility of the courtier not obeying an amoral order and leaving the prince's service.

[51] It is obvious that the courtier will have to converse with other courtiers, just as the novice will have to converse with his equals or inferiors, in Hugh's terminology. After sketching out the courtier's relationship with the prince, Castiglione moves on to his relationship with the other courtiers who are his equals or nearly so, as the courtier will more commonly find himself in this situation. The intertextual link is particularly strong at this point between the two codes, for the *De institutione novitiorum* makes an almost identical statement, in a slightly more peremptory manner.

the *Cortegiano* also provides an arsenal of appropriate material that may be used to entertain the court, including the prince. Castiglione provides rules for the situations in which particular types of joke may be told. Hugh's rules have been transferred to an activity which was certainly not envisaged in his book.

To the reader of the *Cortegiano* the first three types of bodily control described by Hugh of St Victor will be familiar, and indeed are treated at some length in Castiglione's text. It is the fourth category – and one which causes some surprise – that will now be treated. There is hardly a trace of food, or discussion of eating habits, in the *Cortegiano*. Even though it is clear that the meetings take place in the evening, after dinner, the idea of conviviality based around a shared meal makes only one appearance in the text. This particular communal meal marks an important juncture in the *Cortegiano*: 'and then when night began to fall the Prefect decided that they should eat, and led all the gentlemen into supper. As soon as they had finished eating, he went to the rooms of the Duchess' (II, v. 112).

The scene alluded to here represents a significant change in the composition of the group of courtiers: the vacuum created by the absence of the duke of Urbino is filled by his successor elect, Francesco Maria della Rovere, who ambiguously endows the circle with a sense of impending princely power. The future duke (already prefect of Rome) through the reference to eating conveys a fleeting sense of the exigencies of the body, as well as a political need to galvanize the group and bring it under his leadership (the exclusion of the women from the shared meal signals their imminent removal from the political process). Thus the shared meal signals a different unity from that demonstrated during the 'ragionamenti': it is connected with the new duke (a physical presence in contrast to the absence of the 'old' ruler, and the intellectual presences of the courtiers) as a person who imposes his desires on the courtiers ('volse il signor Prefetto').

Given the prominence usually granted to food and its consumption in *De institutione novitiorum liber* and other medieval and Renaissance treatises on social aspects of behaviour, one can only assume that Castiglione was exercising a fully conscious choice in thus breaking with tradition.[52] In medieval and Renaissance treatises on comportment, the customary discussion of table manners often allowed an author the opportunity to write freely in a satiric or comic vein. The instructions frequently take the form of negative imperatives or colourful *exempla* (often with a visual flavour), sometimes acting as a spark to ignite the text. The rituals of eating, because they are such a central part of everyday life, are seen as the key area for testing the criteria of civilized behaviour. Hugh of St Victor is no exception to this: as is appropriate for his environment, table manners involve the entire gamut of social

[52] J. Nicholls, *The Matter of Courtesy: Medieval Courtesy Books and the Gawain-Poet* (Woodbridge, Suffolk and Dover, NH, 1985), notes that the English courtesy poems he had examined 'consider the meal as the most important function in social life and concentrate their precepts on or around it' (p. 14).

behaviour. For example, speech is prohibited at table;[53] the gaze must be restricted to one's food;[54] gesture and dress must befit the occasion as well as the more general ideology of canonical life.[55]

The disorder which can be induced by food is counterbalanced by the order of discipline, and its associated concepts of balance and harmony, so that the danger of natural excess may be avoided. Wrong kinds of behaviour are described in some depth by Hugh, not only to ridicule those who allow themselves to be ruled by base natural passions, but also to prompt the reader to dissociate himself from such flagrant mismanagement of the body and to free himself from a false hierarchy of the senses and intelligence. It is here, perhaps more than in any other place in the treatise, that the writer exploits the possibilities of style and language. His verbal art becomes more concentrated: food is archetypal action which is mirrored in the super-excess of verbal forms which denote too great an emphasis on the natural rather than the symbolic or semiotic body.[56] When Hugh of St Victor describes what happens when the novice loses all sense of 'discretio actionum' (*PL*, col. 941C), the language he uses mirrors such lack and loss of restraint. It seeks to create an illusion of the unusual, of excess, by opening up its vocabulary to less common words, with a greater emphasis on diminutives to indicate the breaking down of social barriers. In fact, the language is reminiscent of the Lucianic dialogue (see *PL*, col. 950A–D). Criticism of excessive behaviour is formulated by the employment of lists structured anaphorically using 'alii' to stress the 'otherness' of such behaviour and lifestyle choices. The life of a canon (in Hugh's view) does not, or should not, include a propensity for fine food – perhaps a means of separating the cloister from the court, and of maintaining its distinctness as a place devoted to God based on the 'rigor disciplinae' (*PL*, col. 950C), that is, on a discipline which subscribes to the notion of prohibition and exclusion as a way of achieving godliness. Discipline also implies the notion of virility, of manliness; a requirement to ensure the necessary control over one's appetites. Moreover, irrational desire for, and excessive interest in, exotic food is compared to the unfathomable desires of pregnant women (*PL*, col. 950C). Masculinity

[53] 'Taciturnitas inter epulas necessaria est' (*PL*, col. 949B).

[54] 'Custodia oculorum inter epulas propterea necessaria est' (*ibid.*).

[55] 'Nihil cum strepitu aut tumultu fiat, sed omnia membra cum modestia, et tranquillitate in disciplina contineantur' (*PL*, col. 949C). Discipline is the equivalent of bodily control, out of which come all those values which render the body attractive: beauty, modesty, balance; instinctual movements are contained.

[56] Excessive desire to eat is equated with the loss of control over the body: 'Non sicut quidam faciunt, qui cum ad sedendum assederint, inquieta quadam agitatione et confusione membrorum intemperantiam animi sui designant' (*PL*, col. 949C). Disturbance and confusion are the exterior signs of inner torment or disorder. The use of 'they' (parallel to 'alii') emphasizes the fact that those who participate in anti-social behaviour exclude themselves from the social body governed by precise rules. The matter of deviant behaviour in regard to eating follows the medieval principle that exterior misrule mirrors inner turmoil. Terms such as 'intemperantia' and 'indecorus' are used to convey the breakdown in the harmony between body and soul as well as between individual and society. The individual here is marked by angst and excessive material desires which neglect the peace and measure of the soul.

is the acceptance of rules, the imposition of boundaries on the body; otherwise the novice becomes an outcast, a subordinated being subject to the sway of the passions, unable to join the élite of society.

A critical part of Castiglione's strategy appears to lie in his summary and infrequent references to the essential act of eating. In no way can it be considered an oversight. Hence the courtiers are partially dissociated from the humanist *convivium*, although retaining sufficient elements (excluding the wine and the food) to lend *gravitas* to the generally considered frivolity of court life. The interlocutors and their imagined courtier are distinguished by this lack of bodily appetite, by the absence of food. They stand apart from the most obvious Italian literary model of the *Cortegiano*, the Boccaccian *brigata* of the *Decameron*, where the *cornice* always describes the activities of the group before they settle down to tell stories. These activities invariably include, often as the centrepiece, the communal meal. For example, the meal on the first day is described as follows: 'Dishes, daintily prepared, were brought in, excellent wines were at hand . . . Everyone was delighted that these things had been so charmingly and efficiently arranged, and during the meal there was pleasant talk and merry laughter from all sides.'[57]

The ritual of consuming food brings together the future storytellers, creating the sense of a shared ethos that can easily survive the surface antagonisms produced by the individual stories. The meal emphasizes those values which are held in high esteem by the adepts of this civilized lifestyle. Eating has become an aesthetic activity and, as such, brings into focus both the sense of order in the micro-society of the *brigata* and the production of pleasure as an integral part of eating in contrast to the chaos wreaked by the plague and the topsy-turvy society of the *novelle*.

Castiglione, in order to remove the courtier(s) from the minutiae of everyday life, rejected the table as the place *par excellence* of pleasurable activity. As a consequence, the status of the courtiers is elevated to a level above that of the common man whose body must be sustained through the ingestion of nourishment. In other words, the courtiers have been sublimated to the realm of Platonic ideas in which nature is subordinated to the power of discourse. The interlocutors (as well as the fictive being they are creating) seem *almost* out of the reach of historical change. The scarcity of references to food only serves to emphasize their eternality in art.

The interlocutors show what is best in court society, both through their own behaviour as embodiments of the courtly ideal and their use of *exempla* and anecdote to illustrate the concepts or rules that are under discussion and sometimes to comment ironically upon wrong kinds of behaviour,

[57] G. Boccaccio, *The Decameron*, trans. G. H. McWilliam (Harmondsworth, 1972), 67. See L. Sanguineti White, *La scena conviviale e la sua funzione nel mondo del Boccaccio* (Florence, 1983), 35–44, and F. Capozzi, 'Food and food images in the *Decameron*', *Canadian Journal of Italian Studies*, 10/34 (1987), 1–13. For a more general analysis of the relationship between the *Cortegiano* and the *Decameron* see V. Vianello, 'Tra "ars" ed "ingenium": il *Decameron* nella critica del primo cinquecento', *Studi sul Boccaccio*, 16 (1987), 361–84.

necessary elements in this kind of treatise, found both in Cicero and in Hugh. In the *Cortegiano* one can detect a further function of *exempla*: that of opening up the text beyond the closed world of the speakers, to enter into the historically imperfect world where errors are committed and are then judged by the interlocutors. Showing performs an essential function in the *Cortegiano*; in a sense it serves not only as a supplement to the bare rules, which are often pared to the minimum of detail and so have need of illustration, but in some cases it almost replaces them, lending a focus and concreteness that would otherwise be lacking because of the generalities in which the interlocutors speak. Indeed, a perennial problem for interpreters of the text has been the rules' lack of precision. In the first place Castiglione has an overriding concern to provide a basis for all kinds of court behaviour, thus furnishing the courtier with the greatest possible flexibility, something that would render him most useful in times of political turmoil. If the courtier happened to be a diplomat in service with a foreign court, then a knowledge of the fundamentals of court behaviour would enable him to carry out his functions in the first instance while he acquired knowledge about the particular features of the court to which he had been posted.

Discourse on rules in the *Cortegiano* generally consists of a twofold process which is not always carried out in the fullest detail: the general rule which generates a number of lesser, dependent rules, which are then normally illustrated by examples. The fact that the general rules are very few in number does not detract from the possibility that they cover the essential aspects of acceptable behaviour in the court. Castiglione presents as the primary rule that of avoiding 'la affettazione' (affectation): 'I have discovered a universal rule [una regula universalissima], which seems to apply more than any other in all human actions or words: namely, to steer away from affectation at all costs' (I, xxvi. 67). The general nature of the foundation rules makes them applicable to situations outside the court environment, helping to explain the popularity of the book all over Europe and not just among members of the aristocratic–courtier class. However, universal rules need to be adapted to individual situations, and it is here that the ecclesiastical codes of conduct come into their own. For Castiglione's text makes clear that a second operation needs to be put in place in order to be able to act profitably at court:

> Next let him consider well whatever he does or says, the place where he does it, in whose presence, its timing, why he is doing it, his own age, his profession, the end he is aiming at, and the means that are suitable; and so, bearing all these points in mind, let him prepare himself discreetly for all he wishes to do or say. (II, vii. 115)

All of Hugh's categories are here. The means to be precise in the application of rules to a given situation are provided. They are not exhaustive, since there are other 'rules' that come into play which are developed by Castiglione to a high degree of refinement. In particular, the notions of 'grazia' and 'sprezzatura' almost render the other rules, if not unnecessary, at least subordinate to them. There is, in any case, one striking difference that complicates their application. For Hugh the aim of his rules was quite clear: the control of the body was in direct relationship with the goals of a religious community. At court there exists only one possible aim, that is, to win the favour of the prince and be able to influence him as an intimate counsellor. Hugh's system certainly does not have social advancement as its declared aim; it places priority on the cultivation of virtue in the context of a religious community.

Although the above seems to cover all possible situations, Castiglione introduces other elements that play a major part in determining one's mode of behaviour in the court environment. Rules are not enough by themselves to ensure success at court; indeed, their indiscriminate application can lead to disaster, as Hugh well knew. Rules that have a metahistorical sense about them, abstract and infinitely applicable, come into contact or conflict with the historical situation of the court, summed up by the term 'la consuetudine' (custom), not just used to refer to Castiglione's position on the language question. In fact the dedication to Alfonso Ariosto, which would have opened the *Cortegiano* but for the later addition of the new dedication to Michel de Silva, alludes to 'la consuetudine' in a non-linguistic context in which everything is subject to the vagaries of historical change.[58]

The contradictory nature of historical change upsets all those areas in which the *De institutione novitiorum liber* and similar treatises were seeking to produce rather rigid rule-based systems of behaviour. Castiglione is rather more reluctant to legislate specifically for all areas of conduct in the light of this preliminary statement on 'la consuetudine'. Or, if he does designate certain general rules, there needs to be the intervention of another kind of category. Rules can only play a part in making sense of court existence, that is why much weight is placed on 'giudicio' (judgement), and to a lesser degree on 'discrezione', lending the courtier psychological substance instead of being merely an amalgam of rules.

The critical significance attributed to conversation and spoken language in the text is in part due to the concept of social intercourse ('il commerzio')[59] the meaning of which can easily be extended to all those locutionary activities engaged in by the courtier.[60] Exchange, real or imaginary, is essential to his success. By giving something to the prince, entertainment first and then advice, he hopes to receive in return favour and authority. Withholding exchange also becomes an important strategy for the courtier in so far as he wishes to gain superiority over any rivals to the prince's favour. Thus, knowing when to participate in an exchange process, and to what extent and with what purpose, is not a matter for rules or discretion alone (signifying, in Hugh's use of the term, knowledge about the application of rules).

[58] I, i. 39.

[59] Dedication to de Silva, II, 33–5.

[60] The activities of the Urbino court are also described as 'commerzio' (II, iv. 112), particularly with reference to the relationship between rulers and courtiers.

Castiglione at times appears to despair of the very efficacy of rules at all, preferring intuition formed through experience and knowledge:

> Thus good usage, so I believe, is established by men of discernment, who through learning and experience have acquired sound judgement, which enables them to agree among themselves and consent to accept those words which commend themselves to them; and these they recognize by means of a certain instinctive judgement and not by any formula or rule. (I, xxxv. 80)

The ideas that Castiglione formulates about language can be extended once more to all fields of activity. The important point to note here is the refutation of rule-bound behaviour in a crucial aspect of court theory. There are certain elements of this theory which Castiglione does not wish to explain fully, even by implicit analogy with other systems. We can notice here that Castiglione is being purposely vague, using phrases such as 'a certain . . . [instinctive judgement]'; this is quite common in the text and creates the impression of a lack of precision in key areas. Perhaps the most surprising example is his introduction of the neologism 'la sprezzatura' thus: '(to use perhaps a novel word for it) to practise in all things a certain nonchalance'.[61] Here the introduction of doubt ('perhaps') leads to a reduction of rigid formulation, suggesting both vagueness and élitist knowledge, and ends up explaining little in the first instance. It is indeed difficult to explain a concept the very essence of which is to keep concealed the manner of its functioning.

The text itself is not unaware of the problems which face the courtier who wishes to advance himself at court, nor of the more general problem of how useful rules actually are in moulding human behaviour. A critical confrontation takes place in the second book of the *Cortegiano* between Unico Aretino and Federico Fregoso on the relationship between rules and 'bon giudicio'. Unico Aretino makes a radical suggestion that does not seem out of place given my previous discussion of the topic:

> 'It seems no great thing to me,' replied the Unico. 'And all that need be said, I think, is that the courtier should possess good judgement, the need for which was rightly mentioned by the Count yesterday evening. If he does have it, then he needs no other instructions about how to practise what he knows at the right time and in the proper manner. To attempt to provide him with more precise rules would be too difficult and surely superfluous.' (II, vi. 112–13)[62]

Here, 'good judgement' is synonymous with 'discretio', as it occasionally is in the *Cortegiano*. It is reduced solely to Hugh's definition of the various

[61] I, xxvi. 67.

[62] In a similar vein, Vincenzo Calmeta challenges the assertion that the courtier's merit by itself will win the favour of the prince: 'but I greatly fear that this rule [regula] is of little use, and I think that experience clearly teaches us the contrary' (II, xxi. 129). The exchange, therefore, illustrates yet another factor that has to be taken into account when assessing the usefulness of rule-bound behaviour.

categories of circumstances which affect behaviour. Federico Fregoso's reply does not completely deny Unico's point. He only suggests that he has taken this position to an untenable extreme.[63] He therefore does not deny that these functions have an important role to play in the development of the courtier, but they do need to be supplemented by other strategies. This procedure ensures that a controversial point is made without having to enter into long explanations. Federico's authority as one of the principal speakers of the second book cannot be underestimated. In contrast, Unico Aretino is one of the 'suspect' characters, similar to Morello da Ortona, in that they both make incisive comments concerning the methodologies of the main speakers, but are characterized in a way that detracts from their weight as serious interlocutors. Morello, advanced in years as we have seen, wants to act the part of the young lover and Unico Aretino claims to be in love with the duchess of Urbino, who does not return his love. In this way Castiglione defuses the radical nature of their criticisms, because it is difficult to separate their serious side from the much more pervasive comical aspects of their characterization. The care taken in the choice of characters to voice these comments (perhaps to camouflage their gravity) makes it natural to hypothesize that the criticisms are not merely frivolous but go to the heart of Castiglione's ambiguous treatment of the courtier.

Certainly, Federico does not dismiss Unico's comment out of hand, only politely suggesting that it does not obey the rule of the golden mean. Federico concurs by suggesting the qualities necessary to succeed at court are 'a certain prudence and wise discrimination' (II, vi. 113). For Federico, intuition and practical reason are not enough, and need to be supplemented by 'some precept', a rather casual and imprecise way of referring to the possible types of rules available to the courtier.

I do not wish to create the impression (fostered, as we have seen, by the writer himself at the beginning of the *Cortegiano*) that Castiglione rejects the educational principles and codes embedded in works such as the *De institutione novitiorum liber*. Neither do I wish to suggest that his relationship with clerical codes of behaviour, as exemplified by Hugh's text, was at all simple – in fact it would be somewhat misleading to suggest that Castiglione's text builds unproblematically on the type of treatise exemplified by Hugh of St Victor. As we have seen, the *Cortegiano* ironically acknowledges its roots in ecclesiastical culture. What is noticeable is that Castiglione sets up a series of terms, 'grazia', 'sprezzatura', 'giudicio', much discussed by the critics,[64] which supplement or direct the use of the rules. It is true that some of the terms are to be found embryonically in such treatises as that written by Hugh of St Victor: Castiglione develops them to such a degree that they have

[63] II, vi. 113.

[64] See, for example, R. Brogue Henning, 'The Paideia of a Renaissance gentleman: Castiglione's *Book of the Courtier*', in R. Schwoebel (ed.), *Renaissance Men and Ideas* (New York, 1971), 109–10, 114; R. Esposito, *Ordine e conflitto: Machiavelli e la letteratura politica del Rinascimento* (Naples, 1984), 99–102; Saccone, *'Grazia, Sprezzatura, Affettazione', passim; idem*, 'The portrait of the courtier', 7–8.

become intrinsic to the explication and operation of the rules which are often subordinated to questions of style. The courtier is allowed a freedom of interpretation that would have been unthinkable to a monk or a novice. The concept of 'sprezzatura' can be considered a comment on the possible rigidity of rules: the element of disdain central to the word itself suggests that the courtier's behaviour is not directed by rules nor by a substantial body of thought ('almost without thinking about it', I, xxvi. 67). The paradox is that the courtier desires to show that he is above rules, yet rules are required to reach that level of behaviour.

Even in the treatment of such a non-ecclesiastical topic as jokes, Castiglione applies the same criteria so clearly exemplified by Hugh of St Victor. It is Francesco Maria della Rovere, the prefect of Rome, who points out that jokes can be treated in the same way as other forms of conversation. Therefore, they are subject to 'disciplina' (II, xliii. 152), that is, rules that shape and restrain their form, including, the 'circumstantiae'. Federico Fregoso's response is to downplay the importance of 'disciplina': 'These rules, my lord,' replied Federico, 'are so universal that they fit and apply to everything' (II, xliii. 152). This is part of Castiglione's problem: the clerical 'regulae' can be transplanted with relative ease from one context to another, but they are not particularly courtly. They do not distinguish court society from other groups or organizations. A compromise is effected by the authoritative figure of Pietro Bembo, the theoretician of literary language. Bembo outlines the process whereby a joke comes into being, tracing its origins in 'Nature and genius' (II, xliii. 152–3). The 'natural' artefact has to be further shaped and corrected by 'judgement and then art' (p. 153), after which the circumstances of its telling are a crucial factor in its success or lack of it. The process could be applied to any number of items treated in the *Cortegiano*. Thus, in many ways Hugh's schema is still seen as valid, but its acceptance creates problems for some of the interlocutors. That is why the concept of 'giudicio' is so important[65] because it does not solely depend on the rules, but on a complex and undefined network of knowledge, distinguished from 'discretio' by subtly moving beyond the principle of rules and their application.[66] There is an expansion of the role of personal judgement in relation to pre-existing rules. Castiglione also works up the concept of 'arte' as a means of gaining advantage over possible rivals, of not revealing everything about one's game. Thus, 'arte' and 'sprezzatura' operate in parallel to such concepts as 'discrezione' and 'disciplina'. The former create a sense of the power ploys being used by the courtier to gain access to the prince. The latter lend respectability to the courtier, ensuring that he can make use of his skills on the right occasions in pursuit of his goal.

[65] It is noteworthy that Emilia Pia, one of the female interlocutors of the Cortegiano, is described as 'gifted with such a lively wit and judgement' (I, iv. 42–3).

[66] 'But above all, he should accompany his every movement with a certain grace and fine judgement if he wishes to earn that universal regard which everyone covets' (I, xxi. 63). Cf. P. D'Angelo, ' "Celare l'arte": per una storia del precetto "Ars est celare artem" ', *Intersezioni*, 6 (1986), 335, 338.

Castiglione has not accepted the concept of 'disciplina' without making changes to it. The courtier's body has been lightened, almost separated from its need for physical nourishment. It is brought into being through language and it is language which provides its sustenance. If one makes a comparison with that other classical sixteenth-century Italian text on behaviour, Della Casa's *Galateo*, the difference becomes even more pronounced. An anecdote is recounted close to the beginning of the *Galateo* which illustrates the tone of Della Casa's treatise. It involves 'messer Galateo', who gives his name to the text so that the episode can be viewed as paradigmatic. Conte Ricciardo had paid a visit to Giovanni Matteo Giberti and, although his host is generally satisfied with his manners, something has caused him considerable concern. It is only when Conte Ricciardo is leaving that the matter is clarified – the culprit is, as it were, apprehended in this mini-detective story. The reader finally learns that Conte Ricciardo's problem is that, when eating, he made a most unpleasant and strange sound with his mouth.[67] Castiglione's text has little or no interest in such matters. Indeed, as we have already seen, he strives to avoid any discussion of eating. Although a clear line of descent can be traced from Hugh's concept of 'disciplina', the *Cortegiano* is ambiguous about this type of systematization of behaviour. Castiglione himself is conscious of the boundaries that separate his texts from other works of practical pedagogy, principally designed for inexperienced young people (boys or novices for instance): 'For this reason, good masters not only teach children their letters but also correct and polite manners in eating, drinking, speaking and walking along with certain appropriate gestures' (IV, xii. 291).[68]

The 'pedagoghi', therefore, are not in the same business as Castiglione. And, by extension, the texts they write are not of the same type as the *Cortegiano*. A fundamental difference is the audience to which the texts are addressed: the 'good masters' are principally involved in the education of children and it is this essential difference that marks off our text from seemingly similar ones. The concept of regulation in Castiglione can be much more complex and nuanced than a text of basic rules, which needs to put forward a number of straightforward precepts to guide the behaviour of young, inexperienced adults in everyday situations. This explains the basic texts' more practical orientation and their emphasis on all-round behaviour, particularly eating, since children may be moulded *in toto*. They need to be trained in the physical aspects of social life as befits their age and possibilities, as well as being trained intellectually. Thus it is no accident that eating and drinking are mentioned in the above passage as the primary physical activities in which boys are to be trained and disciplined. Castiglione's list quoted above is a carbon copy in miniature of Hugh of St Victor's *De institutione novitiorum liber*: the same or similar terms are employed in the medieval treatise and the same or similar subject-matter is covered

[67] Giovanni della Casa, *Galateo overo de' costumi*, ed. E. Scarpa (Modena, 1990), 7–8.

[68] 'Onde i boni pedagoghi non solamente insegnano lettere ai fanciulli, ma ancora boni modi ed onesti nel mangiare, bere, parlare, andare con certi gesti accommodati' (461–2).

(for example, 'bona et honesta' *PL*, col. 935B), reproduced in the *Cortegiano* as 'boni modi ed onesti' (IV, xii. 462); 'in omni gestu modus disciplinae', *PL*, col. 941B), and so on). The 'pedagoghi' have a responsibility for the gestural education of their charges which serves as the basis or implicit foundation on which Castiglione intends to build. The *Cortegiano* marks off its own privileged area of pedagogical concern which, although acknowledging the work of previous educators and utilizing some of their key principles, shifts the perspective from the education of the young to the instruction of a courtier who has already gone through 'basic training'.

In part, the altered perspective of Castiglione is due to an ambiguous attitude to the body which is almost effaced in the *Cortegiano*, though always present. The body is not merely an object on which rules are imposed, but a representation of court society, a symbol of its flexibility and adaptability. The *Cortegiano* is not a straightforward treatise on behaviour. It even exhibits fundamental doubts about the entire project of training a courtier. The rules it enunciates are not always easy to put into practice. The basic beliefs that underpinned *De institutione novitiorum liber* are no longer held with such conviction. The connection between the outer and inner man has become problematic, and as a consequence behaviour cannot be pinned down so easily to a small number of fundamental rules that completely define human behaviour. These rules still exert influence and power, but Castiglione no longer holds the same certainties as Hugh of St Victor. They cannot totally explain how the courtier is to behave. Witness the doubts expressed by a number of the interlocutors that punctuate the text. The *Cortegiano* suggests there is a lack of confidence in rules. For this reason, the *Cortegiano* is a paradoxical text, attempting to provide rules and, at the same time, not believing that such rules can completely explain human behaviour.

IV

GRACEFUL PERFORMANCES: THE SOCIAL AND POLITICAL CONTEXT OF MUSIC AND DANCE IN THE *CORTEGIANO*

Music and dancing are critical components of the Italian Renaissance court's political and social structures.[1] Indeed, Castiglione's *Libro del Cortegiano* emphasizes this aspect of the function of music in court society. Music and dance epitomize the role of the courtier; they are not merely ornamental or additional to more important qualities, but are considered crucial to his social and political existence: 'anzi estimo per le ragioni che voi dite e per molte altre esser la musica non solamente ornamento, ma necessaria al cortegiano'.[2]

This essay will explore the use of music and dance in the *Cortegiano*, concentrating on several areas that have been rather neglected by scholars: the use of Plato's *Republic*, the function of both Plato and Aristotle as historical characters in the text, the *Cortegiano*'s debt to fifteenth-century dance treatises, the 'donna di palazzo' and dance, and the concept of *disciplina* in relation to music and dance. Music and dance, but particularly dance, will be examined from the point of view of the larger problem of the ultimate function of the courtier, in other words, his relationship to the prince and political power.

Music and dance are much more than trivial occupations in the *Cortegiano*. Castiglione may have been aware of Lucian's description of dance as speech

[1] See, for example, B. Becherini, '*Il Cortegiano* e la musica', *La Bibliofilìa*, 45 (1943), 84–96; W. H. Kemp, 'Some notes on music in Castiglione's *Il libro del cortegiano*', in *Cultural Aspects of the Italian Renaissance: Essays in Honour of Paul Oskar Kristeller*, ed. by C. H. Clough (Manchester and New York: Manchester University Press, 1976), pp. 354–69; and J. Haar, 'The courtier as musician: Castiglione's view of the science and art of music', in *Castiglione: The Ideal and Real in Renaissance Culture*, ed. by R. W. Hanning and D. Rosand (New Haven and London: Yale University Press, 1983), pp. 165–89.

[2] I, XLVIII; p. 171. All references to the *Cortegiano* are to the edition of B. Maier, *Il libro del cortegiano con una scelta delle Opere minori di Baldesar Castiglione*, 2nd edn (Turin: UTET, 1964) and will take the form of book, chapter, and page numbers.

without words:[3] it speaks to the prince of the courtier's technical virtuosity, of his self-control and knowledge of society. It helps render the courtier charismatic. Lucian writes: 'his performance is as much an intellectual as a physical exercise: there is meaning in his movements; every gesture has its significance; and therein lies his chief excellence'.[4] The 'consumer' aspects of music (and dancing) are definitely not ignored: entertainment and pleasure were an essential part of the court. But Castiglione, building on the suggestions of Plato and Aristotle, shows the seriousness of such cultural acts and how they relate to questions of social and political interest.

Important in this connection is a complicated anecdote about an ignorant fellow from Brescia who went to Venice to witness the ceremony of the marriage to the sea. It is significant that the geo-political background to the story is that of republican Venice, a detail which underlines the cultural difference between court and republic to the detriment of the latter. The punchline of the joke focuses on the kind of music that most impressed the fellow from Brescia:

> 'Tutte eran bone; pur tra l'altre io vidi uno sonar con certa tromba strana, che ad ogni tratto se ne ficcava in gola più di dui palmi e poi sùbito la cavava e di novo la reficcava; che non vedeste mai la più gran maraviglia'. (II, LIII; pp. 272–73)

As the text explains, the man was describing a trombone. The anecdote might simply be passed off as a humorous sally against an ignorant peasant. However, the description implies that the playing of the trombone is in some way unnatural and requires unpleasing gestures to produce a tune. Such an interpretation becomes more persuasive if we examine the text's attitude towards wind instruments in general, particularly if played by women:

> Imaginatevi come disgraziata cosa saria veder una donna sonare tamburri, piffari o trombe, o altri tali instrumenti; e questo perché la loro asprezza nasconde e leva quella soave mansuetudine, che tanto adorna ogni atto che faccia la donna. (III, VIII; pp. 347–48)

Thus instead of *grazia* we have *disgrazia* (ungraceful movement), implying a breakdown in the harmonious relations of the body. Wind instruments obviously draw attention to the physical being of the player — puffed cheeks might be considered unseemly in refined company. There is ample evidence to show that stringed instruments were considered refined whereas pipes and instruments of that kind were rustic and hence plebeian in a pejorative sense.[5]

[3] See *The Works of Lucian of Samosata*, trans. by H. W. and F. G. Fowler, vol. II (Oxford: Clarendon Press, 1905), para. 62, p. 255. The dialogue *Of Pantomime*, though it deals with a different phenomenon from Castiglione's, has a number of points of contact, including the idea that dancing communicates meaning (Lucian compares it to rhetoric). Dance also indicates social status for Lucian (para. 34; p. 249).

[4] *Of Pantomime*, para. 69; p. 257.

[5] Such a division has a long history and is amply documented in the ancient sources. See on this G. Comotti, *Music in Greek and Roman Culture* (Baltimore and London: Johns Hopkins University Press, 1989), pp. 69–70. Other reasons for the contempt shown for the aulos (flute) were that it was principally the reserve of professional musicians and that it could induce a Dionysiac state, giving free rein to the passions. See Aristotle, *Politics*, 8.1340b20–1341b18, quoted in Comotti, pp. 140–41,

The corollary is that stringed instruments are part of the cosmic harmony whereas pipes are discordant and perhaps even threaten the cosmic and social order. Furthermore, the playing by women of wind instruments might pose a threat of disorder to the world of the male courtier. In ancient Greece, pipes were associated with frenzied dancing, inducing excited and discordant movement.[6] Pipes are part of rustic culture, despised by the court in favour of the Apollonian superiority of stringed instruments.

The fundamental position of music and dance in court society is underlined by Castiglione's appropriation of Aristotle and Plato, not only as theorists of music, but also as practitioners.[7] Towards the end of the fourth book of the *Cortegiano* Ottaviano Fregoso maintains that the art of 'courtiership' ('la cortegiania') was not alien to either Plato or Aristotle (IV, XLVII; p. 509).[8] Indeed, it is claimed that this art was absolutely necessary for them if they were to win the confidence of the rulers whose tutors they were. In reply Gaspare Pallavicino attempts to cast doubt on Ottaviano Fregoso's statement: 'Non so già però s'io mi creda che Aristotile e Platone mai danzassero o fossero musici in sua vita, o facessero altre opere di cavalleria' (IV, XLVIII; p. 510). Pallavicino's implication is that dancing and music were too trivial or lowly occupations for such exalted philosophers. The argument is refuted by the suggestion that the subject of music is treated in some depth in their philosophical texts.[9] Therefore, it can be noted that Ottaviano Fregoso implies that subjects like music and dancing were not 'beneath' the two philosophers and that their understanding of the disciplines was not merely practical, but fundamental to the structure of their philosophies. He is thus inviting the reader to take a closer look at both Aristotle's and Plato's conception of music in their philosophical works. It is no accident that Plato's ideal of the Republic is one of the models to which Castiglione draws attention in order to lend a degree of validation to his enterprise (Dedication, III; p. 76). It should be noted that Castiglione in the case of *The Republic* does not refer to a perfect individual (king, orator, courtier), but to an entity, the ideal state. By so doing, the Renaissance writer adds a further dimension to the formulation of the courtier, namely that the

and M. L. West, *Ancient Greek Music* (Oxford: Clarendon Press, 1992), p. 33. Isabella d'Este refused to play wind instruments since they detracted from her self-image. See W. F. Prizer, 'Isabella d'Este and Lorenzo da Pavia, "master instrument-maker"', *Early Music History*, 2 (1982), 87–127 (pp. 112–16). The conflict is also briefly mentioned in S. Kolsky, 'Images of Isabella d'Este', *Italian Studies*, 39 (1984), 53.

[6] W. D. Anderson, *Ethos and Education in Greek Music: The Evidence of Poetry and Philosophy* (Cambridge, MA: Harvard University Press, 1966), pp. 65, 68.

[7] Castiglione's debt to Aristotle is obvious from a close reading of the *Cortegiano* and has been discussed in other contexts by a number of scholars: L. V. Ryan, 'Book IV of Castiglione's *Courtier*: climax or afterthought?', *Studies in the Renaissance*, 19 (1972), 156–79; in particular p. 158. See also A. D. Menut, 'Castiglione and the *Nicomachean Ethics*', *PMLA*, 58 (1943), 309–21; A. F. Kinney, *Continental Humanist Poetics: Studies in Erasmus, Castiglione, Marguerite de Navarre, Rabelais, and Cervantes* (Amherst: University of Massachusetts Press, 1989), pp. 97, 100–01, 114–15, 125–27.

[8] Cf. S. Kolsky, '"The good servant": Mario Equicola. Court and courtier in early sixteenth-century Italy', *The Italianist*, 6 (1986), 34–60 (pp. 45–46).

[9] 'le intendevano insino alle medulle ed alle più intime radici' (IV, XLVIII; p. 511).

reader is asked to envisage the creation of the perfect courtier as part of the renewal of the state.

Plato entrusts the administration of the perfect state to the Guardians and their leader, the philosopher-king, who would be chosen out of their number. *The Republic* presents a systematic account of the education necessary for the perfection of the Guardian to enable his transformation into the philosopher-king. Plato's perfect ruler must not only be suitably expert in the exercise of political power, but also a philosopher. The Guardians safeguard a constituted order in which social movement is frozen and 'harmony' between the various social strata maintained. The image of music is never far away from Plato's mind: 'It is here, then, I said, in music, as it seems, that our guardians must build their guardhouse and post of watch'.[10] For Plato the soul is a microcosm of the social and political world; it is the 'spiritual constitution'[11] and within it the three orders ('appetitive', 'rational', and 'high spirit')[12] are kept in balance just as are the social classes (Plato talks about the Guardian 'having harmonized these three principles, the notes or intervals of three terms').[13] The perfect musician will become 'one man instead of many, self-controlled and in unison'.[14] Plato treats dance in the *Laws* where he distinguishes between two principal types of dance. The kind of dancing that wins Plato's approval is where the performer maintains 'a graceful style of dancing in a way becoming to the law-abiding man'.[15] He discriminates against those dances which exhibit a bacchanalian frenzy, a total loss of control.

Thus the musician is distinguished from others by his movements, characterized in the *Cortegiano* by the courtier's skill at dancing. His opposite is fully described by Plato and one can recognize all the elements Castiglione is trying to avoid in his construction of the courtier: 'He [the non-musician] no longer uses words to persuade, but accomplishes everything, like a wild beast, by violence and ferocity, and lives without rhythm or grace in ignorance and stupidity'.[16] The non-musician negates all those values that will be taken up by Castiglione's courtier. They define the parameters of acceptable behaviour and carry a judgement on whether a person is capable of being involved in the organization of the state.

[10] *Republic*, 424d. The translation used here is by P. Shorey in *The Collected Dialogues of Plato, including the Letters*, ed. by E. Hamilton and H. Cairns, (New York: Pantheon, 1961), p. 666. On concord see *Republic*, 432a; *The Collected Dialogues*, pp. 673–74.

[11] *Republic*, 444a; *The Collected Dialogues*, p. 686.

[12] *Republic*, 441a; *The Collected Dialogues*, p. 683.

[13] *Republic*, 443d; *The Collected Dialogues*, p. 686. In the *Laws* Plato is equally, if not more, specific about the relations between music and its wider social context: 'He must also possess the requisite preliminary sciences, perceive the links which connect them with music, and apply his knowledge meetly to his moral and legal behaviour' (*Laws*, 967e; *The Collected Dialogues*, p. 1512).

[14] *Republic*, 443e; *The Collected Dialogues*, p. 686. See *Republic*, 442d; *The Collected Dialogues*, p. 684. See also G. Berghaus, 'Neoplatonic and Pythagorean notions of world harmony and unity and their influence on Renaissance dance theory', *Dance Research*, 10 (1992), 43–70.

[15] *Laws*, 814e–816d; *The Collected Dialogues*, pp. 1385–86.

[16] *Republic*, 411d–411e. The translation used here is in *Greek Musical Writings*, vol. 1, *The Musician and his Art*, ed. by A. Barker (Cambridge: Cambridge University Press, 1984), p. 138.

Castiglione carefully modulates his praise of music in the *Cortegiano* (I, XLVII; pp. 169–71), employing as his model the section on music in Quintilian's *Institutio oratoria* (I, X). It is significant that Quintilian prefaces this topic with some remarks on the necessity of a musical education for the orator, especially given his perspective that he reiterates here, having 'in my mind's eye an ideal orator, perfect down to the smallest detail'. One can note Quintilian's approving comment on Plato: 'Plato regarded the knowledge of music as necessary to his ideal statesman or politician, as he calls him'.[17]

The use of music by Plato is essential to his development of a theory of elitist government in *The Republic*. At one point the question is asked: 'but do you recognize that one man is a musician and another unmusical?'[18] The two conditions are equated with intelligence or the lack of it, pointing to a division between rulers and ruled. Plato's aim seems to be the theoretical representation of the *mousikotaton*, the perfect musician, not too dissimilar an aim from Castiglione's own stated intention of creating the perfect courtier. Plato is clear about the first set of benefits that accrue to the musician:

> isn't training in *mousiké* of overriding importance, because rhythm and *harmonia* penetrate most deeply into the recesses of the soul and take a powerful hold on it, bringing gracefulness and making a man graceful if he is correctly trained, but the opposite if he is not?[19]

For Plato music has political consequences, it is by no means an ornament to provide pleasure: 'For the modes of music are never disturbed without unsettling the most fundamental political and social conventions, as Damon affirms and as I am convinced'.[20]

The parallels between *The Republic* and the *Cortegiano* are striking.[21] Both courtier and Guardian are originally soldiers and this function is considered fundamental to their role in the preservation of the state. It is noticeable in the *Cortegiano* that the future ruler of Urbino, Francesco Maria della Rovere, is part of the group of courtiers which is formulating an ideal programme of education for their profession. He does not assume exceptional powers nor does he intervene frequently in the discussions, perhaps because in the fiction

[17] I, X, 15; *The 'Institutio oratoria' of Quintilian*, transl. by H. E. Butler, vol. I, (London and New York: Heinemann, 1921), p. 167.

[18] *Republic*, 349d; *The Collected Dialogues*, p. 599. Relevant studies on Greek music include E. A. Lippman, *Musical Thought in Ancient Greece* (New York and London: Columbia University Press, 1964); W. D. Anderson, pp. 64–110; A. E. Moyer, *Musica Scientia. Musical Scholarship in the Italian Renaissance* (Ithaca and London: Cornell University Press, 1992), pp. 13–24.

[19] *Republic*, 401d–401e; *Greek Musical Writings*, p. 135.

[20] *Republic*, 424c; *The Collected Dialogues*, p. 666. In the *Laws* Plato makes even clearer the connection between musical and social innovation to the detriment of both: 'Now no doubt it would have been no terrible thing if a democracy of free men had arisen just in the field of music: but in fact, from a starting-point in music, everyone came to believe in their own wisdom about everything, and to reject the law, and liberty followed immediately' (701a; *Greek Musical Writings*, p. 157).

[21] See A. Gagliardi, *La misura e la grazia: sul 'Libro del Cortegiano'* (Turin: Tirrenia, 1989), pp. 28, 124. He does not, however, make the connection between music and political institutions, vital to understand the inextricable knot between the *Republic* and the courtier's social and political role.

of the *Cortegiano* he is not yet ruler. If one views his presence from the perspective of *The Republic*, one can draw a parallel between the selection of an outstanding member of the elite to become leader and the 'education' of Francesco Maria, as outlined in the *Cortegiano*, and his later elevation to the dukedom. The fact that Guidobaldo Montefeltro, Duke of Urbino, is absent from the dialogues enables the courtiers to be considered an elite that can exist without the presence of the actual ruler, or at the very least, form an authoritative group around the future prince. There is a blurring of the boundaries: the courtier-class following the Platonic model appears to aspire to the principate or, as a minimum, to train the next leader in their image. It is no coincidence that in the fourth book the courtier is seen by some of the interlocutors to have more knowledge than the prince himself. The comment that the courtier needs to be 'bon filosofo, bon capitano, e quasi saper ogni cosa' (IV, XLIV; p. 504) assumes added significance in this context. Something of this is carried over into the structure of the fourth and culminating book of the *Cortegiano* where the two principal subjects for the final evening's discussion are politics and certain philosophical questions, particularly love treated in the tradition of Neoplatonic speculation.

Both courtier and Guardian are deemed to act on behalf of the state and this is seen as their highest function. In the *Cortegiano* the idea of self-control and harmony (of movements) is most effectively expressed through the proposition of a courtly style of dancing which, as we will see, is an expression of superiority, difference, and definitive cultural norms. Court dance expresses the domination of the body by reason, the repression of sexual desire and the control of bodily movement.[22] The similarities between the two texts seem too striking to be casual. The model of the *Republic* gives a political immediacy to the *Cortegiano*. The fact that the exceptional individual is regarded as a 'saviour of society'[23] has implications concerning the urgency of the courtier's mission. Thus it can be argued that the *Cortegiano* is Platonic, but not solely with reference to Bembo's Neoplatonism. The attraction for Castiglione of the political and social messages of Plato's *Republic* must not be underestimated.

The Republic is not the sole political model for renewal in the *Cortegiano*.[24] Castiglione does not neglect the other philosopher of music, Aristotle, who is paired with Plato, pushing as far as he is able a syncretic ideal in spite of the obvious differences between the two on musical theory: 'E ricordomi aver già inteso che Platone ed Aristotele vogliono che l'om bene instituito sia ancor musico' (I, XLVII; p. 169).[25] And paradoxically in the fourth book, as a counterpoint to the generalized praise of music (in order to demonstrate its usefulness

[22] On the breakdown of bodily harmony see *Republic*, 444b; *The Collected Dialogues*, p. 686.

[23] *Laws*, 689d; *The Collected Dialogues*, p. 1284.

[24] The validity of *The Republic* as a political model is questioned by one of the interlocutors, but he is rebuffed by Ottaviano Fregoso who asserts that is is possible, though difficult, to produce a philosopher-prince (IV, XLII; pp. 500–01).

[25] See Anderson, pp. 111–46.

beyond seducing court women), Aristotle in particular is introduced as a courtier-musician. The example of Aristotle as *musicus* gains in significance at this point because he was the successful tutor of Alexander the Great, who had also been mentioned in the earlier encomium of music. Plato was somewhat of a failure in trying to influence the government of a prince. The theme of music as politics is brought to its climax in Book IV through the discussion of Alexander the Great's achievements. This had been prepared for by his inclusion in the encomium as an example of the power of music over an individual: music had such an effect on him that during a banquet he would rush to arms if the music was of that kind and if it changed he would return (I, XLVII, p. 169). The *exemplum* shows that Alexander's soul was in an intimate relationship with music. Judging by the number of references to Alexander in the text he is perhaps meant to carry particular resonances, especially for the contemporary Italian princes.[26] On one occasion a witty remark made by Alfonso I d'Aragona is described as being 'degno veramente della magnanimità d'uno Alessandro' (II, LXXIII; p. 297). The image that emerges from the text of Alexander is that of a humanist prince whose conquests brought benefits to the vanquished and to humanity in general:

> ed Aristotile, oltre allo indrizzar lui a quel fin gloriosissimo [the reconstruction of Stagira], che fu il voler fare che 'l mondo fosse come una sol patria universale, e tutti gli omini come un sol populo, che vivesse in amicizia e concordia tra sé sotto un sol governo ed una sola legge. (IV, XLVII; p. 509)

The single reference to *concordia* should not be underestimated nor taken out of its musical context since Castiglione seems to be following Plutarch closely on this point. The latter's interpretation of Alexander is of someone who wished to reduce the world to a single unity: 'he believed that he had a mission from God to harmonize men generally, and to be the reconciler of the world'.[27] Political unity, with its musical analogue of harmony, renders Alexander an entirely positive model, someone who was capable of bringing about universal concord. The suggestion that lies behind this example is that a contemporary prince, most likely Charles V, could end the discord so ingrained in Renaissance Europe (if properly advised by his courtier-counsellors).[28]

[26] Substantial references to Alexander are to be found in I, XVIII, p. 113; I, XXV, p. 122 (this allusion introduces Aristotle as his tutor in order to emphasize the point that princes need the best teachers available); I, XLIII, p. 159 (again on his education: 'e non solamente a questi studi [Homer], ma alle speculazioni filosofice diede grandissima opera sotto la disciplina d'Aristotele'. Thus, Alexander can be properly called a philosopher-king); I, XLV, pp. 165–66; I, XLVI, pp. 166–67; I, XLVII, p. 169 (the force of music over Alexander); I, LII, pp. 177–78 (Alexander and Apelles illustrative of his appreciation of the finest painting); I, LIII, pp. 180–81; II, XXXI, pp. 239–40; II, LXVII, pp. 290–91 (a humorous allusion to Alexander's thirst for conquest, the subject of the first reference to him in the *Cortegiano*); III, XXXIX, pp. 392–93; III, XLIV, pp. 399–400 (on his continence as a result of setting himself the highest possible goals in his public life); IV, XXXVI, p. 493; IV, XLVII; pp. 508–09.

[27] Passage to be found in *From Alexander to Constantine. Passages and Documents Illustrating the History of Social and Political Ideas 336 B.C.–A.D. 337*, translated with introductions, notes, and essays by E. Barker (Oxford: Clarendon Press, 1956), p. 8.

[28] 'Aristotile così ben conobbe la natura d'Alessandro e con destrezza così ben la secondò, che da lui fu amato ed onorato più che padre' (IV, XLVII; p. 508).

Similar remarks could be made about dancing which also fulfils both social and political functions in court society in similar ways to music. Castiglione appears well informed about contemporary dance theory and to have read some of the most important fifteenth-century treatises on the subject.[29] His terminology, it will be argued, owes not a little to their work. Let us take as our example Guglielmo da Pesaro's influential treatise, *De Pratica seu arte tripudij*, composed in 1463, the latest in time of the fifteenth-century Italian treatises on dance.[30] Its author was associated throughout his adult life with various Italian courts, including Pesaro, Naples, Milan, Urbino, and Mantua, in the role of dancing-master.[31] What is interesting to note about *De pratica* is that a manuscript of the work was present in the ducal library of Urbino, at least up until 1502.[32] Guglielmo had a long and fruitful relationship with Federico Montefeltro, Duke of Urbino, entering his service in the 1470s as a *ballarino*.[33]

The fifteenth-century writers on dance were determined to elevate the status of their profession by composing treatises that were not merely practical manuals.[34] They introduced a humanistic schema in which dance was considered a noble activity with its own rules. Domenico da Piacenza, whose

[29] For the treatises, see C. Mazzi, 'Il libro dell'arte del danzare di Antonio Cornazzano', *La Bibliofilìa*, 17 (1915), 1–30; see also R. Bruni and D. Zancani, *Antonio Cornazzano: la tradizione testuale* (Florence: Olschki, 1992), pp. 31–33; D. Bianchi, 'Un trattato inedito di Domenico da Piacenza', *La Bibliofilìa*, 65 (1963), 109–49 and *Trattato dell'arte del ballo di Guglielmo ebreo pesarese: testo inedito del secolo* XV, Scelta di curiosità letterarie inedite o rare dal secolo XIII al XIX, vol. XXXIII (Bologna: Romagnoli, 1873; repr. Bologna: Commissione per i testi di lingua, 1968). There is now a modern edition of Guglielmo's treatise, *Guglielmo Ebreo of Pesaro, De Pratica seu Arte Tripudii. On the Practice or the Art of Dancing*, ed., transl. and introduced by B. Sparti (Oxford: Clarendon Press, 1993), henceforth *De pratica*. For serious reservations about the edition see the review by C. H. Clough in *Renaissance Studies*, 11 (1997), 241–69. See also G. Patrizi, '*Il libro del Cortegiano* e la trattatistica sul comportamento' in *Letteratura Italiana*, vol. III, ii, *Le forme del testo. La prosa* (Turin: Einaudi, 1984), p. 868. For a survey of works on dance, consult A. Michel, 'The earliest dance-manuals', *Medievalia et Humanistica*, 3 (1945), 117–31. For the relation of dance theory to painting, see J. Nevile, '"Certain sweet movements": the development of the concept of grace in 15th-century Italian dance and painting', *Dance Research*, 9 (1991), 3–12, and S. Fermor, 'Decorum in figural movement: the dance as measure and metaphor', in *Decorum in Renaissance Narrative Art: Papers Delivered at the Annual Conference of the Association of Art Historians, London, April 1991*, ed. by F. Ames-Lewis and A. Bednarek (London: Department of History of Art, Birkbeck College, 1992), pp. 78–88.

[30] On Guglielmo see O. Kinkeldey, 'A Jewish dancing master of the Renaissance (Guglielmo Ebreo)', in *Studies in Jewish Bibliography and Related Subjects in Memory of Abraham Solomon Freidus (1867–1923)* (New York: Alexander Kohut Memorial Foundation, 1929), pp. 329–72; A. Melica, 'Guglielmo ebreo da Pesaro, maestro di ballo del Quattrocento', *La Rassegna musicale*, 29 (1959), 51–60; D. Bianchi, 'Tre maestri di danza alla corte di Francesco Sforza', *Archivio storico lombardo*, serie 9, 2 (1962), 290–99; B. Sparti, 'Questions concerning the life and works of Guglielmo Ebreo', in *Guglielmo Ebreo da Pesaro e la danza nelle corti italiani [sic] del XV secolo. Atti del convegno internazionale di studi Pesaro, 16/18 luglio 1987*, ed. by M. Padovan (Pisa, 1990), pp. 35–50; P. Castelli, 'Il moto aristotelico e la "licita scientia": Guglielmo Ebreo e la speculazione sulla danza nel XV secolo', in *Mesvra et arte del danzare: Gvglielmo ebreo da Pesaro et la danza nelle corti italiane del XV secolo*, ed. by P. Castelli and others (Pesaro, n. d.), pp. 35–57.

[31] *De pratica*, pp. 23–45, 248–54.

[32] *De pratica*, p. 16.

[33] *De pratica*, pp. 38–41. Castiglione may be referring to Guglielmo's son, Pierpaulo, as an example of a bad dancer (I, XXVI; p. 125)!

[34] *De pratica*, pp. 9–11; Castelli, 'Il moto aristotelico', pp. 35–36.

treatise can be dated to around 1455, and is perhaps the founder of the genre in Italy, makes specific use of Aristotle to lend not only an air of respectability to his work, but also to ground dance in an appropriate scientific theory. Domenico imposes restraint on dancing techniques by having recourse to Aristotle's theory of the Golden Mean ('fugando li extremi'),[35] a position fundamental to Castiglione's portrayal of the courtier. Guglielmo's treatise, as others of the genre, is divided into two parts: the first is a general, theoretical introduction, looking at the basic notions underlying the practice of dance. The second consists of detailed instructions on how to dance particular varieties of the basse dance. Needless to say, the second part has no real echoes in Castiglione's work.

Guglielmo also uses classical myth for the purpose of presenting dance and music as having their origins in humanist culture. He explicitly mentions the Orpheus myth, which never seems far away from the principles of courtly performance:

> ne par che si ritruovi al mondo alchuna si cruda & inhumana gente: che al dolce canto & al suave suono d'alchuno ben concordato instrumento, con summo piacere non si commuova: si come del famoso Orpheo degnamente si scrive. Il quale con tanta gratia la sua dolce cithara sonando non solamente gli humani spiriti a dolcezza commoveva: m[a] il fiero Plutone & gl'infernali idij. (*De pratica*, p. 86)[36]

The fragile status of dance is underlined in the opening section of the second book of *De pratica*. It takes the form of a contentious statement about dance to which the author responds ('Argumentum discipulorum' followed by 'Responsio Guilielmi'). Through this scholastic formula, Guglielmo attempts to answer a deep-rooted criticism of dance and of his own teaching methods. The pupils first of all express their doubts about the morality of the dance, challenging the master's assertion that it is a 'sollenne & vera scienza' (*De pratica*, p. 112). They claim dance is 'indegna et non delettevole a circunstanti chome hai ditto' (*De pratica*, p. 112). It is sinful and wicked and 'inducitrice alla voluptate', they add.[37] Far from being the sign of an ordered society, dancing brings about social disorder ('discordie'). Guglielmo replies by asserting the social and moral values of the dance: 'Ma quando e exercitata da huomini gentili. virtuosi. & honesti, dico essa scienza & arte essere buona et virtuosa et di commendatione & laude digna' (*De pratica*, p. 114). Guglielmo's defence reflects the situation as we find it in the *Cortegiano*, where dance is the sign of a civilized, cohesive, restrictive society, untainted by sin. Dancing is a critical indicator of the reform of the court as a *locus* of moral behaviour.

[35] Bianchi, 'Un trattato inedito', p. 116.

[36] Castiglione has a similar passage in the *Cortegiano*: 'Però non vogliate voi privar il nostro cortegiano della musica, la qual non solamente gli animi umani indolcisce, ma spesso le fiere fa diventar mansuete; e chi non la gusta si po tener per certo ch'abbia i spiriti discordanti l'un dall'altro' (I, XLVII; p. 170).

[37] Castelli, 'Il moto aristotelico', p. 41.

The emphasis in *De pratica* falls on the courtly refinement that music and dance bring to a society. However, for Guglielmo dance is not the symbol of possible social change but rather the confirmation of the social hierarchy as part of a wider harmony. Thus Guglielmo recommends that court dancing should be in stylistic counterpoint to that performed by the 'vitiosi & mechanici plebei' (*De pratica*, p. 90), in keeping with Castiglione's own view. The treatise explains how courtiers are to ensure that their dancing is not be confused with the performances of the other social classes in terms of certain key concepts that help to produce those 'maravigliosi movimenti' (*De pratica*, p. 88).[38]

Castiglione characterizes the courtly dance by a series of adjectives that appear to be vague and imprecise. In the dance treatise some of these terms are explained. The reader, in order to appreciate fully the resonances of Castiglione's adjectivization, needs to be aware of Guglielmo's definition of certain terms. Of particular interest here are *misura*, *aiere*, and *maniera* together with such adjectives as 'suave', 'gentile', 'dolce'. A closer examination reveals their association with the kind of text exemplified by Guglielmo. Guglielmo states that certain dance steps are to be accompanied 'con bella mainiera'; without it 'non haveria la ditta arte la sua naturale & necessaria perfectione' (*De pratica*, p. 98). Although Guglielmo defines *misura* in musical terms, it is not difficult to see that his definition is open to a more philosophical interpretation. When he states that *misura* can be defined as 'una dolce & misurata concordanza di voce & di tempo partito con ragione & arte' (*De pratica*, p. 92) Guglielmo is insisting on the crucial role of reason and moderation in dance. Dance is a discipline where the dancer 'si regoli et misuri' (*De pratica*, p. 92), regulation of the body achieves perfection in the dance. The dancing-master defines the term *aiere* thus: 'il qual e un atto de aiereoso presenza et rilevato movimento colla propia persona mostrando con destreza nel danzare un dolce & humanissimo rilevamento' (*De pratica*, p. 96). Guglielmo recommends that any upward movement of the body must be regulated according to two basic conditions. The first is that 'con ferma discretione' the courtier adapts to the place and circumstances where he is dancing. Secondly, any movement must be performed with moderation: 'et moderatamente quello dimostri nel danzare i passi & gesti con destra legiereza' (*De pratica*, p. 96).

Guglielmo has a specific chapter on 'movimento corporeo' which represents a less sophisticated version of Castiglione's description. In order to dance perfectly (this is the aim of Guglielmo's manual), certain qualities need to be visible in the dance so that bodily movement conforms to a measured pattern: 'bigiogna che sia in se con ogni perfectione misurato. memorioso. airoso. e ben partito. & con dolce mainiera'. And the male dancer, since the text focuses principally on the man, has to be 'giovene. formoso. destro. legiero. & di gratia bene dotato' (*De pratica*, p. 98).

[38] The use of the term 'maraviglia' in the *Cortegiano* has been discussed by W. A. Rebhorn, *Courtly Performances: Masking and Festivity in Castiglione's 'Book of the Courtier'* (Detroit: Wayne State University Press, 1978), pp. 47–51.

One can note a substantial agreement on terminology between the two writers and on the effect that such a theoretical framework might have on practice described in both texts. The term 'aerosa', for example, appears to be essentially permeated by Castiglione's desire to reduce the natural body to a minimum and incorporates the idea of an overwhelming superiority, expressed through lightness, coding authority in such a way as to render it acceptable and pleasing to the spectators.

The *Cortegiano* describes the essential ethos of the dancer's movements: 'che si gli convenga servare una certa dignità, temperata però con leggiadra ed aerosa dolcezza di movimenti' (II, XI; p. 205). Castiglione's lexis here skilfully combines a sense of vagueness with technical accuracy. Castiglione himself specifically introduces one more element into the complex of dance movements, that is, the need for dignified gestures, again used to signify distinction, separating the perfect courtier from other courtiers and from other social classes. Indeed, the ethos of the dance pervades the courtier so much so that, even when he is not dancing, he is emitting signals that come from the ideology of dancing.

There are two occasions in the *Cortegiano* where dancing takes place, once at the end of Book I (LVI; pp. 184–85) and again at the beginning of Book IV (III; pp. 448–49). The first occasion, when Elisabetta Gonzaga calls on two ladies to dance, is pertinent to our discussion. It is no accident that only women are involved at this point in dancing. They are providers of entertainment in an aesthetically acceptable manner. The two women involved no longer have any speaking parts (these have been eliminated by the final version)[39] so that they silently map out their roles before the gaze of an approving audience, indicating that they are capable of achieving *grazia* through stylized movement. The women perform two dances: the first one a *bassadanza*, symbol of refined court society engaged in aesthetic, harmonious activities; the second a dance that remains rather obscure and for which there seems to be no description ('roegarze').[40] The fact that Castiglione feels obliged only to name these dances and not describe them would appear to indicate that he expected a certain familiarity with them from his readers.

The basse dance had been described by Antonio Cornazzano in his treatise on dance (composed in 1455 and then revised about ten years later). It was considered by him to be superior to all other dances and the one most suitable for court society ('*Bassadanza* è la regina dell'altre misure').[41] He contrasts it

[39] See S. D. Kolsky, 'Women through men's eyes: the third book of *Il Cortegiano*', in *The Shared Horizon: Melbourne Essays in Italian Language and Literature in Memory of Colin McCormick*, ed. by T. O'Neill (Dublin: Irish Academic Press, 1990), p. 58.

[40] On the bassadanza see D. Heartz, 'The basse dance: its evolution circa 1450 to 1550', *Annales Musicologiques*, 6 (1958–1963), 287–340; F. Crane, *Materials for the Study of the Fifteenth Century Basse Danse* (New York: Institute of Mediæval Music, 1968), in particular pp. 1–17, with an extensive bibliography; and more generally, O. Gombosi, 'About dance and dance music in the late Middle Ages', *Musical Quarterly*, 27 (1941), 289–305.

[41] C. Mazzi, p. 10.

with the *salterello*, described as 'il più allegro dançare de tutti, et gli spagnoli el chiamano alta danza'.[42] There is a slight insinuation that this type of dance has the potential of breaking the fundamental rule of courtly decorum.[43]

Dance introduces an element that was so obviously crucial to the workings of court society: women, who of necessity played a key role in dance. Guglielmo devotes a chapter to female participation in the dance ('capitulum regulare mulierum'). A defence of courtly dancing had to discipline the sexuality of the dance and neutralize any threat to the gender balance of the court. The 'giovene donna & virtuosa' has to conduct herself 'con piu moderanza assai & piu honestade che al huomo' (*De pratica*, p. 108). For Guglielmo the dance becomes the ritualized enactment of a woman's subservient position in society. Although the same rules apply to her as to the male dancer, her 'movimento [...] corporeo vuole esser humile & mansueto' and, in line with Christian teaching, Guglielmo adds: 'et non sia cogli ochi suoi altiera o vagabunda mirando or qua or la chome molte fanno. ma honestamente e[t e] piu del tempo reguardi la terra' (*De pratica*, p. 108). However, Guglielmo also stresses the intellectual qualities necessary to the female dancer. She maintains a kind of nobility and autonomy in spite of Guglielmo's regulations ('un portamento della sua persona degno et signorile').[44] Castiglione takes over the general thrust of Guglielmo's chapter on the female dancer, inserting the dance into his philosophy of behaviour:

> e però nel danzar non vorrei vederla usar movimenti troppo gagliardi e sforzati, né meno nel cantar o sonar quelle diminuzioni forti e replicate, che mostrano più arte che dolcezza; medesimamente gli instrumenti di musica che ella usa, secondo me, debbono esser conformi a questa intenzione. (III, VIII; p. 347)

The term 'il sforzare' (I, XXVI; p. 124) had previously been employed to refer to the courtier's own need to conform to the notion of *sprezzatura* and similarly illustrated by dance.[45] However, there is a crucial difference: for the courtier singing and dancing are signs of knowledge and as such are indicators of potential ability to advise the prince. For the woman, knowledge is not explicitly mentioned by Castiglione, though it is by Guglielmo. What *is* mentioned is the need to subordinate her performance to the dictates of *dolcezza*: 'quella molle delicatura' (III, VIII; p. 347), 'quella soave mansuetudine'

[42] C. Mazzi, p. 10.

[43] Cornazzano makes a number of value-judgements about dances. His intention would appear to be clear: to document a series of dances that are suitable for performance by the court. His view of the *piva* confirms such an attitude: 'hoggidì, per gl'ingiegni assuttigliati in più fiorite cose, è abiecta e uilipesa da persone magnifice e da bon dançatori' (p. 11). All the dances Cornazano describes are suitable for court consumption: 'Vegnirò mo' a quelli balli et bassedançe che son fora del uulgo, fabricati per sale signorile, e da esser sol dançati per dignissime Madonne, et non plebeie' (p. 16). The same sentiments will also inform Guglielmo's treatise.

[44] *De pratica*, p. 108. Guglielmo notes that the female dancer should also perform the dance steps 'con honestate airosa', and 'legiera in sul pie'.

[45] 'Medesimamente nel danzare un passo solo, un sol movimento della persona grazioso e non sforzato, subito manifesta il sapere de chi danza' (I, XXVIII; p. 129).

(III, VIII; p. 348).[46] Thus the court lady's semiotic possibilities are limited to a single set of signifieds: to project an image of pliable pleasantness, remembering that the courtier has to avoid the stigma of being considered 'molle'. If asked to dance or play music she may accept, but 'con una certa timidità' (III, VIII; p. 348). Also implicit is the understanding that women are not to display their sexuality in a way that would undermine the court's respectability and make people consider it a corrupt and licentious place. As we have already seen, Guglielmo was also at pains to remove the veneer of rampant sexuality from the dance.[47]

Dance can also be considered an extension into the world of the Renaissance court of the concept of *disciplina*.[48] It was originally found in Cicero's *De officiis*, where it had a varied range of meanings,[49] but is beginning to take on the sense of controlling behaviour: 'certaque vivendi disciplina', a lifestyle suitable for the civilized *urbs*, one which emphasizes social responsibility.[50] In the early Middle Ages, Ambrose adapted Ciceronian teaching to the needs of the Church in the influential *De officiis ministrorum* (written in 389–90).[51] Such standards of behaviour were adopted by bishops' courts in the early Middle Ages and, from there were transferred to lay courts, contrary to Norbert Elias'

[46] Guglielmo describes the dancing technique of the female dancer as follows: 'nel suo muovere destra. ligiadra. & continente' (*De pratica* , p. 108).

[47] Guglielmo dedicates his manual 'solamente agli honesti & casti petti' (*De pratica*, p. 90).

[48] The term is used a number of times in the *Cortegiano*: I, XXIV, p. 121 (synonymous here with 'arte' and 'modo'); I, XLIII, p. 159 (equivalent to instruction, 'ammaestramenti'); I, XLVII, p. 170 (close to the modern idea of academic subject); II, XLIII, p. 256 (Francesco Maria della Rovere argues that 'facezie' are subject to regulation and systematic analysis); IV, VII, p. 453 (used in reference to the princely mode of government); IV, XII, p. 461 (control of sense of touch, sight and hearing); IV, XIII, p. 462 ('la radice di queste virtù potenzialmente ingenite negli animi nostri, se non è aiutata dalla disciplina, spesso si risolve in nulla'); IV, XLV, p. 505 (training).

For a general survey see J.-C. Schmitt, 'The ethics of gesture', in *Fragments for a History of the Human Body*, ed. by M. Feher (New York: Zone, 1989), pp. 128–47 and his introduction to *Gestures*, ed. by the same, vol. 1 of *History and Anthropology*, 1984, pp. 1–3. Fundamental to this revised perspective on the relationship between medieval ecclesiastical and Renaissance lay treatises on comportment is the essay by D. Romagnoli, 'Cortesia nella città: un modello complesso. Note sull'etica medievale delle buone maniere' in *La città e la corte: buone e cattive maniere tra medioevo ed età moderna*, ed. by D. Romagnoli (Milan: Guerini, 1991), pp. 21–70. Another important essay which appeared at the same time makes similar points, although it does not specifically analyse the *Cortegiano*: D. Knox, 'Disciplina: the monastic and clerical origins of European civility', in *Renaissance Society and Culture: Essays in Honor of Eugene F. Rice, Jr.*, ed. by J. Monfasani and R. G. Musto (New York: Italica, 1991), pp. 107–35.

[49] Cicero uses it to describe a fundamental change in the foreign policy of the Roman republic: 'Sensim hanc consuetudinem et disciplinam iam antea minuebamus' (II, VII, 27); in reference to Lycurgus' governance of Sparta: 'Lycurgi legibus et disciplinae' (I, XXII, 76). On two occasions 'disciplinae' refers to schools of philosophy (I, II, 5–6).

[50] *De officiis*, II, IV, 15. Cicero similarly uses the term in conjunction with 'leges', 'mores' (I, XLIV, 156). On one occasion, *disciplina* is employed to mean correction of children by parents: some men manage to succeed in life 'sine parentium disciplina' (I, XXXII, 118).

[51] See Schmitt, 'The ethics of gesture', 132–33; Knox, pp. 109, 111–13.

theory of the development of civilized behaviour.[52] Recent scholarship has acknowledged the debt that Renaissance works on behaviour owe to the tradition of *disciplina*, of self-control, regulation of the instinctual body. The body is seen as a crucial vehicle for the transmission of the values which are of major importance to the institution to which the treatise is directed. Obviously, courtly dance is not treated in ecclesiastical treatises on behaviour, the more so since they deal with institutions from which women were excluded. However, they often deal with gait and deportment. In other terms, the emphasis that we find in these medieval clerical treatises on the control of the body, self-government, the repression of particular kinds of gestural activity, is transferred into the realm of the dance seen as the regulated self-expression of the courts. The concept of *disciplina* can be seen to extend to the control of sexuality through rules concerning the correct comportment to be observed in dance routines. Dance is the aesthetic ordering of gesture in order to represent in a stylized manner the basic values of court society. Harmonious movement confirms the ordered power of the court. One of the fundamental purposes served by *disciplina* was the separation between laity and clergy, lending certain distinctive features to clerical behaviour. *Disciplina* would later be transferred to the laity where it would be used to separate the nobility from the other social classes. Distinction is proved by adhesion to a refined set of movements.

One of the most influential of such treatises, *De institutione novitiorum liber*, attributed to Hugh of St Victor, possibly written in the first quarter of the twelfth century, provides a conceptual framework by which one can comprehend more fully the treatment of dancing in the *Cortegiano*.[53] *De institutione* is a training manual for regular canons and is possibly the first to deal with the control of the body in such detail, hence its importance as a turning-point in the history of comportment.[54] Hugh of St Victor's definition of *disciplina* is two-fold: it is the regulation of both social intercourse ('conversatio bona et honesta') and of the body ('membrorum omnium motus ordinatus').[55] The connection between inner turmoil ('inconstantia mentis') and consequent disordered movement ('inordinata motio corporis') is made clear in *De*

[52] See C. S. Jaeger, *The Origins of Courtliness: Civilizing Trends and the Formation of Courtly Ideals 939–1210* (Philadelphia: University of Pennsylvania Press, 1985), pp. 108–10, 259–62; P. Burke, *The Fortunes of the Courtier: The European Reception of Castiglione's 'Cortegiano'* (Cambridge: Polity, 1995), pp. 12–15.

[53] See Romagnoli, 'Cortesia nella città', pp. 38–48; Knox, pp. 113–14; J.-C. Schmitt, *Il gesto nel medioevo*, trans. by C. Milanesi (Rome and Bari: Laterza, 1990), pp. 154–78; C. W. Bynum, 'The spirituality of regular canons in the twelfth century: a new approach', *Medievalia et Humanistica*, 4 (1973), 10–13.

[54] See J.-C. Schmitt, '"Gestus" — "Gesticulatio". Contribution à l'étude du vocabulaire latin médiéval des gestes', in *La lexicographie du latin médiéval et ses rapports avec les recherches actuelles sur la civilisation du Moyen-Age* (Paris: Editions du centre de la recherche scientifique, 1981), pp. 381–90.

[55] The text of *De institutione novitiorum liber* is to be found in *Patrologiae Cursus Completus: Series Latina*, ed. by J.-P. Migne, vol. CLXXVI, ch. X, col. 935b.

institutione novitiorum liber. Movement and gesture, therefore, carry both religious and social/moral meanings.[56] It is crucial that the body functions as a harmonious whole; it is not permissible to misuse the body in ways not sanctioned by the code of conduct developed in the treatise.[57] Hugh introduces the notion that restrained behaviour is not so much for God and religious purposes, but that uncontrolled or inappropriate gestures would be offensive to onlookers.

This concept will be fully exploited and further developed by Castiglione in the *Cortegiano*.[58] Correct behaviour requires *modestia*, restraint, measured gestures.[59] *De institutione novitiorum liber* places considerable emphasis on 'discretio', that is the understanding of the context in which gestures are acted out.[60] The ultimate aim is 'concordia' which for Hugh has musical connotations of harmony as well as political overtones, as defined in Plato's *Republic*. The parts of the body have to work together, just as the organs of the state have to function for the well-being of the *polis*.[61] In terms of the physical body, 'human gesture must be gracious in every act without being effeminate'.[62]

In this context, dance in the *Cortegiano* assumes a range of meanings having to do both with bodily and social control. There is the same contempt, as there was in Hugh of St Victor, for uncontrolled and unrestrained movement. This theme is emphasized in Castiglione's treatment of the 'moresca',[63] which becomes the equivalent of Hugh's disordered gestures ('gesticulationes'). Importantly, the dance must be restricted as far as possible to the confines of the palace and to certain types of dance. In particular, the courtier is not to dance 'in piazza' or 'per le strade'[64] and he is definitely not to take part in a

[56] *PL*, CLXXVI, ch. X, col. 935b.

[57] 'Primum ergo diligenter observandum est, ut singula membra suum teneant officium, neque usurpent alienum', *PL*, CLXXVI, ch. XII, col. 941c.

[58] See, for example, *Cortegiano*, I, XVII, pp. 110–11; I, XXII, p. 119 (prohibits the courtier from taking part in tight-rope walking and the like because 'quasi hanno del giocolare'); I, XXVII, p. 125; II, VI, p. 197.

[59] Hugh does describe the opposite: 'And others (far worse!), when they do something or listen to someone, stick out their tongue like a thirsty dog and revolve it around their mouth like a millstone, twisting their lips from the effort', quoted in C. S. Jaeger, *The Envy of Angels: Cathedral Schools and Social Ideals in Medieval Europe, 950–1200* (Philadelphia: University of Pennsylvania Press, 1994), p. 255.

[60] Castiglione is equally concerned with 'discrezione' and, in the matter of dancing and similar activities, with an intelligent use of gestures ('governandosi con quel bon giudicio che non lo lassi incorrere in alcuna sciocchezza') (I, XXII; p. 119).

[61] 'Est enim quasi quaedam respublica corpus humanum, in quo singulis membris sua officia distributa sunt. Dum ergo unum membrum alterius membri officium inordinate sibi vindicat, quid aliud quam concordiam universitatis perturbat?' (*PL*, CLXXVI, ch. XII, col. 943a).

[62] *PL*, CLXXVI, ch. XII, col. 943c.

[63] This type of dance is not to be confused with a form of courtly entertainment of the same name for which see *De pratica*, pp. 48, 223. It is a wild dance that expresses the 'other' in court behaviour. As the term suggests it appears to have originally been a Moorish dance in contrast to the 'Christian' dances of the court.

[64] Cicero issues similar instructions in *De officiis*: 'Sed ea, quae multum ab humanitate discrepant, *ut si qui in foro cantet*, aut si qua est alia magna perversitas, facile apparet nec magnopere admonitionem et praecepta desiderat' (I, XL, 145; my emphasis).

'moresca' (II, VI; p. 197). Shakespeare's allusion to this kind of dance, which has connotations of the exotic and the forbidden, seems apt in this context: 'I have seen | him caper upright like a wild Morisco'.[65] The adjective 'wild' precisely catches the opposition Castiglione is setting up between the palace as the site of civilization, the 'true' *urbs* ('una città in forma de palazzo esser pareva' (I, II; p. 82) and places exterior to it, the 'real' city and the countryside, where the threat of other kinds of behaviour, that could submerge the court, is always imminent. Thus 'a wild Morisco' is a visible sign of lack of control and an abrogation of the values of court life symbolized by the *bassadanza*.

The classical outsider is the 'madman' at the other end of the spectrum from controlled finesse. And the dance is the site where courtier and madman meet, since it is used to exemplify the extremes of unacceptable behaviour. One of the rejected games involves the discussion of 'publica pazzia' (I, VIII, p. 92). In order to get his point across about the therapeutic effects of public madness, Cesare Gonzaga compares its 'symptoms' to the tarantella, uncontrolled, frenetic dancing leading to the recovery of the victim of the spider's poison.[66] The 'moresca', if performed publicly within the confines of the palace, would signal a confusion of cultures, a contamination with the subaltern classes. Nowhere is this brought out more clearly than in the diatribe against dancing with peasants or members of the lower orders in general. In this context, the courtier is referred to as a 'gentilomo' (II, X; p. 204) since origins and rank are of paramount importance in participation in outdoor activities. Dancing here assumes the aspect of working in the fields, 'tutto 'l dì nel sole coi villani' (II, X; p. 204), breaking one of the most tenacious aristocratic taboos against manual labour, and is implicitly proscribed by Federico Fregoso. Another motive for such an attitude is that dancing in this context places the emphasis on exertion, on the body as a fact of nature, obliterating difference.

The text also strives to defuse the possibility of collaboration and comparison between the diverse strata of society. The dance is one of the principal means by which the court can define itself and distinguish itself from that which lies outside its boundaries. The dance as an exhibition of refinement marks the limits of the court and restricts entry to its ranks. Far from being trivial, the dance, performed in the palace, is a crucial rite in which power is displayed and confirmed. It is princely power that exhibits itself every time a court dance is performed. The dances of the courtier geometrically define the space of the court as the space of power.

Medieval theories of gesture and deportment hinged on the link between the soul ('intus') and the movements of the body ('foris'). Gesture was therefore the reflection of a person's inner life. Such a connection is not so clear in the manner Castiglione analyses dance. Dancing does not necessarily illuminate

[65] Quoted in A. Brissenden, 'Shakespeare and the morris', *Review of English Studies*, 30 (1979), 1.
[66] See P. Spencer, 'Introduction: interpretations of the dance in anthropology', in *Society and the Dance: The Social Anthropology of Process and Performance*, ed. by the same (Cambridge: Cambridge University Press, 1985), pp. 3–4.

the inner workings of the courtier; it does not appear to reflect directly the workings of his soul. It is considered as an activity that images the court. Yet dance itself in Castiglione's formulation does have a double life, a frame of reference that includes an inside and an outside, but in a sense completely different from Hugh's. The Renaissance writer introduces the concept of public and private, almost as a rewriting of the soul–body connection. The link between private and public is not at all straightforward and places the concept of *disciplina* in a new light. The fact that there can exist a discrepancy between the outside and inside, between public and private means that public behaviour is no longer grounded in a spiritual discipline. It opens the way to a more cynical view of human behaviour. Such a vision of human behaviour is only prevented from holding sway in the *Cortegiano* by the introduction, in the fourth book, of the moral 'soul' of the text, the philosophical supports for the behaviour described in the other books. Castiglione makes a distinction between public and private comportment:

> benché in camera privatamente, come or noi ci troviamo, penso che licito gli sia e questo, e ballar moresche e brandi; ma in publico non così, fuor che travestito, e benché fosse di modo che ciascun lo conoscesse, non dà noia. (II, XI; p. 206)

Thus Castiglione has introduced the idea of a double standard whereby the public performance is limited to particular forms of the dance under precise conditions. In private, on the contrary, disordered dances, prohibited elsewhere in the text are permitted. Unlike Hugh, Castiglione sees a place for disordered behaviour in the court system. The private functions as a safety-valve. It can help release pent-up tensions by taking part in the forbidden styles of dance that are only permitted in private performance or when the courtier is 'travestito'. The passage has a number of implications for the *Cortegiano* as a whole. Castiglione allows room for disordered expression, but only in the wings as a kind of ironic commentary on the 'real' court and only when it is clear that everyone knows the rules are being broken, a carnival for the court. Public dancing is the symbol in the text of a revitalized and more 'civilized' court. The dance steps are not explained, but what strikes the reader with force is the image that is created of order and refinement constructed on a ritual catharsis of disordered movements.

The courtier has, it is claimed, as his primary occupation the profession of arms (I, XXVI; p. 109). It is to be supposed that arms connote status in Renaissance society, lending an authority to the courtier which he might not otherwise have. Arms give the courtier a sense of relevance to the military struggles that had been taking place in early sixteenth-century Italy. Yet the soldier who does not adhere to the rules of court society is held up to ridicule in the text. A particularly vivid example is provided of a soldier who refused to dance with a lady because he understood his profession in too narrow terms (I, XVII; pp. 110–11). Apart from its obvious message of the necessity of flexibility, the anecdote implies the necessity of integrating the 'feudal' mentality into the refined pleasures of the court. On another level, dancing symbolizes here the recognition that professional behaviour based on a particularly narrow construction of masculinity is out of place in court society. Thus dance can be construed as a symbol for sociability and adeptness at appearing to belong to an elite group. The military skills of the courtier, like those of Plato's Guardians, are necessary for the defence of the state, but both *The Republic* and the *Cortegiano* concentrate on other aspects of political interaction. The metaphor of music to indicate the harmony of the state, in particular of the ruling class, is present in both works. In the *Cortegiano*, dancing assumes the function of asserting the solidarity of the 'courtier-class' and its ability to share power with the prince. Movement becomes aestheticized; dance represents the ideals of court society contrasting with the sorry state of contemporary Italy.

Castiglione compares some unspecified contemporary rulers to carnival 'colossi', and he makes use of the difference between 'intus' and 'foris' to bring his point home to the reader. The outer magnificence belies inner poverty and moral emptiness, symbolized by the fact that 'dentro erano pieni di stoppa e di strazzi' (IV, VII; p. 454). The writer takes the analogy further by suggesting that, while the 'colossi' manage to stay upright, the princes are 'mal contrapesati e senza misura posti sopra basi inequali'. All sense of balance has gone; *disciplina* is no longer practised. It is the complaint of the text that force (and the image of the 'colossi' imples the ideology of magnificence) has replaced *disciplina*.

The defining principles of dance, such as *misura*, are defied by these princes at their own peril. This is one of the fundamental reasons why music plays such an important role in the text, restoring to court behaviour a sense of dignity and purpose. It is certainly no accident that the principal characteristics of this society are defined by reference to dance and music. When Castiglione introduces the concept of 'sprezzatura', perhaps the basic form of behaviour for the successful courtier, his first example to illustrate its application to the court is one drawn from dancing. 'Il nostro messer Pierpaulo' (I, XXVI; p. 125) breaks all the rules of the dance code and, by extension, the rules of court society. And this example is immediately followed by another in order to show the dangers of affectation (I, XXVII; pp. 125–26). By this negative representation of dance, the text offers an implied ideal of the dance as the cultural yardstick by which the court is measured.

The discussions of music and dance in the *Cortegiano* are certainly valuable for the light they throw on contemporary musical practices, but the function of music and dance in the overall context of the work goes far beyond that of the practical manual. Music and dance validate the enterprise of the courtier because they function as reference points for the classical traditions of philosophy and political thought. They serve to add another dimension to the text in its quest to render more effective the courtier-class. Dance is a semiotic activity that creates a series of meanings for other courtiers involved in the struggle for patronage. It also creates an image of the court as a place of disciplined movement which, by implication, was in a position to offer leadership to the disordered, chaotic body politic of the Italian peninsula. Therefore, the image of the courtier as dancer or *musicus* is not solely one of a leisured, refined gentleman who whiles away his hours in seemingly gratuitous activities. They represent something more — a challenge to other political institutions which have to make a more utilitarian use of time, an emphasis on the power of the courts to control events and to chart their course unperturbed.

V

Old Men in a New World: Morello da Ortona in the Cortegiano

Readers could be forgiven for thinking that the *Cortegiano* is a young person's book. The first three books seem to be an ode to the physically active body. The courtier is always moving: dancing, jousting, exercising, courting the ladies. The characters are mainly young or, having reached maturity at the time of the fictional dialogues are on the point of achieving their full potential.[1] They have been spared the ravages of old age and remain wrinkleless in their literary eternity.

Castiglione managed to survive most of the interlocutors of the *Cortegiano* and it may be that the act of surviving influenced the dedication and the major reworking of Book IV in the latter years of his life.[2] Castiglione notes in the authorial preface to Book IV that Gaspare Pallavicino, Cesare Gonzaga, and Roberto da Bari died "quando di prospera età e speranza d'onore più fiorivano."[3] In the dedication, Castiglione makes the general point about the early deaths of many of the interlocutors: "Morti sono ancor molti altri dei nominati nel libro, ai quali parea che la natura promettesse lunghissima vita" (70–71). In these circumstances, Castiglione can be considered an aging survivor whose thoughts turned to old age as he reflected on the long-gone, youthful court of Urbino.[4] Book IV, it will be argued, has as one of its functions to take cognizance of the aging process experienced by the author but denied to many of the interlocutors, and to suggest survival strategies for the older courtier.[5]

The one elderly courtier in the text, Morello da Ortona, is an outcast who generally attracts the rather hostile attention of the younger characters who form a compact and coherent group. Not much is known about him; not even the date of his birth has so far been unearthed by scholars. According to Cian,[6] Morello da Ortona's presence at Urbino can be documented from 1498. He was employed as a condottiere; Marin Sanudo characterises him as a "strenuo condottiere" of the Duke Guidobaldo Montefeltro. He seems to have become an individual of some importance in the Urbino court, figuring as a witness to the document which validated the Duke's adoption of Francesco Maria della Rovere, successor to the Duchy of Urbino.

In Castiglione's dramatic eclogue, *Tirsi* (written in 1506), Morello da Ortona is referred to as the "pastore antico." His characterisation here could not be more distant from the humorous-grotesque treatment he receives in the *Cortegiano*. In the *Tirsi* his age is *not* used as a means to undermine his seriousness, to make him a figure of fun. Castiglione pictures him in two different guises: the first as a musician, and as such he is compared to Apollo, ensuring that connotations of authority, harmony, elder statesmanship are not lost. Secondly, he is portrayed as a wise counsellor: "Questo agli altri pastor dona consiglio, / ché già del fiero amor provò l'artiglio."[7] Two problems can be noted here in relation to his depiction in the later dialogue. One is that the *Cortegiano* specifically prohibits the older courtier performing music in public . The second is that in the later work Morello does not accept that his lovemaking days are over. And no one in the *Cortegiano* is particularly receptive to his commentary and would-be advice.

The discrepancy in the portrayal of Morello da Ortona between *Tirsi* and the *Cortegiano* could be partially explained by the quasi-official nature of the eclogue, written for the Urbino carnival of 1506. *Tirsi* was composed for a specific occasion and was limited in the exploration of the characters by the constraints of the genre—the stylized pastoral. By contrast, the *Cortegiano* might be regarded as 'semi-private' in that it operates in the wings on an informal level—a group of courtiers meet without the presence of the Duke who would have been present at the carnival performance. The *Cortegiano* only entered the public domain because of Vittoria Colonna's 'indiscretions,' or at least, that is the version Castiglione furnishes in the dedicatory letter.[8] A further complicating factor is the long period over which the *Cortegiano* was composed. Although fictionally set only a year after the composition of *Tirsi*, the *Cortegiano* was not published until 1528. This length of time may help to explain an increasing interest on the part of the author in the effects and mechanisms of old age which are increasingly focussed on the character of Morello da Ortona.[9] In spite of its 'early' setting, the *Cortegiano* is not frozen in time. The experiences of the post-Guidobaldo years are subtly signposted and insinuated into the later redactions of the dialogue.

The characterisation of Morello da Ortona in the *Cortegiano* completely demolishes the sense of Apollonian wisdom that is so clearly suggested in *Tirsi*. There his experiences of love are passed on to other courtiers, but the use of the *passato remoto* and the adverb "già" (in the lines from *Tirsi* quoted above) make it plain that love holds no attraction for him in old age and that he has effectively separated himself from his youthful experiences, having learnt much from them. Although a minor character, Morello speaks and is mentioned by the other characters just enough to create a vivid picture of his activities and proclivities. It is interesting to note that there is an increased presence of the aged courtier in the *vulgata* with respect to the *Seconda redazione* and earlier drafts. Morello cannot simply be described as a figure of fun, despite the laughter at his expense on more than one occasion.[10] His presence challenges some of the positions taken up by the other courtiers. In this way, he represents the repressed consciousness of the court which comes to the surface only in a deformed reflection that can relatively easily be ridiculed by the others.

In both the *Seconda redazione* and the *vulgata* Morello da Ortona's first contribution to the discussion is the same. Significantly, it challenges the very basis of the court society that is being constructed by the main speakers. His criticism of the concept of rules as it is evolving through Federico Fregoso's discourse is intimately linked to the age of Morello da Ortona:

> Allor sùbito,—Queste vostre regule,—disse il signor Morello da Ortona,—a me par che poco insegnino; ed io per me tanto ne so ora, quanto prima che voi ce le mostraste; benché mi ricordi ancor qualche altra volta averle udite da' frati co' quali confessato mi sono, e parmi che le chiamino "le circonstanzie" —. (II, viii, 200)

Morello da Ortona's opening sally is revealing of his characterisation in a number of ways. The brutality of his criticism is barely tempered by the semi-humorous indirect reference to his age through the verb "mi ricordi," a detail which gains in resonance because of Morello's advanced years. He alludes to a developing division between himself and the others who are proposing a mainstream version of the courtier that tends to exclude him. These direct challenges that go to the fundamentals of court culture are often the domain of flawed, unreliable characters, such as Morello, Calmeta, and Unico Aretino. Their validity is undermined because of the way in which such characters are represented. In Morello da Ortona's case, his absurd behavior (so judged by the normalising others) is meant to undermine anything serious he might say. The introduction of such speakers into the text is a way of increasing tensions in its structure, making it less absolute than it might be and thereby preserving its guiding philosophy of almost systematic ambiguity. Criticism from readers who are outside the court system or who are unsympathetic to Castiglione's solutions can be neutralised or even integrated by being anticipated by 'unreliable' characters.

Morello's interjections do not negate the efforts of Federico Fregoso—their purpose is to enable the principal interlocutor to refine and expand his arguments and to admit that there is *some* truth in what the aging courtier has indicated. Morello da Ortona's comment induces laughter in Federico Fregoso, so defusing the situation, but at the same time it forces him to expatiate on the rules in order to convince his audience of their viability and their appropriateness to the society of the court: "Non vi par ora, signor Morello, che le nostre regule possano insegnar qualche cosa?" (II, ix, 202). The elderly courtier exposes two elements in the regularising discourse of Federico Fregoso that present a real danger to its universality and particular application to the courtier. Firstly, Morello claims the rules are too vague to be of any use. It is not hard to deduce that there is an element of truth in this criticism, though purposely expressed in extreme terms so that the objection can be more easily nullified. Secondly, Morello reveals the origins of much of the regulation of the courtier's behavior. He suggests that they are ecclesiastical in origin and uses the example of the manner in which the question and response pattern of the confessional appears to be a model for the discussion on the courtier's comportment. The text shows some embarrassment about this discovery. However, near the end of this encounter between Federico Fregoso and Morello the more authoritative figure almost casually integrates the revelation into his analysis: "In questi errori incorrono coloro che non hanno riguardo alle circonstanzie, che voi dite aver intese dai frati" (II, ix, 203). As far as Federico Fregoso is concerned that is the end of the matter. Federico's condescending tone, emphasising the "voi" further underlines the unreliable nature of Morello's assertion. This will become clearer as the reader's understanding of Morello's behavior develops. Morello's comment is placed in the midst of a detailed analysis of the place of physical activity in court society and is given no particular emphasis. In this way, the original criticism is diminished and the discourse self-consciously attempts to resolve its ambiguous relationship with medieval ecclesiastical literature.[11] The "frati" will come in for extended criticism in Book III of the *Cortegiano*,[12] putting even more distance between ecclesiastical regulation and rules suitable fo rthe court.

Federico Fregoso concludes his discussion of tailoring activity to circumstance by having one last side swipe at Morello: "Né io per me altre regole circa ciò dare gli saprei eccetto le già date, le quali sin da fanciullo, confessandosi, imparò il nostro signor Morello —" (II, xvii, 215). It is immediately noticeable that Fregoso, in order to reduce the impact of Morello's observation, resorts to two stratagems. The first is to make reference to Morello's age: the "sin da fanciullo" needs to be read as as a humorous indication of the courtier's advanced age, juxtaposing an image of Morello as a child and his present age. The second is to use the concept of generic ecclesiastical rules as an excuse to cut short his own disquisition on the courtier's need to match behavior and context. In both stratagems there is more than a touch of comedy which again has the effect of turning Morello into a clown who cannot be taken too seriously. This will certainly impact upon all his other interventions in the dialogue.

The reader, however, should not be fooled by all these subterfuges. Some of the regulations do seem to justify Morello's objections. In fact, the first three books of the *Cortegiano* might be read as a series of exclusions for older men, prohibiting them from taking part in various court activities. Moreover, the preface to Book II is an open attack on the backward-looking tendencies of old men who are inclined to criticise contemporary courts and praise only the courts of the past. There is little positive in Castiglione's representation of old men here. He portrays old age as a time of general enfeeblement, of loss of vitality, of melancholy "di modo che non solamente il corpo, ma l'animo ancora è infermo" (II, i, 188). The preface, which appeared both in the *Seconda redazione* and the *vulgata,* draws a pitiful picture of old age, haunted by its memories of better times, embittered by the loss of physical agility.

This view of old men certainly has implications for the reader's interpretation of Morello. The old courtier wants to live the illusion of youth and tenaciously claims that his physical powers and beauty are no less than those of younger courtiers. The old courtiers of the preface to Book II live by another illusion. What they and Morello have in common is a falsified view of contemporary reality, skewed by an attachment to their own youthful past. The belief that the courts of the past were better than contemporary ones is based on false presuppositions and fails to take into account "la consuetudine," a concept that does not permit the courtier to become fixated on the past, as it asserts change and renewal as the basis of the courtier's behavior ("Però sia licito ancor a noi seguitar la consuetudine de' nostri tempi, senza esser calunniati da questi vecchi" [II, iii, 194]).[13] Such a view represents an extension and exemplification of the theory of court language sketched in Book I of the *Cortegiano* which, in general terms, rejects the fossilised antique Tuscan language in favor of "la consuetudine."[14]

At all levels in the text the emphasis is on youth and change, adaptation to circumstances. It is no accident that the rejected games have to do with love, a sign of the strength of this theme in court society. And the length of the treatment of love in Book III further implies the youthfulness of the participants in these games. The text assumes a belligerent attitude towards Morello da Ortona, the outsider, who tries to take on the appearances of an insider; his clumsy attempts at inclusion lack "la sprezzatura" and are ridiculed by the other courtiers. The principal interlocutors, on the rare occasions when they think about old courtiers, express precise views about the conditions under which they can occupy space in the court.

Federico Fregoso proposes that the old courtier is not to play musical instruments or sing in public: "conoscerà l'età sua" (II, xiii, 210).[15] It is a rather rigid application of the rule of "circonstanzie"—old men singing love songs create an unpleasant impression.[16] Old age of itself violates the fundamental rule of the Golden Mean; it is an extreme and represents a deterioration of the body which, on the surface, indicates a decline in powers. The old courtier is generally out of place in the young court.

Giuliano de' Medici objects to such an exaggerated view: "—Non private, messer Federico, i *poveri* vecchi di questo piacere" (II, xiv, 210; my italics)—but even here a condescending tone and a hint of irony are not altogether absent. Federico suggests that if old men really want to perform music they should do so in private ("faccianlo in secreto" [II, xiv, 211]). Thus, the old courtier is not permitted to become a public figure in the entertainments of the court; he is considered inadequate, even an embarrassment and is thus forced into passivity. Federico does allow the older courtier to appreciate good music because he has learnt to understand its harmonies.

Such a position solicits a response from Morello da Ortona: "—Meglio è adunque,—rispose quivi il signor Morello quasi adirato,—escludere tutti i vecchi e dir che solamente i giovani abbian da esser chiamati cortegiani —" (II, xiv, 212). The sense of exclusion from the activities that are discussed in such detail in the first three books is underlined by the litotes "quasi adirato." Furthermore, Morello makes the connection between courtiership and youthfulness an essential prerequisite for someone wishing to be considered a full member of the court. In spite of the portrayal of Morello da Ortona as an unreliable observer, an outcast, his statement is borne out by the descriptions of the courtier's life. Federico Fregoso's response does not address the issues raised by the elderly courtier. Instead he launches an *ad hominem* attack:

> Rise allor messer Federico, e disse:—Vedete voi, signor Morello, che quelli che amano queste cose, se non son giovani, si studiano d'apparere; e però si tingono i capelli e fannosi la barba due volte la settimana. (II, xiv, 212)

This reference serves to humiliate Morello, especially in front of the women present, since they immediately realise that Federico's pointed remark is directed at the courtier. Morello feels the brunt of the attack and is obviously hurt by its ferocity and by the realisation of the negative impact that such an attack will have on his credibility as a courtier ("ed esso parve che un poco se ne turbasse" [II, xiv, 212]), but he responds in a pointed manner:

—Ma sono ben degli altri intertenimenti con donne,—suggiunse sùbito messer Federico,—che si convengono ai vecchi.—E quali?—disse el signor Morello;—dir le favole?—E questo ancor,—rispose messer Federico. (II, xiv, 212)

The reason Federico Fregoso is so adamant about old courtiers not participating in the physical activities of the court is because he holds dear the tradition which allots to each age appropriate functions. There is nothing original in his assessment of the defining features of youth, maturity and old age, although his taxonomy is not nearly so detailed as one might find in other sources.[17] For Fregoso, early maturity is the most fruitful and productive in a man's life, mainly because it conserves the principle of *mediocritas*.[18]

The question of the role of the older courtier in court society is critical to the reader's comprehension of Book IV of the *Cortegiano*. Morello da Ortona represents everything the aging courtier should not be. He does not acknowledge the changes in his body and when he does, he tries to disguise them. He behaves as if he has learnt nothing from his past experiences. In spite of the living *exemplum* of Morello, Federico Fregoso concludes that aging courtiers have a specific function to fulfil at court, notwithstanding all the negatives associated with their condition. He states that they have three qualities which ought to be fostered (and many more negative qualities which are listed at greater length)[19]: "ché i vecchi, come che siano ordinariamente prudenti più che i giovani, più continenti e più sagaci" (II, xv, 212). These qualities are to be utilised by the court in the following ways:

e valersi di quella prudenzia e cognizion che per lungo uso avranno acquistata, ed esser quasi oraculi a cui ognun vada per consiglio, ed aver grazia in dir quelle cose che sanno, accommodatamente ai propositi, accompagnando la gravità degli anni con una certa temperata e faceta piacevolezza. (II, xv, 213)

Federico Fregoso is outlining here, in the most general terms, the kind of role that will be attributed to the courtier in Book IV. Though he does not actually state that the older courtier could make a perfect adviser to the prince, it is implied that anyone (including the prince) should be able to come and ask the older courtier for counsel. It is possible, Fregoso argues, to lead a balanced life in old age.[20] By contrast, Morello represents the figure of "stultam senectutem."[21] Cato, in Cicero's *De senectute*, disparagingly cites the case of two ex-consuls who "used to lament, because they were denied the sensual pleasures without which they thought life not life at all."[22] He constructs a generally positive picture of old age, despite the recognition that the body is failing. From this point of view Morello da Ortona is the anti-Cato who transgresses all the advice that the Roman gave to his young listeners. The Roman statesman emphasises that "the most suitable defenses of old age are the principle and practice of virtues"—a view that exactly fits the tenor of Book IV of the *Cortegiano*.[23] For Cato sensual pleasures are replaced by intellectual pursuits.[24] But his analysis of the role of the elderly extends to their *auctoritas* in society by virtue of their long political careers. So, in the end, far from representing a decline in powers and political influence, old age is seen by Cicero as a continuation of respectable activities, though along slightly different lines.[25]

In view of a few positive comments on the role of the older courtier in Book II, can we posit a linear development in the treatment of old age between the first three books and the fourth, one which allows us to demonstrate the textual coherence of the *Cortegiano*? In other words, does the *Cortegiano* portray a chronological development of the courtier from youth to old age? There are links of this kind between the two unequal blocks that make up the *Cortegiano*, but they are somewhat tenuous. The few positive comments on old age appear to be submerged by a mass of negative criticisms in the first three books. The text makes it clear that music, dancing, jousting and the like are the means to win over the prince so that the courtier will then be in a position to offer him the best advice. However, if the courtier is already old, he will not be able to *actively* beguile the prince in this way.

This connundrum exercises the minds of the interlocutors in Book IV of the *vulgata*. Such a paradox has the power to undermine the text and to render the instructions found in the first three books virtually useless if a greater role were to be assigned to the elderly courtier. Book IV attempts to resolve this problem with the suggestion that there are two types of courtier. Age becomes a critical factor in analyzing the courtier's relationship with the prince. Giuliano de' Medici posits three types of problematical relationship based on age differentials that for him might invalidate the whole enterprise of creating a courtier. Castiglione complicates what seemed straightforward in the earlier books by focussing on the variations in age that may occur between courtier and prince, thus acknowledging the increasing relevance of age in this most crucial of power relations.

The first of Giuliano's hypothetical cases concerns the prince and courtier who are of similar ages "perché dove è poca differenzia d'età, ragionevol è che ancor poca ve ne sia di sapere" (IV, xliv, 503). The second concerns an old prince and a young courtier, "ed allor il fine che voi avete attribuito al cortegiano è impossibile" (IV, xliv, 503) because the prince would be much more knowledgeable than the courtier. The third pertains to the relationship between a young prince and an older courtier:

> difficilmente il cortegian po guadagnarsi la mente del principe con quelle condizioni che voi gli avete attribuite; ché, per dir il vero, l'armeggiare e gli altri esercizi della persona s'appartengono a' giovani e non riescono ne' vecchi, e la musica e le danze e feste e giochi e gli amori in quella età son cose ridicule. (IV, xliv, 504)

These possible situations become the focus of attention in the last book because the entire apparatus of the *Cortegiano* had led both interlocutors and readers to believe that there was only one way of winning the favour of the prince and that was by performing the courtly games with due "sprezzatura." Now, the terms of the argument are being rejigged. Morello had been harassed by the other courtiers precisely because he did not respect the limitations of his age, limitations that are commented upon quite frequently in the text.

Surprisingly, the fourth book takes a positive view of the older courtier as princely adviser. Paradoxically, Morello acts as a catalyst for an alternative reading of the elderly courtier. Obviously, his personal reaction to old age guarantees a negative response from both courtiers and readers. Morello provides some pointers, through his negative behavior, for the future courtier who will perhaps act in a manner more in keeping with his years. The text makes a great effort to get around the disqualifications of the older courtier:

> Ma se 'l cortegian fosse tanto vecchio, che non se gli convenissi esercitar la musica, le feste, i giochi, l'arme e l'altre prodezze della persona, non si po però ancor dire che impossibile gli sia per quella via entrare in grazia al suo principe; perché se la età leva l'operar quelle cose, non leva l'intenderle, ed avendole operate in gioventù, lo fa averne tanto più perfetto giudicio e più perfettamente saperle insegnar al suo principe, quanto più notizia d'ogni cosa portan seco gli anni e la esperienzia; ed in questo modo il cortegian vecchio,ancora che non eserciti le condicioni attribuitegli, conseguirà pur il suo fine d'instituir bene il principe. (IV, xlvi, 507)

This passage, and indeed the entire discussion on the age of the prince and courtier in Book IV of the final version, were absent in the *Seconda redazione*. The additional material in the *vulgata* marks an awareness, on the part of Castiglione, of the increasing importance of experience and acquired political know-how in advising a prince and its insertion can be read on a number of levels. It would be erroneous, however, to ignore the biographical basis for such changes given the length of time that elapsed between the early drafts and the publication of the *Cortegiano*. During this period Castiglione reached old age and had moved on from the Urbino court since relations with Francesco Maria della Rovere had perhaps reached breaking-point in the aftermath of the Medici seizure of Urbino in 1516.[26] He had served a young prince, Federico Gonzaga, Marquis of Mantua (born in 1500), who came to power in 1519 when Castiglione was forty-one years of age, that is, already an old man by Renaissance standards. Certainly, the relationship was not an easy one; the marquis was ambitious and did not reach the high ethical standards set by Castiglione in the *Cortegiano*. By the time Castiglione was appointed papal nuncio, he had left behind the courts of Italy, both in a geographical and political sense, and was mediating between the emperor Charles V and Pope Clement VII on the international stage. He was by this time operating on a different plane from the relatively claustrophic world of the Italian court societies, and could look back on the Italian court system, if not in an impartial manner, at least in a detached fashion. He was a widower and had taken minor orders. At the date of his departure from Italy he was forty-six years old. He was an old courtier, even though he could not in any way be compared to Morello. The last book of the *Cortegiano* could therefore be read as an attempt to give a proper place to the aging courtier, perhaps based on his own experiences of growing old in various courts and, more generally, on his sense that the Italian courts were no longer the dynamic centers of politics and culture that they once had been. The courts themselves were in decline, growing old as it were.

Castiglione may have been interested in shoring up his own position from a theoretical stand-point: to resist the challenges of the next generation, experience is now considered a key attribute rather than physical prowess and agility. Those figures in the *Cortegiano* who had not been taken by an early death were also growing old. The author was trying to ensure that the older courtier had the possibility of fulfilling a worthwhile role at court, even at the risk of seriously unbalancing the structure of the text.

Aging is intimately connected to the other major theme of Book IV, Neoplatonic love. A basic outline is already to be found in the *Seconda redazione*. As is well known, the theme of love is greatly developed in the *vulgata*. What makes these additions even more remarkable is the role that is assigned to Morello da Ortona in Book IV who acts as an oppositional stimulus to Bembo's perorations.[27] Indeed, it is important to note that the discourse on Neoplatonic love is pitched towards the older courtier as a replacement for physical love. In this way, he is not disadvantaged because he can call upon Neoplatonic love as a means of justifying his position at court and even as a means of asserting his superiority over younger courtiers.

Gaspare Pallavicino, who is certainly not one of the most reliable of the interlocutors, turns the discourse to love by focussing attention on the potential problem it might cause for the older courtier: "'l cortegiano, il quale col valore ed autorità sua ha da indur il principe alla virtù, *quasi necessariamente bisogna che sia vecchio,* perché rarissime volte il saper viene innanzi agli anni" (IV, xlix, 511; my italics). He concludes that "l'amor ne' vecchi non riesce" and love could be the cause for their downfall or ridicule. It is precisely this opposition between young and old loves that induces Bembo to launch into his defense of Neoplatonic love as a solution to the problem of love for the old courtier. Ottaviano Fregoso prompts: "—Poiché tutte l'altre condicioni,—disse,—attribuite al cortegiano se gli confanno ancora che egli sia vecchio, non mi par già che debbiamo privarlo di questa felicità d'amare" (IV, xlix, 512). Such a statement seems to pass over the contradiction inherent in this position. It implies that the old courtier should still be able to perform the various activities expected of someone at court. However, as becomes clear in the discussion on love, the older courtier will have his own specially tailored rules.

Castiglione works a notable variant on the Neoplatonic love schema. The progression from physical passion to disembodied love is linked to the passage from youth to old age. Thus, Neoplatonic love is deemed more appropriate for the older courtier. It obviates the scandals that are potentially present in the figure of Morello da Ortona. Bembo, from the beginning of his speech, implicitly attacks the position of a Morello. Dignity is restored to the figure of the aged courtier:

> ed essendo savio, come noi presuponiamo, non s'ingannaria pensando che a lui si convenisse tutto quello che si convien ai giovani; ma, amando, ameria forse d'un modo, che non solamente non gli porteria biasimo alcuno, ma molta laude e somma felicità non compagnata da fastidio alcuno, il che rare volte e quasi non mai interviene ai giovani; e così non lasseria d'insegnare al suo principe, né farebbe cosa che meritasse la baia da' fanciulli. (IV, l, 513)

Love becomes the solace of old age, a kind of self-fulfilment that does not depend on the sexual love of women.[28] It goes hand in hand with the guidance of the prince, which also tends toward the abstract and the abandonment of some earthly pleasures.

On a number of occasions when Bembo moves to analyse a topic, he is interrupted by Morello whose view-point could not be more polar opposite, coming from a materialist tradition of love. These interruptions were obviously not present in the earlier versions of the dialogue. Bembo condemns any sexual love on the part of the older courtier.[29] It is on this point that Morello challenges Bembo. His view of love seems to be much closer to the opinions of Mario Equicola, as expressed in the *Libro de natura de amore* (published in 1525).[30] Equicola had denied the supremacy of sight in the Neoplatonic hierarchy of love, placing greater consideration on touch, as the vehicle for sexual love.[31] Equicola in the *Libro* attempts to blur his position by espousing a more orthodox version of Neoplatonic love towards the end of his treatise in order to finish the work on a high note, though in reality it carries little conviction.[32] Morello's position is quite clear: "il qual [Bembo] vole che amino d'un certo modo, ch'io per me non l'intendo; e parmi che 'l possedere questa bellezza, che esso tanto lauda, senza 'l corpo sia un sogno" (IV, lv, 520). The debate between Morello and Bembo is much more serious than the mocking tones in which it is couched. It is a question of how the court should present itself: the 'shameful,' overt sexuality of Morello that descends into the ridiculous, or the aloof, noble Neoplatonism that lends direction and dignity to old age. It should be remembered that Ludovico Canossa, who actively intervenes in this part of the debate, was well aware of the gross depiction of love in the *Libro de natura de amore*.[33]

Bembo wants to deny the physicality of the aging body—a reminder of decline—by viewing it as the starting point of another, positive, journey of spiritual redemption. Before Bembo can begin his flight upwards he is involved in a heated debate with Morello and some of the 'sacred' principles of Neoplatonic love come under fire. The inextricable connection that lies at the base of Neoplatonic thought—the conjunction of goodness and beauty, and extended by Renaissance court thinkers to include women, is the object of Morello's deconstructive wit. He maintains that beautiful women can be bad and cruel. Ludovico Canossa points out that Morello calls women cruel because they will not give him what he desires and suggests that Bembo will be able to reform him if he heeds advice about what he can properly request from women (that is, not sexual favours), "non uscendo voi di que' termini" (IV, lv, 520). For a second time the text states that "'l signor Morello si turbasse un poco" and for a moment it appears that he could be converted, but he immediately reverts to his 'old' system: "Quivi il signor Morello,—Il generar,—disse, —la bellezza nella bellezza con effetto, sarebbe il generar un bel figliolo in una bella donna" (IV, lxiii, 529). Morello will not deviate from his belief in sexual love as the true love, parodying one of the central tenets of the Neoplatonic concept of beauty.[34] In this sense, Morello is old-fashioned, harking back to Quattrocento theories of love that did not register or were resistant to the impact of Neoplatonism. His desire for a more substantive "segno" than that permitted to the courtier breaks all the rules of chastity and courtly appearance. Morello is searching for a greater solidity, a "pegno d'amore" that is not just words. His desire is thwarted by the moral commitment of the other courtiers who desire to model a different kind of court and courtier.

The "cortegiano non giovane" (IV, lxiv, 530), a creation of the fourth book, recognizes that the courtier is not an undifferentiated ideal, but changes in and is changed by time. The term is an appreciation of the diversity of those serving at court; inevitably the young courtier at the start of Book I has become old by the end of Book IV. However, the fourth book offers a knotty contradiction, brought about by the extent and nature of the additions in the final text. If Book IV opens by valorising those 'trivial' activities that had been the subject of the bulk of the *Cortegiano*, declaring them to be essential to a courtier's success in winning the ear of the prince, then these same activities are devalued once the emphasis shifts on to the older courtier. Neoplatonic love does not seem to be a solution for all courtiers—it is principally focussed on the Morellos of court life who have learnt only too well the lessons of the first three books, that is, the importance of music, dance, military exercises and love-making in their society. Castiglione is caught in a double bind. The young courtier is unlikely to bring about those sweeping changes in the behavior of the prince that the *Cortegiano* requires because youth is not serious or given to deep reflection. On the other hand, the experienced old courtier can instruct the prince in political savoir-faire, but cannot be actively involved in the routines of court pleasures. A passive knowledge of these pleasures is hardly the same as being able to participate in them. If the prince can only be accessed through these activities, it is clear that the courtier who can take part in them will be able to outperform the older courtier who is then reduced to explaining the finer points through language alone. No convincing solution to the contradiction is presented, an indication perhaps of the profound paradox that underlay court society: levity was its hallmark yet seriousness of purpose was essential.

The character, Morello, could perhaps be read as a sign of the moral confusion of the court. His refusal to conform to the overriding rule of *sprezzatura* and his lack of desire to escape the destructive web of *affettazione*, might be seen as reflecting the culture of a court and a prince, immersed in pleasures (IV, vii, 453). Thus, to create a refined, moral court courtiers like Morello have to be tamed because if they are regarded as extensions of the prince the court becomes a locus of corruption. Morello breaks the fundamental rule of "piacere onesto" (IV, x, 457), endangering the reputation of the prince. This is one of the major reasons why the old courtier is so severely censored by the other courtiers. Courtly skills practised improperly by the aging courtier might have the effect of creating a fractured and amoral court. In the same way, discordant behavior on the part of the prince would have the same effect. It is interesting from this point of view to note the representation in the text of the Duke of Urbino, Guidobaldo da Montefeltro. The Duke has grown prematurely old in his body: "e così restò un dei più belli e disposti corpi del mondo deformato e guasto nella sua verde età" (I, iii, 84). Yet, he accepted the limitations of his situation: "vivea con somma dignità ed estimazione appresso ognuno" (I, iii, 84). He made no attempt to take part in those activities that his weakened body would no longer allow him to perform to the required level of refinement: "pur si pigliava grandissimo piacer di vederle in altrui; e con le parole, or correggendo or laudando ciascuno secondo i meriti" (I, iii, 84). Thus, he was still involved in the activities of the court, but only in so far as his body allowed him. Morello has not learnt this lesson.[35] Indeed, the Duke's absence from the discussion is a further sign of the disintegration of the court that reaches its culmination in the preface to Book IV.

A place has to be assigned to the aging courtier, but not to the type represented by Morello who embodies everything an older courtier should not be. He represents old-fashioned views about the court as a place of licence and grotesque liberty, views that Castiglione is attempting to remold in the *Cortegiano*. Morello's general isolation from the other courtiers, his comic treatment, his insistence on doing things that render him ridiculous and violate the framework within which the courtier has to accommodate himself mark him out as an anti-model. His presence in the *Cortegiano*, which expands as the text gets older, confirms that old age has to be confronted at court even though it places a question-mark over the meaning of court life. Morello da Ortona presents an extreme position on aging; by refusing to relinquish the pleasures of youth, he becomes a warning to other old men, including perhaps Castiglione himself, not to behave in the same manner.

NOTES

I wish to thank Carolyn James for her invaluable assistance in rendering the language of this article more readable and coherent than it would otherwise have been.

[1]Old age in the early modern period can be calculated as beginning at forty so that, of the characters whose dates we know, Bibbiena died at the age of 50, Elisabetta Gonzaga at 55, Francesco Maria della Rovere at 48, Unico Aretino at 77 and Ludovico Canossa at 56. Emilia Pia probably reached old age as Morello da Ortona certainly did. See Gilbert, "When Did a Man in the Renaissance Grow Old?" and Jütte, "Aging and Body Image in the Sixteenth Century: Hermann Weinsberg's (1518–97) perception of the aging body." Mario Equicola argues that in men over forty sexual desire lessens: "Questo intendemo in omini quali non abiano passati li quaranta anni perciò che poi quella età il sangue si refreda" (Equicola f. 215v).

[2]See Ghinassi, "Fasi dell'elaborazione del *Cortegiano*" 155–96.

[3]Maier, ed. *Il libro del Cortegiano con una scelta delle Opere minori di Baldesar Castiglione.* All references will be to this edition, here IV, i; 445. Gaspare Pallavicino died very young: "pur in età molto immatura fornì il suo natural corso" (IV, i, 445) and Roberto da Bari is described as "un giovane di boni costumi" (IV, i, 446). In the dedicatory letter to Michel de Silva, Castiglione notes that the original dedicatee, Alfonso Ariosto, died young and that Giuliano de' Medici "meritava più lungamente dal mondo esser goduta" (70).

[4]Castiglione's comment "Seguitiamo adunque i ragionamenti del nostro cortegiano, con speranza che dopo noi non debbano mancare di quelli che piglino chiari ed onorati esempi di virtù dalla corte presente d'Urbino, così come or noi facciamo dalla passata" (IV, ii, 448). This position appears to come perilously close to that expressed by the old men at the beginning of Book II. There is one significant difference: Castiglione does not deny the possibility that the same quality of courtiers might be found in the contemporary court of Urbino, unlike the old courtiers of Book II who exclusively praise the courts of the past. See Pugliese 175–87 and Carella 473–519.

[5]Beer is the only extensive treatment of old age in the *Cortegiano.* However, Beer's version differs in a number of ways from mine. She rightly pinpoints the "serrata polemica antisenile che prosegue per tutta l'opera" (208), but in so doing tends to minimize the disjuncture that arises in Book IV because of the re-reading of old age in the new circumstances of the last book.

[6]"Dizionarietto biografico" in Cian, ed. *Il libro del Cortegiano del Conte Baldesar Castiglione* (523–24). See also Floriani 66.

[7]*Tirsi* in Maier 566–67; stanza 42.

[8]Maier 68–69. See Woodhouse 62–68.

[9]Morello da Ortona is the bye-word for old-age in the *Cortegiano*: "Perché spero farvi vedere che qui non è omo a cui si disconvenga l'esser inamorato, ancor che egli avesse quindici o venti anni più che 'l signor Morello —" (IV, li, 514).

[10]Beer describes him as "una figura comica," "un personaggio da commedia di tutto riguardo" (214).

[11]For a more detailed discussion of the background see Kolsky, "Making and Breaking the Rules."

[12]III, xx, 363–65. See Scarpati.

[13]See Mazzacurati 28–29.

[14]For a general treatment of court language in the *Cortegiano* see Mazzacurati 42–62 and Marino.

[15]Cf. Ryan 172.

[16]"ché in vero non si conviene e dispare assai vedere un omo di qualche grado, vecchio canuto e senza denti, pien di rughe, con una viola in braccio sonando, cantare in mezzo d'una compagnia di donne, avvenga ancorche mediocremente lo facesse, e questo, perché il più delle volte cantando si dicono parole amorose e ne' vecchi l'amor è cosa ridicula" (II, xii, 210). The stereotype of the old man in love of classical

comedy and a commonplace of the *commedia dell'arte* is viewed in such negative terms that anything that might be considered part of the courting process is forbidden to the old courtier. The fear of being a laughing stock is so great in the text that measures have to be taken in order to reduce or eliminate the risk.

[17]See Gilbert 7–32 and Jütte 259–90.

[18]"Ma di tutte le età la virile è più temperata, che già ha lassato le parti male della gioventù ed ancor non è pervenuta a quelle della vecchiezza" (II, xv, 213).

[19]II, xv, 212–13.

[20]"così in un vecchio è da estimare assai la vecchiezza verde e viva, perché pare che 'l vigor dell'animo sia tanto, che riscaldi e dia forza a quella debile e fredda età e la mantenga in quello stato mediocre, che è la miglior parte della vita nostra" (II, xvi, 214). Castiglione, in the preface to Book II, in the midst of so many negative statements about old age, had left open the possibility for precisely this type of development. The illusion that many old courtiers hold about the superiority of the past is seen as the fatal flaw that invalidates some of the positive qualities associated with old age: "la età matura, la qual con la lunga experienzia suol far nel resto il giudicio degli omini più perfetto" (II, i, 187).

[21]Cicero (ii, 4 , 12). See Beer 208–11.

[22]Cicero (iii, 7, 15). Cato is of the opinion that "the blame rests with the character, not with age" (iii, 7, 17). The conclusions that Cato draws from old men still desiring to act as sexual beings is apposite in any consideration of Morello da Ortona: "where lust holds despotic sway self-control has no place, and in pleasure's realm there is not a single spot where virtue can put her foot" (xii, 41, 51).

[23]Cicero (iii, 9, 17). Cato argues that intellectual qualities become more important in old age: "It is not by muscle, speed, or physical dexterity that great things are achieved, but by reflection, force of character, and judgement; in these qualities old age is usually not only not poorer, but is even richer" (vi, 17, 27).

[24]"Therefore, how can the pleasures of feasting, plays, and brothels be compared with the pleasures which these men enjoyed? But theirs was a zeal for learning" (xiv, 50, 61).

[25]"For spring typifies youth and gives promise of future fruits; while the other seasons are designed for gathering in those fruits and storing them away" (xix, 70, 83).

[26]For Castiglione's biography consult Cian, *Un illustre nunzio pontificio del Rinascimento. Baldassar Castiglione*; Dionisotti, Review of V. Cian, *Un illustre nunzio*; Kolsky, "Before the Nunciature: Castiglione in Fact and Fiction."

[27]Cf. Lanham 162.

[28]Cf. Rebhorn 51–52.

[29]"i pensieri e i modi dell'amor sensuale son troppo disconvenienti alla età matura" (IV, liv, 519).

[30]See Barbéri Squarotti 110–28.

[31]The following comment illustrates Equicola's lack of patience with Neoplatonic love and his adherence to a doctrine that does not deny sexual love, but places it at the centre of his concerns: "Non è cosa fuor di proposito respondere ad alcuni perfidi simulatori, li quali affermano impudentemente amarsi bella donna né oltrail viso e audito loro desiderio extendersi. Il che non è altro che disfare il regno de Amore ed extirpare la radice e soi veri fructi distrugere" (Equicola f. 214r).

[32]"Non po molto crescer in alto l'arbore al quale si permette che li rami latamente si spargano, così è necessario che per lo amor divino ogni altro amore si remova" (Equicola f. 234v).

[33]See Pozzi 151.

[34]Cf. Hager 38, 40–41.
[35]Cf. Floriani, "Idealismo politico" 162–63 and Javitch 42–46.

WORKS CITED

Barbéri Squarotti, Giorgio. *L'onore in corte. Dal Castiglione al Tasso.* Milan: Angeli, 1986.

Beer, Marina. "Le maschere del tempo nel *Cortegiano.*" *La corte e il 'Cortegiano,' I, La scena del testo.* Ed. Carlo Ossola. Rome: Bulzoni, 1980. 201–18.

Carella, Angela. "Urbino e le Marche." *Letteratura italiana. Storia e geografia.* Turin: Einaudi, 1988. II, I: 473–519.

Cian, Vittorio. *Un illustre nunzio pontificio del Rinascimento.* Città del Vaticano: Biblioteca Apostolica Vaticana, 1951.

___, ed. *Il libro del Cortegiano del Conte Baldesar Castiglione.* Florence: Sansoni, 1947.

Cicero. *De senectute, De amicitia, De divinatione.* Ed. E. Capps, T. E. Page, W. H. D. Rouse, L. A. Post, E. H. Warnington. London: Heinemann, 1964.

Dionisotti, Carlo. Review of V. Cian, *Un illustre nunzio. Giornale storico della letteratura italiana* 129 (1952): 31–57.

Equicola, Mario. *Libro de natura de amore.* Venice: Lorenzo Lorio da Portes, 1525.

Floriani, Piero. "Idealismo politico." *Bembo e Castiglione. Studi sul classicismo del Cinquecento.* Rome: Bulzoni, 1976. 162–63.

___. *I gentiluomini letterati.* Naples: Liguori, 1981.

Ghinassi, Ghino. "Fasi dell'elaborazione del *Cortegiano.*" *Studi di filologia italiana* (1967–68): 155–96.

Gilbert, Creighton. "When Did a Man in the Renaissance Grow Old?" *Studies in the Renaissance* 14 (1967): 7–32.

Hager, Alan. "Castiglione's Bembo: Yoking *Eros* and *Thanatos* by Containment in Book Four of *Il libro del cortegiano.*" *Canadian Journal of Italian Studies* 16 (1993): 33–47.

Javitch, Daniel. *Poetry and Courtliness in Renaissance England.* Princeton, NJ: Princeton UP, 1978.

Jütte, Robert. "Aging and Body Image in the Sixteenth Century: Hermann Weinsberg's (1518–97) Perception of the Aging Body." *European History Quarterly* 18 (1988): 259–90.

Kolsky, Stephen. "Making and Breaking the Rules: Castiglione's *Cortegiano.*" *Renaissance Studies* 11 (1997): 358–80.

___. "Before the Nunciature: Castiglione in Fact and Fiction." *Rinascimento* 29 (1989): 331–57.

Lanham, Richard A. "The Self as Middle Style: *Cortegiano.*" *The Motives of Eloquence. Literary Rhetoric in the Renaissance.* London: Yale UP, 1976. 162.

Maier, Bruno, ed. *Il libro del Cortegiano con una scelta delle Opere minori di Baldesar Castiglione*. 2nd ed. Turin: UTET, 1964.

Mazzacurati, Giancarlo. *Misure del classicismo rinascimentale*. Naples: Liguori, 1967.

Pozzi, Mario. "Mario Equicola e la cultura cortigiana: appunti sulla redazione manoscritta del *Libro de natura de amore*." *Lettere italiane* 32 (1980): 149–71.

Pugliese, Olga. "Castiglione's *The Book of the Courtier*: A Matter of Time." *Res publica litterarum* 5 (1982): 175–87.

Rebhorn, Wayne A. "Ottaviano's Interruption: Book IV and the Problem of Unity in *Il libro del cortegiano*." *MLN* 87 (1972): 37–59.

Ryan, Lawrence V. "Book Four of Castiglione's *Courtier*: Climax or Afterthought?" *Studies in the Renaissance* 19 (1972): 156–79.

Scarpati, Claudio. "Osservazioni sul terzo libro del *Cortegiano*." *Aevum* 66 (1992): 519–37.

Woodhouse, J. R. "Book Four of Castiglione's *Cortegiano*—A Pragmatic Approach." *Modern Language Review* 74 (1979): 62–68.

VI

Learning Virtue, Teaching Politics
Some Notes on Book Four of the *Cortegiano*

Book IV of the *Cortegiano* presents the topics of the rule of the prince and Neoplatonic love, material that had received little or no attention in the first three books. In the view of many who have read the fourth and last book of the *Cortegiano*, the introduction of such themes catches the reader unprepared and represents a major change of perspective from the courtier-centered discourse of the earlier books. By contrast, a small group of critics have tried to convince readers that there is not really any 'gap' or disjunction, that the fourth book represents a 'natural' progression from the earlier discussions.[1] Although there is some merit in this view, it will be argued that the transition from the earlier books to Book IV is not as smooth and free from ambiguity as the supporters of this line of thought would wish. There are disjunctions in the way the moral virtues, for example, are treated at different points in the text and these will be examined in this paper. Book IV will not be viewed as an 'aberration' in the *Cortegiano* nor as a completely logical culmination of the dialogues.[2] The present paper examines the discussions concerning love, the moral virtues, and princely power with reference to other key but relatively neglected Renaissance texts. The analysis has the twofold purpose of examining the relationship of these discussions to the rest of the *Cortegiano*, and, perhaps equally important, of testing their internal coherency and significance as statements on their topics.

Classical texts provided Castiglione with examples of how to structure his dialogues. Most of the attention of critics has focused on Cicero's *De oratore*.[3] However, this is not the only work of the Roman writer which served as a model for the *Cortegiano*. Cicero's last philosophical treatise, *De officiis*, is fundamental to Castiglione's text, not only because its contents offer a number of points of contact, particularly in the analysis of 'correct' behavior, but also because it seems to offer a way into the structural complexity of the *Cortegiano* that has so often perplexed readers. The treatise is educational in so far as Cicero purports to provide the necessary information for his son, Marcus, to succeed in life, though in practice it is a much wider ranging ethico-philosophical work about the moral virtues, their relationship to social life and to the notion of expediency. Cicero makes an important statement about the structure of *De officiis* which is particularly relevant to the *Cortegiano*:

> Every treatise on duty has two parts: one, dealing with the doctrine of the supreme good; the other, with practical rules by which daily life in all its bearings may be regulated.[4]

Cicero's description of the structure can be compared to the division of the *Cortegiano* into two (unequal) parts. According to this reading, the fourth book would be concerned with the "doctrine of the supreme good," literally because of Bembo's explanation of Divine Love, and more obliquely, because the moral end of the courtier is to advise the prince to rule virtuously. The first three books had been concerned with the 'practical rules' of court society. What is particularly interesting is that Castiglione reverses Cicero's ideal order so that the reader now moves from the particular, everyday behavior to more general, philosophical matters. As a result of this change, the reader remains partially unaware of the more general concerns and aims of the dialogues until the last book. If Cicero's structural proposition were adhered to, it would be crystal clear that the "practical rules" were grounded in and derived from a specific philosophical doctrine. Castiglione, in ordering the text in this manner, emphasizes the body as a semiotic medium in court life by means of which the courtier can aspire to a higher level of existence.[5]

Crucially, Cicero raises the problem of the relation between the two parts which foreshadows critical debate on the *Cortegiano*:

> But as regards special duties for which positive rules are laid down, though they are affected by the doctrine of the supreme good, *still the fact is not so obvious*, because they seem rather to look to the regulation of everyday life. (*De officiis*, I, iii, 7; pp. 9, 11; my emphasis)

Cicero had earlier stressed to his son the need for two distinct but related areas for attention in his social and philosophical development: "You should be fully equipped with the practical precepts [praeceptis] and the principles of philosophy [institutisque philosophiae]" [*De officiis*, I, i, 1; p. 3]. One can note again the emphasis on the two-fold division ('practical' and 'philosophical') of knowledge reflected in the binary structure of the treatise. Cicero's binary division is a helpful one for providing a coherent rationale for the structure of the final version of the *Cortegiano*.

Such a structure can be found in other Renaissance texts which insert court discourse within a grander design so as to validate court behavior. One such text is Mario Equicola's *Libro de natura de amore*, published in 1525. Its author, Mario Equicola (1470-1525), saw service at the court of Mantua in the period 1508-1525, and was personally acquainted with Castiglione.[6] The first draft of the *Libro de natura de amore* was probably begun in the 1490s, in Latin, and was subject to substantial and sustained revision until it was finally published in 1525.[7] Its subject-matter is germane to the *Cortegiano* since love and its practice at court (the "cortegiano amante") are of critical concern to both texts. Although the treatment of love in the respective works is quite different, there is an undoubted family resemblance: Equicola was deeply affected both by his experience of the court and by Neoplatonism, with which he had a problematic relationship. Ludovico da Canossa, one of the interlocutors of the *Cortegiano*, was highly embarrassed by the contents of the *Libro de natura de amore*, regarding much of it as 'obscene.'[8] In a sense, Castiglione rewrites Equicola's *Libro de natura de amore* eliminating its risqué and naturalistic elements. Equicola emphasized a naturalistic approach to love in which of all the senses touch is privileged. Castiglione is much more careful in his description of the courtier's love life: "il fin ancora di questo amore sarà virtuoso."[9] And in spite of some dissenting voices in the third book of the *Cortegiano* Giuliano de' Medici maintains the Neoplatonic hierarchy of the senses in relation to love by excluding physical contact.[10] In fact, the eyes, in accordance with poetic tradition and Neoplatonic thought, are privileged in Castiglione's vision of courtly love.[11]

Structurally, the *Cortegiano* and the *Libro de natura de amore* have much in common. The fifth book of the *Libro* is a discussion of the 'cortegiano-amante,' inviting comparison with Castiglione's text while the sixth and final book attempts to open out the text to a metaphysical interpretation of love, bringing in the presence of God and ennobling thereby the courtier's role and function. Thus, the last two books of the *Libro de natura de amore* offer a structural parallel to the *Cortegiano* but, more than this, they offer an insight into some of the problems facing a court writer who was trying to improve the reputation of court society and lay down theoretical and ideological foundations for its functioning.

Equicola, confronted by the polysemic possibilities of love, reduces them essentially to a 'realist,' physical view in which classical and Christian morality are used in Book VI to play down the corporeal elements in a last ditch attempt to offer a respectable image of love at court. The emphasis on the physicality of love is tempered by the introduction of reason which brings desire under control. Nonetheless, Neoplatonic terminology is misleadingly employed in order to emphasize the gratification of the senses:

> ma in amore sensuale sempre volemo le prime parti si diano alla belleza, como a quella che è potentissima causa di amore. Ma si como questa ad Amore dà origine et è suo fundamento così le virtù son quelle le quali lo confirmano e sustentano.[12]

Sexual desire and gratification enter into a paradoxical and ultimately ambiguous relationship with the Christian values of chastity and non-sexual love. While Book V of the *Libro de natura de amore* is more concerned with the behavior of the "cortegiano-amante" and the poetic representation of love rather than being a philosophical enquiry, Book VI represents a philosophical justification of court behavior ("fine de amore"). It does not deny as its basic premise the priority of sexual attraction, though it always has to be tempered by a higher goal. For this reason, Equicola prefers to employ the term "la voluptà" in the last book perhaps in the hope of gaining greater acceptability for his concept of love through association with Valla's notion of Christian "voluptas."[13]

Although Equicola's definition of *voluptas* offers a serial progression from physical to mental activities and thence to the spiritual, it is different from Castiglione's version of love in so far as it still places considerable emphasis on bodily pleasures, something that had the power to shock genteel courtiers of the kind found in the *Cortegiano*:

> Non è cosa fuor di proposito respondere ad alcuni perfidi simulatori, liquali affermano impudentemente amarsi bella donna né oltra il viso e audito loro desiderio extendersi. Il che non è altro che disfare il regno de Amore et extirpare la radice et soi veri fructi distrugere. (*Libro*, f. 214^{r})

The sixth book attempts to satisfy conflicting desires: a belief in the absolute necessity of sexual love and the need to represent women in the court system as chaste and, finally, to give a religious perspective to love, through the agency of the chaste woman to find love of God. What can be deduced from such a ramshackle structure is the obvious incompatibility of these desires. Thus, the reader can find the basic assertion of the desirability of physical love expressed in the strongest terms alongside an increasing desire in the last book of the *Libro de natura de amore* to offer a more acceptable version of love.[14]

The contradictions start to become insurmountable when Equicola places at the center of the last book an exhortation to women to be chaste. They are thus placed in the classic double-bind: objects of sexual gratification on the one hand, and the means to salvation on the other.[15] Equicola would have liked to have presented his schema as a natural, linear progression from sexual to divine love. However, there is little indication that the attachment to the senses is ever completely abandoned by the writer.

Castiglione does not have this problem to the same degree since he has ensured that the 'donna di palazzo' eschews any serious hint of physicality. His 'donna di palazzo' can stand at the center of Bembo's concept of Neoplatonic love much less problematically than Equicola's court women. As a result, the 'donna di palazzo' is part of the Neoplatonic ladder, even before Book IV.[16]

Castiglione has smoothed over Equicola's glaring inconsistencies by reducing physical contact between lovers to a minimum. By so doing, he makes the transformation to a Neoplatonic concept of love much easier. However, in spite of Castiglione's best efforts to integrate fully Bembo's discourse on Love into the previous discussions on the practice of love, there are some stresses caused by its presence in the text. Not the least is that Bembo's talk separates him from the other courtiers ("quasi pareva astratto e fuor di sé").[17] In fact, Bembo is literally 'carried away' from the other courtiers present. While it is not true that his speech has no effect on the rest of the company, the terms of its influence on them are heavily circumscribed: "e ad ognuno *parea quasi* sentirsi nell'animo una certa scintilla di quell'amor divino che lo stimulasse."[18] Emilia Pia's much discussed action of pulling at his robe introduces an element of physical contact that might be compared to the importance Equicola attaches to touch in his overturning of the Neoplatonic hierarchy of the senses. However, her action needs to be balanced against the real or imagined effect of Bembo's words which fleetingly create the image of completely rounded, spiritual courtiers.

The treatment of love in Books III and IV does form a coherent unity, in the sense that Book III deals with the young courtier whereas Book IV treats the older one. Such a division reflects the desire for the latter to have a fundamental role at court in spite of the fact that most of the activities in the earlier books would require the energies of a young man. The older courtier of Book IV builds on the experiences of his youth in order to appeal to an implied pleasure-loving prince. The question of age is used to separate logically the practice of love in Book III where it is expected that only a young courtier would participate and the Neoplatonic treatment of love which, as Bembo makes abundantly clear, is best suited to the older courtier who has learnt from experience and is ready to embrace a nobler form of love.[19] If viewed in this way, one can see a necessary progression between these two books of the *Cortegiano* in the matter of love. Paradoxically, Castiglione is at his closest on this point to the views expressed by the Hermit in Bembo's *Asolani*. The Hermit champions old age because it represents the period in a man's life free from the tyranny of the senses.[20] He makes a clear separation between youth and old age in these terms, much as Castiglione's Bembo does in the *Cortegiano*. However, in all other respects, Castiglione transforms Bembo's views of Love into something quite different from that expressed in the *Asolani*.[21] To such a degree, in fact, that Castiglione's Bembo could be regarded as a caricature of the otherworldly Hermit. It would appear that one of the aims of the *Cortegiano* was to demolish Bembo's authority as the author of two pioneering vernacular texts, *Prose della volgar lingua* and the *Asolani*. His position on the vernacular is openly challenged and replaced by a different theory, more oriented to the courts. His theory of love is also subtly subverted, using Bembo himself to revise it in a more Neoplatonic key. These two operations allow Castiglione to 'usurp' Bembo's primacy and replace the Venetian's *oeuvre* by the *Cortegiano*. It is no accident that the text frequently snipes at Venice and stresses the superiority of the court system over the Republican form of government.[22] Bembo's authority, both literary and political is first undermined, and then, he , as it were, capitulates to the courtly vision of the universe by becoming the spokesman for Neoplatonism in the text.

Bembo's speech is interrupted, at least in its early part, by the elderly courtier, Morello da Ortona. The whole of Bembo's discussion appears to be built on the premise that 'i pensieri e i modi dell'amor sensuale son troppo disconvenienti alla età matura' (IV, LIV; p.519). Morello is the object of a sustained attack as the symbol of a morbid attachment to earthly pleasures. He is the Equicola of the *Cortegiano* and has become a figure of fun for the other courtiers.[23] Yet, he fulfils the essential, but discredited function of making a case for sexual love.[24] Although Morello generally only provokes laughter, his objections to Neoplatonism are nevertheless serious and provide Bembo with the opportunity of launching his speech in praise of beauty and love. Morello attempts to turn Neoplatonic thought and terminology on its head: "-Il generar, - disse, -la bellezza nella bellezza con effetto, sarebbe il generar un bel figliolo in una bella donna" (IV, LXIII; p. 529). Bembo might laugh, but Morello's extreme 'realism' does have the effect of somewhat deflating the Venetian writer's rhetorically charged language and confronting him with a more 'commonsense' view of sexual love. Morello's interruptions can also be likened to Emilia Pia tugging on Bembo's cloak. Castiglione contains the threat to his universe by making Morello a courtier of little authority, both old and old-fashioned, but he does represent a coherent attempt to suggest the limitations of Neoplatonism for the court.

If the discussion on love in Book IV can be seen to have strong connections with that in Book III the emphasis on moral questions and on morality in Book IV has been seen by some critics as a new and unexpected development in the *Cortegiano*. While such issues are not ignored in the first three books of the *Cortegiano*, they are certainly not given full treatment in the earlier sections. The question of 'the good' and what constitutes the greatest good are mainly left to the last book of the *Cortegiano*. This strategy had left the reader of Books I-III with the impression that morality did not determine the courtier's behavior. He was more interested in concealing his real intentions, making a show of perfect courtierly comportment. However, there is a moment in Book I when it seems that moral questions will be considered.[25]

After discussing the 'vice' of affectation in Book I, Ludovico da Canossa rounds off this part of his talk by stating that such a defect has a deleterious effect not only on the body but also on the soul. One might think this would be an opportune moment to discuss 'higher' matters.

Canossa confesses defensively that "per ancor" the soul has not received much attention in their debates and the expectation is that it will now become a principal concern of the interlocutors: "né bisogna però lasciarlo" (I, XLI; p. 156). Canossa formulates the ritual response that the soul is more important than the body, a statement that will, in the course of this shortest of chapters (I, XLI), be severely tested. The adjectives Canossa uses to describe the soul "culto" and "ornato" seem to be equally suitable for bodily attributes and it is hard to escape the conclusion that the body is the main (and perhaps the only) concern of the interlocutor at this point in the text and for the first three books of the *Cortegiano*. It would appear that the nexus between bodily action and the soul, so valued by Christian thought, has lost much of its force here. Canossa seems to be paying lip-service to a fundamental element in the theory of human behavior from the Middle Ages onwards: the indisputable connection between physical comportment and the state of one's soul.[26] Although the soul appears to be the pivotal point of the discourse in this chapter, the questions associated with it are treated in a disparaging tone and not without a sense of irony; the discussion that began with an impression of urgency and a sense of duty to cover all possible ground is abruptly foreclosed by the "però di questo non ragioneremo più avanti" (I, XLI; p. 157). Ludovico da Canossa shows considerable hurry to pass over the complex discourses of professional philosophers on the soul, which would have entailed a rigorous taxonomy of the soul and its attributes, in order to deal with the courtier's knowledge of letters (the gerunds "lasciando," "attendendo" reinforce the impression felt by the reader of the lack of sympathy here for abstract, unpractical and self-consuming analysis). In fact, Ludovico sidesteps the whole matter by making his answer dependent on commonsense rather than on more complicated philosophical discussion. The courtier must be 'good' and to achieve that goal "gli bisognano pochi altri precetti" (I, XLI; p. 157), something that both Ottaviano Fregoso and Bembo will demonstrate is patently false if one takes a broader view of things.

There is an obvious attack by Ludovico da Canossa in chapter XLI on the wordiness and lack of practicality of philosophical writing on the soul, censored by the text with the words "così sottilmente" (I, XLI; p. 156) recalling the technical disputes of scholastic philosophers as well as Neoplatonist writers. It is pertinent here to recall Emilia Pia's objection to the use of a technical, scholastic language to talk about women (III, XVII).

Canossa employs everyday language, introduced by "come si dice" (I, XLI; p. 156) to differentiate it from the rarefied language of the philosophers. Thus, the courtier redefines the codes by which he acts by trying to create a new reference system based on the dominance of the body that avoids the traditional discourses of philosophical authority. The courtier is not without morality in his desire to become the prince's closest advisor (he is in possession of the cardinal virtues); it could be asserted that once the courtier has achieved this position of power his moral purpose is revealed, whereby the potentiality of his virtues are realized and made into the driving force of his role as counselor. However, such a position has a number of weak points which will be examined in the course of the discussion.

In short, the courtier must be an "omo da bene ed intiero" (I, XLI; p. 156), a rather vague and general statement that only obliquely makes reference to the more precise categories of moral philosophy. It is noteworthy that of the virtues rapidly reviewed by Castiglione "la prudenzia" (practical reason) is mentioned first to stress the practical nature of courtierly activity. Furthermore, the integrity of the courtier works against the ways in which traditional philosophy dissected the various attributes of the person. It is the primacy of action at this point in the *Cortegiano* that requires a unification of all the courtier's resources in order to succeed. Such a perspective is purposely reductive yet, at the same time, is radical in its possible consequences because the "vero filosofo morale" (I, XLI; p. 157) is equated with the courtier and his world instead of the "tanti savi filosofi" (I, XLI; p. 156) who are more interested in pure theory and intellection than the realm of practical action. The dictum "quel solo esser vero filosofo morale, che vol esser bono" (I, XLI; p. 156-57) exemplifies the pedagogical approach of the first three books of the *Cortegiano*. The statement just cited suggests that goodness is the principal aim of the "filosofo morale" and implicitly of the courtier, as this is one of his essential virtues. In this sense, the text posits the idea that learning the necessary steps to become good does not require a complex manual. Castiglione even employs the adverb "facilmente" (I, XLI; p. 157) to indicate that goodness is something given and understood by all. There is no need for excessively intricate educational rules for the purpose of creating a 'good' courtier. If you desire something enough, innate knowledge will help achieve it, or the courtier's will has the capacity to substitute pedagogical value with less defined, more compelling forces. Although the courtier bears a certain resemblance here to Cicero's "vir bonus", Castiglione seems to be offering a sop to conventional morality. If this chapter represents a partial explanation of the courtier's future behavior it is not solid enough to bear the full weight of the courtier's transformation into the *institutor principis* of Book IV.

The discourse in chapter XLI concerns the individual courtier and his choice of actions in the moral and social fields. The mention of Socrates might be seen to prefigure the function of the courtier as teacher, but no conclusions are drawn from it (I, XLI; p. 157). There is no question here of "l'esere boni" (I, XLI; p. 157) leading to the highest good, the Platonic *summum bonum*. Indeed, there seems to be no space for such a development in the text. This chapter does not, as it could have so easily done, lay the ground for the moral and political discussions of the last book, either implicitly or explicitly. All discussion is truncated here so that when the *Cortegiano* assumes a more abstract approach to the notions of virtue, morality and knowledge, later on, an awkward gap or discontinuity emerges in the text, in spite of the Ciceronian model of the *De officiis*. One explanation could be that chapter XLI is a 'relic' of the massive alterations to the text which saw the inclusion of Bembo's discourse on Love. Ludovico da Canossa's brief moral 'interlude' served as a provisional morality whereby the reader could rest assured that the courtier did have a moral framework in which he operated. Castiglione changed his mind about taking the moral discourse forward. The result is a rather weak link in the analysis of morality. It is true that the idea of 'being good' is capable of dramatic development, yet there is no hint in Book I that such a line will be followed. Indeed, the reader is given the opposite impression.

For a work so much appreciated for its artfulness as well as its artistry, the incongruity between chapter XLI of Book I and the opening of Book IV may well leave readers bemused. Are we meant to employ our understanding of the Aristotelian mean to try and work out some way of lessening the impact of the differences between practical and theoretical knowledge? Can they be considered complementary in the wider scheme of things? The contradiction may only be apparent in that the eternal search for unity can easily produce a binary model in which the active/contemplative paradigm or similar system serves as a means of binding together seemingly irreconcilable opposites. In spite of Aristotelian precedent, Book IV renders the moral discourse slightly 'unreal,' because of the distance between means and ends. The reader is required to integrate the moral ends with the courtly means as if there were no 'gap' or interruption. The generalized explanation of human behavior of Book IV is meant to contain within itself the proposed behavior of the courtier, to frame it completely, but what it does instead is to expose it, emphasizing the difficulties of implementing traditional moral values in court society.

Matteo Palmieri's dialogue *Vita Civile*[27] provides an interesting sounding-board for the Cortegiano's treatment of the moral virtues, especially since it comes from the very different social context of fifteenth-century republican Florence, and represents a more 'straightforward' way of analyzing and categorizing the moral virtues, more in keeping, perhaps, with the civic values it is seeking to inculcate.[28] The *Vita civile* will serve the function of putting Castiglione's discussion of the cardinal virtues into sharp focus. Indeed, Palmieri provides a convenient reference point to judge Castiglione's attitude towards certain aspects of vernacular civic humanism.[29] Such a comparison enables the critic to evaluate the subtle shifts in emphasis effected by Castiglione to accommodate virtue to the court and the court to virtue.

The fifteenth-century Florentine writer is at pains to point out the usefulness of the task he has set himself, that is, in the first place, to have made available in the vernacular the relevant classical authorities on political behavior and the virtues.[30] It is clear that for Palmieri the ancients are not meant to provide stylistic solutions to textual and existential problems but are ransacked for practical resolutions to problems inherent in contemporary life. The structure of Palmieri's text is important in this respect: books II and III are predominately concerned with the cardinal virtues which provide a general coherency and framework for the *Vita civile*. The final book on justice represents the culmination of his discussion of the cardinal virtues.[31] For Palmieri the cardinal virtues cover every aspect of personal and social life. The Christian and classical values incarnated in the four cardinal virtues give a sense of certainty to the action of men; there exists a clear correspondence between the concrete facts of human behavior and the abstract virtues — no crisis has yet appeared to create a gulf between particular and universal values.

The cardinal virtues themselves undergo profound changes in the first book of the *Cortegiano* with respect to their traditional typology. The most crucial of them, justice, is missing from Castiglione's original list in Book I, and is replaced by the less precise "bontà," innate goodness. The list will be rectified in the fourth book but, by then, the courtier will have been almost completely formed for action at the court and justice will take on a significance that seems to be restricted to the prince.[32] The alteration to the classical tradition is a striking one and full of consequences, especially if we remember how important it is to Cicero, who states in the *De officiis* that justice is the "crowning glory of the virtues... on the basis of which men are called 'good men'" (I, vii, 20; p. 21).[33] In the first book of the *Cortegiano*, Castiglione has replaced a universal, social virtue with one that operates on a vaguer, more individualistic plane. Justice appears to have no place in the life of the courtier; it is reserved solely for the prince. Thus, Castiglione maintains the focus in the first book on the courtier's individual morality without having to confront questions of political organization and public morality since no other meaning is given to his key words at this stage. The courtier is concerned with personal advancement which uses morality as one of its means. The slightly suspect air that hovers over the actions of the courtier is no way dissipated by his apparent adherence to the doctrine of the cardinal virtues. Palmieri's brief introduction to justice makes clear the difference from the first:

> Justitia, come regina et dominatrice di tutte l'altre virtù in sé qualunche di queste contiene. Di questa imperadrice delle virtù è proprio conservare le coniunctioni et amicitie degl'huomini, dare a ciascuno quello ch'è suo, et servare la fede nelle cose promesse. (*Vita civile*, II, 24; p. 64)

The function of justice, as defined by Palmieri, is to act as social cement, maintaining social order (the verbs "conservare" and "servare" stress particularly the necessity of social bonds between men). If justice can be considered the most over-arching of the virtues, its absence in Castiglione's list in Book I is all the more disturbing. It may indicate a desire to circumscribe the implications of the courtier's behavior, to ground them in the active present, leaving the moral direction rather vague, especially with regard to his interaction with other courtiers. The emphasis is therefore transferred from the traditional virtues with their clear Christian overtones to the more limited techniques of the body, described with such terms as *sprezzatura*. Castiglione is hinting at a changed perspective on social behavior which implicitly contrasts the court with republican models of political and social life.

Although the discussion of love and the treatment of morality, albeit severely limited in scope, are not absent from the earlier books of the *Cortegiano*, only in the case of the discussion of the amorous relationships between courtier and *donna di palazzo* would it be possible to state that the groundwork is laid for its later development. The treatment of morality, in contrast, develops in unexpected ways because it becomes closely related to politics. Book IV exudes maturity; its change of perspective opens out the text to social and metaphysical responsibility. The rest of the article will be concerned with an analysis of Castiglione's discussion of princely politics and the courtier's role in the education of the prince in order to elicit the principal lines of development and they will then be related to the earlier books of the *Cortegiano*.

The courtier acts as an informant who tells the prince about virtue. He renounces in a fundamental way the practice of a key virtue, justice, and is only concerned with its more general implications. Knowledge which informed all the actions and decisions that the courtier needed to take in the first three books of the *Cortegiano* plays an even greater role in the fourth book, taking on a more theoretical bent. For Cicero, knowledge ("sapientia") is the most important of the virtues: "For what, in the name of heaven, is more to be desired than wisdom? What is more to be prized?"[34] It is no longer just technical knowledge, but a moral and metaphysical understanding, not used for oneself, but for another, the prince:

> Però, come nell'altre arti, così ancora nelle virtù è necessario aver maestro, il qual con dottrina e bon ricordi susciti e risvegli in noi quelle virtù morali, delle quai avemo il seme incluso e sepulto nell'anima, e como bono agricultore le cultivi e loro apra la via, levandoci d'intorno le spine e 'l loglio degli appetiti, i quali spesso tanto adombrano e suffocan gli animi nostri, che fiorir non gli lassano, né produr quei felici frutti che soli si dovriano desiderar che nascessero nei cori umani. (IV, XIII; p. 462)[35]

The imagery of the seed eventually bearing fruit is a metaphor that underpins the whole of Book IV.[36] It serves a variety of purposes, not least amongst them being to describe the transformation of the courtier, his fruition as the instructor of a prince. The image underlines this transformation as natural, as the inevitable outcome of the skills the courtier has acquired in the earlier books. Book IV can be described as the fruit itself, the flowering of which depends on what has been planted before. Yet, while it is to a degree a natural phenomenon, the image cited above places considerable emphasis on human intervention, on the necessity of knowledge and skills to bring about the maturing of the seed into ripe fruit.

The dominant phenomenon of the courtier's comportment is the slippery concept of "sprezzatura," almost despising of 'moral' behavior. "Sprezzatura" is characterized by an insistence on "nasconder l'arte" (I, XXVII; p. 126) and the courtier's progress in general is dependent on "ingegno ed arte" (II, XXXII; p. 241). Its closeness to deception confirms the suspicion in the reader that "sprezzatura"/"arte" have connotations of amorality. "Virtù" is still considered an "arte" in Book IV, but the emphasis on "sprezzatura" is no longer present because the aims are now different. Virtue is defined as "una prudenzia ed un sapere eleggere il bene" (IV, XIII; p. 463). It represents an attempt to give a moral basis to action: "e la virtù, per la quale elegemo quello che è veramente bene" (IV, XIV; p. 463). The "maestro"-courtier teaches both technical skills and moral knowledge. Therefore, the text makes a clear connection between the skills learnt earlier in the *Cortegiano* and their application now to the moral area. The simile employed to define the master is itself drawn from the realm of applied science. The "bono agricultore" has a specialized knowledge (the adjective "bono" is ambiguous, relating both to moral qualities and technical expertise). The philosopher is not intended to be an abstract personality but someone with practical skills whose aim is to ensure the maximum level of achievement in his disciples, an Aristotle or a Plato, as defined in the final version of the *Cortegiano*. Whereas Aristotle tutored Alexander, one of the greatest rulers, Plato, had little success with Dion of Syracuse who could be described as a 'paese sterile' (IV, XLV; p. 505) and no amount of cultivation would produce any tangible improvements.[37]

Virtue is a question of knowledge, but knowledge grounded in practice, as underlined by the term "una prudenzia." Castiglione's definition of virtue underscores such a conception of social life: "però la virtù si po quasi dir una prudenzia ed un sapere elegere il bene" (IV, XIII; p. 463). In this connection, Palmieri's definition of the same term is worthy of examination since it has a number of points in common with Castiglione's usage.

The fifteenth-century Florentine writer emphasized the dichotomy between knowledge and the lack of it:

> tutti gl'huomini, secondo loro natura, desiderono sapere et essere veri cognoscitori di tutte le cose, acciò che per loro ignorantia non conseguitono alcuno errore dove con vergogna siano ingannati. (*Vita civile*, II, 30; p. 65)

Castiglione condemns ignorance much more absolutely and cuttingly than does Palmieri who tends to emphasize the effect of social sanction rather than moral conflict between good and evil. Palmieri defines what Castiglione assumes in the use of his terminology:

> si dice essere proprio del prudente sapere bene consigliare di tutte le cose che sieno laudabili et utili all'universale governo del buono et iusto vivere; et diffiniscono prudentia essere habito vero che con ragione examini et intenda tutte le cose che sono agl'huomini bene o male; simili huomini sono stimati attissimi a' governi delle republice et di qualunche cosa privata. (*Vita civile*, II, 31-32; p. 65)

Palmieri could not be more precise on the use of "prudentia," stating that it is "proprio uficio dell'huomo prudente sapere ben consigliare" (II, 33; p. 66). Castiglione appears to have grasped this notion and made it his own, placing it in the context of the court and the courtier-prince relationship. Thus, Castiglione's moral virtues are quintessentially political virtues. The practices of Books I and II define a social model which is politicized in the course of Book IV. The social space becomes very much restricted in Book IV (a one-to-one relationship with the prince), excluding the uninitiated public performance aspects of the court. The conquest of this new 'princely' space entails a process of separation from the illusory world of the court as theater towards an intimate nexus with the world of power (ideological, theological, political), bringing in its wake a radical change of perspective.

Through the intermediary of the courtier-counselor moral knowledge is brought to bear on princely rule. The problem is that contemporary rulers as a group receive a rather bad press in the *Cortegiano*, although a small number of individual rulers fare better. The use of the conditional tense throughout Ottaviano's discourse on the prince underscores the hypothetical nature of the advice and also the insinuation that it has not yet been possible to actually advise a prince in this manner. The situation is further complicated by the fact that Castiglione, hoping for a beneficent reign, often refers to specific rulers in the future tense, but this hope appears to have dissipated by the final draft of the *Cortegiano*.[38] The example of Federico Gonzaga, who inherited the Gonzaga state in 1519 after the death of his father, the Marquis Francesco Gonzaga, is a good illustration of the point. In the *Seconda redazione*, Federico Gonzaga is referred to as a "fanciullo" (he was born in 1500) — in any case he was not yet ruler of Mantua. The praise of Federico would appear to correspond with Castiglione's desire to re-enter Gonzaga service in 1516.[39] Thus, he is given the highest possible role that a prince could have in contemporary Italy — its savior:

> onde penso che non solamente nel dominio suo, ma in tutta Italia abbia da rinovare il secol d'oro, del qual già tanto tempo fra gli uomini non si vede più reliquia.[40]

Ludovico da Canossa attempts to raise the stakes by comparing the young Federico to Alexander the Great as a young boy. The comparison, therefore, posits Federico as a possible force for the revitalization of the Italian states. By the time of the 'vulgata' all these suggestions have been completely dropped and replaced by a much briefer and vaguer encomium of the now older ruler (IV, XLII; p. 501). The obvious conclusion that can be drawn is that Federico Gonzaga had not lived up to expectations. And indeed, Castiglione had already left his service by the redaction of the last draft of the *Cortegiano*. The reader who is aware of the historical situation might consider Castiglione's admonitions to the prince to be unworkable idealism in the same way as Plato's *Republic*, which was the reason for the introduction of the example of Federico (Frigio had expressed grave doubts on ever finding a prince as described in Book IV).

Castiglione may be implicitly acknowledging the failure of the humanist rhetoric of the good and bad prince and the difficulties of forming a morally responsible ruler. A power beyond morality is Castiglione's fear and his desperation is increased by the fact that such power can make its own rules, depend upon itself and not seek advice from the courtier-counselor of the type outlined in Book IV. That is why the "maestro"-courtier has a conspicuous political dimension. Indeed, the project of the text is to make the intellectual a man of action; in terms of Renaissance philosophy to operate a synthesis between the active and contemplative lives, not only in accordance with canons of balance and harmony, but in order to influence the operation of power.

Castiglione's courtier is forced to recognize the realities of power that at times may deconstruct the ideal, Christian model of rulership. All the lessons of the first three books seem to end in nothing as soon as the courtier is confronted with the realities of absolute power and his own powerlessness. The triumphs of the body in books I-III are not entirely mirrored by the triumphs of the mind in the fourth book. Control of the body politic is much more difficult than governance of one's physical body. Courtiership may have its successes but cannot resolve the basic premise of unequal power.

The early chapters of Book IV allude to the errors of contemporary princes who are so full of themselves that they cannot take advice. This is the unsurmountable problem of the text: if the rulers are not interested in becoming good princes, then, even with all the courtier's attributes, it will be impossible to make any impact. Indeed, this problem was earlier raised by Calmeta who implied that contemporary princes chose questionable courtiers for their intimates (II, XXI; p. 222). The only option for a courtier was to leave the 'bad' prince.[41] Book IV, VII raises the issue in an acute form: the "signori" (p. 459) of the first line are left anonymous, but must surely include the rulers of the Italian city states. Although the word is not mentioned specifically here, such "signori" have become tyrants who are not open to the counsels of their humanist advisers. Castiglione applies to them expressions of excess ("tanto," "talmente") in order to stress that the princes are not behaving reasonably and are hence closed to rational argument, "inebbriati")—their behavior is uncontrolled and perhaps uncontrollable. The writer equates a thirst for absolute power with a desire for absolute, unrestrained pleasure and the use of force to maintain power. Xenophon's dictum from the *Memorabilia*, 'It is not, then, cultivation of wisdom that leads to violent methods, but the possession of power without prudence,' sums up Castiglione's attitude to the proper use of power by the prince.[42] It is no surprise to find the term *disciplina* cropping up in this chapter (IV, VII) on the failings of the Italian princes, including the structures of thought on which their reigns are based:

> e perché credono che 'l saper regnare sia facilissima cosa e per conseguirla non bisogni altr'arte o disciplina che la sola forza. (IV, VII; p. 453)

"La sola forza" implies the absence of discipline/restraint on the political and social levels whereas controlled political behavior would lead to the discovery of the correct equilibrium in society. Castiglione makes it clear that the tyrant acts out of ignorance, puffing himself up with a false sense of infallibility, fatal to Castiglione's project of the empowerment of the courtier. Castiglione seems to frown on grandeur of any kind which is considered dangerous to the political well-being of the state: "perché la ignoranzia loro accompagnata da quella falsa opinion di non poter errare, e che la potenzia che hanno proceda dal lor sapere, induce loro per ogni via, giusta o ingiusta, ad occupar stati audacemente, pur che possano" (IV, VII; p. 454). The use of "loro" lends a note of scorn to the writing, singling out those princes who have espoused political aggrandizement and its concomitant breaking of moral and social rules. Such an attitude vividly contrasts with Machiavelli's naturalization of the process in *Il principe*. For Castiglione, statal aggrandizement activates imbalance and change, and signals tyranny. Thus, a shift in the ideological priorities of contemporary rulers would halt the decline of the Italian city states. Castiglione rejects the politics of magnificence and grandeur as guiding-forces in human affairs. These excesses, as Castiglione sees them, have to be brought under control. This is the role of the courtier-counselor, to challenge the course of contemporary European history.

Ignorance is the principal vice that Castiglione's courtier-educator fights in the final book of the *Cortegiano*.[43] The emphasis on learning is apparent throughout the text — the acquisition of skills being a vital part of the courtier's apprenticeship to power. Letters are considered to be the equal of "la bontà" in the first book.[44] That is a remarkable statement if it were not for the fact that they are used as the primary instrument to enlighten the prince. The moral virtues are necessary to the courtier in so far as they concern a right use of knowledge, to ensure the good government of the prince. Thus, Book IV is intimately tied in with the rest of the *Cortegiano* through its insistence on the link between knowledge and power, either on a personal or a state level. The shift in perspective is brought about by the change in the arena. The courtier first of all uses knowledge to gain access to power and then to moderate that power. Cesare Gonzaga challenges the entire structure of Book IV by putting forward an opposing version of the prince (IV, XXXVI; pp. 491-94). It represents a positive image of the contemporary prince so harshly dealt with elsewhere in Book IV. Cesare Gonzaga puts the case for magnificence being the dominant force in the construction of princely rule. He emphasizes *maiestas*, princely splendor, magnificent building programs and the like. There is no mention of care for one's subjects. Ottaviano Fregoso has no qualms about calling such rulers tyrants. Such an attitude underlines the radical nature of the call to reform of the last book of the *Cortegiano*. It moves against the grain of princely magnificence to suggest a reform of the prince's behavior based on a renewed sense of moral leadership.

The prince's control of the state, its operation for the 'good' of its subjects, is the mirror-image of the courtier's own self-control, not allowing irrational desires to dominate the body. Thus, an underlying theme which binds together the two 'sections' of the *Cortegiano* can be summed up in the term self-restraint or to use the more technical term "disciplina," control of the body to indicate superior mental abilities. All excess is banished from the world of the perfect courtier. Each sign that is emitted from the courtier's body has to persuade everyone at court of his ability, his capacity to integrate and paradoxically to be recognized as exceptional. The nemesis of order for the court is "pazzia," both on a personal and public level, signaled by loss of control, failing to understand the fundamental rules of behavior. Ottaviano explicitly uses the term "pazzia" to refer to the excesses of the ideology of magnificence:

> però è ragionevole che 'l principe ponga mèta ai troppo suntuosi edifici dei privati, ai convivii, alle doti eccessive delle donne, al lusso, alle pompe nelle gioie e vestimenti, che non è altro che uno augumento della lor pazzia. (IV, XLI; p. 500)

The prevalent tendency to excess is criticized by Castiglione on the personal and organizational levels, producing a uniformity of purpose in the *Cortegiano*, rendered complex by the range of activities in which the courtier becomes involved. If it is true, as has been argued by some critics, that the last book represents the culmination of the preparation that the courtier had received up to that point, there are some problems with this view, particularly the transformation of the courtier from someone made for pleasure to someone whose sole interest is now the morality of the state. Obviously, such a transition cannot be completely smooth as the perspective has largely altered: from the courtier's performance before the court to his ability as a teacher. The fourth book itself makes a strong case for a smooth transition of roles and functions (IV, IV-VI; pp. 449-53). Whether the readers believe the text is crucial to their interpretation of the *Cortegiano* as a whole. However, the Aristotelian mean is perhaps meant to be employed in navigating the problem of the fourth book. "Arte" and "disciplina" determine the behavior of individuals and of the courts themselves as political entities. It is these elements that lend a coherency to the text in spite of moral inconsistencies which might have undermined the construction of the courtier as a humanist educator. Unity is not uniform; there are grey areas. But granted the circumstances of the courtier whose authority is not a given, then the rules enunciated in the first three books are considered vital to his achievement of political influence. If such a step is 'natural' for the politically ambitious courtier, it does produce certain discontinuities that weigh heavily on the meaning of the *Cortegiano*. One of Castiglione's most innovative maneuvers is to introduce Plato and Aristotle as courtiers into Book IV of the final version. They had not fulfilled this role in the *Seconda redazione*. Indeed, both philosophers had been examples of the "severo filosofo" (III, VIII; p. 193), exactly the opposite of the case that will be put in the printed text.[45] Castiglione, therefore, reinvents them as courtier-philosophers who are no longer severe, but use courtierly skills, such as dancing, to try and influence the prince to the good. The combination of the two philosophers is suggestive of the structure of the new Book IV. More importantly, Plato and Aristotle now represent a union of court skills and philosophy. Unity of the text is achieved through the juxtaposition of Aristotle and Plato. In this ultimate act of the imagination Castiglione points to the necessary coherence of the *Cortegiano*. It is perhaps also an act of desperation which does not altogether convince the other courtiers and the reader. The introduction of these illustrious 'courtiers' does not resolve all the question-marks hanging over the text, however, it underlines the fact that the writer himself was aware of the discontinuities and gaps in the *Cortegiano* and wished to smooth them over. He was only partially successful.

[1] For an overview of the problem and the relevant bibliography see Eduardo Saccone, *Le buone e le cattive maniere. Letteratura e galateo nel cinquecento* (Bologna: Il Mulino, 1992), pp. 68-70. Saccone himself is of the opinion that the 'problem' has been created by the critics, particularly Burckhardt. J. R. Woodhouse had earlier put forward the view that "the whole of the *Cortegiano* is a build-up, as it were, to the two climaxes now reached in Book IV, the political advice of Ottaviano Fregoso and the spirituality of Pietro Bembo's discourse" (*Baldesar Castiglione. A Reassessment of 'The Courtier'* [Edinburgh: Edinburgh UP, c. 1978], p. 147), modified later in his "Book Four of Castiglione's *Cortegiano* — A pragmatic approach," *Modern Language Review*, 74 (1979), pp. 62-68, which explains the changes and additions in terms of Castiglione's biography. Fundamental to the view that Castiglione did his best to ensure coherence to the text is Lawrence V. Ryan, "Book four of Castiglione's *Courtier*: Climax or afterthought?," *Studies in the Renaissance*, 19 (1972), pp.156-79. Wayne A. Rebhorn, *Courtly Performances. Masking and Festivity in Castglione's 'Book of the Courtier'* (Detroit: Wayne State UP, 1978), pp. 177-204, argues that in spite of the obvious gulf between the two parts of the *Cortegiano* "a conflict of ideas cannot really impair the unity of Castiglione's book, for the substance is the wedding of ideals and personalities, not merely one or the other, and Castiglione celebrates that wedding consistently from beginning to end" (p. 199). The view that the text is fragmented and contradictory is strongly urged by Amedeo Quondam in his introduction to *Il libro del Cortegiano* (Milan: Garzanti, 1981), pp. XXV-XXIX, XXXVI. Piero Floriani had already referred to the "crisi strutturale" of the *Cortegiano* with the addition of Book IV (*Bembo e Castiglione. Studi sul classicismo del Cinquecento* [Rome: Bulzoni, 1976], pp. 122, 153). Simon Friedman, "The unity of Castiglione's *The Courtier*," *Studies in the Humanities*, 6 (1979), pp. 26-29, argues both for and against the unity of the *Cortegiano* depending on how vital one thinks Bembo's speech on love is to the entire work.

[2] The order of topics in Book IV also contributes to this impression, suggesting a break in the continuity of the text. Politics is interposed between the discussions of love in Books III and IV.

[3] See, for example, Floriani, *Bembo e Castiglione*, pp. 132-39; Daniel Javitch, *Poetry and Courtliness i n R enaissance England* (Princeton, N.J.: Princeton UP, 1978), pp. 23-49.

[4] The translation is by Walter Miller in the Loeb edition of Cicero, *De officiis* (London: Heinemann, New York: Macmillan, 1913), p. 9 (Bk. I, iii, 7). The discussion of the cardinal virtues, including practical reason, provides the philosophical backbone of the treatise. Against the practicalities of everyday existence, the attempts to win popularity and the like, Cicero sets higher goals: "We must realize, however, that while we have set down four cardinal virtues from which as sources moral rectitude and moral duty emanate, that achievement is most glorious in the eyes of the world which is won with a spirit great, exalted and superior to the vicissitudes of earthly life" (*De officiis*, I, xviii, 61; p. 63). Thus, it can be seen that Cicero is striving to construct a relationship between behavior and basic philosophical values.

[5] The courtier adopts certain techniques which allow him access to the prince and to an exceptional religious experience. Cicero, in the *De officiis*, focuses on how the discipline of the body is essential for the "vir bonus" to perform his duties: "And yet the body must be trained and so disciplined that it can obey the dictates of judgment and reason in attending to business and in enduring toil" (*De officiis*, I, xxiii, 79; p. 81).

[6] For Equicola's biography see Stephen Kolsky, *Mario Equicola. The Real Courtier* (Geneva: Droz, 1991), pp. 103-226.

[7] On the composition of the *Libro* see I. Rocchi, "Per una nuova cronologia e valutazione del *Libro de natura de amore* di Mario Equicola," *Giornale storico della letteratura italiana*, 153 (1976), pp. 566-85; Kolsky, *Mario Equicola*, pp. 244-46. See also Giorgio Barbéri Squarotti, "L'amante cortigiano" in *L'onore in corte. Dal Castiglione al Tasso* (Milan: Angeli, 1986), pp. 110-28.

[8] See Mario Pozzi, "Mario Equicola e la cultura cortigiana: appunti sulla redazione manoscritta del *Libro de natura de Amore*," *Lettere Italiane*, 32 (1980), p. 151.

[9] All references to the *Cortegiano* are to *Il libro del Cortegiano con una scelta delle Opere minori*, a cura di Bruno Maier (Turin: UTET, 1964, 2ª edizione) and will take the form of book, chapter and page number[s]. Here, III, LIX; p. 422.

[10] "[The courtier] ragionevolmente devrà contentarsi d'ogni minima demostrazione, ed apprezzar più da lei un sol sguardo con affetto d'amore, che l'esser in tutto signor d'ogni altra" (III, LVII; p. 420).

[11] "Però ben dir si po che gli occhi siano guida in amore" (III, LXVI; pp. 429-30).

[12] Mario Equicola, *Libro de natura de amore* (Venice: Lorenzo Lorio da Portes, 1525) 4°, f. 164ᵛ.

[13] See Stephen D. Kolsky, "Theorizing pleasure in the Renaissance," *Spunti e ricerche*, 4-5 (1988-89), pp. 41-42.

[14] "Non refutemo la voluptà de sensi quanto substentatione de natura et nostro bene esser rechiede. Siamo in voluptà de l'animo per le scientie et intellecto et congiongendola con la operatione de la virtù morale procuremo divenire religiosi che per questa strada con guida de amore ascenderemo alla vera felicità" (*Libro*, f. 209ʳ⁻ᵛ).

Equicola never quite moves away from a bodily perspective on love, becoming increasingly desperate to make his concept of love more respectable: "Fine del vero amore et d'ogni amore et d'ogni actione et d'ogni operatione de mortali, deve esser tal termine che ne induca ad considerare che per beneficio di essa sanità potemo usar longamente la voluptà de li sensi integramente et in piacere honestissimo con gloria et honore tradure la vita" (*Libro*, f. 220ʳ).

[15] *Libro*, f. 222ʳ. If Equicola at times utilizes Neoplatonic terminology he is far away from the spirit and sense of Florentine Neoplatonism. Indeed, his use of Neoplatonic language often appears to be a way of rendering sexual love more acceptable: "La cosa dunque laqual amando appetimo et per laqual ne commovemo con desiderio usarla a nostro arbitrio con delectatione dicemo esser principalmente donna che formosa existimiamo" (*Libro*, f. 222ᵛ).

[16] See also Joseph D. Falvo, *The Economy of Human Relations. Castiglione's 'Libro del Cortegiano'* (New York: Peter Lang, 1992), who also argues for the pivotal role of Book III in initiating a changed perspective on court life: "...it is a long road that takes the courtier from the courtly games of love described in Book I and II to the experience of mystical love celebrated at the end of Book IV. At mid-point, the more serious role of women in society and the mature teaching profession of the courtier become a significant link of these two opposite poles." (p. 91). The image of the road obviously implies unity of structure. In my interpretation twisting and bumpy, and sometimes the bitumen even disappears from view!

[17] *Cortegiano*, IV, LXXI; p. 541.

[18] IV, LXXI; p. 541 (my emphasis).

[19] Equicola offers a 'scientific' view on the age of lovers, referring to sexual activity: "Questo intendemo in homini quali non habiano passati li quaranta anni perciò che poi quella età il sangue si refreda, il che cognobe Horatio quando disse: 'Non haver gelosia di colui che la età sua se è affrettata finire li octo lustri" (*Libro*, f. 214^{v}).

[20] "A' quali se la vecchiezza non toglie questi disii, quale più misera disconvenevolezza può essere che la vecchia età di fanciulle voglie contaminare, e nelle membra tremanti e deboli affettare i giovenili pensieri?" (*Gli Asolani* in *Prose e rime di Pietro Bembo*, a cura di Carlo Dionisotti [Turin, UTET, 1966 2nd ed.], p. 490). Morello seems to fulfill this role of the old man still subject to his passions in the *Cortegiano*. On which see Stephen D. Kolsky, "Old men in a new world: Morello da Ortona in the *Cortegiano*," in *Italica*, 75 (1998), pp 330-47. The crucial difference between the *Asolani* and the *Cortegiano* on this point is that the Hermit sees no merit whatsoever in youth because of the dominance of sexual urges: "Per la qual cosa dire si può che sanità della nostra vita sia la vecchiezza e la giovanezza infermità" (*Asolani*, pp. 490-91).

[21] See Guido Arbizzoni, *L'ordine e la persuasione. Pietro Bembo personaggio nel 'Cortegiano'* (Urbino: Quattroventi, 1983).

[22] Bembo defends the republican form of government (IV, xx; p. 471), only to be rebuffed by Ottaviano Fregoso ("Contra la opinione vostra..." [IV, xxi; p. 472). There is a joke in the text that refers to the Venetians' lack of horsemanship (for example, II, lii; p. 271), part of an on-going dispute which focuses on which region has the greater potential for leadership.

[23] "...e parmi che 'l possedere questa bellezza, che esso tanto lauda, senza 'l corpo, sia un sogno" (IV, LV; p. 520). Cf. Alan Hager, "Castiglione's Bembo: Yoking *Eros* and *Thanatos* by containment in Book four of *Il libro del Cortegiano*,"*Canadian Journal of Italian Studies*, 16, n. 46 (1993), pp. 40-41.

[24] See Annick Paternoster, "Il teatro della retorica non-apparente. La struttura del dialogo nel *Cortegiano*," *Lingua e Stile*, 26 (1991), pp. 35-55.

[25] Ludovico da Canossa seems embarrassed by the subject-matter and hurries over it as quickly as possible: "diremo in poche parole, attendendo al nostro proposito" (I, XLI; p. 156).

[26] S ee J ean-Claude Schmitt, *L a raison des gestes dans l'occident médiéval* (Paris: Gallimard), pp. 66-71.

[27] Matteo Palmieri, *Vita civile*, edizione critica a cura di Gino Belloni (Florence: Sansoni, 1982). For a brief discussion of the text in relation to the *Cortegiano* see Eugenio Garin, *L'educazione in Europa (1400-1600)* (Bari: Laterza, 1957), p. 157. For a general survey of Palmieri consult George M. Carpetto, *The Humanism of Matteo Palmieri* (Rome: Bulzoni, 1984).

[28] J.R. Woodhouse, Baldesar Castiglione, pp. 38-58, vigorously argues the opposite case that fifteenth-century educational humanism forms part of a tradition on which Castiglione draws in a relatively uncomplicated manner.

[29] See the perceptive comments of Floriani on Castiglione and Palmieri, *Bembo e Castiglione*, pp. 144-46.

[30] Palmieri wished to perform a useful service to his fellow citizens by making available concepts and precepts of the classical world: "rivolto poi verso i mia carissimi cittadini, in me medesimo mi dolsi, molti vedendone che, disiderosi di bene et virtuosamente vivere, sanza loro colpa, solo per non avere notitia della lingua latina, mancavano d'inumerabili precepti che molto arebbono giovato il loro buono proposito" (p. 5).

[31] "Questa [iustitia] per se stessi è quasi perfecta virtù, et è sufficiente a fare gl'huomini buoni, però che è servandissima delle buone leggi, et iusto è colui che vive secondo quelle" (III, 10; p. 105).

[32] "Appresso gli mostrarei che delle cure che al principe s'appartengon la più importante è quella della giustizia" (IV, XXXII; p. 487). Thus, it is no longer a 'personal' virtue as were the others listed for the courtier, discussed above.

[33] Cicero defines justice as preventing "one man from doing harm to another" and a correct use of public and private property (I, vii, 20; p. 23). In moral terms "the foundation of justice...is good faith — that is, truth and fidelity to promises and agreements" (I, vii, 23; p. 25).

[34] *De officiis*, II, ii, 5; pp. 171, 173.

[35] Plutarch employs farming imagery in his *De liberis educandis* to make the point about virtue being learnt (*Moralia*, 2B-C, 4C, 8B). Plutarch also stresses, in common with Castiglione, the need to suppress the passions through learnt virtue in order to produce a being characterized by self-control and reason. See Vittorio Dini, "Dalla pedagogia delle virtù alla virtù della pedagaogia. Arti, disciplina, virtù morali nel passaggio alla modernità" in *Sapere e/è potere. Discipline, dispute e professioni nell'università medievale e moderna. Il caso bolognese a confronto. Atti del 4° convegno. Bologna, 13-15 aprile 1989*, vol.3 — *Dalle discipline ai ruoli sociali*, a cura di Angela De Benedictis (Bologna: Comune di Bologna, Istituto per la Storia di Bologna), pp. 37-51.

[36] See, for example, IV, IV, p. 450 ("altro frutto"); IV, V, p. 451 ("il vero frutto della cortegiania"); IV, XXXVI, p. 492 ("il frutto delle fatiche ed azioni del cortegiano"); IV, XLV; p. 505 ("abundantissimi frutti"); IV, LVII, p. 522 ("bontà dei frutti"); IV, LXII, p. 529 ("frutti di bellissimi costumi").

[37] “Come ancor indarno s’affaticaria ogni bono agricultore che si mettesse a cultivare e seminare d’ottimi grani l’arena sterile del mare” (IV, XLV; p. 505).

[38] Frigio states with regard to the young Federico Gonzaga who was seven years old at the fictional date of the dialogues: “pregaremo Dio di vedere adempita questa vostra speranza” (IV, XLII; p. 501). No mention is made here of the role of the courtier-instructor.

[39] See Stephen D. Kolsky, “Before the nunciature: Castiglione in fact and fiction,” *Rinascimento*, 29 (1989), pp. 348-49.

[40] *La seconda redazione del* Cortegiano*di Baldasarre Castiglione*, edizione critica per cura di Ghino Ghinassi (Florence: Sansoni, 1968), III, XLIII; pp. 229-30. Cf. Ryan, “Book four of Castiglione’s *Courtier’*,” pp. 166-67.

[41] See Virginia Cox, *The Renaissance Dialogue. Literary Dialogue in its Social and Political Contexts, Castiglione to Galileo* (Cambridge: Cambridge UP, 1992), pp. 51-52.

[42] *Memorabilia*, trans. E.C. Marchant, (London & Cambridge, Mass.: Heinemann & Harvard U.P., 1953), I, ii, 10-11.

[43] Guicciardini makes similar comments on the harmfulness of ignorance as an obstacle to rational rule: “ma la ignoranzia non avendo né fine, né regola, né misura, procede furiosamente e dà mazzate da cechi” (Francesco Guicciardini, *Ricordi*, edizione critica a cura di Raffaele Spongano, Florence: Sansoni, 1951, p. 181 [C168]).

[44] “Ma, oltre alla bontà, il vero e principal ornamento dell’animo in ciascuno penso io che siano le lettere” (I, XLII; p. 157).

[45] “E di queste cose in Alessandro fu autore Aristotile, usando i modi di bon cortegiano” (IV, XLVII; p. 508). In fact, Aristotle is contrasted with Callisthenes who is regarded as a “così austero ministro” (p. 509). Rebhorn, *Courtly Performances*, takes the side of Gasparo Pallavicino who is rather skeptical about the philosophers as courtiers (p. 182).

VII

DID MARIO EQUICOLA WRITE *IL NOVO CORTEGGIANO*?

The work that bears the title *Il Novo Corteggiano de vita cauta et morale* was first attributed to Mario Equicola by Domenico Santoro, the author of the sole full-length monograph that has so far appeared on Isabella d'Este's tutor and secretary [1]. His reason for doing so was his discovery of a copy of this work on which « una mano non moderna » had written that the anonymous *Novo Corteggiano* was in fact composed by Mario Equicola who is referred to as the author of the *Natura d'Amore* [2]. The person who made this attribution does not seem to have been a contemporary of Equicola's to judge by the necessity he must have felt of having to qualify who exactly Equicola was in terms of his best known work [3]. Even though the evidence for attributing the *Novo Corteggiano* to Equicola is really only circumstantial, his claim has been taken up with a vengeance by D. E. Rhodes who strongly urges the reader to accept him as the author of this tract if only for the simple reason that he cannot see a more suitable candidate [4]. Adriano Prosperi also sees Equicola as the most probable author, though he does have some nagging doubts which force him to leave the question open-ended [5]. C. Dionisotti, on the other hand, has greeted the suggestion much more coolly [6].

Until, if ever, documentary evidence turns up, no final and absolute decision about the authorship of the *Novo Corteggiano* can be made. The purpose of this brief contribution to the discussion is not to put forward another candidate, rather it is to ascertain whether Equicola was, indeed, the author of the work in question. Conse-

1 D. SANTORO, *Della vita e delle opere di Mario Equicola*, Chieti 1906, pp. 110-111, 144-148; in particular p. 144. The present writer has recently completed a doctoral thesis for the University of London entitled *Mario Equicola: A biographical Reappraisal* (1981).

2 D. SANTORO, *Della vita e delle opere*..., cit., p. 144. According to D. E. Rhodes, the *Novo Corteggiano* was printed around 1530, that is, five years after Equicola's death (see note 4).

3 The first edition of this work bears the title *Libro de natura de amore* but in the following year (1526) it has already been changed to *Libro di natura d'amore* (cit. *Libro*).

4 D. E. RHODES, *Whose new courtier?*, in *Cultural Aspects of the Italian Renaissance*, C. H. Clough, ed., Manchester and New York 1976, pp. 370-376.

5 A. PROSPERI, *Libri sulla corte ed esperienze curiali nel primo '500 italiano*, in *La corte e il « Cortegiano »*. II, *Un modello europeo*, edited by the same, Roma 1980, pp. 69-72. Prosperi finds the attribution of the *Novo Corteggiano* to Equicola « non inverosimile ma priva di solidi fondamenti » (p. 70). Nevertheless, one has the feeling that Prosperi is cautiously urging us to accept Equicola as the author « come pure fanno pensare certi riecheggiamenti di altri suoi scritti » (p. 70). Prosperi does not take into account passages in the *Novo Corteggiano* that seem, at first sight, to correspond to sections of the *Libro*, but on closer examination, turn out to express exactly the opposite of what Equicola intended in his own work.

6 C. DIONISOTTI, *Gli umanisti e il volgare fra quattro e cinquecento*, Firenze 1968, pp. 112-113. Writing of the various problems facing a student of Equicola's works, Dionisotti states that « e le minori sono o di estrema rarità, o di tarda o dubbia tradizione (*Istitutioni*), o addirittura, come il fondamentale, chiunque l'abbia scritto, *Novo cortegiano de vita cauta e morale*, insieme rare, tarde e di dubbia autenticità » (p. 112, n. 1).

quently, it will be necessary to determine how far the opinions expressed in the *Novo Corteggiano* (as well as the style and language of the text) are in accordance with what we know about Equicola's views from the works that are surely his. It is true that Equicola himself does refer to a work that he composed concerning « quali habiano ad essere le parti di colui, il qual di bon cortigiano pò meritare il nome » [7]. But, whether the work in question is the *Novo Corteggiano* is open to discussion. Even Rhodes has had to admit that Equicola's brief description in the *Libro* does not really correspond with the contents of the *Novo Corteggiano* [8]. The problem becomes yet more confused the moment we begin to examine the contents of the treatise because we find that substantial portions of the *Novo Corteggiano* correspond to parts of the *Libro*, or vice-versa, depending on which work is considered to have been written first. This problem may be seen to arise because in the *Novo Corteggiano* there is hardly any mention of Neoplatonism, a philosophy that dominates the *Libro*. To explain this omission, one could argue that the *Novo Corteggiano* is one of Equicola's earliest works written before he had come in contact with Neoplatonism. However, when one examines Equicola's earliest surviving works we find an Equicola full of enthusiasm for the classical world, overloading his texts with every possible reference to classical philosophies, including Neoplatonism, especially in his work *De Religione* where Christianity is seen as a natural successor to the ancient religions, something alien to the train of thought of the author of the *Novo Corteggiano* [9]. Because of Equicola's attitude towards the vernacular Dionisotti argues that it would have been impossible for the work to have been written before 1508, that is, during the period of the composition of the *Libro* [10]. This does not exclude the possibility that the text as we have it is a translation from the Latin in the same way as the *Libro* is supposed to be. If there were any lingering doubts as to whether Savonarola were the author of the work, as has sometimes been suggested, this correspondence between the final version of the *Libro* and the *Novo Corteggiano* practically rules him out since he would have been alive only when Equicola was preparing the very first draft of the *Libro de natura de amore* in Latin [11].

We can now draw up a number of hypotheses concerning the composition of the *Novo Corteggiano*: (i) The work is an earlier version of the *Libro* which Equicola revised in parts for the later book. (ii) Equicola wrote his study of the « courtier » at the same time as he was working on the *Libro*. (iii) The *Novo Corteggiano* is not by Equicola but he used parts of it before it was printed in the elaboration of the *Libro*. (iv) Both the *Libro* and the *Novo Corteggiano* depend upon an unknown work as a common source. (v) The work is the product of an unknown writer who borrowed passages from the *Libro* to use for his own purposes in the *Novo Corteggiano*. Owing to the

---

[7] D. Santoro, *Della vita e delle opere...*, cit., pp. 144-145. The contents of the *Novo Corteggiano* are not very helpful in elucidating what Equicola exactly means when he states that this work « si espose al grido del volgo et maledicentia de invidi, preponendo al paterno nido il pubblico » (p. 145). In purely biographical terms, it may refer to his employment in the service of the Cantelmo clan and his subsequent rôle as a diplomat-secretary instead of remaining in his native village with his family. Equicola's reference to a work on courtiers may also be an attempt at demonstrating that his analysis of the theme pre-dates Castiglione's first thoughts on the same subject. In any case, the figure described in the *Novo Corteggiano* bears hardly any resemblance to the courtier as described in the *Libro* (cfr. A. Prosperi, *Libri sulla corte...*, cit., pp. 70,71, and L. Savino, *Un precedente del Cortegiano*, « Rassegna critica della letteratura italiana », XV (1910), pp. 102-122).

[8] D. E. Rhodes, *Whose new courtier?*, cit., pp. 374-375.

[9] *De Religione. Oratio dicta Papiae 1498* (Ferrara: Lorenzo de' Rossi, not before 1498), 4°.

[10] C. Dionisotti, *Gli umanisti e il volgare...*, cit., p. 113.

[11] A. Prosperi, *Libri sulla corte...*, cit., p. 70.

lack of external evidence we will have to rely on internal and examine, in particular, those parts of the *Libro* and the *Novo Corteggiano* that are shared in common.

If we were to accept either the first or second hypothesis, namely, that Equicola is the author of both texts, then, we have to confront some real difficulties of interpretation. In the second case we are faced with the acute problem of having to explain why the *Novo Corteggiano*, on a number of occasions, expresses views that run contrary to his longest and most firmly held beliefs. To suggest that Equicola wrote both works simultaneously would require an Equicola torn apart by moral conflict to such an extent that the *Libro*, intended as his intellectual testament, was not « orthodox » enough and had to be corrected by the *Novo Corteggiano*. According to this hypothesis, the *Novo Corteggiano* would represent a change of heart, an ironic reappraisal of his situation. In order to assess the likelihood of such a change, it will be necessary to examine the nature of the differences between the *Libro* and the *Novo Corteggiano*. The fourth hypothesis remains pure conjecture until the common text can be proved to exist. However, the essential point to note is that even if a common text were found, the two works in question still represent different, often conflicting, world-views. Thus, it is the interpretation of his text which would still be the most important matter for the scholar to examine.

First of all, the writer of the *Novo Corteggiano* indicates the methods he has employed in composing his work:

« Et tanto più che non havendo celebrato tutti gli authori né anchora alcuno authore in tutte le parti, habbiamo atteso più alla verità de le cose che allo ossequio et compiacimento de gli homini. Et se scrivendo non abbiamo addutto sempre gli authori né assignato i luoghi alle sententie è stato non già per nostra arroganza né anchora per sottrarci alla fatica ma perché habbiamo istimato più utile il mostrare la essemplarità al vivere che il porgere la occasione al contendere perché leggemo che alcuni havendo voluto locare con ordine distinto tutte le cose che non meno sarebbon state le prefationi che le sustantie » [12].

The writer becomes even more forthright in his views on the correct intellectual line to take and it seems as if he is assuming a polemical position with regard to the *Libro*:

« Confessiamo hora noi medesimi che sì come la parte maggiore de tutte le humane lettere, così il più de le nostre fatiche sia manifestissimo furto il quale si cono-

---

12 *Novo Corteggiano*, fs. A2v-A3r. This passage constitutes a further attack on Equicola's methodology. Equicola is always concerned with listing the variety of opinion that is to be found on any particular matter. Equicola feels that it is the duty of a humanist to record all the conflicting views even if it renders the task of reaching a single solution that much more arduous. The « proemio » to the *Libro* puts forward the principle as something basic to Equicola's thought: « oltra che ancho a niuno sin qui è stata sì benivola la fortuna che dalle opinioni sue molti non habbian dissentito et che non trovi chi contro a lui dica. Donde vedemo philosophice sette, medici, historici esser fra sé contrari et li Theologi istessi in alcune cose non concordi. Né da altro (come credo) questo procede, se non da soverchio amore che alla verità si porta » (*Libro*, f. 3v; I am using the 1526 edition *Libro di natura d'amore*, Venezia, Gioanniantonio & Fratelli de Sabbio, 1526. If indeed, the *Corteggiano* were published in 1530, then this linguistically revised version would have been most likely used by the unknown writer and this version of the *Libro* enjoyed several editions after this date so as to make it the standard edition rather than the idiosyncratic first edition).

scerebbe se non che gli habbian posto altra maschera et altra ghirlanda in cappo che quella che egli si havesse prima »[13].

It should be remembered that Equicola takes almost to the point of obsession his concern over identifying the sources of his information in all the works that are positively written by him. From his first published work until 1525, the year of the publication of the *Libro* and the year in which he died, his method is constant. He *never* seems to have had the slightest intention of renouncing his humanistic training, however unfashionable his own particular brand may have become and whatever doubts he may have had about its applicability to new social situations. Indeed, it gives him great pleasure to show off his immense learning. The author of the *Novo Corteggiano* possesses a different set of priorities which place the emphasis on the moral imperative rather than on intellectual integrity. For Equicola, his humanist methodology is his very life-blood and the least likely to be denied. In fact, he expresses the exact opposite of the statement just quoted above in his most important work:

« Io istimo in niuno esser così freddo et congelato il cuore che essendo in manifesto furto di lett[e]re accolto non se li diffonda il sangue et dimostre per la faccia, potendo esser con ragione dinanzi al tribunale delle Muse citato et costretto a restitutione, como usurpatore dell'altrui fariche et quasi spogliatore di corpi sepolti »[14].

The position of this statement, right at the beginning of the *Libro* (it, in fact, forms the opening lines of the « proemio » to Book I) is indicative of the paramount importance Equicola gives to this concept, whereas the *Novo Corteggiano* represents an open disavowel of such a line of thought. The author of the latter work readily admits to the unoriginality of his and at times goes even further:

« Et se così scrivendo parrà per avventura ad alcuno che ostentiamo troppo le cose nostre, sarà cosa veramente da parerci strana, savendo noi quanta riverenza portiamo a esse cose nel referirle. Ma, rivolgendoci a noi stessi conosciamo i nostri scritti, non per la qualità de le sententie perché sono d'altri, ma per la nostra forse imperitia et inculto Iddioma esser per avventura dignissimi de gli altrui biasmi. Et così diamo a nostri detrattori, in questa parte, ragione »[15].

Although the number of classical references in the *Novo Corteggiano* has been drastically reduced compared to the *Libro*, whenever a passage has an unusually high number of classical allusions it will almost certainly correspond to a passage from the *Libro*. Thus, the « sententie » of the *Corteggiano* are not only the original thoughts of classical writers but, more importantly, are the results of a careful reading of the *Libro* in which these « sententie » appear.

One of the most striking features of the *Novo Corteggiano* lies in the fact that the court, the most obvious place for a courtier, is hardly ever mentioned and when it

---

13 *Novo Corteggiano*, f. A3r. Partially quoted in A. PROSPERI, *Libri sulla corte*..., cit., p. 71, n. 5. In this passage the writer indirectly acknowledges that he has changed, perhaps considerably, his original sources, thus, making them difficult to recognise.

14 *Libro*, f.3r.

15 *Novo Corteggiano*, f. G2r. The writer adds that even though his style may have some defects it should not affect the content of his work because « l'amorevole integrità de l'Animo nostro devrebbe pienamente sopplire là dove sono manchevoli i nostri scritti » (f. G2r).

is the author condemns it (perhaps this is one of the meanings of « novo » in the sense of strange or surprising):

« Ma perciò guarda (volendo tu haver parte con essa virtù) che non procuri ismisurate ricchezze, soperbi theatri né splendide vestimenta perché quinci insorgono veneree delitie, illecite coniugationi et altre enormi vanità »[16].

The very essence of court life is seen as evil, as running contrary to Christian values. Perhaps Equicola is not so very far from this position as we might, at first, think. The Equicola of the *Libro* is caught between two opposing forces: the first sees the court as the centre of a particular culture which he finds interesting and worthwhile (he urges his courtier to take part in the theatrical activities of the court), whereas the second casts doubts on the morality of court life, particularly towards the end of the *Libro*. But never does the court disappear from Equicola's thinking. If one considers the fourth hypothesis to be the most likely, then these considerations would help to explain the attractions of Equicola for a more « orthodox », reformist writer. The author of the *Novo Corteggiano* disregards any part of the *Libro* which refers to the court and its culture. For example, the number of references to poetry is minimal. Dante is cited a number of times in his role as a « religious » poet. « Il celeberrimo Petrarca » is mentioned on a single occasion, but not with regard to his achievement as a poet. It is as a Christian humanist that he finds his place in the *Corteggiano*[17]. There is no room for the frivolity of love poetry; the « pleasing » aspects of the *Libro* have disappeared, to be replaced by a greater emphasis on the « utile et honesta ». « Ben vivere » becomes « honesto vivere ».

At this point, it will be necessary to examine in more detail the fourth hypothesis which gains in credibility when we take into consideration the fact that the anonymous writer seems to have had at his disposal more than one source for his work: the sections that deal with the state in the *Novo Corteggiano* do not correspond to any passages in any of Equicola's known works, let alone the *Libro*. In fact, when the anonymous writer at various points in the book breaks in without warning and addresses a young man to whom he proffers advice, one has the distinct impression that a completely different text is being utilized[18].

The question now arises about how the passages taken from the *Libro* are used in the text. The author of the *Novo Corteggiano* does not simply take a particular passage from the *Libro* and transfer it whole to his own work. Often he makes small changes, usually of a grammatical nature, nor does he limit his interventions on the text to this kind of « correction » but actively interferes with the meaning of Equi-

---

16 *Ibid.*, f.A4r. The writer emphasises the limits that must be placed on worldly pleasures: « ma cerca tutte le honeste delitie (ma, intendi questa parola, honeste) » (f. F2r).

17 « Et gli atti estrinseci dil povero non ascrivere all'intimo dil suo animo perché, come scrive il celeberrimo Petrarca, il poverello digiuno viene ad atto talhora che in meglior stato l'hauria in altrui biasmato » (fs. K3r-K3v). That the writer also introduces the poor into his work is a departure from the closed world of the court, as described in the *Libro*, where they are totally escluded. Although Equicola has no illusions about the difficulties of court life he never feels able to offer an alternative unlike the author of the *Corteggiano*: « anchora ne gli indomiti monti vi è alle volte più a grado il vivere che ne' tumulti dela Città » (f.G4r).

18 « Et tu, specialmente, o giovane ardito, al favore de la inviolabile virtù appoggia la tua trabocchevole giovinezza » (f.A5v).

cola's words. Thus, the argument that because we find passages from the *Libro*, the *Novo Corteggiano* must have been written by Equicola is not so strong as at first sight appeared. One should note that the first chapter after the « Prologo » concerning the « Regole de la Vita » contains a number of echoes of the sixth book of the *Libro*. It is interesting that the sixth book is used first (if not very systematically) because in the fabric of the *Libro* it had the function of lending an air of orthodoxy and perhaps respectability to the work as a whole by ending on a note of Christian belief so as to leave a strong impression of pure Christian faith which the reader would have found difficult to locate in the rest of the work. In this section Equicola papers over the contradictions of court life by an appeal to the Christian faith, and by itself the sixth book may have seemed to be a reasonable Christian response. However, the author of the anonymous work was unable to accept even the sixth book as it stood. Changes were rendered necessary because of the different intellectual stances of the two writers. Thus, while most of the *Libro* seeks in theory, at least, to penetrate the « nature » of things the *Corteggiano* acknowledges right from the start the impossibility of such a desire:

« Sforciandoci sempre de interserirvi alcuna cosa curiosa a contemplatione de gli animi inquieti i quali de più divina ambrosia non si nodriscono che di gire per le ardue speculationi, tanto peregrinando et sormontando che vengano a transcendere (benché impossibile sia) alla somma et assoluta contemplatione de la natura de le cose » [19].

However, in the sixth book Equicola comes close to this point of view when he recommends an ironic attitude towards life, untroubled by too radical an intellectual approach. Thus, the *Corteggiano* embroiders and emphasizes the conclusions of a passage which in a different form is to be found in the *Libro* (Equicola himself is paraphrasing Lucian). The anonymous writer adds to Equicola's passage to emphasize the point even more forcefully: « perchè se la Arithmetica non ti vale a calcular le cose brevi et finite meno ti varrà misurar le immense et a scrutar l'infinite » [20]. He operates seemingly minor changes within a single sentence but which completely change the emphasis. For example, Equicola had written: « non attendere ad altro che star ben nel presente et di ogni altra cosa ridere » while the other text has « né attende ad altro che a star ben nel presente con honestà confidandoti in Dio ne l'avenire et d'ogni altra cosa tu ridi ». Apart from the minor grammatical changes involved, such as removing the latinate construction « ridere » which is replaced by « tu ridi », there is in the second text the introduction of an element absent in Equicola's version — God. Equicola suggests, on the contrary, the attitude someone should take up faced with fleeting reality (« io giudico che del tutto ci debbiamo ridere »). This reality is Equicola's reason for turning to God who represents for him a refuge from the world of the senses which is about to betray him through the onset of old age:

« Consideremo il tempo datoci esser brevissimo...

---

19 *Ibid.*, f. A4r.

20 *Ibid.*, f.A7r-A7v. Immediately following this sentence in the *Corteggiano* we read « né dar fede ad argomenti né a silogismi perché tutti sono furori et arroganze d'homini » (f.A7v) which has an equivalent in the *Libro*: « non dar fede a sillogismi et argumentationi che son pazzie » (f. 207r).

Consideremo il termine del nostro vivere esser incerto, nostre speranze fragili le quali in mezzo 'l corso sono spesse volte interrotte. Più che la sanità cosa alcuna non si desidera ».

The *Novo Corteggiano* offers the reader a paraphrase of this section but without any reference to good-health, a concern of someone who tenaciously hung on to the pleasures of life in spite of his declarations:

« perché se consideri alla brevità della vita depressa in tante pernitie et al termine di quella incerto et alle speranze fragili le quali in mezzo il corso divengono sì sovente interrotte. Conoscerai haverai tempo da effunder tempo » [21].

The message of the *Novo Corteggiano* is less ambiguous than that of the *Libro*: there do not seem to be any regrets or ambiguities about its Christian message. This Christian conception of life provides the framework within which the writer can place other suggestions about the conduct of one's life. He warns against social-climbing of the kind that is likely to force you to become a leader of one sort or another:

« Fuggi anchora la sommità de gradi perché essendo breve la vita de suditti, più breve de Reggi et brevissima de Pontifici » [22].

Equicola is emphatic about the necessity for his courtier to reach the highest position he can:

« Peggiore è lasciarse cadere da suoi meriti che ponersene in più alto luogo che non si deve » [23].

In dealing with the problem of social relations the author of the *Novo Corteggiano* borrows heavily, so it seems, from Equicola's *Libro di natura d'amore*, particularly in the section « De Amicitia ». For his definitions of friendship the unknown writer has recourse to the chapter of the *Libro* entitled *Amor dell'huomo all'huomo.* Here, one can note the reduction of classical references compared to Equicola's text and a general tightening up of the grammar and syntax. If we may take an example, first of all, from the *Corteggiano*:

« Onde mai non fu homo tanto preclaro che uno si elleggesse col quale communicasse et le cose meste et le liete et le gravi et le giocose » [24].

Equicola begins in almost exactly the same way, but then continues with a list of classical examples not to be found in the *Novo Corteggiano*:

« Mai fu homo preclaro che uno non si eleggesse col quale et le cose gravi et giocose, liete et meste potesse securamente communicare. Dicono li antiqui Theseo

21 *Libro*, f. 207r; *Novo Corteggiano*, f. A7v.
22 *Novo Corteggiano*, f.E3v.
23 *Libro*, F.147v.
24 *Novo Corteggiano*, f.C1v.

et Pirithoo, Hercole et Philotete, Pilade et Oreste, Achille et Patroclo. Li due Scipioni hebbero li due Lelii, Alessandro Magno Ephestione. Di Damon et Pithia le carte son piene »[25].

In Equicola's mind the classical ideal of friendship, as exemplified by the attitude of the Roman Emperor Augustus, had been destroyed by many of his more powerful contemporaries who, although Christians, treated everyone as slaves:

> « E intanto ascesa la superbia de Prelati et Signori che in le sottoscrittioni de lettere a loro vedemo servo et schiavo »[26].

In the *Libro* the mention of the words « servo et schiavo » leads Equicola, as if by a natural reflex, to discuss their etymological origins:

> « Il primo facemo ad imitatione de Mori che in Spagna serviano; il secondo de Spagnoli. Il nome schiavo è venuto da Schiaveni popoli in Scithia »[27].

It is obvious that there can be no place for this sort of digression in the *Novo Corteggiano* where the writer would not want to detract from the power of « his » statements about the corruption of the times by adding some trivial academic notions on etymology. There is one major difference between the two texts in the ordering of their respective sections on friendship. The *Novo corteggiano*, instead of beginning the section « De Amicitia » with reference to Biblical examples and dogma, as in the *Libro*, leaves this particular line of enquiry right to the end of the chapter. The writer hopes by this ruse to end on a Christian note, given that the section had been more than usually full of references to classical culture:

> « Et quantunque ne' precetti mosaici diffusamente cosparsi, sia anchora diffusamente iscritto come si deggia amare il prossimo suo ciò è havere Carità, non di meno, così in tale sola parola, come in tutti essi precetti, si contiene tutta la Phylosophia, tutta la dottrina hebrea, tutte le ammonitioni prophetiche et tutti gli Apostolici documenti. Et intorno a questo cardine si rivolge tutta la integrità de la Vita, perché in questo mandato è la plenitudine et osservatione de tutte le leggi et la irrefragibile perfettione dela Salute »[28].

The chapter « De Amore » preaches against « amore eccessivo » which does not contradict Equicola's theories of « mediocritas »[29]. However, the « Osservatione in Amore » opens up a gulf between the two works, principally because this chapter is a compendium of « set-pieces » found scattered throughout the *Libro* and not a coherent philosophical doctrine. The anonymous writer takes over Equicola's attack

---

[25] *Libro*, f.103v.

[26] *Ibid.*, f.104r, and *Novo Corteggiano*, f.C1v.

[27] *Libro*, f.104r.

[28] *Novo Corteggiano*, f.C3r. The equivalent passage in the *Libro* reads: « confessiamo adunque "ama il prossimo tuo come te stesso" non esser nelli precetti Mosaici espressamente, ma in li nostri. Et dicemo in questo solo precetto continerse tutta la philosophia, dottrina hebrea, prophetice ammonitioni, apostolici documenti et ogni christiana verità circa questo cardine rivolgersi. Percioché in questo mandato è tutta la plenitudine et osservantia della legge et ogni abondantia de gratia » (*Libro*, f.100r).

[29] This chapter occupies fs. C3v-C4v.

on the work of « la gran turba » of « versificatori » without specifically mentioning the fact that his examples are taken from poetry. Indeed, the writer enjoys this satirical assault so much that he even adds examples of his own:

« Come veggiamo i sciocchi amanti attribuire di continuo alle loro bagascie moti divini, costumi angelici, portamenti celesti, atti regii, sembianti adorni, gesti da humiliare il tigre, parole da far tranquillo il mare, sguardi da serenar le tempeste, lamenti da far piangere i sassi, suspiri da far arder Giove » [30].

He next describes what constitutes true beauty in a woman; this too has been lifted out of the *Libro* without any reference to the framework of Neoplatonism of which it forms a part [31]. The author of the *Novo Corteggiano* is much more interested in those sections of the *Libro* that seem to have direct social implications and Equicola's philosophical bent has no appeal and is, indeed, replaced by specific social comment.

In order to discuss the relations between lovers our writer copies out verbatim the paraphrase Equicola himself had made of Alberti's *Ecatonfilea* in the *Libro* [32]. This writer does not avail himself of the sections of the *Libro* that deal specifically with these relations in terms of the court. Instead, he prefers to follow the rules of a Florentine, perhaps because he is more inclined to civic Florence than the courts. One can say categorically that the entire subject-matter of the *Libro*, that is love, has been reduced to a shadow of its former self: « virtù » replaces « amore » as the key factor in the *Novo Corteggiano*.

The social element in Equicola's work is, once again, seized upon by the unknown writer in the chapter entitled « De Modestia » in which advice is given about how to present one's image in society adapted from Equicola's own « sententie » on the question. Equicola had written:

« Benché fussero dignissime le lodi di M. Tulio nondimeno perché a quelli a cui eran note, spesso le repeteva, era non meno fastidio et odio il suo consulato che la congiuratione di Catilina » [33].

It seems that the unknown writer has done everything possible to avoid mentioning Cicero, the inspirer of the humanists, in his version of the passage:

« Et benché i meriti de gli homini fossero dignissimi de tutte le laudi; non di

30 *Novo Corteggiano*, fs. C4v-D1r. The equivalent passage in the *Libro* is to be found at f.4r which offers a number of variants; for example, in the *Libro* the adjectives are placed before the nouns. The last three examples in the *Corteggiano* are not to be found in the *Libro*; they have presumably been added by the writer who has imitated Equicola's examples. The distance that separates the author of the *Novo Corteggiano* from the courtly ideals of Mario Equicola is clearly underlined by his uncomplimentary reference to the recipients of love-poetry as « bagascie ». These women who for Equicola and Castiglione represented the essence of court life are now reduced to mere prostitutes who have forsaken the Christian life of married women or of chaste virgins.

31 *Ibid.*, f.D1r-v = *Libro*, fs. 18v-19r. Eauicola himself is here paraphrasing Boccaccio. There are again some changes in the syntax and vocabulary, for example, we find « disgiunte » (f. Dr) instead of « divise » (f.18v).

32 *Novo Corteggiano*, f.D2r = *Libro*, f.27v-28r; *Novo Corteggiano*, f.D2v-D3r = *Libro*, f.159r-159v.

33 *Libro*, f.150r.

meno il rememorargli a cui già son noti non meno è lor fastidio et odio che la Congiuratione de Cathilina »[34].

After « De Modestia » the book pursues a new line which does not depend on the *Libro* as its source until the very last chapter. However, certain attitudes emerge from these intervening chapters which make us doubt very much that Equicola could have been responsible for their composition or compilation. First of all, the two works offer opposing attitudes towards fate and destiny. The author of the *Libro*, even at the end of a troubled life, can still be optimistic about man's power to control his own destiny: « ciascuno è della sua fortuna artefice ». Another typical statement is Equicola's belief that « il savio alle stelle domina et la prudentia ne può governare »[35]. The *Novo Corteggiano* offers no such faith, rather, a stoic acceptance of things:

> « È offitio de l'Animo virile esser sempre cauto et provido contra gli insulti de la fortuna, et di poi, usato ogni provedimento possibile, cedere alla perversa ostinata et ogni aversità che segue, in silentio sopportare et in pace »[36].

On another plane, the *Novo Corteggiano* is more overtly political than the *Libro*. It is addressed to all those who in one way or another control the events of the Italian peninsula. One just has to recall the chapter « Memoriale al sommo Pontifice » in which the Renaissance Popes are castigated for the discredit they have brought on the Church:

> « Tu dei sommamente avvertire che ad attingere alla occupatione di tanto seggio tu non sia impulso più dal livore de l'Animo et da l'Ambitione che da lo affetto di Dio et dal zelo de la salute de gli homini »[37].

Such advice to the pope and other comments on the corruption of the clergy explain why the author wished to remain anonymous[38]. What particularly interests the writer is the theme of corruption in all its social forms. In addition, he is critical of all those

---

34 *Novo Corteggiano*, f.D3v.

35 *Libro*, fs. 193r and 119r.

36 *Novo Corteggiano*, f.E4r.

37 *Ibid.*, f.N4v. The Papacy is further attacked for losing sight of its own dignity and behaving like any other temporal power: « hai apparato l'uso de le lascivie, de decori somptuosi et de le richezze ismisurate et prophane. Onde (quanto a noi paia) puossi al tutto tener per vero chel di che Constantino arrichi Sylvestro » (f.01r). Closely connected to this theme is the idea of the « renovatio » in the form of a crusade: « onde possiamo conchiudere che per exacrabili obbietti sia hoggimai pretermessa al tutto la speranza di ricovrare il Sepulcro et il Nazarethe di Cristo » (f.01r). Equicola had himself written a work exhorting the Christian Princes to recover the Holy Land (*Marii Aequicolae de bello Turcis inferendo suasoriae tres*, 1519). This theme had by Equicola's time become common-place and it provided a good way of releasing any guilty feelings about one's lifestyle or about humanism. The author of the *Novo Corteggiano* probably understood the temptations to which Equicola had succumbed and saw in the *Libro* a half-realized attempt to save himself. Equicola could not and would not throw away all the achievements of his existence. However, the writer of the *Corteggiano* was prepared to complete the necessary task and consign court life to the devil (the republican way of life was the only one acceptable to a Christian).

38 Such assertions as « maggiormente a tempi nostri ne' quali quasi ogni spiritualità se n'è ita al Cielo et in terra è rimasto corrotto l'offitio et la già pura iurisditione de la chiesa catholica ne' moderni pastori » (f.03v), made his anonymity essential and it helps to explain his method of hiding behind other people's works to make detention even more difficult.

types of government that esclude too great a proportion of the « people ». Rule by one man is against nature, so a republic is considered the best kind of government:

« Et tu pari amministratore de la Republica, essendo (come anchora ogni spirto ingenuo è sforciato da innata legge di essere) nemico del privato Imperio et ansio de la publica libertà » [39].

Those in office are urged to do everything in their power « per non lasciar giognere la republica a singulare signoria » [40]. It is difficult to believe that even in his most pessimistic moods Equicola could have expressed such conviction for a republican way of life.

Interestingly enough, the last chapter of the *Novo Corteggiano* corresponds, in general terms, to the last book of the *Libro*. Though there are important alterations, Equicola's final analysis of the human condition is still considered valid and his emphasis on « voluptà » finds its precise echo in the other work. As we have already stated, throughout the *Novo Corteggiano* its author always tries to reduce Equicola's prolixity and endless lists of examples. Thus, if we read the following passages from book six of the *Libro*:

« Diogene pose il fine distintamente: obedire alla ragione in eligere le cose che sonno secondo la natura, Archedemo quasi il medesmo, Cleante pigliò la natura commune, li Stoici de natura difensori sono più tosto differenti nelli vocaboli che nelle sententie. Da li vecchi Academici et Peripatetici è nominato quel bene che è secondo la natura. Quel vogliono esser male che è contra. Né solamente Chrisippo questo diffese, ma M. Tullio mi pare da questa opinione non sia alieno » [41].

The corresponding passage in the *Corteggiano* strikes the reader for its brevity:

« Et Diogene, Archedemo, Cleante, i Stoici, gli Accademici, i Peripatetici, Crysippo, Alesandro, Marco Tullio definirono il medesimo, benché per diverse parole » [42].

The writer only saliages those aspects of « voluptà » which are compatible with Christian doctrine. Hence, it is not difficult to understand why the writer drops all the references to women found in the sixth book of the *Libro*; he purges the concept of « voluptà » of all its worldly connotations.

Even if, as seems quite possible, the texts that were used by the compiler of the *Novo Corteggiano*, were written before the Sack of Rome and do not specifically mention the threat posed by Luther, the compilation would have a readership that had lived through these experiences and which would interpret the work in that light. It was not unknown for works of Savonarolian inspiration to be republished in response to

---

39 *Novo Corteggiano*, f.M1r.

40 *Ibid.*, f.M1v.

41 *Libro*, f.189r.

42 *Novo Corteggiano*, f.P4r; also see *ibid.* f.P4v = *Libro*, f.189v; *Novo Corteggiano*, f.Q1v = *Libro*, f.192r; *Novo Corteggiano*, f.Q2r = *Libro*, f.194r; *Novo Corteggiano*, f.Q3r-v = *Libro*, f.206v-207r.

the challenge to the Papacy from Luther[43]. If the real extent of Luther's threat were not properly appreciated, then a contemporary Italian might not perceive any difference between Savonarola and Luther since the same abuses are attacked by both. The *Novo Corteggiano* is reformist in spirit; it seeks to put Italian life on a more Christian footing. Thus, the court as described by Castiglione and Equicola also needs to be reformed. The writer realizes that his solution does not leave much of the original intact and bemuses the reader who expects to find a different kind of subject-matter. That the term « corteggiano » (its orthography also adds to the sense of « novità ») only appears in the title and that the writer strongly supports the idea of the republic as the ideal form of government indicate that the writer clearly intended to shock his reader into thinking about Italian society. However, try as he might, the author of the *Novo Corteggiano* cannot completely drop his classical education which may be considered as one of the last vestiges of court culture.

To conclude, in my opinion, the *Novo Corteggiano* was not written by Equicola but by someone else who adapted the *Libro de natura de amore* to suit his own purposes.

---

[43] G. Miccoli, *La storia religiosa*, in *Storia d'Italia*, vol. IIi, Torino 1974, pp. 980-981.

VIII

'THE GOOD SERVANT': MARIO EQUICOLA. COURT AND COURTIER IN EARLY SIXTEENTH-CENTURY ITALY

I. Two Renaissance courtiers

Any mention of the word 'courtier' in connection with the Italian Renaissance immediately brings to mind Baldassarre Castiglione as the archetypal representative of court society. Although the nineteenth century view of Castiglione as an 'anima eletta' has been severely criticized in more recent times by bringing to light his relentless ambition and lack of morals in certain political situations, nevertheless there has been a tendency to salvage anything that may possibly distinguish Castiglione's career from that of other, baser, courtiers: in particular, stress has been laid on the breadth of his political vision which extended beyond the desire for personal gain to encompass a plan for universal peace and harmonious co-existence between the great powers. As author of the *Libro del Cortegiano,* Castiglione seemed to many critics to possess a moral imperative lacking in other courtiers; and Castiglione's nobility for them was revealed by the high ethical standards he sets in the dialogues both for the behaviour of the prince and for that of his servants. In spite of these qualities it cannot be denied, however, that Castiglione's career is not so very different from that of other courtiers who have been constantly taxed for their servility and lack of imagination. One such courtier is Mario Equicola who, from the late nineteenth century onwards, has been unfavourably compared with his greater contemporary Castiglione.[1] It is the purpose of this article to concentrate on Equicola's activities as a Renaissance courtier. Insufficient attention has been paid to the so-called 'minor' courtiers of the period, and Equicola serves as an interesting example of this type of courtier. In particular, the article will trace the way in which Equicola, as someone of non-noble birth and an outsider, was able to achieve success, and how his life as a 'servant' affected his cultural production.

II. Equicola's career to 1519

The first thirty years of Equicola's life (he was born in 1470) were shaped by two crucial events. The first was the expulsion in 1487 of the Cantelmo family from the Kingdom of Naples by the King who was intent on centralizing power in royal hands (the head of the family went to Rome and his sons to Ferrara). The second was the French invasion of the peninsula in 1494. The exact nature of Equicola's connection with the Cantelmi is far from clear.

Whether he was an illegitimate scion of the family is impossible to prove, given the present state of the documentation. What is clear, however, is that he was protected by the family and indeed employed by them in the capacity of secretary from an early date. After the French invasion, the Cantelmi divided into two warring factions. Giovanpaolo Cantelmo, Equicola's protector, naturally sided with the French, since he had been in continual conflict with the Aragonese monarchy. His son Ferrante changed sides, but his brother Sigismondo reverted to supporting the French. Equicola followed the politics of his masters; this even involved him in fighting on the battlefield. Sigismondo, Equicola's employer until 1508, was obsessed with the recovery of his estates in the *Regno* and, as a consequence, Equicola had to suffer long, fruitless journeys, particularly to the French court, in order to try and win the French king's approval.[2] As one of a group of intellectuals and writers who found themselves scattered far and wide, Equicola seems to symbolize, for the modern historian, the lack of stability in the entire peninsula. In many ways, Equicola's position was similar to that of a number of southern intellectuals who, still connected with their patrons, were forced to leave the *Regno* and seek refuge elsewhere, either temporarily or permanently (the most notable example was perhaps Jacopo Sanazzaro[3]). Equicola's patron, Sigismondo, however, did have honourable refuge in Ferrara, even if he was more often absent than present there (Duke Ercole I, because of his friendship with Sigismondo's father, had been very generous with grants of land to the family). Yet, this situation was not entirely satisfactory to Sigismondo, who felt that he was in Ferrara on false pretences, and always signed his name as the Duke of Sora. Under these circumstances, it is not altogether surprising that Equicola sought out a new employer. He gained the attention of the person who was to offer him new employment, Isabella d'Este, as a result of the closer rapport which he established with Margarita Cantelmo, Sigismondo's wife and one of Isabella's most intimate friends, as his disaffection with Sigismondo became more marked. He launched what amounted to a propaganda campaign, by producing works designed to flatter and impress the culturally avid Isabella d'Este (in particular the *De mulieribus* and the *Nec spe nec metu*).[4]

Equicola's appointment as tutor to Isabella in 1508 represented a change of direction for him. In the first place, it entailed a move to Mantua, and, secondly, it meant that he was not, for the moment, to be employed in the subordinate position of secretary, as he had been with the Cantelmi. He extended and reformulated the cultural interests of Isabella d'Este in terms of *his* own classical erudition and his desire to show off his pupil to the world. Such an attitude was no doubt pleasing to Isabella who now became, much more clearly than before Equicola's arrival, a great patron able to rival the productions of classical antiquity: 'Ha facta fabricare una Grotta, non simile ad quella del Cyclope homerico, non ad le virgiliane, non inferiore ad quella laquale fabellano essere in Parnaso, ma più augusta, veneranda et sana'.[5]

At the same time, the employment of Equicola as tutor was almost certainly part of a conscious strategy by Isabella d'Este to help create the impression that she was the most learned lady of her times. He was employed to teach her the basics of humanistic culture, particularly Latin, to translate the occasional Latin work into the vernacular, and above all to create an image of her as a woman of no ordinary cultural sensibilities. Such a programme was also to Equicola's advantage: it meant that he could devote a considerable amount of his time to cultural, rather than administrative, matters. Hence Equicola became *the intellectual* associated with the Marchesana, and in this capacity he was able to organize Isabella's patronage so as to reap the greatest benefits for her. He became so closely associated with her cultural programme that it is difficult indeed to say at what point Equicola's influence ends and Isabella's aspirations begin. It is not out of place to note that after Equicola's death Isabella's patronage and enthusiasm seem to decline substantially. Certainly, Equicola was not the sole force behind her interest in culture, and other factors, such as the cultural politics of Isabella's eldest son Federico, the new ruler of Mantua, were involved in this lessening of interest; nevertheless, it can be argued that Equicola's influence seems to have been greater than is generally recognized. It was he that gave her *amateur* predilection for all things cultural a serious façade. Equicola was at the centre of her court, which, culturally and financially, existed independently of her husband's, while being subordinate to it, especially in matters of politics. This did not mean that Isabella did not have political interests: her politics was a personal politics or, at least, presented an alternative to her husband's.

In fact, Equicola was used on occasion to further the political interests of the Marchesana. The question that might be raised in this connection would be why Isabella d'Este felt that Equicola was a suitable representative on sometimes delicate political missions. No doubt Equicola's character played a part. Bandello's much quoted description of Equicola as a 'soavissimo compagno' and a 'buon parlatore' may help us to understand this courtier's attractiveness as a representative. He would have been readily acceptable as someone who could entertain and at the same time be a source of much knowledge ('un archivio di lettere').[6] Bandello portrays Equicola as the quintessential courtier who knows what is expected of him in this society. As Isabella's personal representative, he projected an image of the Marchesana as an erudite woman who entrusted her affairs to an agent who could express them in a very learned style. There was also probably present the equation in Isabella's mind between Equicola's humanistic learning and his skill as a negotiator. It should be noted however that most of Equicola's missions in this period were to Ferrara and in particular to Isabella's brother, the Duke. The above-mentioned qualities would have been enough to assure him of a warm welcome. Different credentials would have been needed, if he had been sent to outsiders who would have expected him to be a member of the nobility and to have some standing in his own right. In using Equicola on such missions, Isabella was clearly drawing a correspondence between her political and cultural positions. It was a recognition of the fact that her politics did not follow the official line but emanated from her own concepts and personal ambitions.

III. Equicola as secretary

Equicola did not always remain in the rather modest position of tutor. After seven years in this post, the death of the Marquis in 1519 presented him with a promotion to Isabella d'Este's secretary. In this year, Isabella was able to take virtual power as co-regent with her brother-in-law, Sigismondo Gonzaga, until her son Federico came of age to rule for himself. Thus, although Federico was Marquis in name, his mother seized the opportunity to win power virtually for herself alone. His was by no means an automatic promotion, and indeed one might have expected the post to be awarded to a member of a noble Mantuan family, as had been the case with his predecessor Benedetto Capilupi. It seems significant that Isabella went for over a year after the death of Capilupi, in February 1518,[7] without filling the post of secretary. It would appear that the Marchesana did not need a secretary in the last year of her husband's reign, possibly because she was by then totally excluded from any political activity. Her decision to appoint Equicola as secretary at this critical juncture was a confirmation of her confidence in his abilities and loyalty to her. At the same time it was an indication that she intended to pursue her own policies with her own men.

To have someone like Equicola as secretary was to ensure that the local nobility did not interfere too much in her affairs; she had temporarily closed the doors to aristocratic advancement by appointing an outsider to a sensitive post in the chancellory. One can quite easily imagine the hostility felt by important noble families in Mantua towards the new appointee. This hostility in part was no doubt due to the awareness of the effective importance of a secretary to whom pleas were made and through whom they could be communicated to the ruler. It would have been much easier if one of their own men had been appointed instead of someone who owed no allegiance to them.

Equicola's new post was a politically sensitive one. The new Marquis had no intention of allowing his mother to rule for long. By the end of 1521, the situation was becoming critical. Up till then, Equicola had acted as a go-between attempting to smooth relations between mother and son. He had been Isabella's agent, keeping her informed of Federico's actions and intentions. Thus, he could be viewed as a co-secretary to two of the co-rulers of Mantua. But Federico's appointment of Equicola as *his* secretary – an appointment made by 1522 (Kolsky, 'Mario Equicola', pp. 199–216) – was meant to be seen as a demonstration of the Marquis's power: he had deprived his mother of her most 'trusted' agent.

There may have been other factors that influenced the Marquis's choice of secretary. Equicola's familiarity with the functioning of the chancellory could now be used to the advantage of the young Marquis who wanted to prove himself. That Equicola had achieved a certain fame in the field of learning was probably also important. Federico undoubtedly understood the uses to which Equicola's learning could be put. His position as tutor had meant that he had written predominantly in Latin and had not published anything in the vernacular. Now as secretary he was required to enhance the prince's reputation and honour more widely, and he did this first with the publication of the *Chronica di Mantua* (after July 1521) and then with the *Libro de natura de amore* (1525). It can be argued, therefore, that Equicola was chosen as secretary not only because of his probably unrivalled knowledge of Federico Gonzaga's mother, Isabella d'Este, which would of course have been invaluable in the struggle for power, but also because of the prestige that would accrue to the prince.[8] For his part, Equicola would have been attracted to the Marquis because of the possibilities that he could open for him. The attractions of princely magnificence would have clouded over moral considerations. Thus, on both sides there were compelling reasons to form an alliance which would be to both their advantages.

Equicola's promotion, however, did have its drawbacks for someone who had been cultural adviser to Isabella d'Este for such a long period, and who had only recently been thrust into the workings of the Mantuan chancellory. His new post made heavy demands on his time and administrative abilities. It is true that he was not the only secretary in the Mantuan chancellory at the time, but the functions of the other secretaries, usually of noble Mantuan families and belonging to dynasties whose names reappear in chancellory records, were more strictly bureaucratic. These other secretaries, for example, Jacobo Calandra or Stazio Gadio, were concerned with drafting chancellory documents that were more closely related to the business of ruling the state. Calandra seems to have been in charge of drawing up decrees, the official documents which sanctioned the favours that the prince might confer on his subjects. The chancellory was a documentation centre run by the secretaries, who had in their charge a number of chancellors who often actually wrote the documents, though we find that the secretaries themselves had to keep the rulers' copy books as a normal part of their duties. It was here that the official business of the state was transformed into documentary form: *grida*, decrees, letters and orders to local officials, copies of all the prince's letters, and directions to ambassadors and other envoys were amongst the documents issued. Documents of a legal standing also fell within the purview of the chancellory: grants of lands to favoured individuals, appointments to offices conferred by the ruler, and so on. To a certain extent Equicola was involved in all this activity, but his position put him in a different category from the other secretaries. He was a private or confidential secretary attached to the *person* of the ruler. Thus, Equicola was chosen to accompany the Marquis when he had to travel for the sake of his health, and, in spite of Equicola's atrocious handwriting, the secretary would have to write the copy books during their absence from Mantua. Further, in the early days of the reign of Federico Gonzaga, when the new Marquis was intent on proving his military valour to all, the hapless Equicola was called upon to accompany him as an essential part of his duties, and not only to write his copy books, but to serve as the link between the Marquis and the Mantuan chancellory. Thus, Equicola's presence in the chancellory was not necessary to its efficient functioning: his duties lay elsewhere. Whilst on the battlefield, one of his more important tasks was to keep the Marquis's mother, Isabella d'Este, 'informed', that is, told what Federico wanted his mother to know. In this way, Equicola became an instrument of the new Marquis's personal politics, which was defined by an aggressive attitude towards his mother, the local nobility, and the other Italian states.

IV. The duties of a courtier

The relationship between the prince and his secretary was thus based on subordination and exploitation,[9] compelling the courtier to seek honourable justifications for what might be considered sycophantic behaviour. Equicola became increasingly concerned particularly with the degradation that a humanist-courtier might suffer because of the court system, as we shall see later. At every stage, the courtier had to come to terms with the sheer power of the prince and with the intense competition among court personnel that this power engendered. For example, Castiglione's emphasis on the moral primacy of the courtier should be seen against the background of the prince's monopoly of power. It was perhaps the only autonomous area that Castiglione could find for his courtier which would enable him, at least in theory, to have some ascendance over the powerful prince. Equicola, on the other hand, did not have such pretensions. He was more concerned with using the court system to his own advantage, whatever the cost in personal terms. But this does not mean that Equicola was not worried by the compromises he had to make to further his career. He also felt the need to explain the behaviour of courtiers in general terms, and, at the same time, to free it from blame and discredit. The fact of their subservience could not be denied. The very term 'courtier' implies a source of power on which well-being depends ('cortegiano' is essentially a more elevated form of 'cortesano', with its clearer connotations of servility). Yet there were degrees of humiliation and sycophancy. The nature of the rapport between the ruler, as the source of power, and his subordinates depended on various factors, such as the status of the official, his rank and the extent of his dependence on the ruler for his material advancement and well-being, or the nature of their private relationship. Furthermore, although the theoretical models of court behaviour that were proposed by courtiers like Castiglione and Equicola might not have had much to do with the workings of real relationships, they are nevertheless important, because they demonstrate the courtier's need to assert a certain degree of dignity and autonomy for himself.

It should not be thought that courtiers of the stature of Equicola and Castiglione were able to specialize happily in bureaucratic activities, either in the chancellory or as ambassadors. Even if Castiglione views his courtier *theoretically* as a knight skilled in warfare and in letters, the actual experience of the battlefield was not exactly a pleasant one for either of these courtiers – and Federico Gonzaga expected at least some of his courtiers to participate actively in the defence of his territories.[10]

In the final analysis, a courtier's duties depended on the attitude the prince took towards him. Federico Gonzaga was very clear about his expectations of a courtier. In a letter to the Bishop of Veroli after Equicola's death in 1525, he made an axiomatic statement about the significance he had attached to Equicola's role: 'In resposta gli dicemo che se Lei ha perso un bono amico noi havemo perso un bon servitore et reputamo havere fatto una grande perdita. Non di meno bisogna acquietarse a quello che vole N.S. Dio.'[11] Thus, the Marquis was quite clear about Equicola's place in the Mantuan court. The latter's malleability did not win him the Marquis's friendship, but merely recognition as someone who was willing to serve: a decree of 1525 mentions Equicola's 'explorata fides et indefessa servitus'.[12] It did not seem to matter that Equicola's association with the Marquis sometimes went beyond the formal limits of a master-servant relationship (one may perhaps imagine a sense of camaraderie between them in the years before Federico became Marquis, because of their escapades involving the 'donzelle'). Perhaps under the orders of Isabella d'Este, who wanted to make the future Marquis dependent on her even for his pleasures, the experienced and worldly Equicola played the part of tutor and go-between to the young, impressionable prince. However, Federico was at the same time playing his own game with Equicola, which worked to both their advantages: while Equicola wished to win the future Marquis's favour, Federico wished to satisfy his lust and to exercise his power over his mother's entourage.

A prince fashioned in the mould of Federico Gonzaga could only think in terms of his utter superiority over all who came in contact with him, and so he simply ignored the rights of his servants. Indeed, everyone was a servant to him. There was perhaps in him the thrill of humiliating those around him and proving his absolute power. It did not matter that Castiglione was a high-ranking official at another court; Federico Gonzaga still insisted on using him as his personal wholesaler. There may have been some sense of professionalism on Castiglione's part, but it did not take much for it to be swept aside by any practical needs of the prince. Other court officials were treated in exactly the same manner by Federico.[13]

Faced with this situation, what was the courtier to do? A too obvious response would be that the courtier should have sought employment elsewhere, but this path was full of obstacles, as Castiglione's case demonstrates, when he decided to change employer. The second avenue might be to leave the court altogether, something that was attempted by Pietro Aretino. However, if social pressures were such that limitations were placed on the possibilities of employment outside the courts (lack of opportunities, or unsuitability for a university appointment, or lack of other professional training, etc.) the courtier would then need to make the best of his situation. Dissatisfaction with court life is a theme that runs through sixteenth-century literature: even those employed at court in apparently good positions felt themselves entrapped or enslaved by the system. However, the risks that a courtier ran by too openly criticizing the court system from the inside are too obvious to need much commentary here. Writers who decided to make their work public usually had to embrace the ethos of their corrupt society. For someone employed at court to criticize the ruler in his writings would require inordinate courage and an acceptance of the fact that one's career might be ruined.[14]

V. Equicola's *Institutioni* and the role of the 'poeta'

Such a state of affairs did not prevent Equicola from theorizing about the role of intellectuals in court society. A work in which he did this, the *Institutioni al comporre in ogni sorte di rima della lingua volgare*, appeared posthumously in 1541, but was completed by 1518. It is Equicola's most serious attempt at demonstrating the importance, if not the superiority, of intellectual endeavour over other activities. Poetry itself becomes a metaphor for intellectual achievement, since in Equicola's view it is the equivalent of philosophy and hence of knowledge.[15] Equicola's readings of the classics probably influenced him in his choice of the poet as the intellectual *par excellence*. Virgil, in particular, was the prime example of what mutual understanding between poet and prince could produce.

The text of the *Institutioni* focuses, in its first part, on the relationship between the ruler and the poet: 'ciascuno sa quanto fosse caro Euripide ad Archelao Re di Macedonia. Simonide fu gratissimo ad Hierone Siracusano' (*Inst.*, fs B1v–B2r). Equicola intends to demonstrate that the ruler cannot do without the services of the poet; in particular, he appears to be addressing his claim to rulers with imperial aspirations. However, through the thick layers of examples, the reader cannot fail to notice that the poet is ashamed of the circumstances in which he finds himself. In other words, a particular kind of poetry is expected of him, a poetry of glorification and commemoration. Indeed, to attempt any other would be foolhardy and would lead to lesser rewards. This is not to say that all poetry was conditioned by these factors, but that Equicola was particularly interested in those poets whom he names as praiseworthy examples: 'Ma come preterirò Vergilio? La cui gloria fece che nè appresso Ottavio Augusto gratia nè notitia gli mancò appresso 'l popolo romano' (*Inst.*, f. B2v). Even if poets could achieve acclaim and perhaps a certain amount of power through their verses, nevertheless, they are always in a subordinate position with respect to the Emperor: Virgil can receive the people's acclaim and be welcomed as if he were the Emperor, but only in the latter's absence. In any case, his power is a mirage.

VI. Equicola on the patronage of intellectuals

Equicola's concern with the relationship between the intellectual and power is shown in the section devoted to interpersonal relations in his *Libro de natura de amore* (1525). This was not a mere academic question. The intellectual's view of the ruler and his attitude towards power were crucial factors in determining the kinds of work he would produce. The view from above was another crucial factor. Certain works, particularly histories, could be commissioned, and these might require even more careful attention to the prince's desire and requirements than an uncommissioned work: it should be noted, however, that whatever work the intellectual was producing he needed to bear in mind such pressures. Equicola was concerned, in theory at least, with providing a theoretical framework in which the dignity of the courtier could be safeguarded:

> Li nostri magiori Romani in gran veneratione haveano questo sancto nome amico. Li vinciuti o socii o amici chiamavano. Da li grandi patritii et triumphanti et consulari homini erano amici chiamati quelli che per honorarli li frequentavano. Li advocati, patroni, causidici haveano clienti, e cliente relativo di patrono come servo di domino che signore dicemo. Augusto non volse nè per gioco, pur da soi, esser chiamato Signore per esser nome in Roma abhominabile. Dice Seneca che per remettere ogni invidia da servi li

> signori erano chiamati patri de famiglia et li servi familiari. De nostri antiqui Caligula primo volse esser adorato como Dio, Domitiano se scrisse dio et domino. Quelli che de le domestice commodità erano ministri in casa de Principi et grandi homini erano servi et ben servendo devenivano liberti, de la grandeza de liquali gran cose et excelse legemo et in favori extremi collocati et posti in alto loco. Però se dice quelli esser stati boni Imperatori, liquali benchè essi fossero non boni haveano appo loro boni servi et boni liberti administratori. Horatio et Vergilio erano di Mecenate amici. Mecenate et Pollione di Augusto amici et familiari. Benchè esser famul, tal vocabulo esser servo significhe. Lo uso lo ha mitigato et quelli che insieme viveno familiari dicemo. Per beneficio de la christiana religione, christiano a christiano non serve. Nondimeno è intanto ascesa la superbia de Prelati et signori che in le sottoscrittioni de lettere a loro vedemo, servo et schiavo [. . .] Retengamo noi, liberi et christiani, il nome de amico, ne consentamo alla perversa consuetudine de vili adulatori. Quelli che in nostro beneficio et honor procurano habiamoli per patroni et noi siamo loro clienti et amici non ficti, non simulati. (*Libro*, fs. 115v–116r)

This passage presents what at first sight appears a bewildering number of terms to describe relations between those who held power and those who served them. Equicola appears to be exploring these relations at different levels of Roman society. From his discussions two key terms emerge: 'amico' and 'cliente'. Beneath his concern for an accurate terminology, however, there is the implication that the reality of power is sometimes hidden by the clever use of language. Such was the case with the Emperor Augustus, who would not have himself referred to as King, seemingly out of respect for the republican tradition in Rome which he was in the process of successfully subverting. The most extreme example of a false terminology is, in Equicola's opinion, when certain emperors designated themselves as gods. In so doing, they demanded to be served in a particular manner: they required adoration of an emperor who no longer considered himself merely human. In spite of these unfavourable circumstances, Equicola points to possible advantages for some sections of the servants of the emperors. In particular, he indicates that there was some kind of social mobility for freed slaves, who could aspire to the highest positions in the imperial administration. Furthermore, Equicola points out, the reputation of an emperor depends on the abilities of his servants: a bad emperor might not be so considered, because his administration had proved capable. Thus, Equicola is singing the praises of servants, who, when treated well, will bring distinct advantages and benefits to the ruler. It should come as no surprise that Virgil is again mentioned in this context. The intricate interpersonal relationships that brought together Maecenas,

Virgil, Augustus, and others are carefully described by Equicola, who tries to find the exact term appropriate to each relationship. The fact that Equicola's discussion of relationships between master and servant in ancient Rome concerns the Empire, indicates that he was interested in developing, modifying, and perhaps applying his findings to the contemporary situation, where he notes that the influence Christianity has had, or, at least, should have had, must affect the way these relations are viewed. However at this point the momentum of Equicola's prose increases, as does his moral outrage at the unchristian behaviour of rulers, both lay and religious, who are implicitly demanding a return to the ancient Roman schema. A return to the master-slave model means that the intellectual has absolutely no power within the system nor any dignity. Thus, Equicola's affirmation that intellectuals are 'liberi et christiani' is a forceful declaration of independence on the part of court intellectuals. This attitude might strike the student of Equicola's life as somewhat strange, since he is often presented as the archetypal grovelling courtier. Yet, from all this, one can surely deduce that Equicola was both concerned with his own self-esteem and with establishing a model which would allow the courtier to reap the greatest advantages without loss of honour. Equicola will have nothing to do, at least in theory, with the 'vili adulatori'. He wishes to re-establish in contemporary court society the patron-client model, but with a signficant change, namely, that the latter-day client, in other words the courtier, will also be the 'amico' of the patron. Thus, Equicola did not view the patron-client model as just a buying-and-selling relationship, advantageous to both buyer and seller. He also added the ingredient of 'amicitia', which would place the relationship on a higher plane. The 'arrangement' that Equicola outlined in the above passage, however, was subject to amendment by the conditions of court society. The courtier of uncertain social origins had but one course at court, and that was to use all the means at his disposal in order to secure a favourable position. Other sections of the *Libro* make it quite clear that Equicola's courtier must subordinate everything to social success. Even the courtier's personality, in this analysis, is considered just another means to attain one's goal (Kolsky, 'Mario Equicola', pp. 261–70). The actual environment of court society led to this contradiction between Equicola's aspirations and the need to adapt to what were the prevailing conditions at court. From this dichotomy was born the sense of unease that suffuses his work.

Equicola only sporadically goes beyond the utilitarian aspects of courtiership; his work seems to be flawed by this absence of a coherent programme which could combine all these disparate elements. It may be illuminating here to compare Equicola's alternating solutions with those reached by Castiglione. What distinguishes Castiglione's theory of the relationship between ruler and courtier from Equicola's is the former's insistence on the moral role of the *cortegiano*, who now becomes the *institutor del principe*. Even if it is understood that the courtier must make every effort to rise through the system, nevertheless, underlying such social climbing is the necessity to be close to the prince, so that the courtier can tutor him in the ways of virtue. In Equicola's version of the courtier as *institutor*, the courtier becomes a reflection of the ruler's power; he has to ensure that his text fits the context of the court. This is not true for Castiglione. The substance of Aristotle's and Plato's philosophy remains untouched by the social conditions of the court: their work almost has the status of a metaphysical entity which is not connected to a particular place or time. *Cortegiania* allows the philosopher to gain access to the ruler:

> Nè penso che Aristotile e Platone si fossero sdegnati del nome di perfetto cortegiano, perchè si vede chiaramente che fecero l'opere della cortegiania ed attesero a questo fine, l'un con Alessandro Magno, l'altro con i re di Sicilia. E perchè officio è di bon cortegiano conoscer la natura del principe e l'inclinazion sue e così, secondo i bisogni e le opportunità, con destrezza entrar loro in grazia, come avemo detto, per quelle vie che prestano l'adito securo, e poi indurlo alla virtù.[16]

In Castiglione's reading, the two incomparable philosophers, Aristotle and Plato, have been transformed into courtiers, and Castiglione's courtier has been transformed into a philosopher, perhaps following the lines of Plato's philosopher-king. As a consequence court culture is seen to be founded on a tradition that has its roots in classical antiquity and can, at the same time, boast two of the greatest philosophers in its ranks. At this, the highest of levels open to the courtier, it must never be forgotten that learning alone is ineffective with regard to the ruler, who needs to be persuaded of certain philosophical tenets by courtly means:

> E di queste cose in Alessandro fu autore Aristotile, usando i modi di bon cortegiano; e che non seppe far Calistene, ancorchè Aristotile glielo mostrasse; chè, per voler esser puro filosofo e così austero ministro della nuda verità, senza mescolarvi la cortegiania, perdè la vita e non giovò, anzi diede infamia ad Alessandro. (*Il cortegiano,* p. 422)

The contrast between the two philosophers does not appear to relate to differences or defects in one or the other's philosophical thought, but rather to the fact that one of the philosophers was not aware of the prevailing differences in a particular court society, and so floundered because of his lack of courtiership. Castiglione is clearly pointing a moral here, that courts require a particular type of thinker who can combine philosophy and courtly manners: one without the other leads to disaster.

The rulers have their sensibilities; conversation at court needs to be elevated to the status of an art so that one's point can be made without offending the ruler. Truth is not an absolute value in itself: at court other considerations are given almost equal value. Without an appreciation of courtly behaviour the intellectual will come to grief. The adjectives that describe Calisthenes, *puro, austero,* and *nudo*, serve to demonstrate the impossibility of being a pure philosopher in court *society* because of its peculiar social circumstances. However this does not mean to say, at least in Castiglione's view, that the philosophy expounded will have undergone a terrible censorship. One can still propound important philosophies, but care must be taken to consider the situation of the ruler and of court society in general.

Equicola subtly suggests a different view of Aristotle in his *Institutioni*. In his view, Aristotle was first of all a poet and secondly a philosopher. Considering Equicola's definition of the poet as someone in the employ of the prince who writes for their mutual benefit, then the idea that the poet-philosopher has values untouched by court society makes no sense. For Castiglione, it is a question of 'dressing-up', whereas, for Equicola, the philosophies themselves are affected by the society in which they are written.[17]

VII. Notions of 'courtiership'

Both Equicola and Castiglione are considered courtiers, the latter more noble than the former who is generally considered a time-server. Castiglione was concerned in his *Libro del cortegiano* to put forward the claims of the courtier, his *rights* to certain freedoms, such as that of movement: in certain circumstances, the courtier should leave the prince he was serving, if unfair demands were made on him. One has the impression that the courtier, in this case Castiglione, was attempting to create a stable institution from which his role would be recognized by the prince. Castiglione introduces a crucial redefinition of the courtier's obligation: 'e commandarle [cose *ragionevoli*] a chi *ragionevolmente* ha da obedire' (my italics) (*Il cortegiano,* p. 394). What is being suggested is a kind of contract through which the courtier preserves his dignity and humanist ideals, reason in particular. It is made quite clear that absolutist behaviour on the part of the ruler is blamed and not praised; the latter must of course act in his own interest, but, at the same time, he must not neglect the interests of his courtiers. Indeed, one can read the *Libro del cortegiano* as a challenge to the Italian princes to make better use of their personnel, given the numerous qualities attributed to the courtier. Expertise should be recognized and not wasted.

These considerations lead us to ask what we mean today by the term 'courtier', when used with reference to the late fifteenth and early sixteenth centuries, and what the nature of a courtier's employment was. Perhaps a first working definition could be along the lines of someone employed at court by the ruler in the capacity of ideologue, protecting and advancing the interests of the prince. This working definition should be understood as covering those people who served the ruler in various capacities, whether on his personal staff or in the court chancellory. It can also be argued that those nobles who attended the prince were being transformed into courtiers: the Marquis of Mantua, for example, considered himself humiliated when he had to serve the King of France in the guise of a courtier. A courtier may have had a specific task, but he could be found involved in other activities which enhanced the reputation of the prince. These functions could include the role of artist or musician, secretary, diplomat, or other type of chancellory official. For each of these posts, the qualifications (formal or informal, for example, a legal training) differed; entry to some posts was restricted to the nobility or even to certain families. It has been noted that in order to enter the Mantuan diplomatic service one had to be either a cleric or a member of the local nobility; there were exceptions, of course, but in general the rule was followed.

Castiglione's birth allowed him to become, albeit after many vicissitudes, a Mantuan ambassador. Such a path was not open to Equicola, who did not possess the requisite citizenship or perhaps even noble origins. In spite of certain similarities between these two courtiers, their birthplaces impelled them towards different careers within the court system. A further hypothesis may be added to the effect that Castiglione's employment as a diplomat influenced the way he wrote, particularly with reference to his most important work, the *Libro del cortegiano*, composed in the form of a dialogue which, it has been suggested, is due to his knowledge and experience of diplomatic practice.[18] Equicola, on the other hand, as secretary, in his major work, the *Libro de natura de amore*, was more concerned to explain a set of doctrines, to provide what would later be considered an encyclopedia of love, something that could be provided by a secretary.

It seems true that the courtiers of this period played some part in forming the courts and more especially in determining their own position in the system. However, we must not forget that it was the prince at the summit of this system who had the final control over his 'servants'. It was his perception of culture in the final analysis that allowed a place for humanist-courtiers. An important ingredient in the cultural make-up of a ruler was his understanding of what was going on in other courts; a sense of rivalry thus played its part in court patronage. It would also seem that an essential factor in the prince's decision to favour particular writers was whether he considered that they would bring him fame and renown. However, at a certain point it becomes legitimate to ask why a prince would take any interest in humanism, especially if he himself was without Latin, and his true interests lay in more obviously princely sports, such as hunting and affairs of the heart, as was the case with Francesco Gonzaga. It is obvious that certain kinds of literary work would find immediate favour with the prince. Historical writing is a case in point. Here the prince might take a very active role indeed in commissioning historical works which would set the regime in a favourable light. Court humanism's association with historiography may be construed as its concern with validating the sources of power. Historiography at court was a more humanistically refined version of the polite letter that princes sent to each other or to other high-placed dignitaries that could be found in the chancellory archives. An example of the esteem in which historians were held is to be seen in the following note that Tolomeo Spagnuoli, the Mantuan first secretary, wrote to the Marquis of Mantua: 'M. Bernardo Rucellai, quel gentilhomo fiorentino che in una sua historia chel compone in uno stile elegante, fa honorata mentione de V. Ex.tia, come divoto che li è, è pervenuto, qui a Mantua cum intentione di andare a Milano'.[19] In this way a humanist could lay the ground for further possibilities of patronage and favour. For other kinds of literary work, it is perhaps more difficult to grasp the rationale. Of course, the prince at times wanted to be entertained and made to laugh, yet often there were other pressures on the ruler as far as literature was concerned. A partial explanation may lie in the idea of a reaction to a stimulus. For example, Francesco Gonzaga, Marquis of Mantua, felt the necessity to reply to the poems of his *fidanzata* Isabella d'Este. In order to do so, the Marquis had to employ a poet to write them for him, and he then passed them off as his own work. It would be easier at this stage to pass a negative judgement on the Marquis's behaviour, claiming it to be indicative of his brutish manner. Yet, it is worthwhile noting that Francesco Gonzaga realized what was expected of him, so that his fame as a ruler would not be tainted by this defect.[20]

The attraction for rulers of encomiastic verse of dubious quality, in Latin and in the vernacular, does not seem to require much explanation. The same might be said for the appearance of their names in the dedications to humanist writings. On one level, it meant that power became equated with knowledge – the ruler was seen to be taking an interest, albeit passive, in the propagation of culture, and, indeed, almost annexing it. On another level, this type of literary production was part of the structures that the rulers were building up for themselves, according to certain key concepts such as *magnificentia*, which stressed the impressive qualities of rule by a prince. After the French invasion of 1494, *magnificentia* was perhaps for the few surviving Italian rulers the sole means of maintaining their dignity, at a time when their powerlessness had never been greater.[21]

VIII. The *Libro de natura de amore* and the court

What intellectual space was therefore open to the humanist? I intend now to study in this light certain aspects of Equicola's *magnum opus*, the *Libro de natura de amore*, a treatise written in the Neoplatonic mould with pretensions to an intellectual meditation on love. In spite of its grandiose aspirations, it cannot help being constantly influenced by considerations of the court. Originality of thought or profound thinking on an abstract, philosophical subject served no purpose: the court was the master and had to be served. Eclecticism was Equicola's by-word, since adherence to one particular philosophy would tie him down too much. One philosophy was not flexible enough to get around the multiple problems, and the moral and social pressures that faced a courtier. Equicola could not often afford to take one particular line to the exclusion of other possibilities, otherwise his vulnerability would show up all too clearly. So, he borrowed from 'all', 'perchè non sia alcuno di sua laude privo' (*Libro*, f. 1r). Taking a stand on an issue, even a literary one, was a dangerous matter. Bembo, Equicola's adversary in matters of linguistic theory, is treated with compassion in the *Libro*, because of the storm raised by the *Asolani*: 'O invidia che non solamente di maldire et detrahere te contenti, ma il nome di coetani extirpare procuri' (*Libro*, f. 33v). Hence the lesson that Equicola seems to have learnt from Bembo is that it is extremely parlous to attempt anything new or original, because it will immediately be attacked by other intellectuals anxious to make their mark in court society. The struggles over the language fought by humanists can thus be seen in terms of a battle to win the right to speak authoritatively on intellectual matters on behalf of their rulers. The aim was to find a set of linguistic choices that was politically acceptable to princes, who might then be influenced, by the arguments of the humanists or by their reputations in such matters, to employ them or at least to favour them. A courtier like Equicola was as interested in the spoken as in the written word, since conversation was one of the principal means of making an impression at court.[22]

The *Libro* contains important evidence of Equicola's attitude to particular kinds of literature, and may serve as an instance of court attitudes towards literary culture. In order for his reader to get the most benefit out of the *Libro*, Equicola paraphrases in its pages those books that will make it more approachable and understandable. These books underline the kind of cultural range necessary to penetrate what seems to be an arcane philosophy. But philosophies and courts can only co-exist to a certain extent: Ficinian Neoplatonism presents quite a different structure, because it is not specifically a product of or directed towards court society. In Equicola's list of books, it is noteworthy that the majority are now regarded as works of literature. Ficino receives no praise as a philosopher but only as a translator. Both Giovanni and Giovanfrancesco Pico are not really singled out for the originality of their thought, the latter's practical skills as a soldier receiving more fulsome praise ('ne li primi giovanili soi anni il vidi conduttero di molte gendarme di Alphonso secondo, Re di Napoli, et quelle governare con molta prudentia') than his skill as a philosopher (*Libro*, f. 22v).

Alongside these and other philosophers, come writers like Bembo, who were not professional philosophers but dabbled with fashionable topics. Significantly, Equicola praised the *Asolani* as 'giocondi per la summa arte, ordine, doctrina et peritia di argumentare' (*Libro*, f. 34v). It is the adjective 'giocondi' that is of interest here — not serious nor profound, but delightful. Even if Bembo's work is composed of highly serious elements, as Equicola admits, they only serve to make the book a 'pleasure' to read (moral implications do not enter into the discussion). Jacobo Calandra is similarly treated. His *Aura*, now lost, serves as an example of the type of writing Equicola himself had chosen: 'de la copia de doctrina resulta l'ornato parlare, come in Joan Jacovo Mantuano si vede' (*Libro*, f. 39v). Although Equicola recommends, 'non scriva quel a cui eruditione manca', a further indication of the equivalence for him between the writer and the humanistically inspired scholar, this identification is perhaps misleading without the additional concept of 'ornato scrivere' (*Libro*, f. 39r). It is not that knowledge becomes mere ornamentation, because the *Libro*, as critics have pointed out, is a marvel of encyclopaedic proportions useful for consultation.[23] The *ornato* is not an extra ingredient, but a product of the content of the writing. It is not a way of embellishing the content; rather it constitutes the core of Equicola's style and method. 'Copia de doctrina' is present at all levels in the court-humanist's work: it is to be found in his rejection of Ciceronianism and his assumption of the eclectic stance which offered him a wider lexical choice, and also in his sentences which are packed with a bewildering variety of classical references. It is with the word 'copia' that Equicola's *modus operandi* is revealed. Clarity and skill in argumentation do not figure so highly, perhaps because Equicola realized the limitations of his philosophical and critical capacities. Perhaps he was also well aware of what would constitute a useful and acceptable work in court society. We find here an emphasis on quantity (of quotations, *exempla*, etc.) which undoubtedly impressed and dazzled the sixteenth-century reader, as it now does the twentieth-century one. The sixteenth-century reader would have appreciated the work as a storehouse of knowledge and as a celebration of courtly civilization. Knowing things seems here to have replaced philosophical thought as a Ficino would have understood it.

The first book of the *Libro* brings together diverse genres, poetry and prose, philosophy and fictional dialogues. The vernacular poets are grouped together at the beginning of the *Rassegna*, thus forming an autonomous section within the list. Equicola's choice of poets indicates mature awareness of the development and high-points of vernacular poetry. The humanist appears open to different sources of knowledge and is willing to take them all seriously. Professional, university philosophers do not appear in the list. Also, love has lost specifically Christian connotations and has become the property of the court. What matters is that the literature has some use for those connected with courts. Speaking about Francesco da Barberino, he mentions in particular that his works 'me par convenga alla vita de cortegiani' (*Libro*, f. 9r). Writings which take a specifically Christian point of view are also absent from this *catalogue raisonné* of philosophies of love, the exception being Dante who is considered in a Neoplatonic light. It is not that the writers Equicola mentions are pagan, but all, in their own ways, seek a syncretist approach which allows them to combine classical and Christian sources.

IX. Equicola and Savonarola

In this connection, the *Libro* may be usefully contrasted with a book on love written from a purely Christian view-point, the *Tractato dello amore di Jesu Christo* by Girolamo Savonarola.[24] This work is straightforward in its message, since there is no need for any painful synthesis of conflicting doctrines: 'che senza l'amore di Jesu non si può salvare alcuno'.[25] Savonarola needs only one text, 'la sacra scrittura', whereas Equicola requires a multiplicity of sources to validate his arguments.[26] It must also be emphasized that Savonarola's *Tractato* represents an attack on certain notions that were prevalent in court society. If, for example, *voluptas* had been taken on board by a certain strand of humanist thinking as characteristic of court society, then Savonarola attempts to re-Christianize the concept: 'gran differentia dalle voluptà del senso a quelle della gratia perochè quelle del senso fanno lo appetito inquieto'.[27]

Voluptas, in Equicola's thought, represents the aspirations of the court as the site of earthly pleasures where contemplation is secondary to gratification. Here the greatest good is the immediate, the sensual, the human. Such a position is not without its difficulties, and Equicola seems to suffer periodically from a 'bad conscience', and tries to Christianize (in Savonarola's understanding of the term) his philosophy. Savonarola has no ambiguities on this point. He speaks out against the unchristian emphasis of court society. For this reason it is the hermit, devoted to a life of Christian meditation, who provides Savonarola with his most positive model: 'che uscire di tal solitudine fussi grande infelicità' (f. a5r). Contemplation of God is the highest goal: 'Colui che ha gustato una gocciola della dolceza di Jesu cercherà sempre di separarsi da ogni altra cura per poter stare con Jesu nella oratione et contemplatione' (*Tractato*, f. a8v). Furthermore, Savonarola also attacks an important element of court society, namely, women. In this he differs greatly from Equicola who, in the *Libro*, attempts to correct certain features of female behaviour at court. Savonarola has no doubts on this matter: 'et maxime debbe fuggire le conversationi delle donne, etiam devote, perchè sono molto pericolose' (*Tractato*, f. 63r).

At first, then, it would seem that the distance between the two works could not be greater. However, at certain points one finds a strange contamination which brings the two works closer together than might have seemed possible. Equicola, having spent the greater part of his life at court, had seen that culture was made subordinate to the wishes of the ruler, and that this was no less true of religion. A suspicion hovers over Equicola's work that he was uneasy about the relation between court behavour and Christian values. Without subscribing to the return to the type of Christianity advocated by Savonarola, he seems to have seen a certain foundation of truth in the position represented by the Florentine. Even if Equicola did not know the *Tractato*, the problem was a pressing one for him in the *Libro*, and one which could not be ignored. However, Equicola was first and foremost a courtier, someone in the service of princes who demanded unchristian behaviour from him at times (as with his involvement with Isabella d'Este's *damigelle*). The continuing impact of Savonarola, and movements to reform the Church, may have contributed to a nagging conscience. Equicola's thought attempts to synthesize these conflicting tendencies, and to bring two distant poles closer together.

It would have been impossible for Equicola to deny his very existence as a courtier, so the best strategy he found was to attempt a Christianization of those courtly values that could be considered 'suspect'. This strategy reaches its culmination in the sixth book of the *Libro*. In this synthesis of his courtier-philosophy, Equicola lays down the foundations of his thought, as well as attempting its justification. The courtier has to grapple with perplexing problems, such as that of the place of the senses in court Neoplatonism. Ficino had not ignored the importance of the senses in his own version of Neoplatonism, but, in comparison with Equicola, he had placed more emphasis on the incorporeal. In contrast, Equicola lingers on the importance of the body in all calculations for eternity. It is as if his experience as a courtier had taught him that this was perhaps the only certainty in the midst of cut-throat competition and rivalry. Neoplatonic philosophy may have appealed to Equicola as a safety-net, since he was acutely aware of the final dissolution of the body, source of all pleasures. At this point, Equicola's major intellectual effort is to insert the body into a grand scheme:

> non refutemo la voluptà de sensi quanto substentatione de natura et nostro bene esser rechiede. Siamo in voluptà del animo per le scientie et intellecto et congiongendola con la operatione de la virtù morale procuremo di venire

religiosi che per questa strada con guida de amore ascenderemo alla vera felicità. (*Libro*, f. 209r)

Equicola seems to be attempting a defence of court life based on the body. Closely connected with this concept is that of 'voluptà'. The tone of the last book of the *Libro* fails to reach that note of Christian ecstasy to which it seemed to aspire, for, at every moment, Equicola recalls the needs of the body: 'Chi vorrà imponere freno alle nostre soverchie voglie vorrà quel che natura non vole, che uno augello non voli mai, la Natura per volar li aperse le ali' (*Libro*, f. 214v). Equicola seems more at home with discussions concerning life on earth. Sexual urges, he suggests, are only relevant for men up until the age of forty. Such attention to detail indicates a greater interest in physical than in metaphysical reality. However, Equicola does his best to defend himself from possible charges of libertinism. He makes every effort to reduce the gulf between Christian purity and sexual pleasure; it is his equal emphasis on the soul and body and their absolute interdependence which perhaps is the only way of giving his theories some respectability. Equicola is taking literally the standard Neoplatonic definition of love ('amore è de l'animo et corpo', *Libro*, f. 221r).

X. Women and metaphysics in the *Libro*

The sixth and last book of the *Libro*, where the culmination of this literal understanding of the combination between body and soul is to be found, is meant to be the last link in the Neoplatonic chain leading to the greatest good. Thus, one would expect the discussion to become more metaphysical and less earthly. And indeed it does, for the most part. So it comes as something of a surprise to find, in the midst of a meditation on the greatest good, a longish section devoted to the subject of women. How can this be?

In the first place, this approach is consonant with a courtly perspective on Neoplatonism. Women were an essential part of the court system: for Equicola, and others like him, they were a way of gaining a foothold in court before being favoured by the prince. Both politically and metaphysically, then, they are the means to a greater good. Thus, women are not present in court for their own sake, but for the opportunities they represent for the achievement of greater ambitions. Their importance is therefore ambiguous, and does not necessarily emphasize their particular place in society.

The introduction of women into the Neoplatonic scheme allows Equicola to combine earthly and heavenly principles in a new perception of the role females play at court. Hence, his male creation, 'il mio nobilissimo et virtuoso cortegiano amante', corresponds to this dual need. The qualities of the courtier are amalgamated with the more metaphysical aspects of love that are discussed in the *Libro*. The process is not dissimilar to that found in the fourth book of

Castiglione's *Cortegiano*. In placing women at the heart of his philosophy, Equicola has to ensure that they are worthy of this elevation. In so doing, he is defending court life from accusations of immorality and excessive indulgence of the senses. It is striking that, while emphasizing women's importance in his version of Neoplatonic philosophy, he needs to remove any taint of sin from court women, and therefore renders them passive: 'Et tu [Jerome] che di lascivia le noti, dimme, qual donna recercò mai homo? (di ben create parlo) Qual novo amante elesse? Ma esse [sono] sollicitate da importuni amanti con ogni sorte di persuasioni [. . .]' (*Libro*, f. 225v–226r). Women, Equicola tells them, have to be careful because of the delicate nature of their honour: 'Considerate che, ad chi, quanto date. Ogni insolentia in amorosi furti, ogni periculo per il quale in Venere si occorre, al homo par sia honor et gloria ma a voi infamia senza alcuna acceptabil excusatione et di morte sete constrette spesso dubitare' (*Libro*, f. 227v). These ideological restraints are not challenged by Equicola. Indeed, chastity is seen as something to be recommended in the midst of the court, which is generally considered unstable, a place of intense competition, deceits, and brutal behaviour: 'Non credate che altro sia che tender la rete quando più che non si conviene sete honorate. Quando lo amante repentinamente miserabil appare, butta alhor l'esca, per sotto lacci comprender chi se fida, per stringer chi crede' (*Libro*, f. 227v). If court society as a whole cannot be changed, some aspects of it at least can be salvaged: men, evil in themselves, have to seek redemption through female intervention. The court is what it is. Equicola seems to be encouraging discernment and caution in women at court. This is perhaps as far as he could go without eliminating his concept of *voluptà* of the senses. He thus falls between an out-and-out libertinism and a return to Christian morality, particularly chastity. Court life is not to be rejected but only modified. Equicola places the greatest emphasis on women loving the right kind of person: 'Ponasi ogni cura in accarezare secundo il grado virtuosi. Attendasi secundo il tempo et loco con dolci ragionamenti et degni de corte nobili intertenere' (*Libro*, f. 229r). In this way women become the ideal repository of what is good in court society: men can continue to assail women, but the latter are now prepared to defend themselves better.

XI. The courtier's body

Voluptas in the end is illusory: the 'cortegiano amante' will have to seek solace in values and beliefs outside the court. Stability and peace of mind, so often absent in that environment, are obtainable through a *deus ex machina*, literally God, 'ameno di ogni quiete et felicità il dator unico'. Thus, the space devoted to health and old age in the sixth book of the *Libro* is clearly connected to the need for a belief in something eternal.

The court could not offer any comfort to an ageing courtier. It perhaps left no lasting sense of one's worth or of the goals of society in general. Old age was particularly fearsome to someone whose pleasures derived from the senses. The body was constantly threatened by ill health, so Equicola laid stress on 'la bona valitudine' (*Libro,* f. 218r). The court is seen in terms of bodies in conflict and competitors for scarce resources. Rivalry and the idea of conquest present a society in which friendship was a rarity and could not be depended upon. The only value was the self, which was subject to the pressures of that society, and had to conform to them. There was an absence of values that did not directly depend on the struggle inherent in court society. Thus, Equicola's attention in the culminating book of the *Libro* to higher matters was a direct response to inner turmoil. Significantly the 'cose divine' did not affect the vision Equicola had of the world; if they had, his pessimism, as far as human relationships were concerned, would have been considerably tempered. The heavens were only used as a last resort, firstly to provide a semblance of orthodoxy in his work and, secondly, and perhaps more importantly, to provide a philosophical framework for himself: 'Preponamo dunque le cose estreme alle fragili, le perpetue alle caduche, le stabili alle mutabili; non ci sollicite speranza di vigilante insomnio non amor lascivo, negocio di ocioso' (*Libro*, f. 235v).

The culmination of Equicola's version of Neoplatonic philosophy, then, does not coincide with a heightening of his praises for a court society. Instead we find a critique of the conditions at court:

> Se de lieto vivere in lei in corte tua speranza reponi, pensa li invidi et delatori et detractatori in quella vivere et calunniatori senza fine. Et per brevemente comprendere tutte le adversità et infelicità che in corte sono, adverti che de Signori la magior parte colle orecchie vede et spesso non chi più merita et serve, ma chi più piace è remunerato.[28]

At first sight it seems that Equicola has committed an error of judgement. Why should he talk about 'le adversità et infelicità che in corte sono' now that he is bound on his voyage to the highest goals to which humans can aspire? It might be that in Equicola's mind the harshness of court life and the desire for 'amor divino' are intimately connected, the one being the origin of the other.[29] The enterprise of regularizing inter-personal behaviour in court society needed to be based on a perception of its failings. The almost anarchic struggle and conflict amongst courtiers for the best positions offered by the prince gave rise to opposing philosophies, the one based on competition and the other based on Christian morality. It was Equicola's task to create a philosophy which could combine the two and at the same time allow a justification for the type of life a courtier was compelled to live.

XII. Aretino and Equicola: Two 'courtiers' compared

From the above it will be seen that it is too simplistic to describe Equicola merely as a subservient courtier who can be taken as a model for that attitude of utter subservience which seems to have been synonymous with the court. He has been compared unfavourably not only with the 'noble' Castiglione, as shown above, but also with the 'rebellious' Aretino; but this contrast too can be shown to be misleading. Aretino's search for independence and his anti-court stance have been seen as setting him above the kind of creature that Equicola has been said to epitomize, since the passages in the *Ragionamento delle corti* which criticize both the court and the effects it has on the courtiers seem to indicate greater moral awareness on Aretino's part. As 'secretario del mondo', Aretino was writing the *other* book, not the propagandistic and eulogistic work of court flattery,[30] but, instead, the view from the other side of the mirror. However, Aretino's dialogue is not so simple as at first sight appears. It should perhaps be seen in relation to the first volume of the *Lettere*, in which there is much flattery of men of high rank and of court members interspersed with some criticism of that same institution.[31] Indeed, in the *Ragionamento* some courtiers are praised by Aretino. There may have been alternatives, such as learned academies, but nevertheless even for Aretino it was impossible not to become involved in the court system, despite what he saw as its shortcomings.[32] Thus, it can be seen that the Equicola-Aretino antithesis does not work as well as one might have thought. Furthermore, as has been argued here, Equicola was a much more complex figure than many critics have granted. His biography is not as straightforward as at first sight appears: it is full of the contradictions of someone who had to come to terms with the society into which he had entered and had to find ways of exploiting it to his advantage. The sacrifices which his attitude entailed in terms of personal autonomy were counterbalanced by a very successful career. Equicola's *iter* allows the critic to trace in some detail the force of court society on the individual intellectual and the response of that same intellectual to court society.

NOTES

1 An extreme example of the tendency to overemphasize Castiglione's policy-making power is to be found in G. La Rocca, 'Il contributo di Baldassar Castiglione alla formazione della politica estera gonzaghesca negli ultimi anni del papato di Leone X: 1519–1521', in *Mantova e i Gonzaga nella civiltà del Rinascimento. Atti del Convegno, Mantova 1974* (Segrate, Edigraf, 1978). See also his 'Il Castiglione diplomatico e politico (profilo ermeneutico)', in *Convegno di studio su Baldassare Castiglione nel quinto centenario della nascita*, (Mantua, Accademia Virgiliana, 1980), pp. 61–80. Typical of the way in which Equicola has been treated is A. Luzio and R. Renier, *La coltura e le relazioni letterarie di Isabella d'Este* (Turin, Bona, 1903), pp. 134–35. Attempts have been made to redress the balance: D. Santoro, *Della vita e delle opere di Mario Equicola* (Chieti, N. Jecco, 1906).

However this work falls into the trap of portraying a too perfect Equicola. A more recent study is S. D. Kolsky, 'Mario Equicola: A Biographical Reappraisal' (unpublished Ph. D. thesis, University of London, 1981), soon to be published in a revised form by Droz, Geneva. For further biographical details, the reader should consult these two studies.

2 On Sigismondo Cantelmo, see T. Ascari's entry in the *Dizionario Biografico degli Italiani* [DBI] (Rome, Istituto della Enciclopedia Italiana, 1975), XVIII, 277–79.

3 For details, see A. Altamura, *Jacobo Sanazzaro. Con appendici di documenti e testi inediti* (Naples, S. Viti, 1951).

4 The exact dates of composition of these two works are uncertain (the *De mulieribus* was probably written in 1501 or before, and the *Nec spe nec metu* in 1505). See also Kolsky 'Mario Equicola', pp. 83–86.

5 Biblioteca Nazionale Universitaria, Turin, Cod. N. III 10, Mario Equicola, *Libro de natura de amore*, autograph ms., fs. 197r–197v. All subsequent references to the *Libro* will be to the printed version of 1525 (Mario Equicola, *Libro de natura de amore* [Venice, Lorenzo Lorio da Portes, 1525] 4°). For details of the work's composition and genesis, see R. Renier, 'Per la cronologia e la composizione del *Libro de natura de amore* di Mario Equicola', *GSLI*, 14 (1889), 212–33, and I. Rocchi, 'Per una nuova cronologia e valutazione del *Libro de natura de amore* di Mario Equicola', *GSLI*, 153 (1976), 566–85.

6 M. Bandello, *Tutte le opere*, edited by F. Flora, 2 vols (Milan, Mondadori, 1952), I, 388 (novella XXX). For an overview of Isabella d'Este, see S. Kolsky, 'Images of Isabella d'Este', *Italian Studies*, 39 (1984), 47–62.

7 On Benedetto Capilupi, see T. Ascari in *DBI*, XVIII, 528–30, and M. L. Doglio, 'Le *Instituzioni* di Mario Equicola: dall'*Institutio principis* alla formazione del segretario', *GSLI*, 159 (1982) 505–35. For the historical background consult G. Coniglio, *I Gonzaga* (Varese, dall'Oglio, 1981), pp. 241–60, and L. Mazzoldi, *Mantova. La storia*, 3 vols (Mantua, Istituto Carlo d'Arco, 1961), II, 269–81.

8 The change of direction that Mantuan politics took in the period 1519–22 is documented in S. Kolsky, 'Castiglione's biography: The courtier and the Italian princes', *Spunti e Ricerche*, 1 (1985), 1–34 (pp. 18–24).

9 It is relevant at this point to indicate that historians have not paid sufficient attention to the post of secretary in the Italian Renaissance (which will be the subject of future studies by the present author). Individual studies of various secretaries would allow the historian to formulate more clearly the extent and effects of bureaucratization in the period. More attention needs to be paid to writings on the duties of the secretary, notably, F. Sansovino, *Del secretario libri VII* (Venice, Altobello Salicato, 1588), 8°. The importance of secretaries in the development of the Italian language and literature cannot be underestimated, especially considering the case of Pietro Bembo, who created the preconditions of a literature which, while being based on a highly developed theory of language, was, as far as the content was concerned, determined to a not insignificant degree by the hierarchies of power.

10 Castiglione's lack of enthusiasm for military activities is discussed by J. R. Hale, 'Castiglione's military career', *Italian Studies*, 36 (1981), 41–57; and for Equicola, see S. D. Kolsky, 'Mario Equicola', p. 258. Federico Gonzaga stated what he expected from those in his employment in a letter of 4 August 1522, Archivio di Stato, Mantua [ASMN], Archivio Gonzaga [AG], busta (b) 2928, Libro 272, f. 33r: 'Secundo loro grado et conditione amamo tutti nostri domestici et familiari. Ma doe virtù precipuamente abramamo di arme et

de lettere. Et del uno et del altro exercitio studiosi desideramo siano non solamente nel nostro dominio ma nel altrui per nostro amore et respecto accarezati'.

11 ASMN, AG, b. 2929, Libro 283, Marmirolo, 7 August 1525, Federico Gonzaga to Ennio Filonardi, Bishop of Veroli.

12 ASMN, AG, Registro dei Decreti, Libro 37, fs. 111r–111v.

13 See B. Castiglione, *Le lettere (1497–marzo 1521)* (Milan, Mondadori, 1978), p. 371. For a similar instance, see Kolsky, 'Mario Equicola', p. 255.

14 An exemplary case of this sort is provided by the Ferrarese poet Antonio Cammelli, known as il Pistoia; see *I sonetti del Pistoia, giusta l'apografo trivulziano*, edited by R. Renier (Turin, Loescher, 1888). For a commentary on his poetry, see R. Pallone, *Anticlericalismo e ingiustizie sociali nell'Italia del 400* (Rome, Trevi, 1975).

15 'Ma lasciamo le cose già tanto tempo invecchiate e delle barbare e longinque nationi, percorriamo la Grecia dove, per esser creduta questa facultà prima di tutte l'altre facultati, fu maggior di tutte estimata, e detta (se a Strabone si crede) prima Philosophia perciochè quivi era ferma opinione (come Platone e innanzi a Platone i Pithagorici dissero) che'l mondo tutto constasse di concento e armonia', *Institutioni di Mario Equicola al comporre in ogni sorte di rima della lingua volgare* (Milan, 1541), f. A4r. All subsequent references to this work will appear in the text. Doglio, in the article referred to in note 7, analyses this work in some depth but has really failed to bring out the consequences of the model poet-patron. The article is further marred by biographical inaccuracies and by the failure to support her statements: for example on a number of occasions she asserts that a particular text was 'ben noto all'Equicola' (p. 519) without producing any supporting evidence.

16 B. Castiglione, *Il libro del cortegiano*, introduzione di A. Quondam (Milan, Garzanti, 1981), p. 421. Subsequent references to this work are given in the text.

17 For Equicola, poetry (and in particular the poetry of celebration) is the most important genre: 'noi stimiamo il Poeta ad tutti gli altri scrittori (come più degli altri ingegnoso) deverse preponere' (*Institutioni*, f. B3r). Thus, poetry, as a courtly act, is given theoretical foundations ('che i gran fatti fossero da' buoni scrittori celebrati', *Institutioni*, f. B2r). Aristotle's appreciation of poetry thus gains significance in this context: 'Aristotele molti suoi luoghi con versi de' Poeti conferma e di poetica scrisse. Si dannano le favole, da quelli che non intendono che importi tal nome, i ragionamenti, ne' quali s'inducono a parlar gl'inanimati non rifiutò Aristotele (*Institutioni*, f. B3r).

18 See J. R. Woodhouse, *Baldesar Castiglione. A Reassessment of 'The Courtier'* (Edinburgh, Edinburgh University Press, 1978), pp. 59–62.

19 ASMN, AG, b. 2475, Mantua, 29 May 1509, Tolomeo Spagnuoli to Francesco Gonzaga. It is clear that rulers of small city states would consider the political benefits of encomiastic and other humanistic literature in terms of their rivalry and competition with other states: a kind of self-perpetuating circle which privileges particular acts of writing and tends to exclude others (public literature to the detriment of private: letter writing becomes a public event with the appearance of numerous collections; chronicles and histories of cities serve to enhance a prince's reputation, and so on. Lyric poetry, in general terms, with the coming of the sixteenth century, tends to be supremely conscious of models which severely limit personal interventions). Glorification of a particular ruler through literature which proposes immortality was an extension of dynastic concerns. Literary patronage was something expected of a ruler who had Augustan pretensions. It moved towards the monumental

because of the tendency to mythologize a prince, to remove him from history which, in the circumstances of the Italian peninsula, meant change, disruption, and possibly political death. Literature was also a means of presenting power in a civilizing guise. Perhaps this is the main thrust of Poliziano's *Stanze per la giostra* in which wild instinctual forces are brought under control by Love and Art. The 'giostra' itself is a virtual representation of the taming of power by cultured princes. 'Civilization' cements together culture and force, hence endowing government with a double validation which by-passes the problem of legitimacy. From this point of view the use of Latin by humanistic courtiers added to the mystique of power.

20 See the appendix to A. Luzio, *I precettori d'Isabella d'Este*, (Ancona, Morelli, 1887).

21 An excellent study of *magnificentia* is R. G. Brown, *The Politics of Magnificence in Ferrara 1450–1505: A Study in the Socio-Political Implications of Renaissance Spectacle* (unpublished Ph.D. thesis, University of Edinburgh, 1982). Equicola was well aware of the importance of *magnificentia.* In his *Chronica di Mantua* (published after July 1521), he mentions the building programme of Ludovico Gonzaga as an example of this princely virtue.

22 The amount of space devoted, first of all, to spoken language and, then, to conversation in the *Cortegiano* is indicative of the key role of oral culture in the struggle for survival at court. Castiglione treats jokes and counselling the prince as the two extremes of conversation – both necessary to win the favour of the ruler.

23 See, for instance, G. Bárberi Squarotti, 'L'amore in corte: il trattato dell'Equicola', *Critica letteraria,* 35 (1982), 211–24.

24 G. Savonarola, *Tractato dello amore di Jesu Christo* (Florence, Antonio Mischomini, 26 June 1492), 4°. For Savonarola's relationship with Florentine Neoplatonism, see D. P. Walker, *The Ancient Theology*, (London, Duckworth, 1972), pp. 42–62.

25 *Tractato* f. a2r. And in a similar vein 'chi non ama dunque Jesu sarà dannato' (f. a3r).

26 'Per fondamento solido della prima conclusione pigliaremo la sacra scrittura' (*Tractato*, f. a3r). Also, 'Et prima per auctorità della sacra scriptura acciochè non parliamo in vento' (f. a4r).

27 *Tractato*, f. a4v. Savonarola goes on to refine his point: 'L'amore della scientia genera tanta consolatione nel core che molti philosophi per quella fruire si sono separati da tutte le delectationi mondani' (f. a4v).

28 *Libro*, f. 235r. (This is a misprint in the 1525 edition and in reality should be f. 233r). See R. Romano, 'L'intellettuale nella società italiana del XV e VXI secolo', in his *Tra due crisi: L'Italia del Rinascimento*, (Turin, Einaudi, 1971), pp. 117–36.

29 See *Libro*, fs. 97r–119v for a discussion of Equicola's categories of love.

30 'Piccenardo: Ma se fossero scritti in un libro i rancori, le invidie, le contese, le nimicitie, i dispendii, le sollecitudini, le querele, le fatiche, l'ire et i cordogli patiti per venire a cotal fine. Vi faria paura l'aprirlo non che il leggerlo' (*Ragionamento nel quale M. Pietro Aretino figura quattro suoi amici che favellano de le Corti del mondo e di Quella del Cielo*, stampato in Novara nel MDXXXVIII, 4°, fs. d2r–d2v).

[31] Pietro Aretino, *Lettere. Il primo e il secondo libro*, edited by F. Flora (Milan, Mondadori, 1960).

[32] 'Dolce: Nè credo che sia giardino nè palazzo che pareggi il piacere che io piglio nel visitare il divino Bembo, il compare, e l'Academia de gli altri amici' (*Ragionamento,* f. q1r).

IX

Appunti sulla biografia di Mario Equicola

Questo saggio prende avvio dalla voce su Mario Equicola del *Dizionario biografico degli italiani*[1]. Il caso biografico dell'Equicola rappresenta non soltanto il rovescio della medaglia rispetto alla biografia troppe volte idealizzata di un Castiglione[2], ma offre allo studioso anche l'opportunità di esaminare il ruolo dell'intellettuale-scrittore nella corte rinascimentale[3]. La funzione dell'intellettuale-scrittore non si limita a produrre solo testi letterari/intellettuali, sia stampati che manoscritti, ma gli si affidano anche altre mansioni altrettanto importanti che non si possono trascurare per poter accomunare tutti gli elementi, spesso eterogenei, della vita dello «scrittore». Si deve infatti tener presente il fatto che in quel periodo, fra lo scorcio del Quattrocento e l'inizio del Cinquecento, gli intellettuali stavano creandosi un'identità attraverso la quale potevano inserirsi nel sistema della corte. Non è casuale che una sostanziosa sezione del quinto libro del *Libro de natura de amore*, pubblicato nel 1525, verta sulla problematica del cortegiano. Né si può supporre che Castiglione ed Equicola siano stati in contatto fra di loro tra 1516 e 1524[4]. Di con-

---

[1] P. Cherchi, «Equicola, Mario», vol. 43 (Roma, Istituto della Enciclopedia Italiana, 1993), pp. 34-40.

[2] Si veda C. Dionisotti, rec. a V. Cian, *Un illustre nunzio pontificio*, in «Giornale storico della letteratura italiana», 129 (1952), pp. 31-57.

[3] Cf. S. Kolsky, *Mario Equicola. The Real Courtier*, Geneva, Droz, 1991. Si veda anche la recensione di Fabio Cimarosti a Mario Equicola, *De natura de amore. Libro quarto*, a cura di Enrico Musacchio e Graziella del Ciaco, Bologna, Cappelli, 1989, in «Filologia e critica», XVI, 1991, fascicolo II, pp. 279-83.

[4] È notevole che Cherchi si serva una sola volta del termine cortegiano in riferimento a un testo pseudo-Equicoliano, *Il nuovo corteggiano*, in cui, come dichiara l'autore stesso, «è tutto assente la corte rinascimentale» (p. 38). Si veda S. Kolsky, *Did Mario Equicola write* Il novo corteggiano?, in «Aevum», 57 (1983),

seguenza è importante esser in grado di tracciare la carriera di un arrivista come Equicola allo scopo di spiegare i motivi del suo successo, nonché i modi impiegati per raggiungerlo. Risulta altrettanto cruciale il ruolo della scrittura, denominata «cortegiana», nella sua ascesi sociale. La definizione della sua produzione letteraria come «cortegiana» denota l'impatto notevole del contesto sociale del tempo sul tipo di discorso che l'Equicola aveva fatto proprio. Peraltro, da un lato la forma del discorso risponde alle esigenze della corte, alla necessità di giustificarla e glorificarla, mentre dall'altro lato propone uno spazio in cui lo scrittore-cortegiano può contribuire alla costituzione della corte e implicitamente a se stesso. Il termine «scrittore» forse non denota le abilità creative e professionali di un Equicola che, fra l'altro, è autore di più di quindici opere stampate, scritte sia in latino che in volgare. Però il segretario dei Cantelmi (più tardi segretario di Isabella d'Este e poi di suo figlio, Federico Gonzaga) fu coinvolto in numerose attività che sono altrettanto valide quanto quelle di uno scrittore, e che per di più facevano parte della sua vita di cortegiano. Fin dall'inizio della sua carriera fu impegnato in iniziative diplomatiche che richiedevano un costante scambio epistolare e una conoscenza delle modalità della diplomazia e delle corti. Si deve prendere in considerazione tutti i compiti che l'Equicola si trovava a svolgere nel corso della sua carriera per completare la sua biografia.

È necessario innanzi tutto stabilire i fatti fondamentali della vita di Mario Equicola. La nascita è datata nel 1470, secondo la testimonianza stessa dell'Equicola[5]. In merito ai suoi primi anni c'è un'assenza di documenti attendibili che ha prodotto varie ipotesi presentateci come «fatti assoluti», senza una sicura base documentata, da parte di alcuni studiosi. Che l'Equicola fosse figlio illegittimo di Giampaolo Cantelmo è un'ipotesi molto attraente, ma quasi impossibile da confermare. Il cognome Caccialupi appare parecchie volte in documenti legali, dunque non può essere un'invenzione o errore da parte dell'Equicola[6] e rende ancora più tenue l'ipotesi di una parentela tanto stretta tra lui e il Cantelmo. Altri luoghi comuni della biografia equicoliana sono altrettanto difficili da confermare per la mancanza di documenti fondamentali. L'asserzione che

416-27 e Id., *Further corrections and additions to the bibliography of Mario Equicola*, in «Aevum», 62 (1988), 310-315.

[5] Per ulteriori particolari si consulti, S. Kolsky, *The Real courtier*, *op. cit.*, p. 17.

[6] *Ivi*, pp. 20-22.

l'Equicola avesse studiato diritto a Napoli, non è probante, ma sembrava accettabile per il fatto che la conoscenza della legge era stata in tempi passati il requisito necessario per un segretario. Analizzando più attentamente la carriera dell'Equicola, il suo coinvolgimento in questioni giuridiche sembra non avere mai un ruolo di spicco, né sembra essere rilevante nell'assegnazione dei suoi vari posti tenuti alla corte. Da un certo punto di vista, quindi, si vorrebbe sminuire il ruolo dell'Equicola a quello di un semplice segretario. Ma gradualmente, mentre l'Equicola acquisisce più esperienza e prestigio, la parte legale della sua funzione sembra essere ridotta al minimo. L'Equicola diventa così segretario-cortegiano e l'aspetto cortegiano prende il sopravvento su quello puramente tecnico-amministrativo. Infatti, ciò che conta di più sono le sue conoscenze umanistiche che assumono un'importanza non tanto perché hanno una particolare incidenza sul suo lavoro quotidiano di segretario, ma perché aggiungono un alone di prestigio e raffinatezza alla cancelleria del principe. Bisogna inoltre considerare che l'Equicola, oltre che espletare le sue mansioni di segretario, era stato selezionato a Mantova, prima da Isabella d'Este e poi da Federico Gonzaga, come «l'uomo» della Marchesana o del Marchese e come tale poteva agire più liberamente ed efficacemente all'interno della macchinosa burocrazia mantovana.

Prima di trovare il posto come precettore a Mantova nel 1508, la vita dell'Equicola ci presenta dei quesiti che rimangono irrisolti. Da stabilire rimane infatti il rapporto dell'Equicola con la vita intellettuale napoletana. Molti studiosi parlano di un suo possibile soggiorna a Napoli negli anni prima del 1500. Un lungo soggiorno a Napoli non si concilia con il fatto che i Cantelmi conducevano sostanzialmente una vita assai movimentata negli ultimi anni del Quattrocento, conseguenza del loro conflitto con la corona aragonese. Solo questo metterebbe in dubbio un rapporto prolungato dell'Equicola con l'accademia pontaniana. Per di più Giampaolo Cantelmo perdette il suo ultimo possesso nel regno nel 1487 (Alvito, luogo natio dell'Equicola, simbolo concreto di una perdita personale). Anche prima dell'«invasione» francese del 1494, l'Equicola iniziò una vita in esilio che durò fino alla morte. Dunque, la sua vita prima del 1508, è caratterizzata dall'estremo movimento e dall'insicurezza. L'esser sempre in movimento è un indizio della precarietà della sua esistenza e spiega il suo profondo desiderio per la stabilità e la sistemazione sicura.

Sembra assumere un particolare rilievo il fatto che Giampaolo

Cantelmo si stanziò a Roma perché qui il giovane Equicola poteva entrare in contatto con l'accademia romana sotto la presidenza di Pomponio Leto, menzionato parecchie volte nell'opera equicoliana[7]. Certo non si può escludere contatti importanti con intellettuali napoletani, ma la domanda da porre è quando e come ebbe la possibilità di fare conoscenza con loro. In certi casi, Equicola avrà con tutta probabilità rinnovato amicizia con certi intellettuali fuori del regno incontrandone anche degli altri per la prima volta (a Roma, in Francia[8] e anche a Ferrara o a Mantova). Più tardi, l'Equicola fu mandato a Napoli più d'una volta come ambasciatore personale di Ippolito d'Este e di Isabella d'Este.

In questo contesto, non si può sottovalutare l'importanza dei soggiorni francesi dell'Equicola. Non si tratta in specifico di un «periodo francese»[9] perché l'Equicola era sempre in movimento, normalmente tra Ferrara e i vari posti in cui si trovava la corte francese per via delle pressioni politiche durante il primo Cinquecento. I Cantelmi sempre speravano, prima della sconfitta del partito francese, di riacquistare i loro feudi nel regno. Ed è per questo motivo che l'Equicola si sentiva così straniato da Sigismondo Cantelmo che, malgrado la situazione stesse peggiorando, il figlio di Giampaolo non negava mai la possibilità di rientrare nei loro territori. L'Equicola non ne era affatto convinto. Era un momento di altissime tensioni politiche e personali, nelle quali l'Equicola doveva sviluppare le sue tecniche diplomatiche sia per il desiderio dei Cantelmi di tornare nelle loro terre che per guadagnarsi dei mezzi di sopravvivenza personale. Le numerose lettere che scriveva in quest'epoca a Margherita Maloselli, moglie di Sigismondo Cantelmo, servirono a sfogare le frustrazioni e i suoi desideri personali in un periodo difficile. Forse già si intravedeva una via d'uscita dalla sua situazione difficile: Margherita era amica intima di Isabella d'Este. Malgrado le pressioni politiche, l'Equicola non abbandonava mai i suoi studi stabilendo amicizie con parecchi intellettuali francesi e italiani[10]. Gli studi rappresentavano la promessa di una vita più comoda e agiata, la prospettiva di

---

[7] *Ivi*, pp. 27-30, 39.

[8] Si veda C. Vecce, *Un'apologia per l'Equicola. Le due redazioni della "Pro Gallis apologia di Mario Equicola e la traduzione di Michel Roté"*, Napoli, Istituto Universitario Orientale, Dipartimento di studi letterari e linguistici dell'occidente, 1990, pp. 19-38. Anche S. Kolsky, *The Real Courtier*, *op. cit.*, pp. 62, 80-86, 90-92.

[9] P. Cherchi, *Equicola Mario*, *op. cit.*, p. 35.

[10] Si veda C. Vecce, *Iacopo Sannazzaro in Francia. Scoperte di codici all'inizio del XVI secolo*, Padova, Antenore, 1988, pp. 24-26.

diventare rinomato e trovare un posto più stabile e meno arduo. Dava sfogo ai suoi interessi personali invece di trovarsi sempre al servizio dei suoi padroni. Questo contatto con la corte francese segnala un momento di grande importanza nella vita dell'Equicola che avrà un'influenza duratura su di lui[11].

In questo primo periodo della vita equicoliana (prima del suo trasferimento definitivo a Mantova nel 1508), l'Equicola intese lasciare un segno della sua presenza sulla scena intellettuale componendo testi latini e facendo così sfoggio della sua erudizione. Però all'interno di «questa prima fase» (Cherchi, p. 34) si può notare un radicale cambiamento di programma. Le prime opere includono *De religione libellus, Oratio de passione Domini,* che dimostrano un certo interesse accademico nella storia della religione, forse parte del retaggio della scuola romana di Flavio Biondo e di Pomponio Leto. È quindi molto sorprendente trovare un testo come *De mulieribus* fra le sue prime opere (pubblicato nel 1501). Anziché rappresentare il futuro dell'«*otium* letterario dell'Equicola» (Cherchi, p. 34), quest'opuscoletto rappresenta piuttosto un fine calcolo politico basato su un apprezzamento del funzionamento delle corti settentrionali italiane. Il suo *rapprochement* con Margherita Moloselli fu lo spunto critico che gli faceva vedere un possibile modo attraverso il quale lei poteva allontanarsi dalla politica fallimentare del marito. Non è un caso che l'opera miri a lodare non soltanto Margherita Maloselli, ma a introdurre Isabella d'Este nell'ambito del suo discorso. L'Equicola non esita a promuovere un ruolo attivo, politicamente impegnato, per le donne d'*élite*. Non c'è neanche dubbio che l'Equicola aveva anche mire personali perché aveva intuito l'importanza che la politica culturale aveva per la marchesa di Mantova. *De mulieribus* presenta esplicitamente l'Equicola come l'intellettuale che capisce i bisogni di Isabella d'Este in quanto lei voleva imporsi nel mondo maschile della politica e della cultura. Questo testo fornisce una base ideologica attraverso la quale una donna poteva giustificare il suo sviamento dalle norme imposte sul comportamento femminile. *De mulieribus*, quindi, segnala una svolta critica per l'Equicola, indicando la sua disponibilità di diventare cortegiano in un ambiente presieduto da grandi donne. È la sua prima scrittura *cortegiana* in cui le metodologie umanistiche adoperate da lui finora vengono adattate alla situazione della corte rinascimentale. A questo punto

[11] Si veda F. SIMONE, *Fonti e testimonianze mantovane sulla civiltà francese del Rinascimento*, in «Giornale storico della letteratura italiana», 104 (1977), pp. 1-44.

l'Equicola fece una scelta a cui rimarrà fedele per tutta la sua vita: esplorerà e farà suoi i temi cortegiani che erano allora correnti (imprese, amore, storia dinastica e così via).

Questi temi cortegiani si ricollegano intimamente con la situazione personale dell'Equicola. Due opere scritte prima del suo arrivo definitivo a Mantova dimostrano chiaramente le mire dell'autore. *Nec spe nec metu*, composto probabilmente verso il termine del suo ultimo soggiorno francese ovvero verso il 1506, ma solo pubblicato nel 1513, e *De opportunitate*, pubblicato nel 1507. Questi due dialoghi esprimono il desiderio cocente dell'Equicola di poter trovare il posto fisso nella corte o di Mantova o di Ferrara. Quindi gli argomenti scelti vertono su due personaggi di spicco di queste due corti: su Isabella d'Este (*Nec spe nec metu*) e su Ippolito d'Este, suo fratello (*De opportunitate*). In entrambi i testi, l'Equicola intende dimostrare le speciali qualità del soggetto, cioè, la scelta del «motto» o dell'impresa, tramite una disamina particolareggiata e minuziosa della frase misteriosa di Isabella d'Este («Nec spe nec metu»), spiegando tutte le possibili fonti e implicazioni classiche del detto isabelliano e dell'immagine visiva, scelta da Ippolito d'Este, per dargli un alone di potere e di onnipresenza.

L'aver percepito che l'impresa svolgeva una funzione importante nel creare la personalità pubblica del principe è un intuito dell'Equicola che sottolinea la sua comprensione della cultura delle corti e il ruolo che ci poteva avere l'intellettuale. L'Equicola presta le sue conoscenze classiche ai principi per dargli una profondità di pensiero, altrimenti assente. La scelta stessa di Ippolito e Isabella d'Este conferma il fatto che i due dialoghi riflettono deliberatamente la conferma di un rapporto finora abbastanza informale nella speranza che uno di loro potesse offrirgli un posto più adatto al suo temperamento e alle sue capacità.

Nel caso di Ippolito d'Este, l'Equicola sfrutta il tema del «privatum signum» in modo da illustrare come la scelta del simbolo personale del falcone su un orologio fosse molto acuta, offrendo al lettore tutta una gamma di significati che si ricollegano al simbolo[12]. L'Equicola così compie una doppia operazione. La prima è di

[12] «Hyppolitus Estensis cardinalis memorandam sententiam ingeniosis patere voluit; et ut omnium oculi voluptate afficerentur» (*De opportunitate*, Napoli [«Antonius de Caneto papiensis»], MDVII, fol. XI Februarii, fol. Blr. L'Equicola anche riconosce la funzione pubblica dell'impresa: «Quod autem nunc ad decus et honorem insignia ponimus. Virtutis ergo imagines ponebantur» (fol. B2v). Per

dimostrare a tutti l'acutezza di Ippolito d'Este, basata sul miglior esempio di Roma antica. La seconda è di rivelare il proprio *ingenium* nonché l'immensità della sua conoscenza sulla cultura antica. Il legame tra i due aspetti è cruciale per il futuro funzionamento del cortegiano perché quest'ultimo propone un'alleanza intellettuale che implica un aumento di prestigio per il cardinale. L'Equicola si offre come qualcuno che può interpretare il comportamento del principe secondo un paradigma umanistico che nobilita anche un aspetto apparentemente minimo della cultura della corte tramite il cumulo di tante fonti classiche addotto in appoggio al tema del testo. La mostra di tanti nomi propri e di tanti concetti servono ad aumentare il prestigio della scelta originale dell'impresa. Per l'Equicola il piacere della citazione consiste non soltanto nel far sfoggio della sua conoscenza, ma anche nel metterla a disposizione del principe, nel farla risuscitare in una visione diretta del mondo antico per mostrare il legame tra il regime estense e gli imperatori di Roma antica.

La pubblicazione del *De opportunitate* coincide con una missione diplomatica a Napoli nel 1507 che l'Equicola aveva fatto come rappresentante personale di Ippolito d'Este[13]. Il dialogo ha anche la funzione di rinforzare i suoi rapporti con gli intellettuali del Regno di Napoli. La scelta di interlocutori è un ulteriore indizio dell'allontanamento dalle posizioni prese dal suo padrone Sigismondo Cantelmo. Siamo vicini a una rottura totale con la politica del Cantelmo e si noti la volontà dell'Equicola di cambiare rotta e di assecondare i piani di un possibile nuovo padrone. Dunque, non è un caso che il suo dialogo sia ambientato nel mondo accademico aragonese. Uno degli interlocutori è Girolamo Carbone, il quale era molto vicino alla corona aragonese[14]. Carbone stesso aveva intrapreso una missione diplomatica a Ferrara, probabilmente prima del 1501[15].

---

quest'opera si veda N. Webb, *Momus with little flatteries: intellectual life at the Italian courts*, in *Mantegna and 15th-Century Court Culture. Lectures Delivered in Connection with the Andrea Mantegna Exhibition at the Royal Academy of Arts, London, 1992*, a cura di Francis Ames-Lewis e Anka Bednarek, London, Department of History of Art, Birkbeck College, University of London, 1993, pp. 56-71 (66-67) e S. Kolsky, *The Real Courtier*, *op. cit.*, pp. 92-7.

[13] *Ivi*, p. 97.

[14] Per cui Pierre de Montera, *L'humaniste napolitain Girolamo Carbone et ses poésies inédites*, Napoli, Ricciardi, 1935, e R. Pastore, *Carbone, Girolamo*, *Dizionario biografico degli italiani*, 19, Roma, Istituto della Enciclopedia Italiana, 1976, pp. 695-98.

[15] Montera, *op. cit.*, p. LIV.

Il tema dell'opportunità[16] ha una forte risonanza nella cultura cortegiana perché segnala che la virtù assoluta sta perdendo valore come guida al comportamento nei confronti della corte per essere complementata o quasi sostituita dall'*opportunitas*[17]. Secondo Castiglione, il comportamento deve adattarsi alle circostanze in cui si trova il cortegiano e certe azioni si possono compiere solo al momento giusto[18]. Qui, nel *De opportunitate* percepiamo l'abbozzo di una tale teoria che conduce a una prassi cortegiana che caratterizzerà la corte rinascimentale. Affinché il cortegiano possa sopravvivere presso la corte o, eventualmente, farsi influente, diventa meno rilevante il merito della persona rispetto ai tentativi per ingraziarsi il principe[19]. Si pensi al discorso «minoritario» del Calmeta nel *Cortegiano,* non accettato dagli altri interlocutori. Della Casa rappresenta il fine logico di un tale ragionamento[20]. Al fine di ottenere il favore del principe, infatti, il cortegiano o qualsiasi altra persona diventa artista e crea quelle circostanze in cui può far avvalere le sue possibilità di premio, stima e favore[21].

La produzione a stampa costituisce solo una parte di quelle che si possono definire le scritture di Mario Equicola. Dare un significato troppo stretto alla parola «scrittura» corre il rischio di escludere troppe categorie di scritti. Durante il corso di tutta la sua carriera di segretario, si nota l'importanza assunta dalle lettere che l'Equicola scrive durante le sue frequenti assenze, prima da Ferrara e poi da Mantova. Prima del suo trasferimento a Mantova, il *corpus* più cospicuo di lettere equicoliane saranno quelle scritte a Margherita Maloselli, durante i suoi soggiorni in Francia. Ovviamente, hanno la primaria funzione di tener la moglie di Sigismondo Cantelmo al corrente degli ultimi sviluppi della situazione critica in cui si trova il marito. In questo giro di anni qualche altra lettera era stata scritta

---

16 «Quicquid acturi sumus captato tempore adendum quasi viva voce pronunciat et opportunitatem tempestivitatemque a nobis non omittendam sapientissime docet» (fol. A3v).

17 «At occasio ut rei militaris scriptores testantur plus quam virtus ipsa iuvare solet fortunamque superat» (fol. E1r).

18 *Il libro del cortegiano con una scelta delle Opere minori di Baldesar Castiglione,* a cura di Bruno Maier, Turin, 1964², II, XIII; p. 210; II, XIX; p. 219.

19 «hinc morale ilud elicitur petituri aliquid a regibus observent tempora quibus laeti sint» (fol. B4v).

20 *Il libro del Cortegiano, op. cit.,* II, XXI; pp. 222-23.

21 «occasioni tanta vis est in rebus omnibus ut saepe ea ad iuti plerique magna ex nihilo fecerint» (fol. D4v).

dall'Equicola al marchese di Mantova, Francesco Gonzaga, nella speranza di dimostrarsi utile e volenteroso nel fornirgli informazioni politiche. Lo scrivere lettere fa parte del suo compito di segretario e costituisce una parte cospicua della sua produzione. Informare i principi degli avvenimenti politici che possono interessarli è un compito che non si deve sottovalutare né dal punto di vista puramente politico né da quello sociale perché fa parte del circuito clientelistico. Inoltre, i Gonzaga, principi di uno stato piccolo che era sempre sotto la minaccia di quelli più potenti durante questo periodo, avevano bisogno del maggior numero di informazioni possibili. In questo senso, qualsiasi informazione valida avrebbe potuto risultare utile oltre che venir considerata come segno di amicizia o futura lealtà.

La lettera era un genere che si addiceva molto bene allo stile «letterario» dell'Equicola (ma non intesa come lettera umanistica da pubblicare, anche se a volte l'Equicola si permette di dilungarsi in temi letterari o filosofici). Il piacere della citazione e degli elenchi che sono così presenti nelle opere letterarie trovano un certo parallelismo nelle lettere: deve esporre in una lettera la più grande quantità di informazioni, forse con un minimo commento, affinché quelli che la leggono possano prendere decisioni sulla base del suo contenuto. In questo campo l'Equicola non è esente da difetti, non sapendo sempre scegliere tra informazioni importanti e altre, il che può condurre a una grande confusione. Un altro aspetto della lettera equicoliana è il bisogno di divertire il lettore, pur tuttavia senza che l'Equicola diventi un clown o giocoliere. Il divertimento, infatti, fa parte integrante della vita di corte.

Connessi alla produzione epistolare sono altri compiti che denotano l'aspetto quotidiano della vita di un segretario: fare copie di lettere per il libro di copialettere, preparare abbozzi di lettere, redigere decreti e altri documenti di natura ufficiale. Nel caso equicoliano si trovano relativamente poche lettere trascritte da lui, forse perché la sua scrittura può essere difficile da decifrare. Pur tuttavia non si può trascurare la routine di ordinaria amministrazione su cui un segretario doveva concentrarsi. Il senso delle parole «scrittore» e «scrittura» si devono allargare per includere testi «non-canonici» e non-letterari. Per un personaggio del tipo dell'Equicola non si può limitare il senso della parola «scrittura» solo a libri stampati o a qualche manoscritto privilegiato dagli studiosi. Più di mille lettere equicoliane sono sopravvissute – una mole massiccia che per la maggior parte si trova nell'Archivio di Stato di Mantova.

Se possiamo definire l'Equicola come scrittore-cortegiano, questo vuole dire che dobbiamo prendere in considerazione *tutti* i suoi scritti di qualsiasi genere per poter analizzare come un intellettuale umanista si adattava ai bisogni della corte e come la corte stessa subordinava la pura conoscenza classica alle sue esigenze contingenti. Nel contempo, lo scrittore-cortegiano contribuiva a creare immagini della corte come centro di erudizione, sviluppando una ideologia della corte, e rafforzando così la propria posizione in alleanza con i principi. L'Equicola si costruisce così un ruolo all'interno del sistema della corte come precettore o segretario, pur essendo un «altro»: non era cioè mantovano, né di nascita nobile. Ma non essendoci lì a Mantova posto per uno studioso, doveva rendersi utile nelle vicende politiche dello stato. Anche quando era precettore di Isabella d'Este non è esentato da compiti prettamente politici. Il termine precettore rivela soltanto una parte del ruolo svolto dall'Equicola nel periodo 1508-1519. C'era, senza dubbio, il compito di insegnare alla marchesana il latino nonché altri elementi della cultura classica. A volte doveva tradurre testi latini in volgare sotto commissione di Isabella d'Este[22]. Però non si può limitare il lavoro dell'Equicola come precettore alle sole operazioni di insegnamento. Il suo ruolo era molto più esteso e profondo.

Diventò il rappresentante personale di Isabella d'Este nella sua politica facendo in modo che lei potesse agire indipendentemente dal marito e dalla sua rete di ambasciatori. Molto probabilmente Isabella d'Este lo utilizzava perché sviluppasse i concetti di fondo che reggevano lo studiolo e la grotta, stanze che erano al centro degli interessi culturali della marchesana[23]. È anche possibile che progettasse certi quadri che si trovavano nello studiolo; esistono documenti che attestano che l'Equicola svolgeva questo lavoro per Alfonso d'Este, Duca di Ferrara e più avanti per Federico Gonzaga[24]. Quindi l'Equicola divenne il perno non soltanto delle espressioni culturali della marchesana, ma anche della sua politica dinastica per cui venne inviato in frequenti viaggi a Ferrara e altrove. Fu portavoce delle aspirazioni culturali e politiche di Isabella d'Este anche

---

[22] S. Kolsky, *The Real Courties, op. cit.*, p. 103.

[23] Si veda S. Kolsky, *An unnoticed description of Isabella d'Este's Grotta*, in «Journal of the Warburg and Courtauld Institutes», 52 (1989), pp. 232-235.

[24] Si vedano R. Lightbown, *Mantegna*, Phaidon. Christie's, Oxford, 1986; Lauro Martines, *Power and Imagination: City-States in Renaissance Italy*, London, Allen Lane, 1980, pp. 319-20.

attraverso le opere latine che componeva in questo periodo: *Nec spe nec metu* che canonizzava un dire di lei; la descrizione del loro viaggio in Provenza; un libro sulla Beata Osanna Andreasi che era la «santa personale» della marchesana, principalmente perché prediceva la nascita del figlio primogenito, Federico Gonzaga.

L'Equicola era coinvolto, volente o nolente, nella politica dinastica, particolarmente dopo la morte del marchese Francesco Gonzaga nel 1519. Prima fu nominato segretario di Isabella d'Este, poi due anni più tardi, di Federico Gonzaga, il nuovo marchese di Mantova. La scelta dell'Equicola non era automatica; anzi, era prassi normale scegliere come segretario uno della cancelleria di nascita nobile mantovana. Isabella d'Este voleva utilizzare l'Equicola in parte per mantenere la sua ascendenza sul figlio con la speranza di impedire che lui governasse da solo senza far riferimento a lei. In questo gioco di potere l'Equicola fu un personaggio-chiave che finalmente cedeva alle lusinghe del «vero» potere detenuto da Federico Gonzaga. Che l'Equicola fosse «sagace consigliere del suo signore»[25] non ha molto significato nel contesto della politica gonzaghesca. In un certo senso, l'Equicola tradì Isabella d'Este, perché l'opportunità di servire il nuovo marchese era troppo seducente; le possibilità di arricchimento e l'aumento del suo potere personale erano troppo reali dopo tanti anni in una posizione molto subalterna.

Come cortegiano l'Equicola si trovava al polo opposto rispetto al tipo di cortegiano teorizzato dal Castiglione. Non era in tutta probabilità di nascita nobile, e promuoveva un'atmosfera di libertinaggio, nonostante il Castiglione facesse del suo meglio per proibirla o almeno renderla più rispettabile. È certo che l'Equicola non ambiva a stimolare il principe ad agire secondo principi morali: gli interessava soprattutto il suo inserimento nella corte oltre che condurre un'esistenza più agiata. Infatti, l'Equicola è in un certo modo la controfigura del cortegiano castiglionesco.

Il *Libro de natura de amore*, pubblicato nel 1525[26], conferma quest'antagonismo con il *Cortegiano*, anche se ci sono certe aree in cui si trovano parallelismi abbastanza significativi. Però le differenze sono più notevoli. L'interpretazione dell'amore diventa il campo di battaglia per due contrastanti analisi della corte. Il Castiglione opera la sua analisi dell'amore a due livelli: a livello, per così dire, «pratico» che tratta i rapporti tra il cortegiano e la «donna di palazzo»,

---

[25] P. CHERCHI, *op. cit.*, p. 36.

[26] L'ultima edizione era di 1626, pubblicato da L. Spineda in Venezia.

insistendo sulla moralità di tali rapporti che non devono abbassarsi alla sessualità (la castità che praticamente domina il rapporto tra i sessi). A livello «teorico», nel quarto libro del *Cortegiano*, l'amore è reso ancora più astratto con l'adesione del testo alle teorie neoplatoniche dell'amore (il corpo che viene negato come veicolo del vero amore).

Secondo l'Equicola del *Libro de natura de amore* il suo «cortegiano-amante» non nega mai il legame corpo-amore. Infatti, il corpo è la meta dell'amore. Neanche però nell'ultimo libro del suo testo l'autore può abbandonare del tutto il concetto di un amore fisico. Se propone, nell'ultima parte del *Libro*, che Dio è la fine di tutto, amore *non* vuol significare la negazione del piacere terrestre. Ci sembra che questo movimento finale verso un amore cristianizzato, più ortodosso, venga spesso e volentieri minato precisamente perché l'Equicola non sa costruire un mondo senza la visione di un amore ancorato ad un concetto materialistico[27]. Il *Libro de natura de amore* suscitò controversie al momento della sua pubblicazione. Infatti, Ludovico da Canossa, uno degli interlocutori del *Cortegiano*, ritenne che – a detta di certe persone – il *Libro* potesse apparire pieno di oscenità[28]. Tale parere coincide con gli sforzi del *Cortegiano* nell'allontanare dalle corti l'amore come fenomeno fisico. Dunque, non sorprende che il *Libro* fosse apparso come «cosa di vecchio stampo»[29]. L'Equicola stesso riconobbe questa possibilità già nel 1521 e per questo voleva far stampare il libro quanto prima: «e se più se differisce, la età non sopporta che da mi se stampino quelle ciancie»[30]. In un certo senso, l'Equicola sta facendo una difesa accanita di vecchi usi, un'azione di retroguardia, dal punto di vista linguistico,

---

[27] Si vedano ENRICO MUSACCHIO, *The role of the senses in Mario Equicola's philosophy of love*, in *Eros and Anteros: The Medical Traditions of Love in the Renaissance*, a cura di Donald A. Beecher e Massimo Ciavolella, Toronto, Dovehouse, 1992, pp. 87-101 e A.J. SMITH, *The Metaphysics of Love. Studies in Renaissance Love Poetry from Dante to Milton*, Cambridge, Cambridge University Press, 1988, pp. 201, 203. Un punto di vista più convenzionale si trova in THOMAS HYDE, *The Poetic Theology of Love. Cupid in Renaissance Literature*, Newark, University of Delaware Press; London e Toronto, Associated University Presses, 1986, pp. 97-98.

[28] Citato in MARIO POZZI, *Mario Equicola e la cultura cortigiana: appunti sulla redazione manoscritta del* Libro de natura de Amore, «Lettere Italiane», 32 (1980), p. 151.

[29] P. CHERCHI, *op. cit.*, p. 37.

[30] S. KOLSKY, *The Real Courtier*, *op. cit.*, p. 208.

culturale e amoroso. È proprio una scelta che fece l'Equicola nei confronti della nuova cultura cortigiana caratterizzata dal Castiglione. L'Alvitano faceva proprio un certo modo di pensare che non era totalmente ortodosso e criticava il neoplatonismo allorché diventava dominante nella cultura cortigiana. Pur utilizzando alcuni aspetti, rifiuta ancora di più questa nuova filosofia. Non rimane convinto che una sola filosofia del tutto astratta possa spiegare un fenomeno sociale come l'amore in tutte le sue varietà. Per questo motivo, presenta svariate teorie sull'amore prese da tante fonti classiche e moderne, inclusi i testi letterari. La *varietas* simboleggia l'adesione all'umanesimo eclettico del tardo Quattrocento, a un concetto della *voluptas* intellettuale che consiste nell'esporre tante citazioni di fonti fuori d'uso e poco conosciute. Le citazioni stesse sono segni di una materialità intellettuale che indietreggia davanti all'astratto, come a qualcosa di inafferrabile.

La biografia di Mario Equicola ci offre alcune lezioni fondamentali per quanto riguarda un approccio critico alla vita di uno scrittore-cortegiano. In primo luogo, il contesto socio-politico delle sue opere assume un'importanza primordiale. Infatti, la loro composizione in molti casi è dovuta in gran parte allo stimolo della vita cortigiana. Neanche il *Libro de natura de amore* si può spiegare solo in termini di un *otium* letterario che permette all'Equicola di divagare, di proporsi uno spazio in cui può esprimersi in chiave personalistica, un divertimento che lascia emergere in superficie il suo amore per l'erudizione. Questo non prenderebbe in considerazione la dimensione sociale dell'opera che, malgrado la sua molteplicità di forme, propone una «filosofia» per le corti, modi di comportamento che caratterizzano il cortegiano nonché una solida base di dati e di informazioni che possono giustificare tali comportamenti. In secondo luogo, nella biografia dell'Equicola non si deve sottovalutare i suoi compiti non-letterari. Quest'aspetto della sua carriera non è da trascurare perché spiega la dimensione cortigiana del suo carattere: l'essenziale apprendimento delle arti cortigiane, la sua *urbanitas*, il suo modo di divertire la corte senza esser considerato come «giocolare». Per queste ragioni, l'Equicola poté stringere amicizia con Alfonso d'Este, Duca di Ferrara e molti altri dignitari ed era ricercato come persona piacevole e divertente. In terzo luogo, la biografia dell'Equicola riflette la vita di un cortigiano affermatosi malgrado le difficoltà della sua carriera con Sigismondo Cantelmo e così via. Inoltre, ci dà la possibilità di tracciare il percorso dell'umanesimo nel momento del contatto con la corte. Non sarebbe corretto parlare di un degradamento della cultura umanistica. Pur non impegnandosi seriamente in edizioni di testi classici e nel commentarli, l'Equicola provò ad adattare l'umanesimo alla corte, ad architettare temi cortigiani. L'Equicola fu uno dei massimi teòrici della corte del primo Cinquecento, un intellettuale che vive l'esperienza della corte con tutte le sue difficoltà. L'attività dell'Equicola coincide con un momento cruciale segnato dall'ascendenza della corte nella storia europea. Il suo contributo, pur essendo problematico, è essenziale alla genesi della figura chiave del cortegiano.

X

The Courtier as Critic: Vincenzo Calmeta's Vita del facondo poeta vulgare Serafino Aquilano

In view of the minor status of both Vincenzo Calmeta and Serafino Aquilano, the relative neglect by scholars of the *Vita del facondo poeta vulgare Serafino Aquilano* may not appear in need of justification.[1] The present study however, will attempt to demonstrate that the *Vita* is an extremely important document concerning the role of the poet in late–fifteenth and early sixteenth–century court society. It will be argued that the *Vita* offers the scholar a rare opportunity to study a contemporary account of the manner in which a poet operated within the patronage system;[2] poetry is regarded not solely as textual analysis, but also as a social process. The *Vita* might even be used to evaluate, in its proper historical context, the more famous case of Ariosto's relations with his patron, Cardinal Ippolito d'Este.

Considering the dominant formulation of the genre in this period, Calmeta's choice of Serafino Aquilano as the subject of a biography is remarkable. In a radical departure from the genre which, up until this time, had usually excluded biographies of contemporary poets (and indeed of most fifteenth–century poets in general), Calmeta has made a conscious decision to elevate the status of a contemporary poet by considering the life and work of Serafino a worthy subject for his writing. The genre at this time was strongest in Florence, a city which could boast of the two most important vernacular poets of the medieval period, Dante and Petrarch. Boccaccio had written a biography of Dante, and in the fifteenth century, Leonardo Bruni had composed biographies of both Dante and Petrarch. It would appear, however, that the 'form' had difficulty in accommodating recent poets: Vespasiano da Bisticci, for example, did not include vernacular writers of any kind in his collection of biographies.[3] It is possible that humanist biographies could only confirm the fame of poets already famous because so few vernacular poets could attain the standard set by Dante and Petrarch or by the classical tradition.

It may be useful to note here that Bruni separates the political from the poetic by distinguishing two kinds of poets, one depending entirely on the mysterious forces of inspiration and the other on "knowledge and study," a humanist distinction which Calmeta will maintain in his own theoretical writings. Calmeta, nonetheless, breaks with tradition by illustrating the life of a professional poet whose principal concern is patronage. Against this background, Calmeta's *Vita* can be seen as bold and innovative. It refuses to become humanist encomium: Serafino Aquilano is not free from criticism. The biography, however, attempts to ensure that Serafino's recent death will not result in his 'achievements' falling into obscurity. It is a recognition, on Calmeta's part, that court poetry has made a significant contribution to poetry in general. The *Vita*, in fact, places the court and its patronage system at the centre of its work.

Calmeta's description of Serafino Aquilano's career illustrates what was later referred to, by Castiglione in the *Cortegiano*, as the "trista valle".[4] In the *Vita*, Serafino's patron Cardinal Ascanio Sforza is presented as the worst kind of patron, a man passionately devoted to hunting with little interest in either music or literature.

While stressing the cardinal's wild, uncivilized nature, Calmeta notes that this particular patronage arrangement was more unequal than most: at best, it would be based on an ideology shared by patron and artist alike. Calmeta, however, recognizes that such an ideal was usually defeated by the reality of the patronage situation: "imperocché, essendo le nature diverse, averia voluto il Cardinale – *como la più parte de li prìncipi*, e non ingiustamente – che Serafino alli costumi suoi se fusse conformato" (61, my emphasis). Here Calmeta exposes the mechanism by which excessive demands or restrictions are imposed on writers. He further demonstrates how inter-personal relations directly affect the production of the client–poet, although Serafino's reaction was perhaps extreme in that he composed satirical verse with the express aim of humiliating the Cardinal.

Such rebellious acts, born of social impotence, are obliquely referred to in the prefatory remarks to this part of Serafino Aquilano's life: "con el quale [Ascanio Sforza] per tre anni con grandissimo sdegno e fastidio ebbe perseveranza" (61). Calmeta is undoubtedly trying to create the best possible impression of his subject and these three years are meant to supply the reader with an example of Serafino's "virtù" in withstanding for so long the uncouth behaviour of his patron.

However, despite the fact that Serafino had achieved considerable fame ("onde in piccolo tempo non solo da lui ma da molti altri citaredi forno le soe rime sparse per Italia", 65), his eventual decision to leave the Cardinal's service was not followed by immediate offers of employment: "Uscito poi de la servitute di Ascanio, molti mesi senza avere certo patrone per Roma andò vagando" (65).

Calmeta implies that the patronage system is all–pervasive and survival without it virtually impossible. For a poet such as Serafino, who did not have the social networks essential for working as a 'freelance' composer and performer, patronage was a vital necessity. Yet, attempts on his life caused him to realize that patronage was not offered lightly; that it was indeed a rare commodity: "e avendo lui medesimamente provato per esperienza che da li prelati di Roma più presto li erano prestate benignamente l'orecchie ad ascoltare le soe composizioni, che offertoli le piatose mani a suvvenire alli suoi bisogni" (66–67).

Serafino's poverty and perhaps a more mature evaluation of his social situation also brought him to the conclusion that " 'l stare senza protettore li era danno e ignominia" (66). Calmeta's barely concealed resentment at the lack of assistance received from "li prelati di Roma" highlights not only the political influence of Ascanio Sforza in Rome but also the inevitability of Serafino's return to the Cardinal's service. In Calmeta's analysis, each participant in the patronage relationship had learnt, by then, to understand his own particular role: Serafino's next departure, ostensibly to visit his family in Aquila, was accepted "con bona grazia dil suo Signore" (67).

His return to Aquila and entry into the court of Ferdinando d' Aragona may be viewed in terms of a search for greater security. Ferdinando, in line for the throne, seemed to represent the possibility of patronage reinforced by ties, if not of feudality, at least of geographical communality. It was an astute move which should have kept Serafino in Naples for more than the three years he actually spent in the service of Ferdinando "con gran favore e remunerazione" (67). However, at this point the poet became a victim of historical circumstances: "Averia Serafino da Ferdinando conseguito alto grado e remunerazione, se insieme con la trista influenza dil Regno de Italia la soa bona sorte ancora non avesse patito alterazione" (68).

With the virtual dissolution of the only kingdom on the Italian peninsula, Serafino was confronted with a choice to which Calmeta does not allude: should he remain loyal to the deposed king or seek employment elsewhere? The text implies that ethical considerations played a minor rôle in the struggle for survival, the term "remunerazione" being used to describe the overriding principle by which the behaviour of the aristocracy (both secular and ecclesiastical) was to be judged. Calmeta ignores Serafino's brief transfer of allegiance to his next patron Elisabetta Gonzaga, Duchess of Urbino, although he implicity tries to justify it by emphasizing her qualities. Also implied is that Serafino, realizing the impossibility of Ferdinando regaining his kingdom, used his Urbino contacts to gain employment in the Mantuan court. Calmeta, however, passes no judgement on Serafino's shameless materialism: "Serafino, de tanta soa speranza destituito, deliberò de più non essere astretto ad alcuna servitù, ma libero andare per Italia a suo beneplacito, magnanimi prìncipi e singularissime donne visitando" (70). It is true that such a calculation would mean ensuring his appreciation by the leading women in these courts. Thus he followed the fashion in amorous verse and competed with the stars of the court circuit, in particular Tebaldeo:[5] one of his most striking characteristics was to be alert to the latest innovation in court poetry and to make it his own. Calmeta may be using this capacity of Serafino's as a subtle criticism of the poet whose style was always in terms of worldly success rather than aesthetic criteria: "Nel quale [li amorosi sonetti] fece tale profitto che non meno che in li strammoti ebbe nome e celebrazione" (69).[6]

It should be noted here that Calmeta distinguishes two classes of poetry. One, which he considers superior, must be original; it must 'fare stile' (22). Petrarch and Dante are the poets most worthy of imitation in this category. The other, which includes the work of Serafino, is defined, at its best, in the essay *Qual stile tra' volgari poeti sia da imitare* (20–25): "quelle con lo instrumento di musica accompagnando, per poterle meglio non solo negli amorosi ma ancora negli eruditi cuori imprimere" (21). It is important that Calmeta considers lyric poetry a legitimate genre which should not be scorned by the 'eruditi cuori': to be accepted and appreciated by them, however, it must conform to certain rules; in particular, the words must be granted greater significance than the music:

> Così medesimamente sono da essere essistimati di sommo giudicio coloro che cantando mettono tutto lo sforzo in esprimer ben le parole, quando sono di sustanza, e fanno che la musica le accompagna con quel modo che sono i padroni da' servidori accompagnati (22).

Calmeta does not dismiss here those forms, such as the *strambotto*, which Bembo will try to abolish; indeed he appears to betray some appreciation of them.

At the end of the fifteenth century, in the last years of Sforza domination, Serafino's quest for some permanent employment led him to Milan: "A Serafino dunque parendo avere un'altra monarchia di Ottaviano ritrovato e un vivere a soa natura tanto conforme che ogni altro piacere li fece uscire de la memoria, deliberò in corte de Milano fermare li suoi pensieri" (72). The reference to the emperor Augustus is a studied one; it is intended to conjure a picture from an idealized past where patronage of poets and scholars produced monumental results. Yet, once again, reality intrudes: fame in the fifteenth and sixteenth centuries was passive and did not automatically attract patrons. The poet was required to promote himself: "e tutto a corteggiare il Duca e la Duchessa se dispose" (72). It is the verb "corteggiare" which suggests the absolute necessity of adapting to circumstances and subordinating oneself to them. Here Serafino found his career turning full circle after those first, futile attempts at rebellion against Ascanio Sforza. He now wished to re-enter Sforza service at all costs.

The death of Beatrice d'Este, Duchess of Milan, saw the dispersion of her court (Serafino had been on its periphery) and marked the beginning of a decline in the Northern Italian court system. While the death of the Duchess (who had acted as a magnet to all manner of men involved in intellectual activities) symbolized the decline of the court system, the reality, for both Calmeta and Serafino, meant the beginning of a search for yet another patron. Changing political conditions on the Peninsula did not make such a task easy:[7] foreign invasion was causing a steady reduction in the number of courts, while those remaining were, for the most part, engaged in a life-and-death struggle for survival. Considering the circumstances, it was perhaps a logical conclusion that Serafino (and Calmeta) obtained patronage from Cesare Borgia: "poi insino a l'ultimo di soa vita sotto la protezione di Cesare Borgia collocò tutti li soi penseri" (74). Cesare, in conjunction with Alexander VI, was the one Italian "prince" who was able to profit, for a time, from the French invasions: he was creating a state while others were losing theirs. It could be argued that in this process of creation Cesare Borgia *needed* a court which would help him appear less a 'cut-throat bandit' and more like a 'Renaissance prince'; it might even lend a sense of legitimacy to a most illegitimate regime.

If the *Vita* is a rich source of information for the patronage system as it directly affects poets, it also provides a commentary on Serafino Aquilano's behaviour as a poet. Calmeta hints at the poet's charismatic qualities which turned a poetry recital into a religious experience: "ogni soa operazione era con ardore misticata" (75). Such annotations may help to explain the power of Serafino's fascination.

Yet, in many respects, he came very close to being an "anti–poet", denying those goals which Calmeta thinks the poet should set himself. Nonetheless, partly through friendship and partly through a recognition of Serafino's natural talent for poetry, Calmeta views the poet's *cursus* as, in a sense, "exemplary". In reading the following statement together with his other surviving critical writings, one gains the impression that Calmeta wants to do justice to his subject, one of his abiding critical precepts being:

> Se vorrai intendere il giudicio loro sopra le altrui opere, non diranno assolutamente: "Questa cosa non mi piace"; ma quelle parti che sono laudabili prima estolleranno, e l'altre che sono da dannare, con modestia et evidente ragione dove si pecca ti faranno comprendere, non curando i romori volgari, ma al giudicio de' pochi adeguandosi (VIII. *Della ostentazione*, 46).

Calmeta's insistence that literature is an elitist activity, best practised by specialists in a select environment, runs counter to Serafino's philosophy as presented in the *Vita*. Throughout the text Calmeta stresses that Serafino had one overriding concern, the greatest possible fame in the present: "Era tanto avido de rumore populare che ad ogni cosa che potesse el vulgo tirare in ammirazione lo ingegno accomodava" (75). It is obvious that Calmeta did not share Serafino's view of literature.

Reading *S'egli è lecito giudicare i vivi o no* and *S'egli è possibile esser buon poeta volgare senza aver lettere latine*, the critic might be tempted to explain the *Vita* as an exercise in irony – the Serafino of the *Vita* appears not to conform to various critical propositions found in these and in Calmeta's other works. Calmeta, however, does not condemn out of hand "la natural vena" in a poet (*S'egli è possibile*, 9), although he is, at the same time, convinced that it must be supplemented by a careful use of erudition ("ma che ancora bisogni lo studio letterale", 9). It appears that Calmeta's simile of "una veste di broccato ricchissimo fatta da inetto sartore" (9) is an attempt to demonstrate that in a court environment it is possible and indeed necessary to weld together "la natural vena" and "accidente" (11). From a number of viewpoints Calmeta seems to be moving towards a theory which blends certain 'Bembian' notions with the practices of court intellectuals. He insists on the concept that "non possono le parole senza precetti oratorî insieme ben congiungersi" (9–10), although this is only half the equation since the subject-matter must not be treated as subordinate to "i colori retorici" (11). It may be that Calmeta was influenced by Cortese and the Roman tradition of humanism since he is clearly advocating an eclectic attitude towards learning: "e le sentenze senza varia dottrina sono frivole" (10). Such a proposition closely resembles the one supported by Equicola and Castiglione:[8] the figure of the orator, which Calmeta borrows from Cicero to enhance the reputation of the court poet, is analogous to the operation carried out by Castiglione in the *Cortegiano*: "essendo tra 'l poeta e l'oratore non poca conformità" (10). The similarities, however, are not based exclusively on the level of "oratorî precetti" (10) since the orator held a privileged status in ancient Roman society while in *Quattrocento* society it was the name used to refer to an ambassador. From this viewpoint Serafino might be perceived as a rather frivolous figure, having no real political function nor writing in the mould of Lorenzo de' Medici, Poliziano or Sannazaro. It is essential, therefore, to read the *Vita* with care in order to discover the positive points Calmeta finds in Serafino's itinerary. It should be noted also that the *Vita* is, to a lesser extent, the story of Calmeta himself.

The *Vita*, then, can be viewed as a work which attempts to present the boundaries of court culture as less fluid: it is a *summa* of the achievements of one of the most important proponents of this culture and an analysis of his shortcomings (only fully appreciated if read in conjunction with Calmeta's other writings). Nonetheless, I would argue that Calmeta does not leave the reader with a wholly negative impression. He stamps his own views on the text despite the fact that they are at the embryonic stage of development. It is suggested, however, that the subtext might not have attracted the attention of Calmeta's contemporaries who perhaps saw in Serafino only a rather unrefined *citaredo*. Such probably was the opinion of Pietro Bembo. The *Vita* might even be regarded as a central (anti–) text in the development of Bembo's literary theories: in this interpretation, Serafino would be a symbol of all that Bembo rejected in court culture. The gulf between the two poets can be measured by comparing Bembo's *Asolani*, the first edition of which appeared in 1505, with the *Opere del facundissimo Seraphino Aquilano . . .*, published in Venice in the same year (for the first time incorporating Calmeta's *Vita* with Serafino's own compositions).[9]

It would have been difficult to avoid interpreting this alliance as approval of Serafino's poetry, despite modern criticism regarding Calmeta's reservations about the poet. Hence, one can consider that, for his contemporaries, Calmeta's name was inextricably linked with Serafino's; the 1505 edition merely reinforced the earlier literary connection of the *Collettanee*. Even Calmeta's own caution regarding the value of the collection as a whole could not have invalidated the enterprise. At the very end of the *Vita* he quotes a single sonnet for reasons which seem to be significant: first, he appears to be passing an aesthetic judgement on the standard of poetry in the *Collettanee* since the Unico Aretino's sonnet is considered "secondo el guidizio nostro, più eletto" (77); second, the Unico Aretino was associated with Paolo Cortese's "unofficial" academy in Rome.

Bembo probably would not have been impressed by Calmeta's choice: the author of the *Prose della volgar lingua* undoubtedly cared little about making too great a distinction between the two poets, particularly since neither writer shared his own conception of literary taste and value. Clearly the *Asolani* represents a decisive break with Calmeta's literary horizons: while Bembo managed to make literature equivalent to theory (both linguistic and cultural), his challenge to the courtly hybrid ultimately led Calmeta to reflect on his own position and in turn to formulate his theory of the *lingua cortigiana*.[10]

Bembo's use of Neoplatonism was the sign of a fundamental change in court culture–the fragmentary spontaneity of the courtly lyric was being challenged by a more serious, 'committed' writing. Bembo was aiming for a sense of coherence, *gravitas* and seriousness, far removed from Serafino's attitude to literature as a game, to be produced for a particular audience, and consumed merely for its momentary pleasure. Calmeta himself notes this aspect of Serafino's poetry: "Tutti li soi concetti furno d'avere in vita nome e celebrazione, ancora che solo tra' mediocri e plebei di sé fusse restato il rumore" (76).

Calmeta and Bembo appear to agree on this point since both have imbibed the ideology of humanism which viewed literature as a monument to eternity. Unlike Bembo however, Calmeta is commenting by inference and does not elevate his thought into a literary system. This is probably why the *Vita* has not been examined thoroughly for its theoretical statements on poets and poetry: Bembo's *Asolani* and the later *Prose* undoubtedly swept Calmeta's contribution to literary thought into obscurity. Linguistically, Calmeta's theory was seen as the 'loser' and since most literary histories take the side of a winner, Calmeta's work is viewed as an interesting "side-show", doomed to inevitable failure. His lack of a fully formulated theory of literature is due not only to his close links with particular social institutions but also to his ambiguity regarding the value of the central one, the court. In the *Vita* he implicitly favours another institution, the Academy, though he does not see it as a replacement for the court. For this intellectual structure Calmeta reserves fulsome praise, for example, Paolo Cortese's Academy: "per modo che non casa di corteggiano ma officina di eloquenza e recettaculo d'ogni inclita virtù se potteva chiamare. Concorrevano ivi ogni giorno gran multitudine de elevati ingegni" (63). It is important to note that Calmeta makes a clear distinction between an ordinary "casa di corteggiano" and Paolo Cortese's residence, thus implying that in the context of court society courtiers are not necessarily interested in things cultural. Cortese is regarded as exceptional in this respect.

Given the brevity of the *Vita*, Calmeta has devoted a considerable amount of space to the Academy. Furthermore, he stresses that in Aragonese Naples, apart from the court, "fioriva in Napoli ancora un'altra Academia de litterati" (67). The introduction of these academies into Calmeta's discourse has the effect of increasing the status of Serafino as a poet by showing him in the company of respected intellectuals who appreciate his poetry: "non sol le orecchie dil vulgo ma ancora quelle de li dotti con suoi poemi demulciva" (67). Calmeta here is acknowledging the value of Serafino's work by suggesting that even though Serafino did not write Latin poetry, his vernacular production, nevertheless, was of a standard acceptable to the academies of the period. This impression is strengthened by the fact that the commemorative poems in the *Collettanee* are written both in Latin and in the vernacular.

It is evident that this acceptance of Serafino by the members of these academies represents for Calmeta the high-point of the former's literary career and, in a sense, justifies his entry into the court system. It should be noted here that a number of Calmeta's essays have as their *cornice* gatherings in private houses which might be likened to academies. *S'egli è possibile* has its origin in discussions involving Blasio da Cella who was "continuo da diversi spiriti acuti visitato, essendo quella casa d'uomini singolari e a virtù dedicati recettacolo" (7). In a similar way, the discussions in *La poesia del Tebaldeo* were generated by Calmeta's stay with learned friends in a villa outside Milan (15). The essay, *Per molti essempi che cosa sia servare il decoro*, employs Cortese himself to provide the starting-point for the discussions: "Disseriva un giorno il nostro Cortese a molti circostanti nel suo portico, tra' quali io ancora era" (32). It appears that Calmeta's 'intellectual' allegiance lies with men and the institutions being developed to foster enquiries into certain areas, particularly literature. He seems to associate women with the 'practice' of poetry rather than with its theoretical implications, the court, presided over by women, being the arena where poetry is performed. Calmeta's preference for the Academy may also be an indication of a greater interest in the theory of poetry rather than in its practice.

The only institution to rival the Academy was Beatrice d'Este's court. This was, however, ephemeral, disappearing "in un subito" (73) on the death of the Duchess: the *Vita* commemorates a court which symbolizes the end of a relatively trouble-free period in the history of the Peninsula. Yet, even if Calmeta has reservations about court life in general, in no way does he see the Academy as a viable alternative. The Academy can do no more than help a poet become better known: "La qual cosa de accrescere più il suo nome li fu assai giovamento, essendo emulazione tra tutti quelli dotti a cui più recondita invenzione di fare strammoti li poteva ritrovare" (64).

Calmeta's notion of the *poeta* can never be married to Bembo's since the latter abolishes 'performance' as a criterion for judging the poet: music is considered as detracting from the intrinsic value of the text which becomes, in Bembo's theory, the goal of all his analysis. A consequence of this radical change in emphasis is the rôle attributed to women by each writer. No reader of the *Prose e lettere* can fail to note the prominent rôle taken by women in Calmeta's writings: of the ten letters published by Grayson seven are addressed to women. One of Calmeta's short critical pieces is a comparison between Cecilia Gallerani and Giulia Farnese with whom he had come into close contact through experience as a courtier and intellectual: "con loro lungamente come amico e domestico ho conversato" (28).

A particularly interesting aspect of Calmeta's analysis of these two women is the use of categories which he generally reserves for poetry: "Ma se Giulia *per natural dote* ha nel vestir qualche poco più grazia, Cecilia *con l'accidente* molto meglio si sa aiutare" (28, my emphases). This mode of comparison is analogous to that used in contrasting Serafino and Tebaldeo. It indicates that Calmeta's criticism of poetry lacks depth and is not the object of a specialized form of interpretation: Calmeta perhaps distinguished the activities characterizing court society only to the extent that they employed different materials.

However, Calmeta's representation of the court clarifies the connection between women and poetry: in the *Vita* it is the women at court who organize poetry as an integral part of their entertainment system. Calmeta thereby implies that lyric poetry gained access to court circles principally through the patronage of the women.[11] Hence, to a certain degree at least, poetry was composed and performed with this audience in mind, and thus accounts for Calmeta's insistence on Serafino's skills as a musician.

Bembo, in the *Prose*, is undoubtedly reacting against the court ethos which he had presented in a refined form in the *Asolani*. It has been noted that the dialogues of the *Prose* take place in a private house. It does not appear to have been observed, however, that women take no part in the discussions, even though the subject-matter is often poetry.[12] Bembo presents learned society in the form of a male academy, refusing to allow the seriousness of his conception of poetry to be undermined by the presence of women. His insistence on this point becomes even more emphatic if we consider that Giuliano de' Medici, as one of the interlocutors in the *Prose*, not only ignores the subject of women but even fails to mention his intimate relations with court society; he is portrayed as a Florentine who patriotically values the language of his city/region.[13] By contrast Giuliano speaks, in the final version of the *Libro del cortegiano*, about the place and status of women.

Although Giuliano's hypothesis is firmly rejected in the *Prose*, it does not receive the same kind of dismissive treatment of Calmeta's theory, ironically meted out by this same arch–courtier ("ma io non so ancora se dire si può, che ella sia veramente lingua").[14] Since Giuliano had been exiled from Florence, the fictional date of the *Prose* enables Bembo to place him in Venice, even though he spent much time in the courts of the peninsula, particularly in Urbino.[15] The *Prose* seem to suggest that Giuliano was more concerned with republican ideals than with the values of court society, thus implying that Bembo has striven to remove Giuliano from the ambience of the court. Indeed, it is the latter who deals the fatal blow to Calmeta's theory of the *lingua cortigiana.*

Bembo's judgement could not be more definitive. Undoubtedly, the severity of his critique has been a major factor in deterring scholars from studying Calmeta's *Vita*; the poetry practised by its "hero" was unceremoniously dubbed *seicentista* by D'Ancona, thus discouraging independent study of the *poesia cortigiana.*[16] While it would be a mistake to exaggerate the importance of the *Vita*, in many ways it stands at the crossroads of court culture, a summation of its achievements in poetry and its potentials. Nonetheless, the *Vita* records the failure of the court poet to elevate his poetry beyond the requirement of a consumer society, as well as Calmeta's failure as a writer to create a dynamic theory of court literature which would have helped ensure its survival.

NOTES

[1]The most recent review of Calmeta's biography is "COLLI, Vincenzo detto il Calmeta", compiled by Marzio Pieri, in *Dizionario Biografico degli Italiani*, XXVII, 49–52. The fundamental text for Calmeta remains Vincenzo Calmeta, *Prose e lettere edite e inedite*, a cura di Cecil Grayson (Bologna: Commissione per i testi di lingua, 1959); on his biography see in particular pp. XIII–XXX. (All references to Calmeta's writings are to this edition). Other useful information is provided by Augusto Campana, "Dal Calmeta al Colocci. Testo nuovo di un epicedio di P. F. Giustolo" in *Tra latino e volgare. Per Carlo Dionisotti*, a cura di Gabriella Bernardoni Trezzini, Ottavio Besomi et al. (Padua: Antenore, 1974), 267–315; 302–10, and Pier Vincenzo Mengaldo, "Appunti su Vincenzo Calmeta e la teoria cortigiana", *Rassegna della Letteratura Italiana*, 64 (1960), 446–469; 450 n.16.

[2]It is true that patronage has received intense scrutiny in recent years. A good starting-point is *Patronage in the Renaissance*, edited by Guy Fitch Lytle and Stephen Orgel (Princeton: Princeton UP, 1981) and, more specifically focused on Italy, *Patronage, Art and Society in Renaissance Italy*, ed. Francis W. Kent and Patricia Simons (Oxford: Oxford UP, 1987). A more specific study is Jerry H. Bentley, *Politics and Culture in Renaissance Naples*, (Princeton: Princeton UP, 1987), which examines the literary patronage of the Aragonese kings.

[3]See *The Humanism of Leonardo Bruni. Selected Texts*, Translations and introductions by Gordon Griffiths *et al.* (Binghamton, New York: Center for Medieval and Early Renaissance Studies, 1987), 85–100 [Le vite di Dante e del Petrarca]. Vespasiano da Bisticci, *Le vite*, edizione critica con introduzione e commento di Aulo Greco, 2 vols, (Florence: Nella sede dell'Istituto. Palazzo Strozzi, 1970, 1976), does write the biographies of Matteo Palmieri, Vittorino da Feltre and other intellectuals but nowhere does he compose biographies of vernacular poets.

[4]See Baldesar Castiglione, *Il libro del cortegiano con una scelta delle opere minori*, a cura di Bruno Maier (Turin: UTET, 1964), 224.

[5]Calmeta himself has an extremely negative opinion of Tebaldeo's poetry (*Prose e lettere*, pp. LXII–LXIII, 15–19) to which he applies Bembesque principles of "gravità" and "maiestà" (16).

[6]On Serafino's poetry see Antonio Rossi, *Serafino Aquilano e la poesia cortigiana*, (Brescia: Morcelliana, 1980) and for his *strambotti* see Barbara Bauer-Formiconi, *Die Strambotti des Serafino dall'Aquila*, (Munich, 1967).

[7]Alessandro Luzio, Rodolfo Renier, *Mantova e Urbino* (Turin–Rome: Roux, 1893), 89–96, record the peregrinations of Serafino, providing details which are absent from the *Vita*. Serafino, it would appear, continued to exploit the dynastic connections of the Gonzaga, staying at various times in Mantua and Urbino after the death of Beatrice d'Este. Perhaps Calmeta omitted this part of Serafino's *iter* to avoid the poet (and himself) being accused of ingratitude or even treachery by transferring their allegiance to Cesare Borgia. Calmeta intentionally minimizes Serafino's later changes of employer to avoid suspicions regarding the morality of his choices.

[8]See, for example, my " 'The good servant': Mario Equicola. Court and courtier in early sixteenth–century Italy", *The Italianist*, 6 (1986), 34–60; 41–45, 49–51.

[9]See *Prose e lettere*, pp. XXXI, 59.

[10]Consult Pio Rajna, "La lingua cortigiana" in *Miscellanea linguistica in onore di Graziadio Ascoli* (Turin: Loescher, 1901), 295–314; P. V. Mengaldo, 446–50 in particular but *passim*; Giancarlo Mazzacurati, *Misure del classicismo rinascimentale* (Naples: Liguori, 1967), 62–67 and by the same writer, "Pietro Bembo e il primato della scrittura" in *Il Rinascimento dei moderni* (Bologna: Il Mulino, 1985), 65–147.

[11]Calmeta is explicit about the rôle of women in promoting "la vulgare poesia e arte oratoria" (*Vita*, 72). He dates the Renaissance in vernacular poetry to Lorenzo de' Medici and his group but the second stage in the revival is credited to Beatrice d'Este and other leading court women (including Elisabetta Gonzaga and Isabella d'Este): "poi mediante la emulazione di questa e altre singularissime donne di nostra etade, su la pristina dignitade essere ritornata se comprende" (72). It is also noted that Calmeta's view here closely resembles Bembo's theory of the imitation of Boccaccio and Petrarch, mentioned explicitly, just prior to the beginning of my quotation. Calmeta, however, believes that the decline of vernacular literature has been rectified. Bembo, of course, could not agree. Cf. Mazzacurati, *Misure*, 75 n.1.

[12]See Pasquale Sabatino, "Ideologia e scrittura: Le *Prose della volgar lingua*", *Riscontri*, 5, n.3–4 (1983) 9–25.

[13]For biographical details consult Giuliano de' Medici, Duca di Nemours, *Poesie*, a cura e con uno studio di Giuseppe Fatini (Florence: Vallecchi, 1939), VII–XCI.

[14]Pietro Bembo, *Prose e rime*, a cura di Carlo Dionisotti, (Turin: UTET, 1966), 110.

[15]Consult Giuliano de' Medici, *Poesie*, XII–XXXIII. Giuliano had considerable contact with the Sforza court (XV–XVI) as well as Urbino (XXII–XXXIII).

[16]Alessandro D'Ancona, "Del secentismo nella poesia cortigiana del XV secolo" in *Studi sulla letteratura italiana de' primi secoli*, (Milan: Treves, 1891), 151–237.

XI

LELIO MANFREDI TRADUTTORE CORTIGIANO

Intorno al *Carcer d'Amore* e al *Tirante il Bianco*

E un caso fortunato che la produzione delle opere principali (traduzione e opere originali) del *corpus* manfrediano sia registrata nelle lettere, ancora esistenti, nell'Archivio Gonzaga di Mantova, scambiate per lo più tra Manfredi stesso e i Gonzaga o i loro funzionari[1]. Queste lettere non soltanto ci permettono di stabilire la cronologia delle opere, e a volte i titoli di opere perdute o ritenute perdute, ma anche le condizioni in cui erano scritte (come per esempio l'intenzione o meno di stamparle) e qualche ragguaglio sulla loro accoglienza (circolazione manoscritta). La corrispondenza tra il Manfredi e i Gonzaga - motivata dal fatto che inizialmente il Manfredi risiedeva a Ferrara e faceva parte del circuito culturale ferrarese - attesta un vivo scambio culturale tra Ferrara e Mantova. Già nel 1513 il duca di Ferrara, Alfonso d'Este, si riferiva a «Lelio di Manfredi familiare nostro dilectissimo» in una richiesta di assistenza fatta per conto del Manfredi stesso alla marchesa di Mantova, Isabella d'Este[2]. I rapporti del Manfredi con Mantova rappresentano inoltre la diffusione della cultura ferrarese (ad esempio, l'interesse nella cavalleria, non assente a Mantova ma certamente non molto sviluppato in senso letterario rispetto agli Estensi sotto il patronato dei Gonzaga) e non è fortuito che i primi contatti di cui siamo informati coinvolgano Isabella d'Este e poi, solo in un secondo momento, suo figlio Federico Gonzaga[3]. Isabella d'Este, figlia di Eleonora d'Aragona, e cognata di Lucrezia Borgia, s'interessava in modo particolare a qualsiasi fenomeno culturale che potesse considerarsi raro o nuovo; ed inoltre Lucrezia Borgia, rivale della marchesa di Mantova, aveva portato con sé damigelle spagnole nonché cultura spagnola[4]. Per di più, se la cultura napoletana aragonese era più aperta all'influenza ispanica, Ferrara all'inizio del Cinquecento fu una calamita che attraeva esuli napoletani, tra cui l'ex-regina e i suoi seguaci[5]. Quindi è possibile ipotizzare che lo spazio culturale esistesse per quelli che percepivano un "mercato" per la letteratura spagnola a Ferrara ed altrove, e questo sarà il contesto in cui agirà Lelio Manfredi.

La sua traduzione più riuscita, a giudicare dal numero di edizioni stampate, fu quella del *Carcer d'amore* «traduto dal magnifico miser Lelio de Manfredi ferrarese, de idioma spagnolo in lingua materna»[6]. È da notare, fin dall'inizio, che sul frontespizio il nome dell'autore spagnolo originario è stato sostituito da quello del traduttore. Quindi non sembra che al pubblico interessasse né l'autore originale (D. Hernandez de San Pedro) di questo romanzo sentimentale nè il contesto socio-letterario di esso, ma soltanto il contenuto generico, di potenziale interesse per i lettori italiani, avulso dalle sue origini e rivestito di forma italiana[7]. Secondo quanto il Manfredi afferma nella lettera del 21 novembre 1513, indirizzata ad Isabella d'Este, la traduzione del *Carcer d'amore* era stata caratterizzata da due momenti: in primo luogo l'esecuzione della traduzione stessa e in secondo luogo la ricerca della persona a cui dedicare il lavoro:

> «Sempre ho desiderato che quella [Isabella d'Este] cognosca quanto io gli sia affectionato servitore e al presente mi si è offerta la causa oportuna che havendo traducto il *Carcer de amore* da l'hispanica lingua mi parve dedicarlo a Vostra Celsitudine come a Fautrice e vero lume e albergo de la virtute[8]».

Qui, è importante notare che non sembra che la decisione di tradurre il *Carcer* sia stata imposta dalla marchesa, ma sia piuttosto stata una decisione indipendente e non influenzata in modo diretto dai Gonzaga. Questi ultimi dimostrarono però un notevole interesse per l'opera una volta che questa fu portata a termine. L'interpretazione di un impegno preso autonomamente dal Manfredi è confermata dall'aggettivo «oportuna»: nella visione del Manfredi Isabella d'Este avrebbe potuto soddisfare tanto il desiderio di lui di prendere contatti più concreti con i Gonzaga quanto la propria ambizione di avere un gran numero di opere a lei dedicate. Manfredi forse si sentiva sicuro di arrivare al suo scopo per le seguenti ragioni: aumentare in questo modo la fama d'Isabella d'Este in quanto committente di cose nuove, cioè la letteratura spagnola. Inoltre l'essere Isabella d'Este la destinataria della dedica avrebbe contribuito a rendere più facile la circolazione del libro. Per di più, dedicare la traduzione alla donna che si professava molto colta e interessata alla cultura letteraria in fattispecie, la letteratura volgare di più certa accessibilità ad una persona sprovvista di conoscenze approfondite di altre lingue contribuiva a precisare il pubblico del libro. Il *Carcer d'amore* sembra scegliere un pubblico che in primo luogo consiste di cortigiani e di donne della corte e in secondo luogo della società borghese; quanto al suo argomento letterario, l'opera è di una raffinatezza tale da piacere ai circoli presieduti da donne avide di ascoltare racconti d'amore. Un ulteriore motivo per cui la traduzione non avrebbe mancato di far effetto in questi ambienti rarefatti e in particolare di riuscire gradita alla marchesa è l'abbondanza dei suoi facili allegorismi (spiegati peraltro dal testo stesso), che la rendono paragonabile ai quadri con i quali pian piano Isabella stava riempendo in modo programmatico il suo *Studiolo*. Simbolismo a parte, l'argomento del superamento delle passioni, cioè l'uscire dalla «pregione d'amore» e il lasciar regnare la ragione, fu un tema caro ad Isabella d'Este, il che è dimostrato dai suoi enunciati in proposito e ancora una volta dai quadri dello *Studiolo*[9]. Lo scrittore spagnolo crea una trama piena di peripezie che sembra aver una stretta parentela con il materiale che Boiardo e Ariosto adoperano nei loro episodi piu "romanzeschi" i quali piacevano cosi tanto alla marchesa (non è un caso che l'Ariosto utilizzerà un racconto spagnolo, verosimilmente tradotto dallo stesso Manfredi, nell'*Orlando Furioso*)[10].

Comunque la traduzione dell'opera spagnola non era soltanto un'avveduta scelta editoriale che andava incontro alla sensibilità dei suoi/sue lettori/lettrici ideali, ma faceva anche parte di una corrente cortigiana e erudita che s'interessava in modo eclettico ad espressioni culturali piuttosto esotiche o almeno non comuni, come si presume che ancora per molti fosse la letteratura spagnola in quei luoghi e in quel periodo. Dunque è significativo che il Manfredi faccia riferimento al rappresentante più alto di questo tipo di cultura nell' ambiente mantovano, prima nella lettera del 21 novembre 1521: «e benché prima ne havessi parlato al suo virtuosissimo preceptore meser Mario» e poi nelle parole del traduttore che chiudono il *Carcer*:

> «La qual [Isabella d'Este], se bene è occupata in cose di non poco momento et importanzia - ne li studii e muse, al sacro fonte de le quale per via ormai a lei facile e piana, gli ha dimostrato e dimostra continuamente aurire le divine linfe il dottissimo ed eloquentissimo messer Mario Equicolo, de le cui laudi meglio è chiuder le labra che non parlare a sufficienzia». (*Carcer*, p.269)

La persona di cui si parla è Mario Equicola, precettore della marchesa dal 1508 e primo consigliere dei suoi progetti culturali[11]. Il linguaggio fin troppo latineggiante pare inteso come omaggio sia all'Equicola come ottimo precettore sia ad Isabella d'Este come buona studiosa della cultura preminentemente classica. L'Equicola è lodato in modo generico e vago, ma la sua funzione è resa esplicita in quanto persona che *rivela* alla marchesa i tesori del patrimonio classico, il che implicitamente mostra il bisogno di lei di aver intorno a sé intellettuali che rendano più accessibili culture remote ma presenti, offrendole progettualmente i loro servizi in questo senso. Qui il termine che sottolinea il ruolo dell'intellettuale di corte come traduttore è «servitute» («affettionato desiderio di servire»), dato che la scelta del testo è dovuta a fattori - come gli interessi culturali affermatisi nella corte - parzialmente estranei ai traduttori in quanto mediatori culturali. Per il traduttore il testo non offre grandi spazi di libertà intellettuale. Infatti il Manfredi si diletta del suo stato di servitore, in un susseguirsi di iperboliche laudi della *domina*, che mettono in rilievo l'elemento del *serio ludere*:

> «avendo cum non poca diligenzia e fatica ridutto questo picciol volume da lo externo idioma in nostra vernacula lingua, a Vostra Excellenzia - vivo lume de la virtute, sola beltà de l'unica bellezza, verità aperta del vero, equale bilancia de la iustizia, splendida grandezza de la liberalitade, ferma colonna de la clemenzia, stabile fortezza del casto pensiero, lucida gemma in oro nitido e prezioso, amenissimo fonte in florido giardino, micante luce ne le tenebre, guida, governo, albergo e abitaculo de le nove muse - l'ho dedicato, avendo forsi abiuto manco rispetto a la grossezza del mio ingegno e a la inezie de la lingua che a la altezza Sua». (*Carcer*, pp.169-70)

Nonostante il fatto che *l'encomium* sia posto fra parentesi, avendo quindi l'apparenza di qualcosa di non del tutto essenziale, il lettore sente il piacere giocoso della scrittura che pecca per il suo gusto dell'eccesso, dello squilibrio: l'autore della prefazione mette in risalto differenze di condizione, tra lui e la destinataria della dedica, tra «questo picciol volume» e il linguaggio grandiloquente e fiorito di metafore iperbolizzanti dell'intervento in prima persona del traduttore, quasi questi volesse superare la distanza sociale con la sua lingua ampollosa e latineggiante. Perciò l'elenco degli attributi segue un ritmo ben preciso, basato sull'assonanza e sull'allitterazione in una sequela di similitudini comuni ma ugualmente lusinghiere; il tutto culmina nella rappresentazione di Isabella come centro di un *revival* culturale. Per questo il nome d'Isabella d'Este funge da simbolo di autorità nell'avvento d'una nuova cultura che qui si propaga tramite il libro stampato («cum deliberatione di farlo mettere in stampa [...] il quale insignito de suo Illustrissimo nome venirà in publico», lettera del 21 novembre).

La storia del libro, per quanto riguarda la marchesa, continua nell'anno successivo ed è un segnale della volontà del Manfredi di compiere il suo "dovere":

> «Illustrissima et Excellentissima Madonna mia observandissima. Poi ch'io ho fatto stampire il *Carcer de amore*, Vostra Celsitudine mai non è stata in queste parti e per questo mai gli ne ho potuto corretto come ho determinato che sia. Ma poi che è venuta gli ne mando uno e ben mi duole non sia in charta di capretto perché havendone fatto stampire duodece a Vinegia (come dissi a meser Mario [Equicola]) mi furno mandati tutti atachati insieme per non esser l'inchiostro asciutto e viscoso. E il deffetto fu del portatore che tanto gli strinse che fu causa di fargli guastare»[12].

Il "dovere" del Manfredi è stato stimolato dal fatto che Isabella d'Este contribuì alle spese della pubblicazione del libro ed è per questo che aveva fatto stampare esemplari di lusso (equivalenti della copia di presentazione manoscritta ma moltiplicati), ma come sempre il Manfredi, perseguitato dalla sfortuna, in parte conseguenza dei suoi mezzi economici molto modesti, non riesce a far bella figura: questa volta gli esemplari di lusso sono stati rovinati[13]. In questa lettera si nota un nuovo elemento, che riapparirà anche nella lettera del 21 novembre 1513: il Manfredi, verso la fine, mette in rilievo una sua opera originale, da lui composta per l'occasione con l'intenzione di dedicarla alla marchesa. Egli tenta dunque di mostrarsi anche sotto un altro aspetto se non uno scrittore vero e proprio, almeno qualcuno che sa innalzarsi al di là della funzione di traduttore. Egli le presenta un'opera che dice, in un gesto di pura cortigianeria, scritta apposta per via dei libri "rovinati":

> «Ma per satisfare a quel manchamento mando a Vostra Illustrissima Signora quel pallazzo che già fece far cum tanta spesa Lucullo, da me cum mancho prezzo e facilitate più assai, rehedifficato».

Particolarmente significativo è il gioco che fa il Manfredi accostando i mezzi economici di Lucullo, l'uomo più ricco di Roma antica, con la propria situazione; il suo scopo è tanto presentarsi come molto meno abbiente ma dotato di un'intelligenza che forse potrà supplire alle ricchezze, quanto ironizzare in modo raffinato su se stesso, dimostrando il proprio spirito di corte. L'opera (ritenuta perduta ma si trova nella Biblioteca Marciana), che rivela un altro aspetto del Manfredi come mediatore culturale della civiltà classica latina, ha per titolo appunto *Pallazzo di Lucullo* ed è effettivamente dedicata ad Isabella d'Este[14]. La si può descrivere come testo di divulgazione mirante a portare ai contemporanei i gusti architettonici esoterici di un romano eccezionale dell'età classica e corrispondente agli interessi della marchesa, interessi che comprendevano l'architettura. La curiosità che una descrizione di una villa antica avrebbe stimolata nella marchesa non sarebbe stata poca data l'importanza delle *delizie* ferraresi e mantovane nella vita aristocratica. In primo luogo il Manfredi spiega chi fosse Lucullo, presentando un riassunto tratto da fonti latine come per informare un'interessata studentessa a cui manchino gli strumenti filologici:

> «Lucio Lucullo, splendidissimo romano, Illustrissima et Excellentissima Madonna, fu ne le cose di guerra illustre assai et in quelle de la pace incomparabile a tutti li homini de la etate sua». (f.244ʳ)[15]

Il Manfredi si concentra sul programma edilizio che Lucullo intraprese ritornato dalle guerre, mettendo in risalto la magnificenza e l'audacia delle sue dimore, ammettendo di avere trovato tutti i relativi particolari su libri: «le qual cose legendo io alcuna volta per diletto mi posero in core di comporre la descriptione de uno casamento fabricato da lui in Tusculano» (f.244ᵛ). Lo scrittore sembra stimolato da interesse d'ispirazione umanistica, cioè dal desiderio di ricostruire con le parole, una parte del passato classico:

> «Hora legendo io questo come già dissi cum non pocha diligentia e fatica mi sum sforzato de intendere come fatta fusse questa sua casa estivale, facendo a similitudine di quelli che li fragmenti de rotti marmi componono insieme per vedere li antiqui epitaphii e li edifficii prisci dal tempo e da la vetustà corrosi guasti e consumpti». (ff.245ʳ⁻ᵛ)

Non è affatto casuale il paragone tra il lettore attento di testi latini e l'archeologo che prova a ricostruire il passato a partire dagli elementi disponibili, perché il Manfredi, così facendo, può far sembrare il suo compito più arduo di quanto non fosse in realtà. Benché in effetti le sue fonti si limitino a pochi, e piuttosto noti, testi, lo scrittore-divulgatore intende dimostrare la sua perizia scientifica in materia, la sua maturità come interprete delle vestigia della cultura antica (aggettivi come «antiqui» e «prisci» ed anche il termine «la vetustà» vorrebbero sottolineare le sue capacità nel campo umanistico, certo più prestigioso, secondo il canone culturale dominante del periodo, dei suoi tentativi di traduzioni spagnole e catalane contemporanee. Quest'opera del Manfredi mette a punto il desiderio allora prevalente nelle corti di far rispondere la cultura umanistica alle esigenze dei principi: ed infatti il Manfredi non manca di accennare al rapporto di concorrenza tra l'epoca moderna e la civiltà classica:

> «Quale ho deliberato per quanto mi serà possibile chiaramente dimostrare cum parole e cum dissegno et dedicarlo a Vostra Celsitudine, la quale a l'età nostra miraculo di natura non solamente volentieri intende li giesti de li homini excellenti ma cum opera contende de oguagliarse a quelli o superchiargli in parte di virtute e magnanimitate». (f.246ʳ)

Con questa dichiarazione il Manfredi insiste su un doppio rapporto che potrebbe sussistere tra la marchesa e gli *uomini* di Roma antica: prima fase di questo rapporto è lo studio dei testi antichi, seguito dalla messa in pratica - ma con la chiara intenzione di migliorare e superare i modelli - di quanto si è appreso.

In questi sforzi divulgativi è da notare il desiderio del Manfredi di mostrarsi degno umanista, che ha un'ottima padronanza della lingua latina, anche se tecnica, e del greco, e che pertanto spiega tutti i termini esotici o tecnici perché vengano intesi da un pubblico non esperto in questo campo. Un esempio: «Latinamente serebbe lo Ornithone nominato Aviario et Occellera ne la lingua che usamo al presente. Però che li greci Ornis dicono a lo occello» (f.248ʳ). Ma questo duplice desiderio di spiegare e allo stesso tempo vantarsi di estese conoscenze si rivela particolarmente in una nota finale aggiunta alla sua descrizione della villa:

> «Perché la dissignatione che descripta habiamo è tutta per le antique misure compartita mi è parso ponere qui di sotto qualche instructione ad essa apertinente». (f.263ʳ)

Per dar ulteriore prova della sua erudizione, cita una pletora di *auctores*, fra i quali «il beato Augustino et Ugo da San Victore», Erodoto, Columella, Varrone e così via. Però il Manfredi desidera dimostrare che non si perde in mezzo a tutte queste misure diverse:

> «certo l'Asia e tutto lo Oriente per cubiti ha sua misura, la Italia e Romani per piede, il quale secondo Junio Columella contiene sedece dita ne la misura de la terra e venti quattro ne la architettura secondo Varone. E di cotale piede credo io essere stato lo edifficio di L. Lucullo». (f.263ᵛ)

E difficile non accettare la definizione stessa dell'autore di questa nota come «instructione» ad una persona assetata di sapere anche se impedita da una preparazione nozionistica e linguistica non molto approfondita. Perciò non dovrebbe sorprendere il fatto che il Manfredi parli di Mario Equicola a questo punto:

> «Et questo è quanto ho ritrovato ne l'antique misure, le quale forsi superfluamente sono poste, essendo certo che molte volte siano state dimostrate a la Vostra Celsitudine da messer Mario Equicolo suo virtuoso et doctissimo preceptore al cui juditio e castighatione sempre mi rimetto volontieri». (f.264ʳ)

Diventa quasi d'obbligo l'accenno all'Equicola, in quegli anni precettore della marchesa, incaricato della formazione classica di lei e consequentemente in grado di influire sulle sue scelte culturali. Il Manfredi riconosce apertamente il ruolo dell'Equicola come *leader* di una corrente intellettuale, di cui, sebbene come figura di secondo piano, fa parte egli stesso: questa corrente, che si potrebbe chiamare umanesimo eclettico di corte, punta non tanto su edizioni di testi classici quanto sull'interesse per gli aspetti culturali trascurati dall'umanesimo "ortodosso", per abbracciare culture e letterature europee (ad esempio, provenzale e spagnolo) tutte ancora da scoprire e da analizzare come una volta il latino e, ancora in quel periodo, il greco. La funzione precipua attribuita alle traduzioni - incarico da cui non sarà esonerato lo stesso Equicola - e l'importanza data a partire dal primo decennio del Cinquecento al volgare come mezzo di comunicazione privilegiato tra i principi e gli intellettuali di corte sono caratteristiche essenziali di questa corrente, ovviamente ancora molto ristretta. Attestazione notevole dei princípi teorici e metodologici di questa corrente è il *Libro de natura de amore*, l'*opus magnum* dell'Equicola, che consiste in misura cospicua di parafrasi - a volte parziali traduzioni - di opere varie sull'argomento in questione. La scelta dell'Equicola è di dedicarsi a un'attività compilatoria piuttosto che curare edizioni degli autori classici o analizzare a fondo questioni filologiche che forse avrebbero richiesto un impegno assai maggiore, impossibile nelle condizioni peculiari di questi intellettuali[16].

Queste problematiche condizioni spinsero il Manfredi a rivolgersi ad altri potenziali protettori o committenti anche se la sua traduzione del *Carcer d'amore* aveva riportato un certo successo. Egli non si mise in contatto col marito della marchesa, Francesco Gonzaga, sapendo che i suoi interessi culturali non si estendevano a questo tipo di letteratura in quanto egli non sembrava condividere gli entusiasmi della moglie e del primogenito, Federico Gonzaga, che diventò l'oggetto delle mire del Manfredi poco dopo l'inizio del rapporto di quest'ultimo con la madre; non sarebbe inappropriato parlare di un progetto ideato dallo stesso scrittore che intendeva così collegare la sua attività culturale alla curiosità ed avidità intellettuali di questi Gonzaga. Il secondo progetto fu la traduzione di *Tirant lo Blanch* dello scrittore catalano Juan Martorell, traduzione a cui il Manfredi già accennava nella lettera del 5 ottobre 1514:

> «E cum maggior dono che serà *Tirant lo Blanch* il qual al presente traduco dimostrarò a Vostra Signoria l'affectione e la reverentia ch'io gli porto a la cui bona gratia di continuo mi racomando».

Questa lettera indirizzata al futuro marchese di Mantova indica la costruzione di un mito che servirà nell'avvenire a dar un certo peso alle aspirazioni politiche di Federico Gonzaga. Questo mito è basato su una valutazione positiva dell'ideologia cavalleresca, percepita come fondamento del potere principesco, che essa rende più degno di ammirazione innalzando il principe all'altezza dei guerrieri mitici medioevali, come quelli rappresentati nell'opera catalana. Si può perfino constatare che l'interesse dimostrato per la letteratura spagnola da parte del Gonzaga non era estraneo ad un vivo apprezzamento dell'influenza di quello stato nella politica europea[17].

Come abbiamo già visto, la traduzione del *Carcer d'amore* dedicata ad Isabella d'Este si intreccia con quella del *Tirante il Bianco* dedicata a Federico Gonzaga. Anche se le due traduzioni non sono state inizialmente concepite come un unico progetto non c'è dubbio che l'anno 1515 segni il culmine delle sue aspirazioni alla protezione gonzaghesca con due lettere che portano la stessa data, l'una alla marchesa, l'altra al figlio (Ferrara, 29 marzo 1515): mentre quella già presa in esame testimonia la fine di un rapporto letterario con la pubblicazione del *Carcer*, quella a Federico mostra l'inizio di un rapporto che durerà oltre la vita del Manfredi, fino alla pubblicazione postuma del *Tirante* nel 1538. La storia del *Tirante* in questo senso non segue la strada piuttosto lineare del *Carcer* ed è piena di lentezze prodotte da difficoltà pratiche, dunque non c'è da stupirsi che questa lettera dia notizie di un ritardo dovuto a cause di forza maggiore per il traduttore:

> «E accepti Vostra Signoria questa scusa la quale se bene non è a satisfactione di meriti e del desiderio suo, pur è di veritate evangielio. Ma se ad ogni quindece dì gli ne havessi mandato un quinterno non haverei forsi fatto tanto quanto in questa volta sola che gli me mandò quattro quinterni. Né d'altro doler mi posso se non che non ho scriptor veloce. Ma quelli che nei tempi futuri gli mandarò seranno bellissimi e dilectevoli ad udire perché cominciarà la bellezza del libro. Et cum quella maggior prestezza ch'io potrò, mi sforzarò dargli fine per satisfare al desiderio di Vostra Signoria alla cui bona gratia humilmente mi racomando». (ASMn, AG, b.1245, Ferrara, 29 marzo 1515, il Manfredi a Federico Gonzaga)

Si vede quindi che dovranno trascorrere più di venti anni prima che la traduzione sia stampata. Le varie cause concrete dei ritardi, a cui il Manfredi accenna, non serviranno ad altro che a spazientire il principe abituato a volere che i suoi desideri siano realizzati all'istante, caratteristica forse ereditata dalla madre. Una difficoltà non insignificante può essere stata la lingua del testo originale, cioè il catalano. Esiste una traduzione castigliana del *Tirante* che il Manfredi avrebbe potuto adoperare come controllo, verificandolo rispetto alla prima edizione catalana. Una prova di questa teoria sarebbe il fatto che le versioni castigliana ed italiana sono divise rispettivamente in 5 e in 7 libri, mentre non esistono divisioni in quella catalana[18].

Non mancano nei documenti altre spiegazioni del lento progresso della traduzione, addotte dal Manfredi per giustificarsi. Un tema che ricorre abbastanza spesso è quello delle sventure capitate al traduttore, sventure che questi usa abilmente per destare nel principe un senso di compassione:

> «Illustrissimo et excellentissimo Signor mio, se Vostra Signoria al presente non ha il *Tirante* da me traducto sum certo che, havendo inteso il caso mio come fui ferito e come sum stato in periculo di morte per cui steti multi e multi mesi prima ch'io mi convalessi, mi haverà per escusato». (ASMn, AG, b.1246, Ferrara, 10 marzo 1518, "Laelius de Manfredis" a Federico Gonzaga)

La lettera spiega in parte tanto il silenzio della durata di quasi tre anni, quanto il motivo del mancato completamento del *Tirante*. Nondimeno per conservare l'"amicizia" del giovane Federico, il Manfredi ha composto un'altra operetta, fatto sorprendente data la sua precedente confessione relativa al mancato progresso dell' *opus magnum*. Ma una semplice spiegazione è offerta dal titolo di questa "nuova" opera, *L'ordine di cavaglieria*[19]. A nessuno sfuggirebbe che il titolo dell'opera manfrediana equivale a quello scritto da Ramon Lull, *Libre de l'orde de cavalleria* che servì da base per la parte teorica sulla cavalleria del *Tirante*[20]. Sembra però certo che il Manfredi abbia elaborato il suo lavoro principalmente in funzione del *Tirante*, con altre aggiunte di cui parleremo in seguito. Il concetto del «cavagliero» come «homo eletto» (f.6^{v}) in quanto «debe haver in sé tal virtuti che ad altri homini non appartengono» (*L'ordine*, f.7^{v}) è comune sia al *Libre* che al *Tirante*[21]. Tanto il *Tirante* quanto *L'ordine* danno rilievo al dovere cristiano del cavaliere: «Il cavaglier debe coprire, defendere e salvar la santa matre chiesia» (*L'ordine*, f.8^{v})[22]. È ovvio a questo punto che il Manfredi non ha minimamente cambiato l'ordine del trattamento della materia del *Tirante*, che a sua volta rispecchia la sequenza del *Libre*. Ciononostante il Manfredi si sentiva libero di aggiungere dettagli che mancano nel *Tirante* o di propria iniziativa o attingendo ad altre fonti, cosa chiaramente visibile nella sezione sul significato delle armi[23]. La seconda parte del trattato manfrediano segue il *Tirante* (il cap. XXXVI equivale con qualche minore aggiunta alla sezione dell'*Ordine* «come si degrada il cavagliero», ff.18^{v}-22^{v}). Ora *l'Ordine* cambia prospettiva e diventa, per così dire, più acceso e personale, distaccandosi dal *Tirante*: il Manfredi si dilunga ad analizzare le più svariate cerimonie d'investitura (*il Tirante* per contro s'interessava esclusivamente all'ordine della Giarrettiera): «l'usanza del Turcho, Imperatore di Constantinopoli» (ff.23^{v}-24^{r}), le cerimonie di Ungheria (ff.24^{r}-25^{r}), di Francia (f.25^{r-v}) di Spagna (ff.25^{v}-26^{r}), d'Inghilterra (ff.26^{r}-29^{v}), evidente per quest'ultimo paese il legame con il *Tirante*) e finalmente di Germania (ff.29^{v}-31^{r})[24]. A differenza degli altri paesi, la Germania svolge nell'economia dell'opera, una funzione precisa, che acquista significato nel corso dell'opera:

> «De la Alemagna. Non mi estenderò in molte parole perché si come vogliono li astrologi e

spetialmente Julio Firmico che l'Imperatore non sia subietto al corso et al moto de le stelle per essere persona unica eletta al mondo. Cossi le cerimonie sue non debbono essere equali alle altre perché tanto è grande la potentia de la Maestate sua che dicendo ad uno, "Tu serai cavagliero", quello è cavagliero, e dicendo ad uno altro, "Tu serai doctore", quello è doctore». (*l'Ordine*, ff.29^v-30^r)

Non è difficile riconoscere il fondamento ironico di questo brano: rispetto alle altre autorità, l'Imperatore è in grado, in primo luogo, di fare a meno di cerimonie. Ed è per questo che il Manfredi non gli risparmia la sua ironia, perché nella sua visione ideologica la cerimonia in sé riveste di dignità e di un senso di *elitismo* l'ordine cavalleresco. Inoltre la facilità con cui l'imperatore può nominare cavalieri e notai rende meno elitarie e più aperte queste "professioni", i cui membri concorrono con i cavalieri più affermati di vecchio stampo; l'ordine cavalleresco è pertanto svalorizzato[25]. Per questo, il Manfredi, concentrandosi sul passato piuttosto che sul presente, si compiace di indicare la decadenza dell'epoca attuale:

«Antiquamente non ardiva né presumeva homo di condictione alcuna portare oro in veste, in apparato né in ornamento alcuno s'el non era cavagliero». (*l'Ordine*, f.31^r)

Questo stato ideale relegato ad un passato non ben definito, quasi mitico («antiquamente») non esiste più:

«E all'età d'hoggi è venuta una consuetudine che l'oro è fra ricchi e non fra poveri. E per questo i ricchi, non havendo rispetto a virtù né a fama, lo portano, e li poveri virtuosi magnanimi e valent'homini che non l'hanno no 'l portano. E questo è chiarissimo exempio che dimostra quanto sia poco estimata la virtute e mancho cognosciuto il vitio e l'ignorantia». (*l'Ordine*, f.32^r)[26]

Solo verso la fine del trattato il Manfredi si decide a descrivere le origini dell'istituzione della cavalleria, come per confermare la struttura dialettica di questa parte dell'opera (cioè la distanza tra passato e presente) rifacendosi alle origini pure e mitiche della cavalleria, simboleggiate da esempi proposti come modelli al corrotto mondo contemporaneo[27].

In un atto di mitomane autoesaltazione, il Manfredi, nelle ultime pagine dell'opera, collega il suo passato ai tempi mitici del *Tirante* ed allo stesso tempo alla storia gloriosa degli ex-imperatori bizantini della dinastia Paleologa. Non c'è alcun dubbio che in questo passo l'ideologia cavalleresca sia usata per fini personali. L'autore, non soddisfatto di riferire che Taddeo Paleologo, imperatore di Constantinopoli, aveva creato cavalieri i Manfredi, o almeno i membri legittimi della famiglia, aggiunge un ulteriore dettaglio significativo: «la casa di Monferrato la qual hebbe l'origine dal'Imperio constantinopolitano [...] la prima casa che hoggi sia al mondo» (f.39). Questo parebbe un tentativo di creare un connubio tra tempo quasi mitico e tempo presente (i Paleologhi già imperatori ora principi di Monferrato) nella speranza di mettere in rilievo il prestigio di cui i Manfredi erano onorati. Quindi la conclusione dell'operetta si può leggere sia a livello generale teorico sia come apologia di un gruppo sociale in pericolo di scomparire, sia come preghiera personale da parte del Manfredi:

«Si pò comprendere che l'ordine di cavaglieria è la maggior dignitate che si possi dare al mondo, la qual quanto è riceputa da persona più degna et illustre tanto è di maggior riputatione e fama». (f. 39)

Non sembra che l' *Ordine di cavaglieria* abbia entusiasmato minimamente Federico Gonzaga; se il suo autore mirava a migliorare con essa i propri rapporti con il Gonzaga, non riuscì nel suo intento, anzi ottenne l'effetto contrario. Nella lettera del 10 marzo chiese al Gonzaga di rispondere alla sua iniziativa:

> «Ma Vostra Excellentia si dignarà di farmi intendere e cognoscere per sue littere quanto la fatica mia gli sia stata agrata. E una altra volta mi sforzarò cum altra più bella opera satisfare al diffetto e manchamento di questa».

Il silenzio del Gonzaga costituisce la sua risposta:

> «E sia come si voglia supplico a quella, voglia dignarsi di rispondermi perché quando non gli sia grata farò conto di non glie l'haver scripta, dolendomi di haverla fastidita cum quella. E scio certo che cognoscendo Ella il dispiacere ch'io ne haverò voluntieri mi rimetterà questo errore». (ASMn, AG, b.1246, Ferrara, 23 marzo 1518, il Manfredi a Federico Gonzaga)

E forse troppo facile parlare dell'«ingrato Signore» (Zilli, p.47) e dipingerlo a fosche tinte - tendenza moralistica frequente più nella critica del secolo scorso che in quella contemporanea - senza indagare più da vicino il sistema di rapporti istituiti tra principe e letterato. Parlare di «demeriti artistici» (Zilli, p.48) non ha molto senso se questo concetto non viene inserito nel contesto cortigiano; si deve piuttosto parlare in termini della formazione e funzione del gusto letterario nell'ambito della corte, esaminando attentamente le condizioni reali tanto della produzione letteraria quanto del consumo di testi letterari. Se dunque ci si chiede perché Federico Gonzaga non sembrasse interessato all' *Ordine di cavaglieria*, bisogna notare che, in primo luogo, probabilmente aveva avuto una netta impressione di *déjà vu*, avendo già incontrato l'argomento nelle pagine manoscritte del *Tirante* che aveva già ricevute dal Manfredi. In secondo luogo, l'opera è prettamente ferrarese d'ispirazione nella redazione pervenutaci e non offre spunti d'interesse gonzaghesco, ma sembra piuttosto scritta per il pubblico ferrarese ed estense. Questa seconda considerazione ci porta a riflettere su un brano della lettera sopracitata, in cui il Manfredi dice chiaramente che l'opera è dedicata a Federico Gonzaga:

> «E per questo gli ho voluto replicar questa mia accioché non habbia causa di riprehendermi di temerità e di prosumptione che habbia havuto ardire *intitulargli* simil cosa non degna di pervenire al conspecto suo». (23 marzo 1518, il Manfredi a Federico Gonzaga)

Ma questa asserzione è contraddetta dalla testimonianza dell'unico manoscritto dedicato non al principe gonzaghesco ma ad un certo «Vincentio Musto, ducale consotio» (f.1), cioè, ad un gentiluomo *ferrarese*. E difficile decidere con certezza se la dedica dell'*Ordine* abbia subito mutamenti resi necessari dal nuovo destinatario; però, considerando il tono vago e generale di essa non sembra che ce ne siano stati molti, forse l'autore si è limitato a sostituire Mantova con Ferrara. Tuttavia, è chiaro che il Manfredi non ebbe mai una risposta positiva e favorevole circa l'*Ordine*, altrimenti non avrebbe dovuto trovare un'altra persona a cui dedicare l'opera; si può ipotizzare che egli abbia dedicato l'opera contemporaneamente ad ambedue i potenziali committenti nella speranza che almeno uno di essi accettasse il dono con piacere e gratitudine[28]. A parte la mancanza di fedeltà verso un solo committente, si può anche notare un altro aspetto delle tecniche manfrediane per far colpo sul lettore; il Manfredi vuole suggerire che *l'Ordine* sia il frutto di molte e recondite ricerche e che per questo Federico Gonzaga gli dev'essere grato:

«E quella [una operetta de l'ordine di cavagliera] ho racolto da auctori latini, hebrei, alemmani, inglesi, spagnoli e francesi». (ASMn, AG, b.1246, Ferrara, 10 marzo 1518)

Però non è affatto da escludere che Federico Gonzaga abbia riconosciuto la fonte principale dell'opera e sia stato infastidito da questo tentativo di autoincensamento da parte del Manfredi. Non è che il Manfredi programmi le sue mosse in modo diverso da altri cortigiani-intellettuali però è forse più ingenuo e, quel che è peggio, incapace di leggere bene il mercato, in quanto non si rende conto della gerarchia di valutazioni differenziate per ciascun prodotto. Il Manfredi ci appare inoltre sia intellettualmente in malafede (in quanto è ben conscio di aver usufruito soprattutto del *Tirante*, e forse anche di altri pochi testi) sia ingenuo (quando tenta di rappresentarsi come un altro Tirante o come un cavaliere di uno degli ordini più prestigiosi). Resta da dire che, a parte gli aspetti negativi già esaminati, l'*Ordine* ha la sua importanza culturale nel contesto ferrarese perché mette acutamente a fuoco il valore sociale dell'ordine cavalleresco ed esprime il punto di vista di un ceto oppresso che ha perso i suoi antichi privilegi. Contro questa valutazione positiva non si può non pensare all'ironia espressa in materia dall'*Orlando Furioso*; anzi, le critiche dell'Ariosto rivolte alle pratiche cavalleresche prendono corpo se paragonate a difese del tipo di quelle del Manfredi.

Passa un anno prima che ci pervenga una lettera di Federico Gonzaga, che nel frattempo è diventato marchese e che chiede ancora notizie della traduzione:

«Ni raccordamo che altre volte ne mandaste alcuni quinterni dil *Tirante* tradutto di spagnolo in italiano da voi, promettendoni di mandarci il resto. Et perché hora siamo venuti in desiderio di vederlo tutto tradutto et legerlo [...]». (ASMn, AG, b.2926)

Federico Gonzaga abilmente scarica sul Manfredi tutta la responsabilità del mancato completamento della traduzione in quanto questa era stata promessa da lui, "fedele cortigiano". Quindi, il tono della lettera prende avvio dalla mancata promessa e dal fatto che parla adesso *il marchese*, il quale sembra rinnovare il suo interesse per questo genere di letteratura nel momento in cui arriva alla vetta del potere politico dello stato mantovano. Il nuovo marchese parla in quanto marchese, come avrebbe fatto ad un suo funzionario, considerando alla stessa stregua i servizi resi da entrambi. Infatti per il momento il Manfredi, non avendo niente di nuovo da offrire, non ritiene opportuno scrivere direttamente al marchese, ma si rivolge piuttosto al segretario del marchese, Stazio Gadio, profondendosi in scuse e promesse lusinghiere:

«E per questo di verghogna non gli [a Federico Gonzaga] rispondo per non haver desiderio di satisfargli cum scuse perché io portarò la risposta e il *Tirante* insieme e prestissimo il quale io voglio che sia di Sua Celsitudine e a quella dedicato venghi a luce e cossi sia posto a stampa se quella non si ne sdignarà»[29].

La traduzione non è stata completata in seguito a circostanze - come una nuova ferita - che il Manfredi descrive con abbondanza di particolari: circostanze probabilmente vere ma insufficienti a giustificare un ritardo di anni. Il marchese però insiste per avere la sua traduzione, spedendo un'altra lettera in questo senso[30]. È importante mettere in risalto qui che il Manfredi aveva sempre l'intenzione di far stampare il *Tirante* («e cossi sia posto a stampa») per soddisfare il suo desiderio di accrescere sia la sua reputazione che quella del marchese. Ma, come vedremo, di qui al *Tirante* stampato passeranno dieci anni, fatto socioculturale di non poco significato.

Adesso tutto sembra avviato ad un lieto fine, ma passerà quasi un anno prima che il Manfredi possa venire a Mantova portando con sé la traduzione finalmente ultimata. Viene senza preavviso, alloggiando in albergo dato che la società cortigiana non è disposta a ospitare chi non produca a tempo debito, o non sia di rango abbastanza alto, o non abbia altro di vantaggioso da offrire. Dal punto di vista metodologico non è però produttivo né biasimare i Gonzaga né Manfredi; è cruciale notare che Federico Gonzaga non esprime compassione per il Manfredi malato che, riammalatosi, decide, accettando umilmente la sua posizione sociale subalterna, di far ritorno a Ferrara senza avere visto il principe, o avergli chiesto aiuto, e addirittura senza nemmeno averlo informato del suo arrivo. Il Manfredi racconta in seguito al marchese le sue sventure, cioè la malattia unita alla mancanza di denaro. Il fatto che abbia finito la traduzione serve solo da sfondo al suo dramma personale:

> «E cossi cum ogni diligentia, studio e cura come scia tutta Ferrara mi possi all'opera. Lo fornì e glie 'l portai. Ma dal disgratiato dì che mi desimbarchai in Mantua in sino all'ultimo dì che me imbarchai per venire a Ferrara alloggiai a l'hostaria del sole dove fra quattro dì mi venne la doglia de la costa e tre volte mi fu tratto sangue. E subito ch'io poti mi ne venni a Ferrara. Ma mi fu forza pagar l'hostaria e per non haver denari da pagarla e da levarmi fui sforzato di lasciare non solamente gli panni ch'io mi havevo comprati ma insino alle camise all'hoste»[31].

E fin troppo evidente che lo scopo della lettera è di farsi restituire denari e vestiti, ed è interessante vedere come il Manfredi procede nel ribadire la responsabilità del marchese («cum quanta instantia e preghi mi scrisse che volessi traddure il *Tirante*»): tentativo di costruire un rapporto in cui il committente non si limita a dare ordini, ma mostra un vigile paternalismo. A ciò si aggiunge un debole tentativo di ricatto, con il riferimento a «tutta Ferrara», che nonostante l'esagerazione, allude alla pubblica natura della sua impresa, nota agli intellettuali e cortigiani ferraresi: per questo, qualora il principe si sottraesse alle sue responsabilità, gliene deriverebbero vergogna e perdita d'onore. Lo scrittore peraltro non risparmia un accenno all'*imago* principesca di Federico Gonzaga:

> «Vostra Excellentia la quale è liberalissima e non scia alcuna di queste cose né vole che alcuno la venghi a servire a sue spese e spetialmente nel gran caso e longa fatica che ho fatto io. La supplico di gratia voglia fare che le robbe mie mi siano restituite».

Una seconda lettera sull'argomento ripete la sostanza del suo dilemma aggiungendo l'amara verità della distanza tra *fictio* e realtà:

> «Se alla venuta ch'io feci a Mantua fussi cossi andato da Andrinopoli a Costantinopoli e fussi stato Tirante facevo el fin suo di doglia di costa, ma per non esser quello e in simil viaggio fui riserbato ad altri tempi». (ASMn, AG, b.1247, Ferrara, 4 giugno 1520)

Una terza lettera, anche se rivela una certa consapevolezza che il romanzo cavalleresco idealizza il principe e si riferisce ad un'epoca ben lontana dal presente, mostra nondimeno qualche nota di speranza, facendo riferimento implicito al canone comportamentale del principe del Rinascimento e alle nozioni di liberalità e splendore, che devono guidare la committenza culturale:

> «E perché io cognosco Vostra Celsitudine liberalissima come ha dimostrato in minor cosa di questa e in minor dono e a servitore minor di me». (ASMn, AG, b.1247, Ferrara, 27 giugno 1520)

Con questa lettera il Manfredi asserisce l'importanza dello scrittore-traduttore rispetto ad altri che ricevono favori gonzagheschi e, a parte i tentativi di pressione finanziaria, rappresenta una formulazione del ruolo da attribuire al testo scritto nella società cortigiana, per niente «minor», ma qualcosa di rispettabile che comporta ben precise responsabilità (un «dono» che si aspetta un altro dono). In questi termini, Federico Gonzaga si sarebbe dimostrato poco interessato alla sua immagine d'*imperator in minore* se fosse venuto meno ai suoi obblighi. Non si può secondo me parlare in termini personalistici del rapporto Gonzaga-Manfredi come fa lo Zilli («ciò che da queste lettere è invece più facile intuire è quanto poco sollecito si mostrasse il duca [sic!] della sorte del Manfredi», art.cit., p.48). Il Manfredi dimostra una certa abilità nell'attaccare i presupposti ideologici del marchese, e, se le sue lettere vengono lette in questa chiave, la risposta del Gonzaga sembra prevedibile, quasi automatica:

> «Siamo contenti che facciati pagare a conto nostro la spesa che fece a l'hostaria dal sole Lelio di Manfredi da Ferrara mentre el stete a Mantua quando el ne portò el *Tirrante*. La qual spesa intendemo è circa libre quaranta tre perché non volemo el paghi cosa alcuna d'essa spesa. Et le robbe sue lassate in pegno per tal debito li siano restituite»[32].

Non c'è dubbio che la traduzione stesse a cuore al giovane marchese che arrivò perfino a richiederla durante una spedizione militare: «mandami anche appresso il *Tirante*»[33]. Poi, ci sono altri testi spagnoli da tradurre di cui non abbiamo ulteriori dettagli ma che rivelano un Manfredi impegnato in un compito che il Gonzaga forse non avrebbe affidato ad altri e che di necessità esige un rapporto un po' più intimo tra di loro:

> «Messer Lelio di Mamphredi ne ha comminciato a tradur un libro che ni è di grande piacere e già ci ne ha portato cinque quinterni. Et perché el ne fa intendere che il ditto libro è vostro et che l'haveti mandato a torre mentre che esso messer Lelio è stato qui con noi, pregamovi che ne lo vogliati prestare fin che' si possi finir di tradure»[34].

Questa maggiore, anche se di poco, benevolenza da parte del Gonzaga non contribuisce sensibilmente a migliorare le condizioni finanziarie del Manfredi, tema di pressoché tutte le lettere dal 1521 al 1528, che si aggiunge all'altro tema ricorrente, quello delle sue precarie condizioni di salute. Del premio di cui aveva parlato il marchese non c'è traccia in queste lettere, e la restituzione dei danari per la visita a Mantova del 1520 diventa cosa complicatissima, forse in seguito all'incompetenza del Manfredi[35]. In ogni modo, il Manfredi non perde mai speranza, anzi, pensa che valga la pena di continuare a prestare la sua opera per Federico Gonzaga quasi senza interruzione: forse non aveva alternative o forse - visto il fallimento dei suoi precedenti tentativi di dedicare opere al re di Francia - il rapporto con il Gonzaga gli sembrava relativamente più promettente. Per di più le lettere scritte al marchese dal 1525 fino al 1528 non sono state mandate da Ferrara come tutte le precedenti, ma hanno origine sia da Mantova sia «dalla pallazzina di campagna»[36]. Il Manfredi descrive la sua situazione in termini del tutto negativi asserendo che qualsiasi speranza di miglioramento dipende dalla volontà del marchese di Mantova:

> «Io mi sum ridutto a l'ombra di Vostra Excellentia per finire seco questi pochi anni che mi restano a vivere. E non ho provisione né terre che mi mantenghino né amici che a gli bisogni mi soccorrino. Unde non scio da qual altro riccorrere che da Vostra Illustrissima Signoria unde la supplico che mi vogli havere per racomandato. Che non posso haver vino alla Canova né ho denari da comperarne né mai ho cosa alcuna al venere né al sabato. E perhò la pregho che voglia far che mi sia dato quel che mi ha promesso. Et alla bona gratia sua di continuo mi racomando». (ASMn, AG, b.2508, Mantova, 26 ottobre 1528)

Il tono della lettera passa dall'umile al quasi perentorio. L'inizio mostra la sua assoluta dipendenza dal marchese come se tutte le altre possibilità gli fossero precluse («io mi sum ridutto») con un accenno implicito al suo trasferimento a Mantova («finire seco»). Non è neanche evitata una ovvia retoricità che gioca sul *topos* del letterato a cui non resta molto da vivere (*topos* in questo caso non lontano dalla realtà) e che è senza denaro (*e non ho* [...] *nè amici* [...] *non scio* [...] *non posso haver* [...] *né ho denari* [...] *né mai* è la struttura dominante del brano).

Dopo aver ricapitolato quegli aspetti della sua esistenza che meglio dimostrano la sua miseria, il Manfredi passa alla parte positiva, alla richiesta, alla supplica («mi vogli havere per racomandato»). A questo punto niente di specifico, nessuna domanda di un posto, il che forse è dovuto alla consapevolezza della sua età probabilmente avanzata e delle sue condizioni di salute; ma, subito dopo, un riferimento preciso porta per un momento un tocco concreto e realistico nel tono generalmente convenzionale dell'epistola, «non posso haver vino alla Canova». Nell'ultima frase il Manfredi non può nascondere il suo risentimento contro il marchese per la mancata ricompensa, promessa, a quanto pare, mai concretizzata («che mi sia dato quel che mi ha promesso»). E difficile scindere la retorica dalla situazione reale del Manfredi, ma nondimeno ci si può fare un'idea dello sfruttamento di questo traduttore pagato con promesse mal mantenute, anche se non completamente trascurato. Le cose non migliorano perché un anno più tardi il Manfredi scrive al marchese con lo stesso tono e con gli stessi lamenti:

> «Io scio certo che Vostra Signoria scia il grande male che ho habiuto questo anno e che hebbi l'anno passato per modo che più non mi restai cosa alcuna da impignare»[37].

Le ultime tre lettere del Manfredi, datate settembre e ottobre 1528, continuano a elencare le sue sofferenze, in particolare la debolezza fisica che sembra indicare l'avvicinarsi della sua fine.

La corrispondenza tra il Manfredi e Federico Gonzaga mette in risalto una lacuna, un silenzio, se, come abbiamo già stabilito, il Manfredi terminò il *Tirante* nel 1520 con l'intenzione di farlo stampare in quello stesso anno. Invece dopo quella data non si accenna più a un'edizione stampata del *Tirante*, che circola soltanto in versione manoscritta[38]. In questo il *Tirante* differisce dalla traduzione del *Carcer* per la stampa della quale Isabella d'Este aveva fornito aiuti concreti, dato che il Manfredi non poteva finanziarlo da solo. Sia alla marchesa che al traduttore derivavano vantaggi immediati dalla pubblicazione del libro: alla prima andava la fama più diffusa di innovatrice culturale (con la sua *côterie* come centro d'interesse per la letteratura spagnola, il che forse rappresenta una risposta a Lucrezia Borgia); il secondo, associandosi con Isabella d'Este, veniva ad avere prestigio e forse, col tempo, guadagni finanziari. Se dunque ci si chiede perché il *Tirante* non sia stato pubblicato che nel 1538, a circa dieci anni dall'ultima lettera e presunta morte (1528) del Manfredi - fatto ancora più enigmatico dato il grande successo del romanzo cavalleresco in versi durante questi anni - si deve concludere che probabilmente il responsabile è il marchese di Mantova più che il Manfredi. Questi, secondo la lettera dedicatoria del testo stampato, sarebbe morto prima di potere far pubblicare l'opera:

> «Ma, sì come spesso avviene che non possiamo a nostri dissegni fornir di dare perfettamente tutti i colori che vorremmo, così non fu concesso a messer Lelio di vedere le fatiche e le notturne sue vigilie poste in luce sotto l'illustrissimo nome di vostra eccellentissima signoria, conciosiaché preparandosi egli per istampare l'opra sua, fu intercetto da morte e cadde prima che potesse pervenire al segno ove havea il suo corso indirizzato»[39].

Non esiste nessun'indicazione che il marchese si sia preoccupato di portare a termine l'opera del Manfredi, facendo stampare il *Tirante*. Solo due anni prima della morte del Gonzaga, Federico Torresani intraprende quest'operazione come per puro caso, a quanto pare senza l'intervento diretto del duca di Mantova: «hor, essendomi venuta alle mani questa sua tradottione» (p.45). Infatti l'intervento del Torresani non consiste solo nel finanziamento, il che potrebbe spiegare il ritardo e la riluttanza del principe a far stampare il libro: il Torresani scrive nella sua prefazione che «l'ho fatta io con nuova lima ripolire e con somma diligenza stampare» (p.45), cioè la lingua manfrediana aveva bisogno di essere aggiornata e messa in regola con i sistemi linguistici dominanti. Ma prima di tutto un testo della lunghezza del *Tirante* richiedeva l'investimento di una somma non insignificante, che probabilmente il duca non poteva o non voleva permettersi; questo investimento spettava quindi ad un *businessman* che conoscesse il mercato e i suoi *trend*. È importante notare che il Torresani pubblicò nello stesso anno un'edizione del *Cortegiano* e sembra che vedesse le possibilità di un allargamento del pubblico di opere che prima interessavano precipuamente la corte[40]. La stessa prima edizione del *Tirante* conserva la prefazione originaria del traduttore, scritta anni prima, che fa riferimento a una situazione culturale diversa: sono infatti morti tanto il Manfredi stesso quanto l'intellettuale di rilievo di cui si fa menzione, Mario Equicola (morto nel 1525, cioè 13 anni prima della pubblicazione del *Tirante*).

Questa prefazione (pp.46-47), probabilmente uguale a quella manoscritta, conferma quanto fosse ironica la posizione di un intellettuale sempre costretto a scrivere al principe per chiedere grazie quasi mai concesse ed è ormai un anacronismo. Non c'era più un Equicola alla corte di Federico Gonzaga che potesse servire da punto di riferimento per il Manfredi come scrittore riuscito. La carriera stessa del Manfredi è un esempio delle incertezze e dell'ambiguità della posizione sociale dell'intellettuale in questo periodo: egli si trovava isolato e senza la protezione di alcuna struttura portante nel mezzo di un sistema di committenze che in gran parte dipendeva dalla volontà del principe. La lettera, in quanto documento che testimonia del potere dell'uno e dell'impotenza dell'altro, è il mezzo di comunicazione per chi, trovandosi per qualsiasi motivo lontano dalla corte, non possa avvalersi della presenza principesca. La corrispondenza tra il Manfredi e Federico Gonzaga richiama alla mente quella tra Luigi Pulci e Lorenzo de' Medici, se si tengono in debito conto la diversa epoca e la diversa situazione degli scrittori (Pulci è più aperto e meno arrendevole). L'autore quattrocentesco e quello cinquecentesco condividono la paura di essere esclusi o anche dimenticati e quella di trovarsi in ristrettezze finanziarie, ma quello che caratterizza il Manfredi è la sua insistenza nel dichiarare di non avere assolutamente legami concreti con altri che possano aiutarlo[41]. Non parla mai di un incarico né all'università, né alla corte estense (è difficile guidicare se l'essere "familiare" fosse fonte di guadagni concreti), né a quella mantovana, né sembra che fosse notaio o avvocato. Quindi, a parte proprietà di cui non siamo informati, per migliorare la sua posizione doveva presentarsi come "offerta interessante" per la corte, puntando tanto sul potere dei cortigiani quanto sul loro desiderio di svago intellettuale. E il colpo di genio è il suo essere pronto ad assecondare il desiderio di testi spagnoli da parte dei Gonzaga e addirittura il suo incoraggiare questo desiderio, istituendo un vero e proprio mercato di testi. Ma la letteratura spagnola costituisce solo una parte del consumo; il Manfredi lotta quindi anche per farsi riconoscere come scrittore, ma in questo campo non era senza rivali, dei quali il marchese era in grado di guidicare i relativi meriti. Un rivale di questo genere fu ad esempio Pietro Aretino, che negli anni '20 riuscì ad incantare il marchese di Mantova. Paragonando i carteggi dei due scrittori ci si può rendere conto della distanza che li separa. In primo luogo il numero delle risposte di Federico Gonzaga all'Aretino è piuttosto alto; inoltre le lettere del Gonzaga contengono valutazioni positive se non adulatorie, ad esempio, «tutte [vostre lettere] mi sono state gratissime et iocondissime. He per essere cose dotte et piacevole, et ne ho preso gran spasso et piacere, come faccio de tutte le vostre belle compositioni le quali mi delettano tanto quanto credo che voi sapiati»[42]. Sembra che il marchese non trovi parole per esprimere la gioia orgiastica da lui provata nel leggere opere dell'Aretino («et come che simili novità sogliono piacere sempre ad ogniuno, nondimeno dilectano me sommamente», doc. VI, p.71). Questo, in buona parte, spiega l'indifferenza e il silenzio del Gonzaga nei riguardi delle opere letterarie del Manfredi[43]. Questo silenzio è totale soprattutto nei riguardi delle commedie manfrediane, (una delle quali, la *Filadelfia* è giudicata dallo Zilli «priva di una qualsiasi nota di vivacità»). La reazione negativa da parte del Gonzaga risalta ancora di più se la si confronta con il giudizio positivo da lui espresso sulle commedie inviategli dall'Ariosto:

> «Però vi ne ringratiamo con tutto il core, certificandovi che la legeremo con summo piacere et delectatione, sperando che l'habbi ad essere simile a tutte le altre opere da voi dottamente et eruditamente composte»[44].

Anche se il rapporto che legava il Gonzaga all'Aretino e all'Ariosto - non essendo questi ultimi senza appoggi politici abbastanza rilevanti, e non dipendendo quindi essi totalmente dal marchese - era ben diverso da quello fra il Gonzaga e il Manfredi, non si può prescindere dal *piacere* che il marchese provava nella lettura delle loro opere, in contrasto con la sua reazione tiepida e fredda alle opere manfrediane[45]. Infatti, la forma prevalente della lettera manfrediana è la supplica, il che indica la posizione completamente impotente del traduttore. Ciò che il Manfredi intuì fu l'importanza della letteratura spagnola nel produrre nuovi testi su temi particolarmente cari al pubblico delle corti. Questa sua prima attività fu sempre connessa a quella di fornire testi cortigiani nella speranza di guadagnarsi premi dai potenti delle corti (o mantovana o ferrarese o francese). Si può dire con certezza che solo il *Carcer* sia stato un totale successo; il *Tirante*, nonostante fosse circolato manoscritto per molti anni, fu pubblicato solo dopo la morte del Manfredi.

Il caso Manfredi mette a fuoco le difficoltà che all'inizio del Cinquecento doveva affrontare un intellettuale isolato e non in grado di inserirsi a pieno in una struttura che lo proteggesse e consentisse un accettabile tenore di vita. Il ruolo del traduttore, sempre un po' anonimo e nascosto dietro il testo altrui, si dimostra particolarmente increscioso in questo caso. Per questo il Manfredi, nonostante le sue scarse predisposizioni voleva uscire dall'anonimato per essere scrittore vero e proprio. Infatti, il lavoro del traduttore è considerato dai Gonzaga lavoro meccanico che non deve subire ritardi, il che riduce il prestigio dell'atto di scrivere. In termini generali sembra che lo scrittore non possa affatto far prevalere la sua posizione nei riguardi del committente, qualcosa che *non* è eccezionale in questo periodo. Le lettere del Manfredi, che sono a volte talmente patetiche da sembrare comiche, consentono di intravvedere le condizioni in cui lavorava un intellettuale medio.

Il caso Manfredi è anche importante per altri motivi. Esso rappresenta una tappa interessante nella storia culturale italiana del primo Cinquecento: non solo la sua scelta dei testi da tradurre, ma anche le sue opere originali, connesse alle traduzioni, dimostrano scelte culturali ben precise. Sotto Federico Gonzaga, in particolare, la cultura mantovana si trova in fase di transizione. Le sue esperienze come ostaggio presso la corte romana e quella reale di Francia, senza dubbio stimolarono il Gonzaga a ripensare ed a superare i paradigmi culturali sostenuti dal padre Francesco. Se quest'ultimo considerava la sua funzione di condottiero in modo commerciale, il figlio era più incline a romantizzare l'elemento guerriero e ad esagerare la sua importanza nella macchina politica della penisola. La sua attività militare si prestava ad un'operazione di glorificazione di sé attraverso la decorazione dei suoi palazzi e, in chiave minore, attraverso le sue letture dei romanzi cavallereschi[46]. Il marchese si vedeva come eroe mitico, più valente dei capitani suoi rivali e degno di ammirazione da parte di tutti: è in questo contesto che si inserisce il suo entusiasmo per il *Tirante*. Inoltre i suoi contatti con le corti più brillanti dell'Europa lo avevano colpito al punto di fargli desiderare di essere alla loro altezza sul piano culturale, creando intorno a sé a Mantova una delle corti più eleganti e raffinate, sul modello della Spagna imperiale e di Roma papale. Il Manfredi dunque fa parte di questo disegno, anche se svolge un ruolo minore. L'iniziativa manfrediana di tradurre testi chiave della letteratura spagnola è manipolata per motivi dinastici dal Gonzaga, che sfrutta la situazione abbastanza precaria del traduttore. Quest'ultimo trova difficile in queste condizioni cambiar rotta, siccome la sua funzione è stata stabilita fin dall'inizio dei suoi rapporti con i Gonzaga; egli è costretto ad una specializzazione dalla quale non poteva liberarsi. Il Manfredi finalmente non è un caso particolare, ma merita di essere studiato in quanto rappresenta un punto d'intersezione tra la letteratura e la corte, tra sistema di letteratura e sistema di potere.

Sono assai grato a Mirna Cicioni per la sua assistenza nella stesura definitiva del testo italiano di questo lavoro.

SUMMARY

The Translator at Court: Lelio Manfredi. Notes in *Carcer d'Amor* and *Tirante il Bianco*. Lelio Manfredi was active in the first thirty years of the sixteenth century at the courts of Mantua and Ferrara. His principal activity was translating Spanish and Catalan texts into Italian, an activity which was encouraged first of all by Isabella d'Este and later by her son, Federico Gonzaga. His role as translator although in demand did not bring him financial security. He tried to curry favour by composing a range of 'original' works, but that strategy was even less successful. The *Pallazzo di Lucullo*, though lost, throws light on the way an intellectuall thought he could appeal to Isabella d'Este's artistic and classical sensibilities. Other texts written by him were not even acknowledged by Federico Gonzaga. The article traces Manfredi's *iter* as he slides deeper into poverty and discovers that the patronage system only despenses 'welfare' if the prince is truly entertained or the aspirant has provided a useful service. However, Manfredi's longest and most complex translation *Tirante il Bianco* was only printed after his death.

NOTE

1. Il contributo più recente su questo personaggio alquanto trascurato è quello di C. ZILLI, *Notizia di Lelio Manfredi, Letterato di Corte*, in "Studi e Problemi di Critica Testuale", XXVII (1983), pp. 39-54. Sono ancora utili F. FLAMINI, *Viaggi fantastici e 'trionfi' di poeti*, in *Nozze Cian=Sappa-Flandinet*, Bergamo 1894, pp. 279-299; F. FLAMINI, *Le lettere italiane alla corte di Francesco I re di Francia* in "Studi di storia letteraria italiana e straniera", Livorno 1895, pp. 197-337 (p. 244); A. LUZIO e R. RENIER, *Niccolò da Correggio*, in "Giornale Storico della Letteratura Italiana" ["GSLI"], XXII (1893), pp. 65-119, 70-73; A. LUZIO e R. RENIER, *La coltura e le relazioni letterarie d'Isabella d'Este Gonzaga*, in "GSLI", XXXV (1900), pp. 244-245.
   Per quanto riguarda le lettere si veda G. BERTONI, *Nota su Mario Equicola bibliofilo e cortigiano*, in "GSLI", LXVI (1915), pp. 281-283; A. BERTOLOTTI, *Varietà archivistiche e bibliografiche*, in "Il Bibliofilo", V (1884) pp. 163-166; VI (1885) pp. 39-41; VIII (1887) pp. 90-91; IX (1888) pp. 70-73, 160-162.
2. Archivio di Stato di Mantova, Archivio Gonzaga (da ora in poi: ASMn, AG), busta 1195, Ferrara, 21 novembre 1513, Alfonso d'Este a Isabella d'Este.
3. «Quando mandai il *Carcer d'Amore* a la Excellentia de la Sua Illustrissima genitrice intesi come Vostra Signoria summamente desiderava de haverne copia». ASMn, AG, b.1245, Ferrara, 5 ottobre 1514, «Laelius de Manfredis» a Federico Gonzaga, citato da A. BERTOLOTTI, op. cit., a nota 1, V (1884), p. 163.
4. Vedi G. BERTONI, *Catalogo dei codici spagnuoli della biblioteca estense*, Erlangen 1905, che traccia i rapporti tra gli Estensi e la cultura spagnola con particolare riferimento al *Cancionero di Modena* portato a Ferrara da Lucrezia Borgia; W. F. PRIZER, *Isabella d'Este and Lucrezia Borgia as patrons of music: The Frottola at Mantua and Ferrara*, in "Journal of the American Musicological Society", XXXVIII (1985), pp. 1-33 (22-24); M. BELLONCI, *Lucrezia Borgia: La sua vita e i suoi tempi*, Milano 1967 (11ª edizione), pp. 271-272; A. FARINELLI, *Italia e Spagna*, Torino 1929, vol. II, pp. 81-83.
5. A mo' d'esempio, *La seconda redazione del «Cortegiano» di Baldassarre Castiglione*, edizione critica a cura di G. GHINASSI, Firenze 1968, pp. 257-258, registra indirettamente la presenza napoletana nell'Italia settentrionale come conseguenza delle invasioni francesi e spagnole, le «procelle di fortuna» (p. 257). Al Castiglione non sfugge la presenza di Antonia del Balzo a Gazzuolo che prima «per le sue virtù merita esser celebratissima» (p. 258) e poi è ricordata per la quantità di figlie da lei partorite ma non è da dimenticare che nel 1500 Antonia del Balzo aveva dato in prestito a Isabella d'Este una copia presa dalla propria biblioteca del *Tirante* in lingua catalana. Questo fatto è ricordato da A. LUZIO e R. RENIER, *Niccolò da Correggio*, in "GSLI", XXII (1893), pp. 65-119; 71-72.
6. Per un elenco delle edizioni del *Carcer* vedi *Càrcer d'amor.Carcer d'amore. Due traduzioni della «novela» di Diego de San Pedro*, a cura di V. MINERVINI e M. L. INDINI, Fasano di Puglia 1986, pp. 144-151.

7. Di seguito alla lettera dedicatoria troviamo nelle edizioni a partire dal 1521 quest'indicazione «incomencia la ellegante opera, dicta *Carcer d'amore* del magnifico meser Lelio de Manfredi» (*Carcer*, 1524, f. a3).

8. ASMn, AG, b.1245, Ferrara, 21 novembre 1513, il Manfredi a Isabella d'Este.

9. Riguardo ai quadri cfr. E. Verheyen, *The Paintings in the Studiolo of Isabella d'Este at Mantua*, New York 1971 e R. Lightbown, *Mantegna: with a complete catalogue of the paintings, drawings and prints*, Oxford 1986, pp. 186-209.
Il romanzo non solo sembra scritto per un pubblico cortigiano ma si svolge addirittura nell'ambiente della corte; l'autore che accettò di provare a far liberare Leriano dalle prigione fa in proposito il commento che segue: «trovai esser il megliore expediente communicare cum alcuni gentilomini, gioveni corteggiani principali che ne la corte vedevo» (*Carcer*, p. 183). Verso la fine del romanzo è trattato il tema delle donne, che sarebbe piaciuto molto a Isabella d'Este, la quale aveva già incoraggiato parecchi intellettuali a scrivere in materia. Prima di morire «l'eroe» Leriano esclama che «le ultime parole mie siano in laude de le donne» (*Carcer*,p. 249). Infatti, il romanzo diventa un trattato organizzato secondo i criteri del *genre*:
Voglio mostrarti per quindice cause come errano quelli che in questo sexo poneno la lingua, e venti ragioni come gli sono li omini obligati, e diversi exempli de la lor bontate. (*Carcer*, p. 249)
Cfr. J. Ormstein, *La misoginia y el profeminismo en la literatura castellana*, in "Revista de Filologia Hispanica", III (1941), pp. 219-232; J. F. Gatti, *Contribucion al estudio de la Carcel de amor": La apologià de Leriano*, Buenos Aires 1955; C. Fahy, *Three early Renaissance treatises on women*, in "Italian Studies", XI (1956), pp. 30-55.

10. Cfr. P. Rajna, *Le fonti dell' Orlando furioso. Ricerche e studi*. Firenze 1900 (2ª edizione), pp. 149-153, 156-158 e P. Valesio, *Genealogy of a staged scene (Orlando Furioso, V)*, in "Yale Italian Studies", n.s., I (1980), pp. 5-31.

11. Per questo personaggio cfr. D. Santoro, *Della vita e delle opere di Mario Equicola*, Chieti 1906; D. Santoro, *Images of Isabella d'Este*, in "Italian Studies", XXXIX (1984) pp. 47-62; D. Santoro, *'The good servant': Mario Equicola. Court and courtier in early sixteenth-century Italy*, in "The Italianist", VI (1986) pp. 34-60; S. Kolsky, *Mario Equicola. The Real Courtier*, Ginevra 1991.

12. ASMn, AG, b.1245, Ferrara, 29 marzo 1515, "Laelius de Manfredi" a Isabella d'Este.

13. Due anni prima, Isabella d'Este aveva scritto al Manfredi per informarlo di avere ricevuto la traduzione del *Carcer d'amore* in manoscritto:
Messer Lelio. Havemo recevuto la nobil opera vostra che per il nepote vostro ce haveti mandata. Et damovine quelli ringratiamenti et laudi che meritati, parendoni per quanto comporta il iudicio nostro la traductione bella [...] (ASMn, AG, b.2996, libro 30a, Copialettere d'Isabella d'Este, Mantova, 29 novembre 1513, a "Domino Lelio de Manfredis").
Il corso della transazione richiede che, una volta approvata la merce, si parli del prezzo, e così la lettera prosegue:
Vorressimo essere apte a dimonstrarvi la gratitudine che vi ne sentimo cussì in effetti come siamo in parole che lo faressimo molto voluntieri. [...] Ma per hora acceptareti da esso vostro nepote questi pochi denari che per lui vi mandamo acciò habbiati melio il modo di mettere l'opera in stampa, insieme con quell'altra lettera vostra.
Dunque, il denaro serve da polizza d'assicurazione per far sì che il libro si stampi davvero (ansia di fama da parte d'Isabella d'Este?), e non deve servire ad arricchire in nessun modo il lavoratore culturale. Forse per sdebitarsi in un altro modo Isabella termina la lettera con qualcosa che somiglia a una promessa concreta a favore del traduttore:
Circa quanto ne scrive lo Illustrissimo Signor Duca nostro fratello [Alfonso d'Este] in vostra commendatione per la causa che haveti contra il debitore vostro qua. Siati certo che non vi mancarimo di favore né di bona iusticia. Et alli piaceri vostri ce offerimo paratissime.
Isabella promette di accettare una richiesta fattale da suo fratello dal momento che ha nelle mani la traduzione-manoscritto (per la lettera del duca di Ferrara vedi nota 2). E un impegno limitato di protezione che forse Isabella non avrebbe preso senza l'intercessione del fratello. Possiamo intravvedere la costruzione di un sistema per cui la marchesana non si abbassa a spendere soldi per diffondere la sua fama, ma promette invece di usare l'apparato dello stato

a vantaggio del suo protetto.

14. La dedica è come segue: «Alla Illustrissima et Excellentissima Madonna. Madonna Isabella Estense da Gonzagha Marchesana di Mantua Laelio de Manfredi D.S.» (f. 243ʳ). Il *Pallazzo di Lucullo* si trova in un manoscritto miscellaneo che consiste prevalentemente di testi veneziani. Zilli, art. cit. a nota 1, dice che per quest'opera «manca qualsiasi testimonianza e precisazione» (p. 50) ma essa è stata già segnalata nel vol. 81, *Venezia - Marciana* degli *Inventari dei manoscritti delle biblioteche d'Italia*, Firenze 1956, pp. 116-117; 117. Il manoscritto proviene dalla biblioteca di Apostolo Zeno (403) e ora porta la collocazione Mss.Italiani classe 7, n.363 (7873).
15. Il Manfredi non nasconde le sue fonti, anzi le esibisce, come per vantarsi della sua erudizione sia per quanto riguarda la grande varietà delle sue letture sia per il suo senso del passato che sa riempire le altrui lacune: «unde ritrovai ne la quarta e ne la undecima epistola di Pomponio alcuna mentione di questo ma non tale che si potesse se non per coniectura designare lo edifficio» (f.245ᵛ). Quindi dovette ricorrere ad altri autori: «ma chiarissimamente per messer Varone è descripta una parte di questa casa ne lo ultimo libro de la rusticitate al quinto capitolo» (ff.245ᵛ-246ʳ; il riferimento preciso è *M. Terenti Varronis Rerum Rusticarum*, lib.III, cap. V); si notino i riferimenti bibliografici precisi che fanno pensare a un maestro di scuola scrupoloso verso i testi originali che spera di stimolare a letture più approfondite la destinataria della dedica.
16. L'uso da parte del Manfredi del termine «castighatione» mette in evidenza la distanza tra l'umanesimo filologico, di cui uno dei più noti rappresentanti quattrocenteschi è Ermolao Barbaro, autore appunto delle *Castigationes plinianae et in Pomponium Melam* (a cura di G. Pozzi, 4 voll., Padova, 1973-1979) e l'umanesimo eclettico di, tra gli altri, Mario Equicola. Interessanti sono i commenti dell'Equicola nel *Libro de natura d'amore* sulla lingua e letteratura spagnola in generale; egli nota che non ci sono grandi differenze fra lo spagnolo e l'italiano («et alcune loro parole non immute, trovando quelle già accettate per nostri et usarsi», *Libro*, Venezia: «nelle case di Pietro di Nicolini da Sabbio», 1536. Cfr. G. L. Beccaria, *Riflessi linguistici dello spagnolo sull'italiano del primo Cinquecento* in *Doce consideraciones sobre el mundo hispano-italiano en tiempos de Alfonso y Juan de Valdés*, prologo de M. Sito Alba, Roma 1979, pp. 103-114) e questo commento si può interpretare come l'origine dell'interesse equicoliano per lo spagnolo, interesse da dilettante stimolato dalla facilità di apprendimento della lingua oltre che, ovviamente, dalle influenze che la politica e i rapporti cortigiani avevano sulla cultura.
17. Per vedere quali libri fossero in voga cfr. B. Croce, *La Spagna nella vita italiana durante la Rinascenza*, Bari 1922 e A. Croce, *Relazioni della letteratura italiana con la letteratura spagnola* in *Letterature comparate*, a cura di A. Viscardi *et al.*, Milano 1948, pp. 101-144. Federico Gonzaga, una volta marchese, non perse il suo interesse per i libri spagnoli e riuscì ad accumulare una biblioteca abbastanza fornita di libri spagnoli. Secondo l'inventario dei suoi libri redatto dopo la sua morte nel 1542 possedeva 43 libri spagnoli su 179 libri inventariati (latino, volgare e francese) (Vedi A. Luzio e R. Renier, *La coltura*, in "GSLI", XLII (1903), pp. 75-111; 81-87) di cui una buona percentuale consisteva di romanzi cavallereschi.
18. Cfr. J. Martorell, Martì Joan de Galba, *Tirant lo Blanc*, proleg i text de M. De Riquer, 2 voll., Barcelona 1979 (2ª ed.). Parlando della versione italiana, De Riquer scrive, «Encara que aquesta rubrica hagi fet creure que la versio italiana es feta sobre la traduccio castellana del 1511, l'examen dels textos demostra que Lelio di Manfredi féu la seva tasca, prou reexida, sobre l'edicio de Valéncia del 1490» (p. 99) ed anche *Tirante el bianco*, version castellana impresa en Valladolid en 1511 de la obra de Joanot Martorell y Martì Joan de Galba, vol. I, a cura di M. de Riquer, Madrid 1974, p. CIII. Per l'edizione critica della traduzione manfrediana vedi *Tirante il bianco*, a cura di A. M. Annicchiarico, M. L. Indini, M. Majorano, V. Minervini, S. Panunzio, C. Zilli, introduzione di G. E. Sansone, Roma 1984. Sansone non ha dubbi sulla «indipendenza della traduzione italiana da quella castigliana» (p. 21) e noi condividiamo questo parere, con la piccola riserva che abbiamo già notato.
19. Il manoscritto si trova nella Biblioteca ariostea di Ferrara ed è stato elencato dall'Antonelli (*Indice dei manoscritti della civica Biblioteca di Ferrara*, Ferrara 1884, n. 300); è discusso

brevemente dallo Zilli (op. cit. a nota 1), che però non approfondisce abbastanza il significato del trattato. Benché asserisca, correttamente, che quell'opera «non può essere stata composta che sotto l'influenza e la suggestione del *Tirante*» (Zilli, p. 44), il critico lascia alquanto incerto il lettore dato che nella pagina precedente afferma che l'opera «chiaramente non risulta essere una traduzione» (p. 43) e poi, sempre a pagina 44, paragonando due brani tratti dalle due opere, osserva come «certi passi del trattato siano pari pari presi dal *Tirante*» (p. 44). Se il trattato non è precisamente una traduzione vera e propria, è certamente un'antologia della sezione teorica sulla cavalleria della prima parte del *Tirante*.

20. Zilli, op. cit. a nota 1, p. 44, n. 13, allude al debito che il *Tirante* dimostra nei riguardi dell'opera lulliana, ma non riconosce quanto siano vicini i due titoli. Non sembra fuori luogo suggerire che il Manfredi cercasse di riproporre un ideale medievale filtrato dalla prospettiva del Quattrocento (*Tirante*) e dalle esperienze ferraresi del Rinascimento. Da questo punto di vista è possibile che il Manfredi abbia consultato l'opera lulliana, eliminando ogni riferimento contrario alla sua idea di civiltà cavalleresca come, ad esempio una delle idee fondamentali di Lull, quella della superiorità dell'uomo rispetto alla donna, idea parzialmente riveduta nei romanzi cavallereschi d'origine ferrarese (*Obres de Ramon Lull*, I, *Doctrina pueril. Libre de l'orde de cavalleria*, a cura di M. Obrador y Bennassar, Palma de Mallorca 1906, p. 209). Ma senz'altro la fonte più importante è il *Tirante*, da cui ha tratto molti particolari che non si trovano nell'opera lulliana.

21. *Tirante*, cap. xxxii sull'origine dei cavalieri e *Libre*, «part primera: la qual tracta del començament de cavalleria» (pp. 208-11).

22. *Tirante*, cap. xxxiii e *Libre*, «offici de cavaller es mantenir e deffendre la sancta fe catholica» (p. 212). Nel *Tirante* si trova a questo punto l'episodio di Quinto, che serve da esempio di fede cristiana militante (cap. xxxiii-xxxiv). Vedi Zilli, op. cit. a nota 1, p. 44, che non approfondisce però le strutture parallele dell'opera catalana e di quella italiana.

23. Il Manfredi scrive, «E perché le armi cossi offensive come difensive non furono ritrovate senza gran significato, dirò quello che significano» (f. 14r). La sezione corrisponde in linea di massima al cap. xxxv del *Tirante*, che presenta un ordinamento diverso rispetto al *Libre* lulliano («Cinquena part: de la significança qui es en les armes de cavaller», p. 232). La distinzione che il Manfredi fa tra armi offensive e difensive sembra esser innovativa rispetto al *Tirante*; il Manfredi inoltre introduce nuovi elementi nella simbologia cavalleresca dell'armatura.

24. La descrizione nel *Tirante* dell'ordine della giarrettiera (capp. lxxxv-xcv) può essere interpretata come un ulteriore motivo per cui quest'opera costituisce un indice dell'*ethos* delle corti dell'Italia settentrionale. E ben noto che il duca di Urbino, Guidubaldo Montefeltro, apparteneva a quell'ordine: Cfr. C. H. Clough, *The relations between the English and Urbino courts, 1474-1508* nel suo *The Duchy of Urbino in the Renaissance*, Londra 1981, art. XI e G. Colon, *Premiers échos de l'Ordre de la Jarretière*, in "Zeitschrift für Romanische Philologie", LXXXI (1965), pp. 441-453. Analogamente, Federico Gonzaga apparteneva all'equivalente ordine francese. E chiaro che gli ordini cavallereschi sono una delle componenti di una ideologia di *élite*, di innalzamento di ceti sociali desiderosi di consolidare il loro potere tramite la creazione di gruppi esclusivi basati su concetti del feudalesimo riesumati e rimessi in auge. W. Barberis, *Uomini di corte nel Cinquecento tra il primato della famiglia e il governo dello stato* in *Storia d'Italia*, Annali 4: *Intellettuali e Potere*, a cura di C. Vivanti, Torino 1981, pp. 855-894, commenta appunto il *Tirante* in modo da chiarire gli elementi di base della cultura cortigiana. Anche se non privo di errori di fatto riguardo alla traduzione del Manfredi, il saggio ha il merito di riproporre il *Tirante* nel suo contesto italiano e di indicarlo come «un'immagine della società quale la proponeva un testo quattrocentesco» (p. 878). Qui pare opportuno precisare che il *Tirante* proponeva alla società della fine del Quattrocento un ideale medievale capace di attrarre anche la società cortigiana italiana del Cinquecento (cfr. W. J. Entwistle, *Tirant lo Blanch and the social order at the end of the fifteenth century*, in "Estudio Romanics", II (1949-50), pp. 149-164).

25. Il Manfredi trova difficile frenare la sua rabbia:
E però taccierò de' doctori per non fare una Syrene che havendo cominciato de la militia finisca in dir male. (*L'ordine*, f. 31r)

I "doctori", secondo il Manfredi, fanno parte di una società civile che tende a sottovalutare le virtù cavalleresche se non addirittura a renderle di impossibile attuazione, imponendo leggi diverse da quelle della cavalleria.

26. Dopo avere fatto riferimento come ulteriore esempio del divario tra passato e presente («al tempo antiquo», f. 32^{v}), al privilegio, limitato ai cavalieri, di portare la spada il Manfredi ritorna al tema ossessivo dell'accrescimento del numero dei cavalieri, senza tener conto dei valori di gruppo:
Et all'età nostra si fa il contrario che, ritornando il duca over capitano dal gran conflitto del fatto d'armi, fa cavaglieri, più per letitia che per virtute, tutti quelli che adimandano d'essere illustrati de ordine tanto famoso. (*L'ordine*, f. 33^{r-v})

27. Come ci si aspetterebbe, nel *Tirante* le origini dell'ordine cavalleresco sono trattate logicamente, all'inizio (cap. xxxii); più tardi, Martorell fa la rassegna dei cavalieri riputati più valorosi dalle epoche passate (cap. xxxvii). Il Manfredi invece adopera una procedura umanistica per provare ad arrivare alla verità:
Quali fussero e' primi che usassero dar l'ordine di cavaglieria [...] diverse sono le opinioni de le quale mi sforzarò narrare quanto mi ne è pervenuto a notitia. (*L'ordine*, ff.34^{r-v})

28. Il problema della doppia dedica si pone per altri testi manfrediani. Il suo *poema in terza rima*, per esempio, esiste in due redazioni, l'una dedicata a Federico Gonzaga e l'altra al re di Francia, Francesco I.

29. ASMn, AG, b.1247, Ferrara, 5 giugno 1519, «Laelio de Manfredi» a Stazio Gadio. Un altro brano della lettera è riportato dal Bertolotti, op. cit. a nota 1, V (1884), 164. Le peripezie della traduzione sottolineano l'ambiente ostile in cui lavorava l'intellettuale che non era direttamente impiegato dalla corte ma allo stesso tempo il Manfredi sembra divenire mitomane, raffigurandosi come un eroico Ulisse che supererà tutti gli ostacoli: «Pensati ch'io mi vidi disperato ma non mi persi d'animo per non haver perso l'ingiegno e la memoria». Lo stesso giorno, indizio rivelatore di una strategia trasparente e disperata, il Manfredi scrive a Mario Equicola. Il primo parla di un favore fatto all'Equicola, cioè, l'avergli procurato una copia in lingua originale del *Carcer d'amore*, forse posseduta prima da Niccolò da Correggio (ASMn, AG, b.1247, Ferrara, 5 giugno 1519, parzialmente citato dal Bertolotti, op. cit. a nota 1, V (1884), 164).

30. Speciale amice noster carissime. Havendo inteso quanto scrivete a Statio nostro secretario di volerci portare tutto il *Tirante* tradutto in italiano ne havemo preso grande piacere. (ASMn, AG, b.2926, libro 258, Mantova, 14 giugno 1519, Federico Gonzaga a Lelio Manfredi).
In questa lettera e in quella precedente Federico ripete decisamente che è ora di finire *tutta* la traduzione (nella lettera del 31 maggio scrive: «hora siamo venuti in desiderio di vederlo *tutto* tradutto et legerlo. Vi pregamo siati contento mandarcilo *tutto* che vi accorgereti che vi saremo grati et premiaremo la virtù vostra et l'apiacere che receveremo da voi in ciò» (ASMn, AG, b.2926, libro 258, Mantova, 31 maggio 1519, il corsivo è nostro). Non bastano più «alcuni quinterni».

31. ASMn, AG, b.1247, Ferrara, 22 maggio 1520; lettera parafrasata dal Bertolotti, op. cit. a nota 1, V (1884), 64.

32. ASMn, AG, b. 2963, libro 11 (copialettere riservati), Marmirolo, 9 luglio 1520, Federico Gonzaga a Antonio da Bologna. Questa lettera è stata mandata una quindicina di giorni dopo la terza lettera manfrediana (27 giugno 1520).

33. ASMn, AG, b.2977, libro 2, «In expeditione contra statum Mediolani», «Ex castris ad pontem Lencie», 19 settembre 1521, Federico Gonzaga a Ippolito Calandra. Circa un mese più tardi il marchese richiede altri romanzi cavallereschi italiani (Pulci, Boiardo ed Ariosto), forse mettendoli tutti sullo stesso livello (ASMn, AG, b.2977, libro 4, «Ex castris», 30 ottobre 1521, Federico Gonzaga a Ippolito Calandra, citata dal Bertolotti, op. cit. a nota 1, IX (1888), 160).

34. ASMn, AG, b.2928, libro 274, Mantova, 22 aprile 1523, Federico Gonzaga a Giovan Pietro Obizo, f. 51^{v}, lettera citata dal Bertolotti, op. cit. a nota 1, IX (1888), 160, ma con errori di trascrizione. La risposta del secretario del duca di Ferrara, Alfonso d'Este, testimonia il crescente interesse per la letteratura spagnola dimostrato dagli intellettuali d'avanguardia:

Il libro che Vostra Excellentia per le sue me recercha a dì pasati prestato a messer Lelio deli Manfredi et lui me lo havea impegnati. Me lo scosi et lo prestai al Reverendo domino Petro Bembo che con grandissima instantia me lo havea recerchato et cusì è adesso Sua Signoria in Padoa dove io fra 4 iorni, a Dio piacendo andarò. (ASMn, AG, b.1248, Ferrara, 6 maggio 1523, *ut supra*).

35. Il semplice tentativo di ricuperare i suoi vestiti comporta un gran numero di equivoci e di complicazioni, nonché ripetuti e contraddittori appelli sia al duca di Ferrara che al marchese di Mantova. (ASMn, AG, b.1247, Ferrara, 22 aprile 1521, «Laelius de Manfredis» al marchese di Mantova)

36. Da Mantova sono le lettere del 4, 6 agosto 1525, e del 26 ottobre 1526; invece le ultime lettere manfrediane che sopravvivono, quelle del 26, 29 settembre 1528 e del 13 ottobre 1528 vengono dalla «pallazzina di campagna», area geografica non meglio identificata, ma probabilmente Marmirolo, data la loro collocazione in queste buste. Non perde contatto con Ferrara, ma si intuisce leggendo fra le righe che si è stabilito a Mantova e/o nel Mantovano. Scrive al marchese:
E mando anchora quattro salami a Vostra Excellentia che mi son venuti da Ferrara. Se non sono come merita la pregho che mi perdoni e che accepti la mia bona voluntate. Ma mi è scripto che l'ha fatti la meglio maestra di Ferrara. (ASMn, AG, b.2506, Mantova, 4 agosta 1525)
Come vedremo, questo dono serve da preludio a una richiesta urgente da parte del Manfredi.

37. ASMn, AG, b.2508, Mantova, 26 ottobre 1528. In seguito alla presentazione della sua situazione disperata, il Manfredi fa il punto e viene alla specifica richiesta di aiuto, in questo caso collegata al pagamento della dote di sua moglie: «per questo mando la qui alligata supplicatione a Vostra Excellentia preghandola voglia far che mi sia signata come io adimando accioché a questo bisogno mi possa prevaler dil mio perché a quel ch'io ho aprovato le liti mi pareno immortali in questa terra».

38. Nella corrispondenza manfrediana del periodo successivo al 1522 c'è un unico riferimento al manoscritto del *Tirante*:
Illustrissimo et Excellentissimo Signor mio, io non mandai heri sera il *Tirante* per la pioggia che non si guastasse, ma hora lo mando per il presente latore, mio famiglio. (ASMn, AG, b.2506, Mantova, 4 agosto 1525)

39. *Tirante il Bianco*, p. 45.

40. Cfr. D. Bernoni, *Dei Torresani, Blado e Ragazzoni*, Milano 1890, ristampa Farnborough 1968, pp. 112-128, 315-317. La scelta di Pietro dei Nicolini da Sabbio si può anche spiegare con il fatto che in quegli anni costui pubblicava vari romanzi cavallereschi (1535 e 1539 Boiardo, *Orlando Innamorato*; 1538, Caviceo, *Il peregrino*; 1540, Ariosto, *Orlando Furioso*). Vedi *Short-Title Catalogue of Books Printed in Italy, now in the British Museum*, London 1958, p. 899. Il Torresani in quanto *entrepreneur* badava ai profitti e anche se il *Tirante* era in "dono" (Bernoni, pp. 115-16) non poteva ignorare altre transazioni di natura economica col duca; l'Agnello, ambasciatore mantovano a Venezia scrive a Federico Gonzaga:
Mando a Vostra Excellentia il qui alligato libro chiamato el *Tirrante el bianco* che mi ha dato messer Federico da Asola [Torresani] da mandarle et così faccio. M'ha anche detto che con questa occasione voglia raccordar a Vostra Excellentia del quel credito ch'egli ha seco di ducento ducati et però non ho potuto mancare per le calde preghere ch'egli me n'ha fatto. (ASMn, AG, b.1472, Venezia, 12 agosto 1538)

41. Cfr. L. Pulci, *Morgante e lettere*, a cura di D. De Robertis, Firenze 1962, ad es. lettera IX (p. 953): «lo ti mando parecchi versi perché ti ricordi di me», lettera XIII (p. 957): «perch'io non ho havuto moneta da spendere da uno tempo in qua, ho spesa la tua riputatione.»

42. Citato in A. Luzio, *Pietro Aretino nei primi suoi anni a Venezia e la corte dei Gonzaga*, Torino 1888, p. 63 (lettera del 28 maggio 1527). Per altri simili commenti cfr. pp. 71-79 (documenti V-XV).

43. Le affermazioni dello Zilli (op. cit. a nota 1) riguardo alle opere letterarie sembrano assai esagerate e non documentate. Egli fa riferimento all'«atteggiamento di totale e perdurante noncuranza che il Manfredi, a nostro avviso, dové subire a carico di quella parte del suo

repertorio cui mostrava di tenere di più, e proprio ad opera di coloro che furono i primi e più assidui lettori delle sue traduzioni» (p. 48). Non esiste la minima indicazione che il Manfredi tenesse in modo particolare alle sue opere letterarie e, come abbiamo già visto, il loro modo di produzione è un fattore che è impossibile trascurare nel valutarle. Ciò che lo Zilli chiede al lettore è di vedere nel Manfredi una vittima dei Gonzaga, rifiutandosi di considerare la questione del gusto letterario e di discutere le eventuali gerarchie di tali gusti. Lo Zilli ha quindi creato di fantasia un quadro poco convincente, e la sua conclusione rappresenta un'ulteriore conferma della sua impostazione basata su un giudizio aprioristico; egli parla dell'«antipatia quasi preconcetta in cui soprattutto i Gonzaga tenevano il Manfredi come autore, alle dipendenze dei quali egli tuttavia lavorava come traduttore assai apprezzato» (p. 54). Questa dicotomia tra le due attività non è profonda quanto sembra a prima vista, altrimenti Federico Gonzaga avrebbe assicurato senza alcun ritardo la pubblicazione del *Tirante* ed avrebbe dato un premio più notevole per questo lavoro.

44. Pubblicato da M. Catalano, *Vita di Ludovico Ariosto*, II. Ginevra 1931, n.372, p. 204 (lettera del marchese datata 12 giugno 1519, concernente *La cassaria*).

45. Un'ulteriore attrattiva dell'Aretino era forse il fatto di esser venuto da Roma, che Federico Gonzaga, dopo la sua nomina a capitano generale della Chiesa romana, stava cominciando a considerare modello di tutte le sue aspirazioni culturali.

46. Vedi S. Kolsky, *Castiglione's biography: The courtier and the Italian princes*, in "Spunti e Ricerche", I (1985), pp. 1-34: 20-23 e E. Verheyen, *The Palazzo del Te in Mantua. Images of Love and Politics*. Baltimore - London 1977.

XII

IMAGES OF ISABELLA D'ESTE*

The exceptional personality of Isabella d'Este, Marchioness of Mantua, has ensured that no scholar who has come to study her does so half-heartedly. All too often, the student of this remarkable woman falls under her spell and will always be ready to defend her in the face of any attack on her character. One such scholar was Alessandro Luzio, whose work still remains indispensible for its documentation of Isabella d'Este's life. However, the great mass of archival material Luzio brings to light in no way affects Luzio's own view of the 'Marchesana'.[1] Isabella is Luzio's idol. She can do no wrong. When considering a potential rival, such as Lucrezia Borgia, he makes no secret of his belief in the 'decretata superiorità d'Isabella sotto ogni rapporto'.[2] At times he will go so far as to suggest that the Marchesana presents the image of the perfect woman: 'un ideale muliebre, oso dire, insuperato finora'.[3] The vitality and dynamism of her character, in the interpretation of this historian, epitomize the possibilities of Italian society in anticipation of the Risorgimento.

Luzio never tires of telling his reader that Isabella's interests were not confined to her cultural activities. In his opinion, Isabella's role in the political events of her period is not to be undervalued. She is a 'Machiavelli in gonna', able to succeed where men have failed. Luzio, indeed, attributes almost mythical qualities to Isabella's political interventions, referring to 'questa sua azione benefica di Ninfa Egeria politica'.[4] He does not doubt that greater significance must be granted to her political activities than to her cultural ones. In contrast, her husband is often treated unkindly by Luzio and most other historians. The Marquis is at once beyond the civilizing effect of culture and moreover he is politically inept. To reduce him to a nonentity or a bumbling fool serves all the more to impress the strength of Isabella d'Este upon the reader.

* An earlier version of 'Images of Isabella d'Este' was read at the Italian History Seminar of the University of London chaired by Professor N. Rubinstein in February 1980. Since then it has undergone extensive revision. The advice and comments of Clifford Brown, William Prizer, Brian Richardson and Mark Davie have been particularly helpful.

[1] On Luzio, see *La figura e l'opera di A. Luzio*, edited by M. Bianchedi (San Severino Marche, 1957).

[2] A. Luzio, *Isabella d'Este e i Borgia* (Milan, 1915), p. 81.

[3] A. Luzio, 'Isabella d'Este e la corte sforzesca', *Archivio storico lombardo*, third series, 25 (1901), 176.

[4] Luzio, 'Isabella d'Este e la corte sforzesca', p. 145.

In England, interest in Isabella grew through the work of Julia Cartwright. This enraged Luzio, who saw her book on the Marchioness as an unfair compilation of the material which he had been unable to bring together into a single work. The reasons behind Luzio's failure to do so may have been the sheer mass of the documentation he had accumulated and the lack of an overall, unifying vision for his 'deliziosa creatura'. Cartwright disagrees with Luzio as to what constitutes the more important element of her subject: 'it is above all as a patron of art and letters that Isabella d'Este will be remembered'.[5] Thus a more genteel picture emerges, better suited to the sedate atmosphere of Edwardian England, where Luzio's image of a virago needed to be toned down. Cartwright's Isabella is also a model of female perfection. She talks about the 'innate nobleness and loyalty of Isabella's nature' and, all told, she sees nothing that changes her mind about her estimate of Isabella's 'fine character'. Again, it is Francesco who suffers in comparison, trespassing on his wife's good-will with his constant nagging; Cartwright notes 'the patience with which Isabella bore his caprices, and the faithfulness with which she carried out his wishes'.[6] Isabella is considered to have overcome the faults of her age by adhering to the solid virtues of home and family. The final impression we have of her from Cartwright's analysis is one of moderation and balance: 'her nature was singularly complete and well-balanced, and it may be said with truth that she saw life steadily and saw it whole'.[7]

In more recent years a number of objections have been raised against these images of the Marchesana. Carlo Dionisotti expressed in no uncertain terms his dissatisfaction with the traditional idealized picture of Isabella. His few lines aim to reduce considerably her stature: no mention is made of her art patronage; instead the unattractive side of her personality is emphasized. He does not hesitate to call her 'una donna per quanto si sa non bella e sufficientemente frigida e viperina'.[8] Her personality matches her taste for power and intrigue. The long-felt affection for Isabella is, in his opinion, misplaced and hard to understand. From this point on, the traditional picture of Isabella has gradually been revised, though the older views of her character have never been completely discarded: for an attack on Isabella d'Este can be seen as nothing less than an attack on a certain comfortable view of the Renaissance. Hence, we find many of the old prejudices about Isabella still surviving. Her 'fascino irresistibile' continues to make a balanced interpretation almost impossible. The complexity of her character leads writers into

[5] J. Cartwright, *Isabella d'Este Marchioness of Mantua 1474–1539: A Study of the Renaissance*, 2 vols (London, 1904), I, viii.

[6] Cartwright, II, 86.

[7] Cartwright, II, 391.

[8] C. Dionisotti, 'Recensione a *Un illustre nunzio pontificio*', *Giornale storico della letteratura italiana* [hereafter abbreviated to *GSLI*], 129 (1952), 53.

making contradictory statements about her behaviour. In her book on Lucrezia Borgia, Maria Bellonci was certain that Isabella d'Este displayed the characteristics of her own family, that she was a 'vera Estense', but in a more recent publication, Bellonci has come round to the view that 'risulta in realtà una Gonzaga'.[9] It is not just a case of changing one's mind; Bellonci seems to be admitting to a fundamental uncertainty as to what constitutes the driving force of Isabella's character. Other writers have refused to face up to these contradictions. Lauts, for example, does not conceal the fact that his admiration for Isabella forms the basis of his study: 'Toutes les qualités que Castiglione exige de la Dame parfaite, elle les incarne naturellement'.[10] Lauts is willing to discuss facets of her personality that cast grave doubts on the validity of his judgement, and yet he passes no comment on the more extreme forms which Isabella's behaviour sometimes takes, especially with regard to her female offspring. Finally, in George R. Marek's ineptly titled book *The Bed and the Throne*, 'il fiore più squisito del nostro Rinascimento' no longer fulfils a merely decorative function.[11] Here, in a generally entertaining and perceptive work, Isabella d'Este becomes a symbol of the future struggles of the feminist movement. He concludes that ' most important, she gave a new meaning to what it was to be a woman'.[12]

In the light of the interest currently shown in Renaissance women, particularly by writers favourable to feminism, it is important not to exaggerate the 'radicalism' of Isabella in respect of 'feminist' issues. The purpose of this article is to suggest the major factors that need to be taken into account and to suggest that existing images are inadequate or misleading for a number of reasons. The article seeks to reassess Isabella's image as presented by her contemporaries and by herself. It will concentrate particularly on her cultural and political activities as well as her family life.

If any of Isabella's learned contemporaries wished to sing her praises, the most obvious way of doing so was to compose a literary work which emphasized her special qualities as a woman. In this case, the writer had a standard schema: he would laud her beauty, learning, culture and moral rectitude. Perhaps there is no one less restrained that Giangiorgio Trissino in the praise of Isabella's beauty. Her very name is significant in this respect:

'Il nome suo è Isabella.' 'Convenevolissimo veramente,' disse Macro, 'e bellissimo nome è questo, il quale la sorte o la divinazione paterna le pose; perciò che Isa ne la

[9] M. Bellonci, *Lucrezia Borgia* (Milan, 1939), p. 294; and for her later comment see 'Isabella d'Este a cinquecento anni dalla sua nascita' in *Mantova e i Gonzaga* (Mantua, 1977), p. 56.
[10] J. Lauts, *Isabella d'Este 1474–1539*, French translation by G. Welsch (Paris, 1956), p. i.
[11] The description is Cian's, in his 'Isabella d'Este alle dispute domenicane', *GSLI*, 67 (1916), 376. G. R. Marek, *The Bed and the Throne: The Life of Isabella d'Este* (New York and Toronto, 1976).
[12] Marek, p. 234.

lingua greca (come sapete) suona, quanto ne la nostra equale, tal che così composto, altro non dice che equalmente et in ogni parte bella'.[13]

Even Isabella had to express her doubts as to the truthfulness of Trissino's description, stating that his work was 'al nostro iudicio elegantissima et ingeniosa, sebben troppo et fori della verità excede in laudarmi et perché il vulgar proverbio è: "so che tu non dici il vero, pur mi piace"'.[14] Isabella realized that truth was not the essential element in the composition of her images provided that they corresponded to the ideas she had about herself and wished to convey to others. One aspect of the work would have especially pleased her, namely, that it was Bembo who had been chosen to praise her intellectual qualities. Isabella had never been able to forgive Bembo for having dedicated the *Asolani* to Lucrezia Borgia and for having refused her invitation to come to Mantua.[15] *I Ritratti*, then, can be seen as an act of complicity between Trissino and the Marchioness: Bembo is made to praise Isabella to the skies in Lucrezia Borgia's own city, Ferrara. It seems to me that Trissino is also availing himself of the opportunity of attacking Bembo's linguistic theories by having the author of the *Prose* praise Isabella's spoken language in accordance with Trissino's own theories: 'La loquela sua, poi, non è patria pura Toscana, ma il bello de l'una e de l'altra ha scelto, e di quello insieme mescolato, dolcissimamente favella'.[16] Thus, in the year before the publication of the *Prose* Trissino is trying to defend his own position in the language dispute. Bembo is also made to single out for praise those accomplishments that were particularly dear to Isabella and through which she enjoyed celebrity: 'Se voi l'haveste una sola volta udita cantare son certo che vi sarebbe come coloro che udirono le sirene, e la patria e la propria casa uscita di mente'.[17] In exchange for this demonstration of his loyalty Trissino makes it plain that he expects a reward:

[13] *Tutte le opere di Giovan Giorgio Trissino, gentiluomo vicentino, non più raccolte*, edited by Scipione Maffei, 2 vols (Verona, 1729), II, 269–77 (p. 273).

[14] B. Morsolin, *Giangiorgio Trissino: Monografia d'un gentiluomo letterato nel secolo XVI*, second edition (Florence, 1894), p. 392.

[15] See V. Cian, 'Pietro Bembo e Isabella d'Este Gonzaga: Note e Documenti', *GSLI*, 9 (1887), 81–136; in particular, pp. 93, 95. It should be said that, although friendly relations seem to have been maintained, Bembo was not successful in trying to obtain a painting from Bellini for the *Studiolo*, and he did not dedicate any of his major works to her.

[16] *I Ritratti*, in *Tutte le opere*, II, 274.

[17] It is interesting to note that Bembo himself refuses to allow his daughter to learn how to play a musical instrument because 'il sonare è cosa da donna vana et leggiera. Et io vorrei che tu fosti la più grave casta et pudica donna che viva' (*Delle lettere di M. Pietro Bembo*, Volume IV (Venice, Giovanni Alberti, 1587), 124–25); none the less, Bembo's paternal concern for his daughter reveals his profoundly conservative view of the position of women in society. He ends the letter in a way which throws light on what he must have thought about Isabella, famous for her skill as a musician: 'Et contentati nell'esercitio delle lettere et nel cuscire, i quali due eserciti se tu farai bene non havrai fatto poco'.

Né di cosa che si faccia tanto s'allegra o tanto si gode [referring to Isabella d'Este] quanto di quello che in far bene a le genti dispensa; e non molto a buffoni, a pazzi et a trombetti o a simili canaglie dona, ma a persone buone, virtuose e dotte; da le quali non aspetta che le siano danari, panni o simili cose richieste, anzi, dove il bisogno loro intende prestamente soccorre. E così largamente gli dà che dissolve loro ogni cura che a procurarsi il vivere s'appertenga; per la qual cosa alcuni di costoro cercano sempre che il nome suo in versi et in prose consecrato rimanga; e di qui a mille e mill'anni in bocca de le genti dimori.[18]

Trissino wished to impress upon his reader that Isabella d'Este had no equal in the past or present.[19] Isabella thought the same and acted accordingly. Indeed, Isabella herself did everything in her power to avoid coming off second best and to demonstrate her singularity and supremacy in all things. This desire to have no equals finds expression even in matters of religion; when she received a 'confessionale' from Rome it did not meet her expectations 'per essere troppo vulgare et comune con altre persone nominate'.[20] Thinking in these terms she demanded the correct treatment from all who came in contact with her. For example, in 1517, she wanted to visit a sanctuary at Chambéry, for which permission was necessary from the Duke of Savoy. Unfortunately, the Duke did not reply to her request: 'Essendo anchor stata ferma là tutto el giorno sequente, mai venne. Per il che assai mal contenta mi partii di là, parendomi essere iniuriata'.[21] The damage had already been done when the Duke decided to send a special messenger: 'Io ringratiai assai quella, dicendoli che quella mi excusate havendo deliberato far la via de Asti'. It was only when the Duke granted her permission to visit the sanctuary whenever she liked that Isabella relented, though even now she postponed the visit to another time.

A corollary of the same attitude is Isabella's determination to surround herself with objects of the highest quality: 'desideramo havere un spechio grande di azalo che sii bono et in excellentia perché de tristi et mediocri siamo copiose'.[22] If she was willing to lend Don Cesare d'Aragona her precious copy of Eustathius she, none the less, laid down certain conditions; she told him to 'Fare che non capiti in mano di troppe persone perché essendo cosa rara è da tener caro né lassarlo vedere a molti per non diminuirli la reputatione'.[23] Connected with her desire to be surrounded by rare and precious objects is her desire to be innovative, that is, to create and control her own rarity. The

[18] *I Ritratti*, in *Tutte le opere*, II, 276.

[19] Macro, in *I Ritratti*, remarks 'essendo costei tale che sol se stessa e null'altra simiglia' (*Tutte le opere*, II, 276).

[20] Archivio di Stato, Mantua, Archivio Gonzaga (hereafter abbreviated as ASMN, AG), busta (b.) 2996, libro 30, Mantua, Isabella to Bernardo Bibbiena, 9 May 1513.

[21] For the whole episode see ASMN, AG, b. 2997, libro 33, Isabella to her husband, 23 June 1517.

[22] ASMN, AG, b. 2996, libro 28, Isabella to Taddeo Albano, 9 August 1510.

[23] A. Luzio and R. Renier, 'La coltura e le relazioni letterarie d'Isabella d'Este', *GSLI*, 33 (1899), 24–25.

Marchesa constantly desired to have new things and always to have them as quickly as possible, in order to forestall any opposition and perhaps, equally importantly, to satisfy her imperious 'appetito'. Isabella uses this suggestive word to refer to that ever-present need of hers to acquire, possess and hoard all kinds of objects, but especially classical artefacts: 'perché sapeti quanto siamo apetitose di queste antiquità'.[24] The word suggests her vast energy which must be brought under control. Interested in the purchase of goods from Cairo, she wrote, explaining her position: 'Non siamo de così poco animo che per uno appetito nostro vogliamo restare per la perdita de otto o dece percento de havere le cose che desideramo'.[25] Related to her 'appetito' there is what Isabella calls 'la sensualità', which may be defined by reference to its opposite, 'la rasone'.[26] The humanist concept of reason placed various restraints on behaviour which Isabella recognized as having some validity. Nevertheless, the importance of the senses, indeed of all physical reality, could not be denied, and in Isabella's case the need to assert her right to physical space occupied by men meant that this side of her was particularly in evidence. It perhaps found a natural outlet in her constant desire for new possessions.

The most important projections of her self-image are connected with Isabella's tendency to hoard objects: the *Studiolo*, at first the repository for her 'objets d'art' and then later used to exhibit her allegorical paintings, and the *Grotta* which became the room where the collections were housed. The decoration of the rooms was meant to reveal Isabella's 'presence' at every level.[27]

Everything in the *Grotta* serves to underline the sense of balance which Isabella sought to impress upon her visitors. One of the most important features of the imagery of the *Grotta* is the 'impresa', a device used to create admiration, wonder and a sense of the enigmatic, a puzzle posed by a superior intelligence as a kind of distinguishing mark, a 'privatum signum'.[28] It is

[24] ASMN, AG, b. 2993, libro 10, Mantua, Isabella to Jacopo d'Atri, 29 March 1499. See also C.M. Brown, '"Lo insaciabile desiderio nostro de cose antique": New Documents on Isabella d'Este's Collections of Antiquities', in *Cultural Aspects of the Italian Renaissance*, edited by C.H. Clough (Manchester and New York, 1976), pp. 324–53.

[25] Quoted in C.M. Brown, '"Una testa de Platone con la punta dil naso di cera": Unpublished Negotiations between Isabella d'Este and Niccolò and Giovanni Bellini', *Art Bulletin*, 51 (1969), 372–77 (p. 375, n. 16).

[26] These terms are to be found in a letter to the Marchioness of Monferrato (ASMN, AG, b. 2991, libro 4, letter 137, Ferrara, 17 March 1494, f. 39^{v}), condoling with her on the death of her husband: 'cognoscemo che amaramente lo poterà tolerare consiliandose solamente cum la sensualità, ma essendo prudente V. S. como è, non negarà a la rasone el loco suo, attenta che questa è una lege comune et che persona non è exceptuata'.

[27] C. M. Brown, 'The Grotta of Isabella d'Este', *Gazette des Beaux-Arts*, 89 (1977), 155–71, and 91 (1978), 72–82.

[28] The term 'privatum signum' is Equicola's (*De opportunitate* (Naples, 1507), 4°, f. a2^{r}).

easily transferable since it can descend from the walls of her rooms and form the pattern of a dress to puzzle and impress greater numbers of people at once; such was the case with the 'impresa delle pause' which represents one of the Marchesa's favourite themes, that of music. For her music is the supreme symbol of harmony, balance and tranquillity of mind.[29] Indeed, the paintings on the walls of the *Studiolo* illustrate the theme of music in a variety of guises, from the rhythmic dancing to a lyre of Mantegna's *Mars and Venus* to Costa's *Comos* where the groups of musicians and singers look secure and peaceful in spite of a furious attack by the vices. Similarly, the *Coronation of a Lady* has a number of musicians, one of whom is determinedly looking heavenwards, suggesting the celestial harmony. Correggio's *Virtue* is holding a celestial lyre whilst the *Vice* is playing the pipes.[30]

It has been observed that the motif of the opposition between wind and string instruments is ubiquitous in the paintings of the *Studiolo*.[31] Wind instruments are regarded with disdain; they are discordant and inharmonious, as can be seen by the puffed-up cheeks of the pipe-player in the *Vice*.[32] Isabella was undoubtedly aware of the Ovidian myths attached to these two kinds of musical instrument. Two episodes of the *Metamorphoses* involve challenges to Apollo's musical supremacy, the first by Marsyas and the second by Pan. In each the theme of rivalry predominates and particularly in Pan's case the challenger is depicted as an uncultured rustic whose pipes can be no substitute for the lyre.[33] Although the idea of the superiority of string instruments was by Isabella's time rather commonplace this does not mean that Isabella paid any less attention to it in the composition of her images. On the contrary, it was all the better if this kind of theme were easily recognizable, since the implication of Isabella being a new Apollo would not be lost on her admirers and rivals.

Harmony is the result of a successfully fought battle over the forces of evil. The *Coronation*, although apparently devoid of moral significance, seems to have been used by Isabella to represent this victory of harmony over chaos and

[29] See P. Williams Lehmann, 'The Sources and Meaning of Mantegna's *Parnassus*', in P. Williams Lehmann and K. Lehmann, *Samothracian Reflections: Aspects of the Revival of the Antique* (Princeton, 1973), pp. 59–178; I. L. Mumford, 'Some Decorative Aspects of the Imprese of Isabella d'Este (1474–1539)', *Italian Studies*, 34 (1979), 60–70. For more general discussion and on the 'impresa delle pause' see Luzio-Renier, 'La coltura', *GSLI*, 33 (1899), 50–52.

[30] P. Egan, 'Poesia and the Fête Champêtre', *Art Bulletin*, 41 (1959), 305. Equicola was aware of this aspect of the myth as can be seen in his *Libro de natura de amore* (Venice, 1525), f. 170^r: 'La docta Pallas li flauti butta perché la faccie li deformava'.

[31] For example by I. Fenlon in *Music and Patronage in Sixteenth Century Mantua* (Cambridge, 1980), pp. 19–20.

[32] G. Gould, *The Paintings of Correggio* (London, 1976), pp. 127, 239–42.

[33] In an Italian translation of the *Metamorphoses* (Ovidio, *Metamorphoseos vulgare*, Venice, Giovanni Rosso, 1497, fo.). Pan is described as 'dio de villani' and his music as 'contadino e rustico' (f. 93^r). For other occurrences of this theme see I. V. G. Mallet, 'Mantua and Urbino: Gonzaga Patronage of Maiolica', *Apollo* (September 1981), pp. 162–69 (p. 165).

vice.[34] However, art historians have not yet fully unravelled the complexity and intricacy of the painting. Perhaps this was precisely Isabella's intention so that she would be the only one capable of explaining *all* its details, even if the general outline was clear enough; hence her greater interest in the meaning of the paintings than in their artistic quality.

Isabella d'Este's cultural interests are usually taken on their own terms. None the less, it is true that, however exceptionally avid she may have been in collecting *objets d'art*, her behaviour can be more fully understood in the light of general cultural patterns that had been taking shape in the second half of the fifteenth century. What was exceptional was the fact that a woman had taken up this fashion and added it to her own energy and verve. In his treatise *De splendore* Pontano set himself the task of describing the 'splendid' man whose wealth enables him to indulge his taste for luxury according to certain well-defined rules. In particular, the splendid man should possess objects that are not inherently useful. This luxury does not exist for its own sake, but has a precise social function, namely to create a good impression of oneself before the other people; and this in turn presupposes an awareness of one's 'dignitas'. 'Splendor' represents the private side of the more public concept of 'magnificentia'. But the notion of 'splendor' was not without political significance.[35] In 1515, for example, Venetian envoys were taken on a guided tour of Isabella's apartments and were much impressed by their splendour. That Isabella was not present in person would have helped increase the envoy's sense of wonder since all the mysteries of the rooms could not be revealed to them.[36] On the other hand, her apartments were not merely a political tool; they formed a necessary part of her personality. In part, the politics of splendour are a result of her uncertain position in the government of Mantua. She is in a position analogous to that of a second son whose only chance of wielding power is in the absence of his elder brother. But Isabella was constantly reminded that she was a woman and so she contrived to make the best of her position.

There can be no doubt that the title of 'la prima donna del mondo' well pleased Isabella.[37] For to be first was always her primary objective. Yet at the same time, the reference to her sex suggests the limitations of her position. In Isabella's mind first place would have meant nothing less than being able to rule in her own right. From the moment of her birth that possibility had been

[34] R. Klein, 'La Bibliothèque de la Mirandole et le concert champêtre de Giorgione', in *La Forme et l'intelligible* (Paris, 1970), pp. 193–203; E. Verheyen, *The Paintings in the 'Studiolo' of Isabella d'Este at Mantua* (New York, 1971), pp. 30–51 (p. 45 n. 92).

[35] G. Pontano, *I trattati delle virtù sociali*, edited by F. Tateo (Rome, 1965).

[36] Cartwright, II, 136–38.

[37] The title is used for the first time in 1494 (Luzio-Renier, 'Niccolò da Correggio', *GSLI*, 21 (1893), 239).

taken away from her, simply because she was a female. She may have been the first-born but was destined to take second place in affairs of state. An extension of this situation is to be seen in the marriage arrangements of her younger sister Beatrice, the second daughter of the family. Because of her father's refusal to break the marriage agreement that had already been made between his eldest daughter and Francesco Gonzaga, Marquis of Mantua, Isabella saw the greater prize of Milan fall to her sister through Beatrice's marriage to Lodovico Sforza. Mantua must have seemed second-rate in comparison to Milan. Yet Isabella's determination to rule in her own right was such that she even kept her own 'copialettere', something highly unusual amongst Italian women married to the ruler of a state. Far from being satisfied with her role as a princess, Isabella d'Este wished to be recognized as a prince.

Her most persistent pamphleteer, Mario Equicola, had pointed out Isabella's qualities as a ruler as early as 1501 in his *De mulieribus*: 'Nemo pensius cogitat, agit consultius, maturius expedit, cives suos circumspecta providentia protegit et defendit'.[38] The incisiveness of Equicola's words indicates Isabella's firmness and command in matters of state. Moreover, Equicola intimates that her cultural activities, in this case exemplified by music, fill the time when she is not occupied with her other duties: 'siquid autem ab œconomicis politicisque resipiscit negotiis citharam sumit'.[39] Unlike Equicola's praise of her beauty there is no exaggeration here. Apart from her skill as a musician, Isabella was at the centre of a revival of vernacular music, that is, music in an Italian style as opposed to the northern style which dominated the peninsula.[40]

Whenever she could, Isabella took an active role in Mantuan politics, even involving herself in business which her contemporaries must have considered to be interfering in her husband's affairs:

> Scrivemo per l'alligata de la conclusione et stipulatione del contracto de la conducta del Signore Marchese .... Et quantuncha dicamo dicta conducta essere passata facilmente, tamen, non è stata senza difficultà. Circa la quale siamo stati in disputa in Camera però, et presente solo la Ill. Madama Marchesana et 4 overo 6 de li principali soi col predetto Signore Marchese, per bono pezzo.[41]

Isabella took the greatest pleasure in the intricacies of negotiation whether in political or cultural matters. Indeed, her bargaining over the acquisition of an

[38] M. Equicola, *De mulieribus* (Ferrara, 1501), 4°, f. b2^{v}.

[39] *De mulieribus*, f. b2^{v}.

[40] Fenlon, pp. 16–17, 21–22; C. Gallico, *Un libro di poesie per musica dell'epoca d'Isabella d'Este* (Mantua, 1961), pp. 21, 33; N. Bridgman, *La Vie musicale au Quattrocento et jusqu'à la naissance du madrigal (1400–1530)* (Paris, 1964), pp. 151–52.

[41] Archivio di Stato, Milan, Archivio Ducale Sforzesco, Potenze Estere, Mantova, cartella 1013, 24 June 1498, 'Gaspar de S.^{to} Severino, Corradolus Stanga et Joannes Galleratus' to the Duke of Milan.

objet d'art may be in part a redirection of some of her energy which she might otherwise have used in governing Mantua. Her passion for the minutiae of life was satisfied by being able to collect objects which she could hold and touch. At the same time, this passion turned her into an able administrator since she always felt the need to be informed about everything and anything that was going on: 'Ni avisate così minutamente quanto occorse quel dì, di hora in hora, che se fossimo stato personalmente in campo non l'haveressimo potuto intendere più minutamente'.[42]

As a ruler, Isabella d'Este did not behave like a tyrant. On the contrary, she felt it was her duty to act justly towards the people of Mantua. Her concept of the ruler was no doubt influenced by the memory of her mother and by the example of her husband.[43] She herself often invoked the word 'compassione' at the news of some disaster that had befallen Mantuan citizens. Above all, she had a clear idea of how a ruler of a state should behave towards her subjects. Her eldest son, Federico, on the other hand, was anxious to make his power felt, whatever the consequences. On one occasion he wished to deal out punishment to certain of his men who had deserted: 'tagliar l'orecchie, il naso, bandirli et confischar li lor beni'.[44] Isabella did not carry out his orders but instead she replied: 'ni è parso andare alquanto retenute et de intendere le ragioni se alcuni ne havessero in suo favore'. Moreover, she objected to the prescribed punishment: 'Quando cussì piacia a Vostra Signoria la pena de tagliarli il naso et le orechie et bolarli farimo comutarla in cinque boni tratti de corda, ultra il bando et la privatione di beni. Ad questo ni move il respecto d'essere Mantuani che il vederli con quelli segni pur troppo vergognoso ala Patria'.[45]

For most of her life, however, Isabella was excluded from Mantuan politics. Her husband felt threatened by Isabella's refusal to enter into a working partnership with him which would have enabled them both to share power. He found her too ambitious, too quarrelsome and unwilling to compromise her ideas on the political strategy Mantua should follow. In the first place, the sense of being an Este never left her. Indeed, this sentiment was strengthened by the fact that she was forced to seek political alliances outside Mantua. She seems to have had a strong affection for her immediate family which extended as far as the rebels Don Giulio and Don Ferrante. After they had been in prison for years she was glad to hear that the Duke of Ferrara, her brother Alfonso, had decided to move them to better quarters: 'si pono

[42] ASMN, AG, b. 2998, libro 38, Isabella to Equicola, 19 October 1521.

[43] Francesco Gonzaga once wrote to the vice-legate of Bologna: 'Havemo in ciò voluto come che officio de bon Principe et Signor verso li soi subditi fare la scusa d'essi' (ASMN, AG, b. 2925, libro 256, 5 September 1518).

[44] ASMN, AG, b. 2978, libro 1, Federico to Isabella, 12 January 1522.

[45] ASMN, AG, b. 2964, libro 15, Isabella to Federico, 25 January 1522.

sperare alla giornata meliori segni di clementia verso quelli poverelli'.[46] Isabella's concept of family politics included a sense of the dynastic that her husband could not afford to cultivate through force of circumstances. Illustrative of this point is the incident that arose over the naming of their second son. Isabella was adamant that he should be called Ercole after her father (just as her first daughter had been named Eleonora after Isabella's mother). Francesco insisted on calling him Luigi after the French king in order to demonstrate his loyalty, a loyalty that could not last in the ever-changing conditions of the Italian peninsula. This difference of opinions is emblematic of the wider gulf separating the couple.[47]

When she heard the news of the French king's entry into Milan in 1499 she automatically recalled Beatrice to mind: 'ricordandomi che per quella medessima porta et modo fece la intrata sua la felice memoria de la Illma Madama mia sorella quando andò a marito'.[48] This was no doubt partly in remembrance of her sister and the glory she had represented: for as she was dead she was no longer a rival, and in any case Milan had lost its independence. But Isabella probably also had a political motive. She saw the possibility of reviving the dynastic line in the person of Beatrice's eldest son, Massimiliano Sforza, when he was installed as Duke of Milan in the period immediately following the Diet of Mantua (1512). She made every effort to try and reconstruct the network of northern Italian states, all linked together by dynastic bonds, so that it would have been possible for Milan, Ferrara and Mantua to act in unison. But such an attempt was doomed to failure because of the increasing power of the nation states in the peninsula.

The death of her husband in 1519 provided her with the opportunity that she had been seeking since her brief period of government during Francesco's imprisonment by the Venetians when 'ella sola resse il stato'.[49] However, the new ruler, Federico Gonzaga, was not to allow her to govern Mantua long by herself — he wished to share power with no one, least of all with his mother. In this respect at least, it is true to a certain extent to say that Federico was a caricature of his mother.

Isabella, indeed, found the role of mother the most uncomfortable and perplexing of the duties she had to perform. The very term she uses to express

[46] ASMN, AG, b. 2998, libro 43, Isabella to the 'Factor Ferrariae', 27 August 1523.

[47] Francesco Gonzaga had become very cynical about married life in general because of his personal experiences of it: 'Il pigliar moglie è sempre cosa laudabile e da bono cristiano, perhò non possemo se non laudar le disposition tua a questo . . . . Ben ti anuntiamo che entri in uno novo modo de vivere che tanto ti parrà strano quanto non ti porresti imaginar e tanto più a te ché ni pari pocho prosperoso a contentar una femina e credila a noi che siamo in tal vita già XXV anni in titulo e già decesette in effecto' (ASMN, AG, b. 2914, libro 193, Francesco Gonzaga to Giovan Francesco Tridapale, 13 October 1506).

[48] ASMN, AG, b. 2993, libro 10, Isabella to Francesco Gonzaga, 9 October 1499.

[49] M. Equicola, *Chronica di Mantua* (after 10 July 1521), 4°, f. ?2^{r}.

childbirth in general is significant in this context: 'scaricare dil peso'.[50] But more revealing is her attitude to her female offspring. Isabella's refusal to allow Eleonora, her first-born child, to be placed in the cradle meant for the first-born son, seems almost vindictive. Just as Isabella had had to forfeit the rights and privileges that would have naturally fallen to the eldest son, so would her daughter.[51] The fate of her daughters was decided almost before they were born and few escaped the convent. Even after the birth of Federico her attitude did not change. It had been her sister-in-law, Elisabetta Gonzaga, who had pointed out to Isabella that her behaviour was hysterical and illogical: 'recordandoli che la Illma Madama sua matre, bona memoria, hebbe prima de le femine, poi fece de li maschi e così deve haver speranza farà epsa similmente'.[52] To give birth to a daughter produced a flaw in Isabella's view of herself; it reduced her to the level of ordinary women, since, if all women need to bear children, then at least she should be able to give birth to princes, cardinals and warriors. In her mind to have a daughter was a defect, a humiliation. This attitude did not change as the child grew older and consequently it produced a blind spot in her political strategy. The advantages to be gained by a well-married daughter were outweighed by Isabella's own personal motives. One of these was perhaps her fear of the possible rivalry of a daughter who had a richer and more powerful husband. A similar rivalry is reported between her mother and Beatrice at the time of the latter's marriage.[53] But to have a son was a completely different matter. Francesco's jubilation was probably not so great as Isabella's at the birth of their first son and his disappointment was certainly not so profound at the birth of a daughter.

Isabella was naturally inclined to extremes, which may explain why she was concerned with giving the impression of moderation and balance in the *Grotta*. She herself understood how unhealthy were her obsessions. The idea of a stoic Isabella d'Este, as presented by Mario Equicola in his treatise *Nec spe nec metu*, is undermined by that same writer in his *Oratio* devoted to the Beata Osanna Andreasi: 'Quotiens Estensi Isabelle Mantue Principi tempestas animo ingruebat ut ex rerum temporisque varietate necessario contingit, Osannam petebat ex eius aspectu nunquam tristis abibat ut imminens malum vitandum'.[54] The Marchesana always seems to be throwing tantrums like a spoilt child who cannot have her own way. She appears to us as a very

[50] ASMN, AG, b. 2994, Isabella to Ippolito d'Este, 21 November 1503.

[51] Marek, p. 57.

[52] ASMN, AG, b. 1067, Urbino, Elisabetta Gonzaga to Isabella, undated but probably 1496.

[53] For a detailed history of Isabella's relationship with her sister see Luzio-Renier, 'Delle relazioni di Isabella d'Este Gonzaga con Ludovico e Beatrice Sforza', *Archivio storico lombardo*, second series, 7 (1890), 74–119, 346–99, 619–74.

[54] M. Equicola, *In conservatione (sic) Divae Osannae Andreasiae Mantuanae oratio ad D. Isabellam Estensem Mantuae Principem* (1515?), 4°, f. B6^{r}.

embittered, resentful figure. Such resentment was caused by an inability to live up to the image that she and her humanist collaborators had so skilfully created. Indeed, one could go further and suggest Isabella's behaviour was conditioned by the values propagated by the humanists. This becomes particularly clear if we examine her attitude towards her own physical beauty. No one was more painfully aware of her plump figure than Isabella herself. She once complained to her husband that if she were more fully involved in the government of the state she would not have grown so fat.[55] In this connection, we should reconsider the reasons for the frequency of Isabella's vows, since her piety, as far as we can tell, did not warrant the number of vows she made. An explanation may be found in the fact that once a vow was made it was necessary to dress in white or black; and black is often considered to be a help in making a person look slimmer than he or she really is. The Marchioness always wished to be considered a woman as defined by the male humanists. On the other hand, Isabella's attempts at gaining recognition as a woman of learning sprang from a desire to go beyond the limits imposed by tradition upon the education of a lady. Isabella's stand on this matter had been well noted by her contemporaries, one of whom wrote that women 'se insuperbiranno contra gl'huomini, dicendo che le dottrine non sono solamente loro, ma ancho de le donne, et si gl'huomini ce voleranno replicare, subito li faranno tacere nominando la dottrina de Vostra Signoria'.[56] It cannot be denied that Isabella made a determined effort over a long period of years to improve her knowledge of classical culture, evident from the number of tutors she employed for her own personal use, again something unique amongst the wives of Italy's rulers. However, despite this unceasing effort the results were less than encouraging. Though it would have been due to her efforts if a statue in commemoration of Virgil had been erected in Mantua, Pontano, who had been commissioned to write the inscription, is reported to have praised the Marchesana for her action which he considered all the more commendable since she was 'senza lettere'.[57] To substantiate Pontano's assertion, we need look no further than Isabella's correspondance, where she does not conceal her absolute dependence on

[55] A. Luzio, *La Galleria dei Gonzaga venduta all'Inghilterra nel 1627–8* (Milan, 1913), p. 233. See J. M. Fletcher, 'Isabella d'Este, Patron and Collector' in *Splendours of the Gonzaga: Catalogue*, edited by D. Chambers and J. Martineau (Exhibition 4 November 1981–31 January 1982, Victoria and Albert Museum, London) (Milan, 1981), pp. 51–63. Miss Fletcher's final view of Isabella is the conventional one: that of someone obsessed by art patronage to the exclusion of everything else.

[56] ASMN, AG, b. 809, Naples, Jacobo Perillo to Isabella, 20 June 1518.

[57] Luzio-Renier, 'La coltura', *GSLI*, 40 (1902), 299. One should also see W.J. Ong, 'Latin Language Study as a Renaissance Puberty Rite', *Studies in Philology*, 56 (1959), 103–24, where Latin culture is considered part of the male-dominated world; so that Isabella can be seen here as wishing to enter it.

translations from the Latin. As early as 1492 she admitted her lack of Latin to her husband:

Lo venerabile frate Petro dal Carmine, predicatore deputato a fare el sermone del Sangue de Christo, me ha dimandato ch'el voria sapere se lo havesse di fare latino o vulgare perché alcuni dicono essersi consueto fare latino, altri che meglio seria per universale intelligentia farlo vulgare. Esso dice haveva pensato farlo prima latino poi vulgarizarlo. Gli ho resposto che se perderia troppo tempo, ma che scriveria a la Ex. V. per intendere la voluntà sua, sopra la quale se poteria gubernare, sì che prego me ne dia, raccordandoli che se Lei intende poco latino, io mancho.[58]

It might be thought that Isabella's remark on her little Latin could be construed as a piece of flattery designed to bolster up her husband's ego in the face of his too clever wife. However, her admission, which no self-respecting disciple of humanism would have made, should be taken seriously. At no stage does Isabella seem to have mastered the Latin language so that she could read it freely.[59] But she did none the less express a preference for the kind of Latin that she should be taught. Not for her the restrictions of Ciceronianism with its sharply defined boundaries and rules. Isabella preferred the freedom to use the words she wanted, and especially words that were not in general circulation. Hence when Ercole Strozzi recommended the 'doctissimo' Battista Pio as her tutor because he would be able to teach her 'squisiti vocabuli', Isabella eagerly seized the opportunity. However, Isabella did not keep him in her employment for very long (perhaps he was too pedantic for the Marchesana and more suited to a university career). The tutor who had the most success with a difficult pupil was Mario Equicola, employed in this capacity from 1508 to 1519. He too was an eclectic though unlike Pio he was prepared to place limits on the type of Latin he used.[60] In general terms, Isabella's tastes in literature were dictated by her desire for the new and rare. Nevertheless, she wanted to possess as complete a library as possible: Latin works as well as those written in the vernacular.

It was a deliberate policy on Isabella's part to extort praise from everyone who came in contact with her: 'io ho sempre creduto de reportarni benevolentia et laude'.[61] The use of the word 'benevolentia' is interesting here because it is a word frequently employed in the diplomatic language of the

[58] ASMN, AG, b. 2991, libro 2, lettera 84, Isabella to her husband, Mantua, 26 May 1492, f. 21^{v}.

[59] For example, in 1505, she admitted that she was unable to read a Latin text without the assistance of a tutor (G. Zarri, 'Pietà e profezia alle corti padane: Le pie consigliere dei principi', in *Il Rinascimento nelle corti padane*, con una premessa di P. Rossi (Bari, 1977), p. 230, n. 98).

[60] C. Dionisotti, *Gli umanisti e il volgare fra quattro e cinquecento* (Florence, 1968), pp. 81–116. It is interesting to note that in a contemporary satirical attack on Apuleianism, Pio and Equicola are the principal protagonists (R. Sabbadini, 'Una satira contro Battista Pio', *GSLI*, 27 (1896), 185–86).

[61] A. Luzio, *Isabella d'Este e il Sacco di Roma* (Milan, 1908), p. 96.

period where it indicates the aim of winning favour from those more powerful than oneself. In Isabella's case, it is a confession of her own vulnerability and weakness. It is a recognition of the fact that there are people in the world whose good opinion it is necessary to win. This realization together with her own desire to be the focus of attention dominated her behaviour. Thus, if we attempt to penetrate beneath the surface of Isabella's character we find that this 'surface' is, in fact, not just a veneer but the very marrow of her personality.

Isabella d'Este rarely allowed herself to be alone. She always surrounded herself with her 'donzelle'. In this way, she created a self-contained world where she could truly be the prince, and 'lord' it over her ladies. Her husband was completely excluded and if he did try to interfere here he met with Isabella's sternest opposition. Here, a different morality prevailed, encouraged by Isabella herself. Her eldest son, Federico, spent many hours in the company of the 'donzelle' who had become notorious as the 'ministre di Venere'.[62] On Federico's engagement, his mother told him marriage was not as bad as he imagined: 'Né deve extimare molto d'essersi in questa sua adolescentia maritato, parendogli forsi d'essersi troppo presto privata de libertà, perché essendo la sposa di tenera età haverà tempo di darsi piacere per qualch'anni senza essere altramente sottoposto al obligo coniugale'.[63] The Marchesana, however, wanted it to be known that *she* had risen above her own sexuality and attained a higher level of harmony; she had defeated it after a fierce struggle, if the paintings on the walls of the *Studiolo* are to be believed.

It is difficult to draw together the many threads that made up Isabella d'Este's life. It seems likely that she inherited her cultural models from her mother, who would have served as an example to the Marchesana. It is not hard to imagine that even her mother was considered a rival and that Isabella's achievements were aimed to outdo her.[64] Any woman who looked like challenging Isabella's supremacy was thought a rival. In this way, there is no real sense of solidarity with other women (except perhaps in the case of Elisabetta Gonzaga), which suggests a lack of a 'feminist consciousness'. Isabella was not concerned with the promotion of women in general. On the contrary, she effectively blocked their progress, as in the case of her daughters. She wanted to be praised by everyone of importance, no matter what the cost. Even *she* felt that she had acted wrongly in certain cases, particularly

[62] B. Castiglione, *Il Libro del Cortegiano*, edited by V. Cian, fourth edition (Florence, 1947), p. 385, note to line 7.

[63] ASMN, AG, b. 2997, libro 33, Isabella to Stazio Gadio, 19 February 1517.

[64] W. L. Gundersheimer, 'Women, Learning and Power: Eleonora of Aragon and the Court of Ferrara', in *Beyond their Sex: Learned Women of the European Past*, edited by Patricia H. Labalme (New York and London, New York University Press, 1980), pp. 43–65.

towards her daughter Eleonora.[65] After 1527, Isabella no longer was as active as she had been up till then. Her secretary Mario Equicola, who had encouraged her in various cultural enterprises, had died in 1525. Federico Gonzaga, her son, intended to exclude her from both the political and cultural scene so that he might become the unique centre of attention.[66] Other powers were now in control of Italy and this ageing woman was being overlooked in the changed situation of Counter-Reformation Italy.

Isabella d'Este had a clear idea of what it meant to be a woman and particularly of the limitations imposed by men. Instead of openly revolting, Isabella tried to extend the possibilities available to her, with the aid of her humanist advisers. It is significant that the highest praise contemporaries could bestow on the 'prima donna' was that she had an 'animo virile'.[67] It seems that it was impossible to praise Isabella d'Este for her own especial qualities as a woman.

[65] Cartwright, II, 364–66.

[66] For the power struggle in Mantua and Equicola's part in it, see by the present writer, 'Mario Equicola: A Biographical Reappraisal' (unpublished Ph.D. thesis, University of London, 1981).

[67] Equicola describes Isabella's resolve on taking over the government during her husband's imprisonment (1509–10) in the *Chronica di Mantua*: 'Questa, raffrenato il dolor et lacrime al che lo amor et l'affectione la constrengeano, pigliò animo virile et quella virtù che fino alhora era stata sopita se excitò con duplicato valore' (ff. ?i^{v}–?ii^{r}).

XIII

AN UNNOTICED DESCRIPTION OF ISABELLA D'ESTE'S *GROTTA*

It is well known that Isabella d'Este moved from her rooms in the Castello San Giorgio to apartments in the *Corte Vecchia* after the death of her husband, Francesco Gonzaga Marquis of Mantua, in 1519. The new quarters included a replacement for her 'cavernous' tunnel-vaulted first *Grotta* by a room more rectangular in design.[1] The panegyric or short description edited here (see Appendix) refers to the first *Grotta* and can be related—in part—to the circumstances of Isabella's removal; it appears in the autograph manuscript of the *Libro de natura de amore* composed by Mario Equicola, Isabella's tutor (1508–19) and secretary (1519–c. 1522).[2] The manuscript is datable to the years 1509–11, and the passage in question was struck out in the autograph, so that it comes as no surprise to find it missing from the first printed edition (1525).[3]

Equicola's purpose was generally to enhance Isabella's reputation as a woman of learning, by using his classical erudition in her service and to her praise, so it is understandable that he had first included in the *Libro* a description of her *Grotta*. He seems to have viewed it as a place of greater significance than any other of Isabella's rooms (implicitly including her *Studiolo*) which likewise housed her collections of paintings and antique statuary;[4] in part, too, he may have wanted to associate it with his own special contribution to her projects. Although the first use of the term *Grotta* in this context is attributable to Niccolò da Correggio in 1498, Isabella's *Grotta* does not appear to have gained special prominence until about 1507–08,[5] and it may be

[1] On the *Grotta* see G. Gerola, 'Trasmigrazioni e vicende dei Camerini di Isabèlla d'Este', *Atti e Memorie della Reale Accademia Virgiliana di Mantova*, n.s., xxi, 1929, pp. 253–90; A. Martindale, 'The patronage of Isabella d'Este at Mantua', *Apollo*, lxxix, 1964, pp. 183–91; C. M. Brown, '"Lo insaciabile desiderio nostro de cose antique": New documents on Isabella d'Este's collection of antiquities', in *Cultural Aspects of the Italian Renaissance. Essays in Honour of Paul Oskar Kristeller*, ed. C. H. Clough, Manchester 1976, pp. 324–53; idem (with A. M. Lorenzoni), 'The Grotta of Isabella d'Este', *Gazette des Beaux-Arts*, lxxxix, 1977, pp. 155–71 and lxxxxi, 1978, pp. 72–82; idem, *La Grotta d'Isabella d'Este. Un simbolo di continuità dinastica per i duchi di Mantova*, Mantua 1985; J. M. Fletcher, 'Isabella d'Este, patron and collector' in *Splendours of the Gonzaga*, [cat. exh.], eds D. Chambers and J. Martineau, London 1981, pp. 51–63.

[2] On Equicola see D. Santoro, *Della vita e delle opere di Mario Equicola*, Chieti 1906. Other bibliographical references are given in S. D. Kolsky, *Mario Equicola: A Biographical Reappraisal*, unpublished Ph.D. thesis, University of London 1981 and idem, '"The good servant": Mario Equicola. Court and courtier in early sixteenth-century Italy', *The Italianist*, vi, 1986, pp. 34–60.

[3] On the manuscript see R. Renier, 'Per la cronologia e la composizione del *Libro de natura de amore* di Mario Equicola', *Giornale storico della letteratura italiana* (hereafter *GSLI*), xiv, 1889, pp. 212–33; I. Rocchi, 'Per una nuova cronologia e valutazione del *Libro de natura de amore* di Mario Equicola', *GSLI*, cliii, 1976, pp. 566–85; G. Castagno, 'L'autografo del *Libro de natura de amore* di Mario Equicola', *Lingua Nostra*, xxiii, 1962, pp. 74–77; idem, 'L'autografo del *Libro de natura de amore* di Mario Equicola', in *Arte, pensiero e cultura a Mantova nel primo Rinascimento in rapporto con la Toscana e con il Veneto*, Florence 1965, pp. 133–43; M. Pozzi, 'Mario Equicola e la cultura cortigiana: appunti sulla redazione manoscritta del *Libro de natura de amore*', *Lettere italiane*, xxxii, 1980, pp. 149–71. The manuscript, which is definitely autograph, is Biblioteca Nazionale Universitaria, Turin, cod. N.III.10; the passage with which we are concerned is on fols 197^{r}-98^{r}. It is difficult to determine with any degree of certainty when Equicola eliminated the passage from his manuscript. For the reasons I outline below, however, it would seem most likely that he removed it after 1519 when Isabella had changed rooms.

[4] Cf. Brown, 1976 (as in n. 1), p. 349, n. 48, who considers it 'disconcerting' to find Margherita Cantelmo making a distinction between the *Studiolo* and *Grotta*. This was probably under the direct influence of Equicola who was anxious to maintain their separate identities. If there was a blurring, it was possibly more obvious after his death in 1525 or when he could not be so influential.

[5] Cf. Brown, 1976 (as in n. 1), pp. 331–32. See also A. Luzio and R. Renier, 'Niccolò da Correggio', *GSLI*

First published in: the *Journal of the Warburg and Courtauld Institutes* 52, 1989.

significant that it was in 1508 that Equicola became her tutor. Previously the *Grotta* may have been more simply regarded as just a secret retreat, a place of retirement from the world. Evidence that it thereafter acquired a deeper meaning is provided by two letters of late 1507, both written in Equicola's hand. Even though one of them is signed as from Margherita Cantelmo, a close friend of Isabella d'Este and the wife of Equicola's employer, Sigismondo Cantelmo, it bears the hallmarks of an Equicola composition, with its use of Latinizing adjectives and of hyperbolic language concerning Isabella. Margherita (or rather, Equicola) writes:

... not for this reason is removed my desire to be in the sacred *Grotta*, to be in the venerated sight of the divine image of she whom on earth I rightly worship.[6]

By use of this exalted vocabulary of reverence ('veneranda' is also used of the *Grotta* in the panegyric: see Appendix) a mundane room thus seems to be transformed into a place of worship. In the other letter, dated the following day, Equicola wrote (in his own name) to Isabella, alluding to one of his own previous compositions which celebrated the *Grotta*. His salutation 'to the divine *Grotta*' in this letter[7] points to his authorship of Margherita's letter already quoted and typifies his manner of amplifying Isabella's cultural achievements.

Equicola's description of the *Grotta* comes at the culminating point of a discussion about the pictorial and sculptural representations of Cupid in the fourth book of the *Libro* manuscript (the second book in the 1525 printed edition). It forms a suitable back-drop for one of Isabella d'Este's prize treasures, a statue of Cupid which Equicola believed to be the work of Praxiteles, a claim he uses as supporting evidence that Isabella's reputation for taste and expertise in matters of classical art was well founded. However, Equicola had reduced this section quite considerably by the time he finished revising the manuscript for publication.[8] The reasons why he did this are not so obvious as they might at first appear. It was not merely because Isabella had subsequently moved apartments; if this alone had been the explanation, Equicola could have described instead her new *Grotta*. There may have been, firstly, a political motive behind his alterations. The printed text announces that it is Equicola's work as secretary of Federico Gonzaga, Marquis of Mantua (1519–40), which may suggest that there existed in the last years of the secretary's life, if not outright hostility between himself and the Marchioness, at least some acrimony. For Equicola seems to have changed patrons as soon as he perceived that the new Marquis offered him greater possibilities of advancement (c. 1522).[9] Secondly, there may also have been an intellectual motive for changing the text of the *Libro*. Immediately before the manuscript passage on the *Grotta* Equicola had written a brief *excursus* on the nature of digressions, attempting to justify them if they do not adversely affect the economy of a piece of writing. In the printed version this section is extended and firmed up with classical *exempla*, and indeed it and the discussion of the Cupid take the place of the omitted description of the *Grotta*. Although committed to that kind of eclectic erudition which is characterized by information continually breaking down the framework in which it operates, Equicola may have felt that the passage describing the *Grotta* was itself too much of a digression; he could not justify its inclusion, since it broke his own rules concerning logical cohesion and the

(as in n. 3), xxi, 1893, pp. 205–64; p. 253; and the entry on this courtier in *Dizionario biografico degli italiani*, xxix, Rome 1983, pp. 466–74.

[6] 'Non per questo ad me se leva il desyderio de essere nella sacra grocta, nel conspecto venerando de la diva imagine de quella, la quale in terra meritamente adoro' (Archivio di Stato, Mantua [ASM], Archivio Gonzaga [AG], busta [b.]1813, Gazzuolo, 15 November 1507, Margherita Cantelmo to Isabella d'Este).

[7] 'Ad Vostra Excellentia et alla divina Grocta me recomando' (ASM, AG, b.1813, Gazzuolo, 16 November 1507, Equicola to Isabella d'Este).

[8] *Libro*, 1525, fols 73^{v}-74^{r}; *Libro*, MS, fols 198^{r}-202^{v}. Most of the encomiastic references to Isabella d'Este have been eliminated in the printed text, for example: 'Te o Cupido di Praxitele in dignissimo loco [*in più digno che mai fusti* crossed out] collocato et da quella che omni laude excede laudatissima Dia Isabella [*da più illustre persona* crossed out] posseduto col hymno de Orpheo così chiamo et invoco o magno dio!' (*Libro*, MS, fol. 201^{v}). For other texts describing Isabella d'Este's Cupid see E. Verheyen, 'Eros et Anteros. *L'éducation de Cupidon* et la prétendue *Antiope* du Corrège', *Gazette des Beaux-Arts*, lxv, 1965, pp. 321–40; 331–32, 338–39.

[9] See Kolsky, 1981 (as in n. 2), pp. 192–99.

proper separation of topics in sequence without interruption by extraneous material.

Before the description of the *Grotta* Equicola puts forward a view of Mantua as virtually synonymous with civilisation, meaning artistic achievement in particular. In eulogizing Isabella d'Este he then concentrates on those accomplishments of hers which found expression in the *Grotta*, particularly Latin learning and music. This art, avidly practised by Isabella, was there represented both in the form of a device and in the intarsia panelling.[10] The *Grotta* comes to represent the triumph of civilization over brute nature, incorporating the 'natural' form of a cavern into its design. Thus Equicola puts forward classical precedents only to reject them, implicitly because of the barbarous purposes for which some *grotte* were used (the Homeric and Vergilian Cyclops's caverns in particular). Some of the analogies with the caves of classical antiquity seem rather forced and the point may have struck Equicola, this dissatisfaction also contributing to his decision to cancel the passage.

The short description of the *Grotta* does not seem to deviate from fact. Equicola stresses certain aspects that are intended to present a particular image of its maker: the Golden Mean is observed throughout the structure. The decorations' primary function, according to Equicola, is to give pleasure to the eye: '[the *Grotta* is] skilfully composed of every kind of delight' ('artificiosamente composta de omni generatione de delitie abundante'). The objects depicted on the intarsia panelling are an essential part of this strategy because 'they delight and are not bothersome to the mind' ('delectono non fastidischeno la mente'), and again 'they are a relaxing sight' ('Recreano ... il viso'). Here there is some comparison implied between Isabella's choice of wood panelling and the practice of placing cloth and tapestry over bare walls, greatly in favour of the former. But Equicola goes further, stressing that this exquisite inlaid wood is far superior to any of the overlavish, overelaborate forms of decoration used in the apartments of the most extravagant Roman emperors, naming Titus, Tiberius, Nero and Heliogabulus. He may have had in mind a passage from Alberti's *De re aedificatoria* in this choice of emperors who personified magnificence gone awry,[11] and the contrast between their degenerate taste, and Isabella's divine excellence, and the marvel of her *Grotta* could hardly have been more pointed.

[10] See S. Kolsky, 'Images of Isabella d'Este', *Italian Studies*, xxxix, 1984, pp. 47–62; 52–53; and I. Fenlon, 'The Gonzaga and Music', in *Splendours* (as in n. 1), pp. 87–94; 87–88.

APPENDIX

Panegyric to Isabella d'Este's first *Grotta* in Mario Equicola, *Libro de natura de amore*, autograph in Biblioteca Nazionale Universitaria, Turin, cod. N.III.10, fols 197^{r}-98^{r}:

In Gallia cisalpina, da Longobardi hogi Lombardia dicta, in la regione veneta è una terra da Mintio circumdata. Syllio Italico[12] casa delle muse la nomina, nota per fama sopra il celo per lo doctissimo canto del nostro Italo Homero. De questa inclyta cità[13] de Gonzagi sede et dominio è Marchesana la Magnificentissima Dia Isabella da Este. La quale unitamente[14] possedendo quanto per gratia del celo in le altre laudabile et formoso se retrova[15] di lettere latine et musica scientissima.[16] Chi questo nega è maligno, chi lo afferma è senza adulatione veridico. Questa ultra le altre habitationi per se commodissime, de antique statue et excellentissime picture ornate, ha facta fabricare una Grotta,[17] non simile ad

[11] See *De re aedificatoria*, IX, viii.

[12] Silius Italicus, *Punica*, viii, 593–94: 'Mantua, Musarum domus atque ad sidera cantu / evecta Aonio et Smyrnaeis aemula plectris'. The rest of Equicola's sentence is indeed a paraphrase of Silius Italicus's lines and sentiments.

[13] 'è principe la' is deleted immediately after.

[14] In the margin at this point there is a deletion, referring obviously to Isabella d'Este: 'di omni laude digna, omni laude excede'.

[15] 'de omni virtù, precipuamente' is deleted immediately after.

[16] *scientissima* replaces the deleted 'cumulatissima'.

[17] For the various uses of the word *grotta* consult the *Grande dizionario della lingua italiana*, vii, Turin 1972, pp. 75–76.

quella del Cyclope homerico,[18] non ad le virgiliane,[19] non inferiore ad quella la quale fabellano esser in Parnaso,[20] ma più augusta, veneranda et sana. So certo se le muse volissero in Italia habitare elegeriano questa per perpetua loro habitatione, per essere artificiosamente composta de omni generatione de delitie abundante.[21] La luce più da oriente che da meridie piglia et del suo aere contenta, ultra non ne desidera. Ha in se inchiuso il frescho et il temperato calore. La volta in lamnia[22] con le pause del musico concento che ad tempo tacere denota[23] et le cartule delle sorte insieme colligate in candidissimo colore impie non satia li occhi. Li lati ornati de tersie con figure minutissime in ligno di proprio non adulterino colore con musici instrumenti, portici, templi, cità, paesi, et prospective, delectono non fastidischeno la mente. Recreano multo più il viso che se fossero paramenti di brocat[o] li quali naschenno riccho li pò havere et in varii usi[24] servirsene. Questo è più pretioso ornato che le incrustature di Tito Cesari,[25] de petre como cristallo risplendenti, più sumptuoso che'l Camerino di Tiberio[26] con lastre di specchi, più grato chel ornare prodigo di Nerone,[27] più iucundo al' aspecto che l'aurea astrecatura[28] di Heliogabalo.[29]

[18] Homer, *Odyssey*, ix, 116–566.

[19] *Aeneid*, iii, 570–691, on the cavern see in particular 616–19. Note also *Aeneid*, vii, 568, where there is mention of the 'specus horrendum', the entrance to Dis.

[20] A reference to the Corycian cave for which see Pausanias, *Description of Greece*, x, vi, 3 and x, xxxii, 2, who claims that this cave was the most splendid in all of Greece.

[21] *abundante* replaces the deleted 'piena'.

[22] This refers to the gilded stucco of the vaulted ceiling on which there are various *imprese* personal to Isabella d'Este. On the *impresa delle pause* see A. Luzio and R. Renier, 'La coltura e le relazioni letterarie d'Isabella d'Este Gonzaga', *GSLI* (as in n. 3), xxxiii, 1899, pp. 50–52 and I. Fenlon, *Music and Patronage in Sixteenth Century Mantua*, I, Cambridge 1980, p. 21; and 'The Gonzaga and Music', in *Splendours* (as in n. 1), p. 88; in general consult I. L. Mumford, 'Some decorative aspects of the *Imprese* of Isabella d'Este', *Italian Studies*, xxxiv, 1979, pp. 60–70, Kolsky (as in n. 10), pp. 52–53.

[23] Equicola elaborates on this theme later in the MS when he discusses the virtue of keeping silent at the right time: 'Habia in memoria il sapientissimo Biante di haver parlato, esserse più volte pentito né mai de haver taciuto. Questo in figure ingeniosamente ha significato la prudentissima Isabella da Este de Mantua Marchesa [principe deleted] con tucte le pause della musica pratica le quali ci admoniscono et quelli ad viva voce ne dicono "ad tempo taci"' (*Libro*, MS, fol. 240ʳ).

[24] 'possed[ere?]' deleted immediately after.

[25] L. B. Alberti, *De re aedificatoria*, IX, iv, refers to Titus's building practices: 'In *crustationibus* parietum nulla picturae coniectatio erit gratior atque spectatior, quam quae lapideas columnationes exprimat. Porticum qua spatiari consuesset, Titus Caesar tersis Feniceis lapidus distinxerat, quorum *splendore quasi ex speculo* omnia viderentur' (my italics to indicate the key-words which Equicola 'translates' into his text).

[26] *Camerino* was the usual term to refer to the private apartments of a ruler or distinguished person. For Tiberius, see M. E. Blake, *Roman Construction in Italy from Tiberius through the Flavians*, Washington D.C. 1959, pp. 16–18; A. Maiuri, *Capri. Its History and Monuments*, Rome 1956, pp. 76–87; G. Iacopi, *L'antro di Tiberio a Sperlonga*, Rome 1963, which recalls that the grotta 'cui Speluncae nomen est' (Suetonius, *Lives of the Caesars*, Tiberius, iii, 39) was a series of caves which underwent radical transformation. Alberti himself does use the term *grotta* but it is always with reference to coastal structures unlike Isabella d'Este's which has no connection with water. See also on this N. Neuerburg, *L'architettura delle fontane e dei ninfei nell'Italia antica*, Naples 1965, pp. 35–38.

[27] Alberti, IX, viii, provides precise details which Equicola does not use: 'Quae aedificabat Nero, cuncta erant auro tecta, distincta gemmis.'

[28] Alberti, IX, viii, mentions the golden paving 'qui stravit auro pavimenta'. Cf. 'Antoninus Heliogabalus Aeli Lampridii' in *Scrittori della storia augusta*, ed. P. Soverini, Turin 1983, pp. 614–15. The Praxiteles Cupid was housed 'nella tua aurea grotta in aurata cuna' (*Libro*, 1525, fol. 73ᵛ and *Libro*, MS, fol. 198ʳ with the first adjective not yet present). In the manuscript there is a 'digression', which appears shortly before our passage, on the nature of gold, obviously intended to provide more levels of meanings for the 'aurea Grotta'. First of all, Equicola states that it is an enduring metal: 'Potriase dire verisimilmente lo oro metallo prestantissimo che non patisce ruzine al quale predomina il sole, signore del sangue propria, complexione di amore' (fol. 196ʳ). The gold-tipped arrows of love are used as a telling example of the power of gold: 'ogni cosa cede a l'oro' (fol. 196ᵛ). 'Aurea' may have conveyed further meanings, apart from (imperial) power, such as the Golden Mean or the Golden Age, concepts which were part of the ideology of Isabella d'Este's apartments.

[29] In the margin at this point 'del'Inferno' underlined, perhaps a reference to this Emperor's vicious habits.

XIV

THEORIZING PLEASURE IN THE RENAISSANCE

> Words like "hedonism" - terms of large and vague comprehension - above all when used for a purpose avowedly controversial, have ever been the worst examples of what are called "question-begging terms"; and in that late age in which Marius lived, amid the dust of so many centuries of philosophical debate, the air was full of them. Yet those who used that reproachful Greek term for the philosophy of pleasure, were hardly more likely than the old Greeks themselves (on whom regarding this very subject of the theory of pleasure, their masters in the art of thinking had so emphatically to impress the necessity of "making distinctions") to come to any very delicately correct ethical conclusions by a reasoning, which began with a general term, comprehensive enough to cover pleasures so different in quality, in their causes and effects, as the pleasures of wine and love, of art and science, of religious enthusiasm and political enterprise, and of that taste or curiosity which satisfied itself with long days of serious study.(1)

In this passage from *Marius the Epicurean* Walter Pater pinpoints one of the perennial difficulties associated with defining pleasure - what exactly is it?(2) Marius' version is based explicitly on the doctrines of Aristippus who comes closest to expressing the "popular" conception of Epicureanism. Diogenes Laertius, in his biography of Aristippus, illustrates Aristippus's love of pleasure by recounting the following anecdote:

> Polyxenus the Sophist once paid him a visit and, after having seen ladies present and expensive entertainment, reproached him with it later. After an interval Aristippus asked him, "Can you join us today?" On the other accepting the invitation, Aristippus inquired, "Why, then, did you find fault? For you appear to blame the cost and not the entertainment".(3)

It is interesting that in Pater's novel pleasure is just one amongst a number of conflicting philosophies - all of which need to be experienced and rejected before Marius can understand fully the message of Christianity. *Marius the Epicurean* expresses the need to go beyond aestheticism; pleasure for pleasure's sake. In the end he sacrifices himself for his friend Cornelius, having learnt that there are higher values than the self.(4)

In researching and recording philosophies by which to conduct one's life Pater is, of course, working within a recognizable tradition of philosophical argumentation which seeks either to reconcile classical and Christian thought or to separate the two completely in order to demonstrate the total superiority of the latter. Pater, it will be remembered, was a scholar of Renaissance thought and art and, as such, believed that Italian Renaissance philosophy had attempted to seek a syncretistic solution to the problem of the conflicting demands of "pagan" philosophy and Christianity. Hence we find in *Marius the Epicurean* that the protagonist's embrace of Christianity is not so much an outright rejection of pagan philosophy, as an acknowledgement that a particular kind of Christianity does not offend pagan sensibilities. For Pater this represents a shift in emphasis - away from "the desire of beauty, the love of art for its own sake" (*Conclusion* to his collection of essays, *The Renaissance* - omitted in the 2nd edition because of the author's fear that "it might possibly mislead some of those young men into whose hands it might fall").(5) Pater however never renounces entirely these ideals.

It can be argued here that Pater was projecting his own obsessions on to the Renaissance which became, in his writing, an "ideal" where the tensions between paganism and Christianity were resolved; where art was a "religious object". Nevertheless, from a historical point of view, the most challenging of the philosophical doctrines circulating in the fifteenth century was that centred on the term *voluptas* (pleasure); a term relating in varying degrees to Epicureanism.(6) Pleasure, in whatever context, presented a challenge to Christian thought, particularly to ascetic Christianity. Hence, it provides a good "litmus test" for Renaissance syncretism.

The most detailed, and at the same time most problematic, treatment of pleasure is Lorenzo Valla's *De Voluptate* (*On Pleasure*), a text written and rewritten over a period of some eighteen years (1431-1449); it was only in 1509 that an attempt was made to produce a text which reflected to some degree Valla's later revisions.(7) Thus, the complete text, although circulating in manuscript, had its fullest impact only at the beginning of the sixteenth century with repercussions being felt in texts produced by and for court society *and* on the wider European plane (Erasmus and More). The *De Voluptate* was open to the most diverse interpretations, and the first reactions resulted in widespread criticism and animosity. Thus Valla felt compelled to defend his treatise and clarify his intentions.(8) Although he blamed personal enmity and labelled some of the interpretations as perverse, there remains a lingering suspicion that the dialogue itself may generate conflicting messages. Indeed Valla himself, on more than one occasion, had suggested a simple and straightforward reading of the text, amply supported by the dialogue: the first two books present a clash between two classical philosophies, Stoicism and Epicureanism, with an outcome favourable to the latter. The third book which sees the intervention of Christianity dismisses classical philosophy as insignificant and demonstrates the overwhelming superiority of Christian Revelation.(9) Such an interpretation posits an almost unbridgeable "gap" between the first two books and the third. Indeed Antonio da Rho, the Christian apologist in the last book clearly demonstrates that this *is* the *authorized* reading; both Stoic virtue and Epicurean pleasures being misguided systems and hence sinful:

> Therefore, we must abstain from the pleasure here below if we want to enjoy the one above. We cannot enjoy both of them, because they differ from each other as do heaven and earth, soul and body. Our pleasure here is more uncertain and deceptive: that pleasure above is certain and stable (*On Pleasure* , p. 267)

As if the message were not clear enough, the reader is given instructions on how to enclose the text within specific semantic parameters: "You (Vegio - the defender of pleasure), as I said, were a simulator or an ironist - more Socrates than Epicurus".(10) Indeed it is easy enough to deconstruct certain speeches made by Vegio because they are obviously outrageous and would be difficult to take at face-value: an example is his *declamation* on wine: "men are superior to all other animals on two counts: we can express what we feel, and we can drink wine, sending out the one and ushering in the other." (*On Pleasure*, p. 105). At this point, Vegio, following Aristippus, becomes an unreliable narrator by allowing exaggerated praise of food and drink to vitiate the other arguments favourable to Epicureanism:(11)

> In my opinion, the man who has spoken best and most wisely on this subject is the one who wanted to be given a neck like a crane so as to savor at greater length the pleasure of taste, if it be granted that from the longest neck

> the longest pleasure of eating and drinking is derived (*On Pleasure*, p. 105).

In the first two books of *De Voluptate* a series of *declamationes* by Vegio produce a destabilizing effect on the text by turning "upside down" fundamental Christian beliefs: Vegio pours scorn on virginity ("nothing in human affairs is more intolerable torment than virginity" (*On Pleasure*, p. 125), on chastity, and on marriage in general ("there is absolutely no difference between a woman's going to bed with her husband or with her lover" [*On Pleasure*, p. 119]). His praise of wine, likewise, may be considered the inversion of an essential Christian symbol. Such parodic verbal compositions overtly degrade the high spiritual ideals of Christianity by the use of a grotesque realism which reduces the discourse to a level of bodily materialism: the rational procedures of the dialogue are undermined as elements of disorder are introduced into the text. This strategy will serve to enhance the Christian discourse embedded in concepts of order, in particular, a clear-cut moral system.(12) However, Vegio's position is not consistent (another strategy used to demonstrate the failure of ancient philosophy) and he occasionally reverts to intermediate stages in an effort to render Epicureanism more acceptable to a Christian audience: "I shall not gorge myself with food to the point of indigestion; I shall not take to wine to the extent of falling asleep while doing business" (*On Pleasure*, p. 121).

It is relatively easy to dismiss some of Vegio's claims, but not so all of them. Socratic irony seems to be used in a selective manner to ensure that Epicureanism, as expressed by Valla, in the second book, can demolish the Stoic philosophy of virtue being its own reward. Although the bridges between the two unequal parts of the dialogue are rare, they do, nevertheless, exist: Valla's conception of Christianity as a reward-system is adumbrated in the structures of Epicureanism. Vegio clearly states this principle: "no one is aroused to great and difficult enterprises except by the possibility of a prize" (*On Pleasure* , p. 179). Admittedly, the context runs counter to Christian teaching in that Epicureanism is concerned with the "immediate reward" rather than the heavenly. But even here Vegio is ambiguous: he is unwilling to exclude *a priori* the ultimate reward of Heaven; a position which opens up the text to the possibility of completion within a Christian frame. Vegio would not accept any idea of an afterlife which excluded "the pleasures of the body":

> Therefore, as long as possible (would that it were longer!), let us not allow those bodily pleasures to slip

away that cannot be doubted and cannot be recovered in another life (*On Pleasure* , p. 221).

Paradoxically, Valla's interpretation of Christian doctrine lays to rest that particular doubt. To him, as we have seen, the reward of Heaven, is the result of "abstinence" during one's earthly life and, closely following St. Augustine, Antonio da Rho stresses the physical nature of the Christian paradise. It is at this point that scholars confront obstacles to a satisfactory interpretation of the Vallian heaven since "true pleasure" appears so closely aligned with the pleasure of Epicureanism.(13) Valla, however, emphasises the view that heavenly pleasures know no limits of duration; thus echoing the earthly paradise (in Dante, *Purgatorio*):

> Mentr'io m'andava tra tante primizie
> dell'*etterno piacer* tutto sospeso,
> e disioso ancora a più letizie.(14)

Dante's "etterno piacer" and his later description of the "carro" as "triunfale" (*Purgatorio*, XXIX, 107) may have provided Valla with a literary model suitable for his purpose. Literary devices and precedents which could conjure up the eternal as present through an emphasis on the visual were necessary to the balance of the dialogue which might otherwise be threatened by the seductive narrations of Vegio:

> what then should be suspected of the speech of Vegio [asks Antonio da Rho], who filled our ears with a multitude of arguments and stole deeper within with his delight? He broke into our intimate feelings with strength and impetuous violence and *nearly removed the mind from its proper state.* (15)

The danger of Epicurean discourse lies in its appeal to the senses - in its power of seduction. To counter these effects the senses are raised to a higher level and "colonised" by Christianity; where they are in the service of the one, true religion, distant yet present but no longer posing a threat. Hence Valla can write "hic triumphus" (*De Voluptate*, p. 310) - just as a victorious general showed off his booty and prisoners, the Christian writer can show the submission of the physical to God's rule. Order has been restored.

It is evident that the description of Paradise provides Valla with the opportunity to display his rhetorical skills. Such a climactic representation of the Christian Heaven asserts the power of Vallian poetics to capture the ineffable. His Latin becomes superior to that used by the classical writers, placing him on the same level as the Church Fathers. The description is notably visual; in some ways it could be interpreted as the triumph of Art, Christian Art. It represents, in essence, the return to the Father, the final validation of order. The God-Man ["Deus-homo", p.314] is compared to "a father filled with most expectant impatience, ready to receive his son returned from a long, distant journey" (*On Pleasure* , pp. 315, 317). It is a return to that writing which guarantees the repression of the senses - an oratorical art that sublimates awkward sensual presences. But even in Valla's Heaven where one cannot deny the essential Christianity of the description it does seem also a place where earthly pleasures reach their apogee: "in the state of eternal felicity that kind of pleasure will be much richer and more plentiful" (*On Pleasure* , p. 301).(16)

The concluding statement of the final version of *De Voluptate* is left to Guarino da Verona, the well-known humanist educator. The choice is significant in a number of respects. Importantly, Guarino's long association with the Ferrarese court serves to open up the text to a different environment and a different set of priorities, and his speech clearly demonstrates a contrasting intellectual viewpoint. He believes that the classics are a perfect training for young people and sees no real conflict between this and Christian teaching. Thus we see a significant change in style and tone. Although acknowledging Rho's discourse as effective in producing *voluptas* , Guarino's interpretation nevertheless seems rather unexpected given the Christian emphasis of Rho's *panegyricum* . The Ferrarese humanist does not view the debate in terms of a victory for Christian ideology; for him it must be analysed in terms of difference:

> Both you and Vegio, in the manner of the best orators, have called upon all the powers, arms, and arts that help one to win; but to indicate the difference between you properly I shall introduce a kind of comparison that is humble but not absurd, and (as I believe) is also novel and unfamiliar. Maffeo [Vegio] and Antonio each seemed to be singing the praises of pleasure most sweetly in his own way (*On Pleasure* , p. 321).

Guarino compares Vegio to a swallow, a bird "associated with urban eloquence, which is exercised between walls, in the curia, and in the courts [in subsellis]" (*On Pleasure* , p. 321). Antonio da Rho, he likens to a nightingale which "was associated with the sylvan eloquence of the poets". The latter's inspiration is clearly superior, being defined classically by reference to the Muses. Guarino nevertheless makes room for Vegio's Epicureanism:

> Vegio introduced us bodily into paradise (for "paradise" is the Greek word for Garden); and Raudense, speaking in this garden, rapt us away in spirit into another, more excellent paradise (*On Pleasure* , p. 321).

While accepting that Rho has a higher level of awareness, Guarino nevertheless considers the "gap" between the two interlocutors as one of quality rather than substance. Thus, in contrast to Rho's suggestion, he implies that the two systems are not irreconcilable. The introduction of this contradictory element moderates the criticism of humanist thought implicit in the third book of the dialogue, although it does create problems for the text's final attitude to the Vegio/Rho relationship. Guarino's conciliatory tone however may be a partial recognition of the place Epicureanism holds in the development of a Christian apologetic. It is, nevertheless, somewhat disturbing to find such an attitude at all in a work by Valla. The later revisions may have been affected by his contacts with court society, including Ferrara and the royal court of Naples. But in themselves they do not help to explain why the *De Voluptate* , on a number of occasions, expresses views that would not be sanctioned in other works, as for example, the *De Libero Arbitrio* . One explanation might lie in the fact that *De Voluptate* was a youthful work which, almost in spite of itself, allowed some of the contradictions inherent in the subject-matter to surface. His point regarding the connection between the court's and Vegio's edited version of Epicureanism will not be lost on later writers.

As stated earlier, the initial reactions to *De Voluptate* were widespread, negative and direct.(17) The second wave of interest occurs more indirectly and coincides with the printing of the work in the early sixteenth century. Within Italy an implied dialogue with the text can be detected on the part of court-humanists who were living through and theorizing about pleasurable activities. Indeed, the court necessitated reflection on pleasure since courtiers were often expected to function as entertainers. In many ways, court society existed for pleasure; a view clearly stated in a text such as Castiglione's *Libro del cortegiano* where terms such as "piacevolezza", "piacevole", "piacere", and numerous other synonyms, are a frequent and obvious feature. The vernacular term "piacere", of course, has different connotations and originates from a different source than the more illustrious Latin *voluptas* . Indeed, the principal inter-textual referent is Boccaccio's *Decameron* in which "piacere" often occupies a specific semantic field;

sexual pleasure in the *novelle* , in contrast to the *cornice* which offers a more refined view of pleasure, one more congenial to Castiglione's tastes and ideological position.

While granting a certain, necessary status to "piacere onesto" Castiglione however, does not make it the goal of court society. For him, it becomes the *means* to a higher end. Thus he seems to have constructed an elaborate justification for courtly pleasures, ensuring they have a central place in the courtier's ontology - and if pleasure must yield to a Neoplatonic interpretation of the greatest good the distance between the two "philosophies" is not so great as it might at first appear.

Castiglione operates a fundamental revision of Ficinian Neoplatonism. The most obvious change can be seen in the influence of court culture on the raw philosophical material. Even so, the court seems, in the person of Emilia Pia, rather sceptical about so abstract and idealist a philosophy. Equally important is the fact that women, almost the bodily signs of a court, have a function in Castiglione's Neoplatonism which they certainly did not have in Ficino's. It is through love of the woman that one begins to climb the ladder towards divine love. Castiglione notes that the first steps on the path towards the "mistress"/beloved).

This process dramatizes the way in which pleasure is gendered in Renaissance theory. It always appears as a male definition in which the woman is the pleasure-object. If women pose a sexual threat, if they are considered objects to be feared, the texts examined in this article stress male power and domination - they speak male pleasure. Castiglione is no exception even though pleasure is not the final goal of the courtier's activities:

> Se adunque le bellezze, che tutto dì con questi nostri tenebrosi occhi veggiamo nei corpi corruttibili, che non son però altro che sogni ed umbre tenuissime di bellezza, ci paion tanto belle e graziose, che in noi spesso accenden foco ardentissimo e con tanto diletto, che riputiamo niuna felicità potersi agguagliar a quella che talor sentimo per un sol sguardo che ci venga dall'amata vista d'una donna, che felice maraviglia, che beato stupore pensiamo noi che sia quello, che occupa le anime che pervengono alla visione della bellezza divina!(18)

Thus pleasure has been displaced, but not eliminated. In this way, Castiglione seeks to find a resolution to the problem posed by the necessity of endowing the court with a grandiose philosophical/metaphysical structure - an acknowledgement of the physical basis of court life necessitates its justification and sublimation. Thus we notice a "gap" (perhaps exaggerated by some critics) between the third and fourth books of the *Cortegiano* , in some ways, similar to that opened up by the third book of *De Voluptate* .(19) These texts are not alone in exhibiting such a conceptual "leap". Let us here examine briefly one such text written by a contemporary of Castiglione - Mario Equicola's *Libro de natura de amore* , published in 1525.(20) Situated in a court environment, this treatise which takes up the discourse on pleasure attempts to work through the moral predicament of (Aristippean) pleasure as perceived by a committed courtier. It is interesting to note that the fifth book (from a total of six) is concerned with the practice of courtiership *and* with a survey of lyric poetry from Roman antiquity to the present. Thus, the courtier is above all a lover whose main purpose is to entertain (women). The sixth book attempts to transpose these concerns onto a more philosophical plane, in order to create a courtly ontology - Equicola it seems is like Vegio whose discourse is not meant to be interpreted ironically. The sixth book takes even further, if possible, the Epicurean position of utilitarianism which implies exceptional duty to self. For Equicola "di tutti effecti che in noi sono et naturalmente possono sorgere esser cagione principio et origine amore che noi a noi stessi portamo".(21) The culmination of that love is *voluptà* . Although acknowledging that "amor è de l'animo et corpo" the writer nonetheless manipulates the concept in such a way as to ensure that the cares of the body are not neglected.(22) In the final section of the *Libro* Equicola repeatedly insists on the hypocrisy of those who claim that in loving a woman one's interest "fermarsi disio amoroso in viso et odito soli". For him "è impossibile".(23) Based on a careful reading of Cicero's *De Finibus* and Diogenes Laertius' *Life of Epicurus* (and perhaps Valla's *De Voluptate* as well), Equicola's Epicureanism appears almost canonical. Unlike Castiglione, pleasure for him is not a means but an end - the highest end. This view closely resembles Valla's "Christian Epicureanism" where Heaven represents the continuation of pleasure for all eternity, contrasting with earth - forever subject to time and dissolution.(24)

Equicola's work is more easily read than Valla's since the former's project merely aims at the confirmation of earthly pleasures: for him the courtier/lover has no pretensions concerning his role in the institution of power. Although ambition is revealed as a motivating force in the last book of the *Libro* , it is viewed in terms of making the private public in a rather aggressive fashion: the images of possession and control refer to the male domination of the lover, hence emphasizing the act of conquest rather than the consequences of such action.[25] Love is intimately connected with the present; it is a sign of actual activity. However, it is not the only pleasure. Equicola alludes to another, 'intellectual' pleasure, also connected to power and position at court - those courtiers "dediti alla scientia, ornati de sapientia" play a crucial role in channelling intellectual energies towards *their* interpretation of *voluptà* .[26]

The pleasure of knowledge ("piacere del savere" [*Libro* , f.229v]) is however, not central to Equicola's concerns. For him it is a possibility not fully explored, although for other writers it will become the chief pleasure. Erasmus, in his colloquy, *The Epicurean* , severs the body-soul nexus and takes perhaps a stand more extreme than Valla's.[27] Implicit reference is made to the position assumed in the third book of *De Voluptate* when Hedon declares: "In plain truth, there are no people more Epicurean than godly Christians" (*The Epicurean* , p. 538). But Erasmus is not interested in the resurrection of the flesh. Instead he wishes to force home one point above all: (Hedon) "Then you admit that the principal pleasure comes from the mind, as from a fountainhead?" (*The Epicurean* p. 540). Mental powers, according to Hedon, can control bodily instincts and are considered the most important expressions of the soul: "For so great is the power of the mind that frequently it takes away the feeling of physical pain" (*The Epicurean* p. 540). "The real pleasures of the mind" (p. 541) involve a separation of the roles of intellectual and courtier - indeed, one of the anecdotes related in the dialogue concerns a trick played on certain "court ladies" (*The Epicurean* pp. 542-43). Thus, unlike Equicola, Erasmus wishes the "intellectual" to stand apart from court society - to seek satisfaction only in "the true goods of the mind" (p. 544). If old age is Equicola's obsession signifying the end of the enjoyment of the body, Erasmus' interpretation of Epicureanism allows Hedon no fear concerning senility or death: "What would they [young men who are crazed by pleasures] not do to lay up against approaching old age the provision of a good conscience and an unstained honour!"(*The Epicurean* , p. 550) Erasmus' rejection of all worldly goods and the expression of an obvious nostalgia for Franciscan poverty (a clear attack on papal politics of grandeur) seems to be both an answer to, and a criticism of, other versions of Epicureanism as well as of general modes of behaviour.

The emphasis on the mind as the chief pleasure can be found also in More's *Utopia* : "Of all the different pleasures, they seek mostly those of the mind, and prize them most highly, because most of them arise from the practice of the virtues and the consciousness of a good life".(28) The body, however, is not completely neglected. It is understood that the health of the body is essential to the [health] of the mind: "Most of the Utopians regard this health as the foundation of all the other pleasures, since by itself alone it can make life peaceful and desirable, whereas without it there is no possibility of any other pleasure" (*Utopia* , p. 59) - an "orthodox" Epicurean view, not touched upon by Erasmus, and emphasised by Equicola for his own purposes.

In conclusion, it is not true to say that discussion of pleasure was an insignificant part of intellectual debate in the Renaissance. Rather one can note the differences in emphasis: the role of Christian doctrine in defining the semantic space given to pleasure, and the tensions existing in relation to bodily pleasures. Interest in Epicureanism was not due solely to the discovery of the *Life of Epicurus* , though this did stimulate debate. The growth in importance of court society and its attraction for intellectuals must be taken into account: the prince and his pleasures needed either justification or moderation, while even the life-style of the courtiers needed some kind of defence. Debate on pleasure involved both personal and institutional choices. On one level it was an attempt to re-evaluate the concept of virtue and to insist on the life of the mind. Importantly, these texts do not represent an isolated moment in European culture - the discourse on pleasure is one with a long history; being the object of further investigation in the seventeenth and eighteenth centuries when pleasure becomes libertinism. Burckhardt's image of the Italian Renaissance as a period of individuality receives a degree of confirmation from the interest in and manipulation of Epicurean philosophy; itself an aspect of individualism. However, pleasure was often viewed as a problem, to be resolved by syncretism, suppression of particular elements or by challenging accepted norms. In some circles, it became vital to Christianize pleasure in order to demonstrate that the two modes of thought were not irreconcilable. In others, particularly courtly ones, pleasure needed justification for its own sake. Perhaps one of the lesser known contributions of early sixteenth-century court society was to make some people feel less guilty about pleasure.

NOTES

1. Walter Pater, *Marius the Epicurean* (Harmondsworth: Penguin, 1985; first published 1885), pp. 119-120.

2. See J.C.B. Gosling, *Pleasure and Desire. The Case for Hedonism Reviewed* (Oxford: Clarendon, 1969), pp. 21-27.

3. Diogenes Laertius, *Lives of Eminent Philosophers* , with an English translation by R.D. Hicks, 2 vols (London: Heinemann, 1959), vol. 1, p. 205. The anecdote related here is just one amongst several employed to illustrate Aristippus' open-mindedness and lack of hypocrisy extending to sexual *mores* : "A courtesan, having told him that she was with child by him, he replied, 'You are no more sure of this than if, after running through coarse rushes, you were to say you had been pricked by one in particular' "(p. 209).

4. See U.C.Knoepflmacher, *Religious Humanism and the Victorian Novel* (Princeton, N.J.: Princeton University Press, 1965), pp. 214-16. The author considers that *Marius the Epicurean* "reflects the plight of an artistic temperament unable to reconcile the physical world of the senses with the ideal world of morality and religion" (p. 222).

5. Walter Pater, *The Renaissance Studies in Art and Poetry. The 1893 Text*, edited by Donald L.. Hill (Berkeley: University of California Press,1980), p. 190. Pater's comment on the young men is on p. 186 n.1. In the same footnote Pater draws out the connexion between the *Conclusion* and *Marius* . Hence, it can be argued that his thoughts on the Renaissance are at the heart of the debate taking place in the novel.

6. See Don Cameron Allen, "The rehabilitation of Epicurus and his theory of pleasure in the early Renaissance", *Studies in Philology*, 41 (1944), 1-15; Eugenio Garin, "Ricerche sull'Epicureismo del Quattrocento", in *La cultura filosofica del Rinascimento italiano. Ricerche e documenti* (Florence: Sansoni, 1961), pp. 72-92.

7. The critical edition is edited by Maristella de Panizza Lorch as De *vero falsoque bono* (Bari: Laterza, 1970). For further analysis of the various redactions, consult, by the same writer, "Le tre redazioni del *De Voluptate* del Valla", *Giornale Storico della Letteratura Italiana* , 121 (1943), 1-22 and Eadem, "Le tre versioni del *De vero bono* del Valla, *Rinascimento*, 6 (1955), 349-64. The title of Valla's dialogue is rather problematic. After starting out with the more radical and direct *De Voluptate* Valla preferred, in subsequent versions, the more "philosophical" and less tendentious *De vero bono* . See Giovanni Di Napoli, *Lorenzo Valla. Filosofia e religione nell'umanesimo italiano* (Rome: Edizioni di Storia e Letteratura, 1971), pp. 177-82, for some discussion of the title. I have preferred to use the title *De Voluptate* since it clearly demonstrates Valla's concerns and the direction of his thought. The work has been translated by A. Kent Hieatt and Maristella Lorch, *On Pleasure. De Voluptate* (New York: Abaris Books, 1977). This will be the translation used in the article. Three early sixteenth-century editions of the *De Voluptate* are worthy of note because they witness the availability of Valla's dialogue in a period when courtier-writers were actively formulating treatises on the subject of court society: (1) *De vero falsoque bono accuratissime recognitum et a mendis non parum multis repurgatum* (Coloniae: In domo Quentell, 1504). 4º (2) *De voluptate ac vero bono libri III* (Parisiis: In aedibus ascensianis, 1512). 8º (3) *De voluptate ac vero bono libri III* (Basileae: Apud Andream Cartandrum, 1519). 4º

8. See G. Zippel, "La *Defensio quaestionum in philosophia* di Lorenzo Valla e un noto processo dell'Inquisizione napoletana", *Bulletino dell'Istituto Storico Italiano per il Medioevo e Archivio Muratoriano* , 68 (1957) 319-47 and Lorenzo Valla, *Scritti filosofici e religiosi* , a cura di Giorgio Radetti (Florence: Sansoni, 1953), pp. 429-54 (*Apologia Ad Eugenium IV*). For a brief critical survey of criticism on the *De Voluptate* consult Hieatt and Lorch, pp. 44-46. Girolamo Mancini, *Vita di Lorenzo Valla* (Florence: Sansoni, 1891), gives details both of the dialogue and its reception. See in particular, pp. 45-64.

9. The most recent of such interpretations is Brian Vickers, "Valla's ambivalent praise of pleasure: Rhetoric in the service of Christianity", *Viator* , 17 (1986), 271-319.

10. *On Pleasure* , p.261. See also Vickers, pp. 273-74.

11. Other statements made by Vegio might be acceptable in certain circumstances. His early definition of Epicureanism is a good example:

> Pleasure, then, is a good, from whatever source, located in a sense of delight felt by the soul and the body. This is approximately what Epicurus meant, and what the Greeks called edonén. ... All people everywhere include two things under this word: joy within the soul through pleasurable emotion, and cheerfulness in the body (*On Pleasure* , p. 89).

12. It appears that Valla could not, at the time of writing the first version, have had any knowledge of Ambrogio Traversari's Latin translation of Diogenes Laertius' *Lives of the Philosophers* (Charles Trinkaus, *In our Image and Likeness. Humanity and Divinity in Italian Humanist Thought* , 2 vols [London: Constable, 1970], I, p. 110). However, when Valla decided to revise the text it would not be altogether unlikely that the translation had come to his notice, particularly taking into account the number of years needed to carry out his revisions. If such is the case, Valla was more interested in producing a caricature of Epicurus in the first two books in order to ridicule particular aspects of Epicureanism rather than a historically exact representation.

13. I cannot agree with Brian Vickers' analysis of the *De Voluptate* . It is perhaps too simplistic to see the work in black and white terms: "Valla's concern to validate the Epicurean notion of pleasure, detach it from its almost universal association with the body, and appropriate it for the promised joys of Christianity, must be taken as the animating force of *De Voluptate* " (p. 317). In the first place, Valla is concerned with the resurrection of the body and secondly, one can detect a sensual note in his description of Paradise.
A consensus seems to be growing amongst scholars that the *De Voluptate* is relatively unproblematic. For example, Jill Kraye states in her contribution to *The Cambridge History of Renaissance Philosophy* , general editor Charles B. Schmitt (Cambridge: Cambridge U.P., 1988), "moral philosophy", pp. 303-86; p. 384, that "only when pagan ethical doctrines were

completely turned on their head, replacing earthly by heavenly values, could they have any relevance for Christians". It is the "completely" of this statement with which I take issue and which is the subject of the present contribution.

14. *Purgatorio* , XXIX, 31-33 (my emphasis). A recent study of Dante's attitude towards Epicurus is Valerio Lucchesi, "Epicurus and Democritus: The Ciceronian foundations of Dante's judgement", *Italian Studies* , 42 (1987), 1-19.

15. *De Voluptate* , p. 279 (my emphasis). The insidious nature of pleasure and its discourses is emphasized by Rho. He understood the power of pleasure so that he underlines the need for it to be incorporated into Christianity:

    If in defending pleasure's side of the argument, Vegio thought that he not only should teach his hearers how great a pleasure is but also tried his hardest to delight and move them, so as to induce assent in our minds, is it not required by the worth of our, as I may say, dogma that this side of the argument should have its defender? (*De Voluptate* , p. 279)

16. For detailed discussions of Valla and his Christian views (plus bibliographical information) see Mario Fois S.I., *Il pensiero cristiano di Lorenzo Valla nel quadro storico-culturale del suo ambiente* (Rome: Università gregoriana, 1969); Di Napoli, *Lorenzo Valla* , pp. 221-37, 243-46; Maristella de Panizza Lorch, *A Defense of Life: Lorenzo Valla's Theory of Pleasure* (Munich: Fink, 1985).
    Physical pleasure is nowhere denied in Book III. Indeed, certain kinds are enhanced by Rho's discourse:

    How much pleasure there is, each time that we are restored and refreshed by shade or breeze during the hottest summer, or by a fire when we have been pinched and nipped by snow and wind. To my way of thinking this is the most gratifying of all the kinds of pleasure (*De Voluptate* , p. 301).

17. See, for example, Di Napoli, *Lorenzo Valla* , pp. 30-42.

18. Baldesar Castiglione, *Il libro del cortegiano*, ed. Bruno Maier (Turin: UTET, 1964), p. 537.

19. Numerous critics have commented upon the change of perspective initiated by the fourth book of the *Cortegiano* . We can mention here Wayne Rebhorn, "Ottaviano's interruption: Book IV and the problem of unity in *Il libro del Cortegiano* ", *MLN* , 87 (1972), 37-59 and Lawrence Ryan, "Book IV of Castiglione's *Courtier* - climax or afterthought?", *Studies in the Renaissance* , 19 (1972), 156-79.

20. See I. Rocchi, "Per una nuova cronologia e valutazione del *Libro de natura de amore* di Mario Equicola", *Giornale Storico della Letteratura Italiana* , 153 (1976), 566-85; Mario Pozzi, "Mario Equicola e la cultura italiana: appunti sulla redazione manoscritta del *Libro de natura de amore"* , *Lettere Italiane* , 32 (1980), 149-71; Maria Luisa Doglio, "Le *Instituzioni* di Mario Equicola: Dall'*Institutio Principis* alla formazione del segretario", *Giornale Storico della Letteratura Italiana* , 159 (1982), 505-35; Giorgio Bárberi Squarotti, "L'amante cortigiano" in *Idem*, *L'onore in corte. Dal Castiglione al Tasso* (Milan: Angeli, 1986), pp. 110-28; Stephen Kolsky, "'The good servant': Mario Equicola. Court and courtier in early sixteenth-century Italy", *The Italianist*, 6 (1986), 34-60.

21. All references are to the 1525 edition of the text published in Venice. Equicola argues that "l'homo in tutti soi effecti et actioni non pensare né operare altro che amar se stesso et di questo amare dicemo essere ultimo fine la voluptà" (f. 210^{v}). Thus, his basic definition of love refers to love of ourselves in the first instance and is his guiding philosophy.

22. In spite of such a declaration (f. 221^{r}) Equicola's discussion stresses the importance of physical concerns. Health is a major issue for the writer because it enables him and others to lead an enjoyable life:

> che per beneficio di essa sanità potemo usar longamente la voluptà de li sensi integramente et in piacere honestissimo con gloria et honore tradure la vita (f. 220^{r}).

It is noteworthy that Equicola sees no contradiction between the two propositions expressed in the sentence quoted above. Indeed, he can be quite cynical about those people who claim to live without pleasures, that is, refuting the courtly mode of existence.

His final comment "costui, secondo il mio parere, è ornato de divini doni" (f. 216^{v}) is certainly ironic. Equicola is most careful, in the sixth book, to show a slightly more moral side to court life, yet, at the same time, he is unwilling to denounce physical pleasures.

23. *Libro* , f. 221^{r}. This is a recurrent theme in the sixth book and Equicola does not hesitate to emphasize it:

> Non è cosa fuor di proposito respondere ad alcuni perfidi simulatori, li quali affermano impudentemente amarsi bella donna, né oltra il viso e audito loro desiderio extendersi (f. 214^{r}).

24. See Kolsky, " 'The good servant' ", pp. 54-55.

25. One can note the adaptation of Neoplatonic terminology to" the circumstances of the court. Equicola stresses the "taking" of what one is after "amata la desiderano, desiderata la sperano, sperata cercano haverla" (f. 214^{r}). The conquest of the beloved has a precise aim: "con desiderio usarla a nostro arbitrio con delectatione" (f. 222^{v}).

26. *Libro* , f. 209^{v}.

27. *The Epicurean* in *The Colloquies of Erasmus* , translated by Craig R. Thompson (Chicago and London: Chicago U.P., 1965), pp. 535-51.

28. Sir Thomas More, *Utopia* , translated by Robert M. Adams (New York: Norton, 1975), p. 60. See also Edward Surtz S.J., *The Praise of Pleasure . Philosophy, Education and Communism in More's "Utopia"* (Harvard U.P., 1957).

XV

MALE DESCRIPTIONS, FEMALE INSCRIPTIONS (*ORLANDO FURIOSO,* XLII, 73-96)

THE complexity of the issues concerning the women characters in the *Orlando furioso* is too well known to need illustration.[1] Any attempt at classifying women in the poem always has to take account of their diversity.[2] Yet, Ariosto's female constructs, in all their variety, do not exhaust the possibilities of the feminine in the *Orlando furioso.* For the poet introduces historical and contemporary women, often known to him personally. They are not characters in the same way as Angelica or Bradamante are, but are introduced for the express purpose of strengthening the encomiastic, dynastic and feminist themes of the poem. This note will examine one particular passage (XLII, 73-96) in order to ascertain the effects of male discourse on the representation of women in this part of the poem.

The passage under examination forms part of a larger episode which traces Rinaldo's departure from Carlomagno's camp until his tardy arrival in Lipadusa (XLII, 42-XLIII, 150). The journey marks an ironic return to the epic mode for this hero of the chivalric romance. He arrives in time only to bury Brandimarte, having missed the combat between the Christian and Moslem champions. Before his arrival on the island, the poem has sought to emphasize Rinaldo's

[1] For example, Robinson states, almost in desperation, that "woman's character, as it emerges from these references, is not subject to ready generalization" (115). See also, Günsberg 7-12 and Benson 138-53.

[2] Shemek addresses the problem of the variety of female representations in the poem in terms of "Ariosto's intervention in the *querelle des femmes*" (75). In this interpretation, the *Orlando furioso* surveys the many possible subject-positions available to women revealing "Ariosto's views concerning gender relations to be among the most complex and discerning of his time" (87).

newly won maturity, through the *nappo* episode and the boatman's tale.[3] Hence his status is enhanced in the latter stage of the poem much in the same way as Ruggiero's. In fact, both knights gain in standing through a cross-fertilization of their chivalric qualities: "e se d'un ventre fossero e d'un seme, / non si potriano amar più tutti insieme" (XLIV, 5, ll. 7-8). Rinaldo's association with the dynastic theme, the abjuration of his past passions and the emphasis on a virile maturity, render the paladin a suitable observer of the statues representing famous contemporary women (connected to the Estensi). Yet, at the same time, Rinaldo does not have a high opinion of women in general and of his wife in particular: "Mia donna è donna, et ogni donna è molle" (XLIII, 6, l. 5).

In spite of such reservations about Rinaldo's attitude toward women, the description of the statues appears to be a straightforward example of encomiastic poetry supporting the dynastic theme. However, I will argue that this description posits the necessity of male writing to inscribe women within its boundaries. The poet's writings are considered the essential element in any possible political alliance between the male writer and his female subjects. Indeed, the poet finds some justification for his role in court society by writing about the dynastic theme and especially the function of women in respect of the foundation of the House of Este.

These women are framed in stone; they take the form of monumental statues, part of the ornamentation of a fountain in the shape of a "loggia" or "padiglion" (XLII, 79, l. 3). The last-mentioned term anticipates the conclusion of the *Orlando furioso*: the place where Bradamante's and Ruggiero's marriage is consummated, the "genïal letto fecondo" (XLVI, 77, l. 1), is located "in mezzo un padiglione amplo e capace" (l. 2). Even if one takes into account the poem's pervasive irony, the reader cannot fail to notice that Ariosto emphasizes through Bradamante the crucial concept of union and submission to one's role in the dynastic order.[4] Although Bradamante still

[3] See the discussion by Santoro 140-51. DeSa Wiggins (33-37) emphasizes the irony of the *nappo* episode: "If the magic goblet episode portrays Rinaldo as prudent, it does not suggest that Ariosto held prudence in very high esteem" (36).

[4] Feinstein asserts that "all is subordinated to irony in Ariosto" and that Bradamante is no exception to this rule (56).

has a certain amount of power invested in her because of her detailed knowledge of the future progeny of the House of Este, from this point on she will be principally considered as the bearer of Estensi sons.

The negative implications of the passage under examination are further strengthened by examining it in the light of the declarations made in the *exordium* to canto XXXVII. Here, the poet implies that his position in the *querelle des femmes* is open, modern and 'supportive.' He criticizes "gli antiqui" (3, l. 7) for censuring the role of women in their writings and suggests indirectly that the modern poet would do no such thing. To support his claim Ariosto lists a number of contemporary writers (XXXVII, 8-13) who are positive about women. The poet does allow that women have begun writing for themselves. He, however, provides only one example (Vittoria Colonna) in contrast to the dense display of male names.

The statues themselves seem, at least on a superficial reading, to lend support to the poet's assertion made in the *exordium* in so far as women do have a place in the cultural system. The male sculptors are not identified, unlike the poets who have furnished the inscriptions, thereby suggesting the greater significance assigned to the word in defining women. The eight statues of women, all contemporaries of Ariosto, are not properly individualized. They are not the principal objects of Rinaldo's gaze. In fact, physical description is kept to a minimum, and as a consequence, the statues remain vague, almost invisible: "Son d'abito e di faccia differente . . . . / ma grazia hanno e beltà tutte ugualmente" (XLII, 80, ll. 6, 8).

One could hardly find a more generic and less interesting description of a group of statues than these two conventional lines. Far from being a simple example of *ekphrasis*[5] the text appears unwilling to permit the women to have an autonomous presence; therefore, this description might be termed *anti-ekphrasis*. In fact these statues of women are part of a larger structure. Each woman is supported by two men, who are both writers. Conceivably, these women are in a position of command, and assume the pose of conquerors. However, just the opposite appears to be true. Without the men, these women

[5] On Renaissance uses of *ekphrasis*, see Alpers 190-215, Shapiro 192-239 and Terpening 55-64.

would have no identity of their own, since they are literally and metaphorically supported by the male poets. The passage affirms the power of male discourse to inscribe women, to set limits on their fields of action, and, at the same time, to confirm the dignity of the *poeta.*

The first-mentioned woman is Lucrezia Borgia, Duchess of Ferrara: "La prima inscrizïon ch'agli occhi occorre, / con lungo onor Lucrezia Borgia noma" (XLII, 83, ll. 1-2). She is granted one specific attribute which informs her identity: namely, chastity, explicitly recalling her Roman namesake Lucretia, according to a most conventional procedure. Next, two poets are named, one more expert in vernacular poetry (Antonio Tebaldeo) and the other better known for his Latin verse (Ercole Strozzi). The insistence on both languages may be due more to Ariosto's concern with the linguistic registers of poetry, the discourses available to the poet, than to a desire to indicate that women are worthy subjects of Latin as well as Italian poetry.

The women that follow are treated in a similar fashion: Isabella d'Este, Elisabetta and Eleonora Gonzaga, Lucrezia, Diana and Beatrice d'Este. These high-born ladies represent the strength of the Northern Italian dynastic system, with a special focus on Ferrara and Mantua, and demonstrate the possibility of an alternative patronage network, ideally independent from male power-brokers, for poets who sought fame and material benefits from the court system. Nonetheless, the poets ensure the continuation of male values by emphasizing that the women are in no way independent. Lucrezia d'Este, for example, has one major claim to fame: ". . . fra le lode / pone di lei, che 'l duca di Ferrara / d'esserle padre si rallegra e gode" (XLII, 88, ll. 2-4). Thus, she is not praised for any special qualities she might have as a woman. The emphasis is placed upon the role she played in the power game of dynastic politics (her father Ercole I, Duke of Ferrara, married her off to Annibale Bentivoglio of Bologna).

Equally important, the sense of balance present in the stanza dedicated to Lucrezia Borgia (four lines on her qualities and four on the poets) has disappeared by the time Ariosto reaches Lucrezia d'Este. If four lines are enough to delineate her absence, twelve are hardly sufficient to declaim the skills of her two poets (Camillo Paleotti, the principal speaker on women in the *seconda redazione* of Castiglione's *Libro del cortegiano* and Guido Silvestri).

The passage in question (XLII, 88, ll. 5-8 - 89, ll. 1-8) also illustrates Ariosto's concern to be recognized as a poet with a certain command of the classical repertory. The result is that Lucrezia is soon left far behind as Ariosto searches for an appropriate Latinizing style. A similar procedure takes place in the description of the statue of Diana d'Este (90, ll. 1-4; her two poets take double the lines, 90, ll. 5-8 - 91, ll. 1-4). Even though one might argue that the two poets require double the space, nevertheless Ariosto obviously structured these descriptions in order to favor male discourse.

The pattern Ariosto has set up is disturbed by the description of the last woman, who is unnamed but, in all probability, can be identified as Alessandra Benucci, Ariosto's wife. The unnamed woman has only one poet to sing her praises "(non so perché)" [XLII, 95, l. 6], a poet to be identified as Ariosto himself. Auto-irony affects Ariosto's assessment of his abilities as a poet ("umil canto," 95, l. 3), Such irony might be extended to include a critique of those high-born women who have been praised by the other court poets. For the unknown woman is distinguished by her unadorned appearance, an implicit rejection of courtly dress: "senza oro e gemme, in un vestire schietto, / tra le più adorne non parea men bella" (93, ll. 6-7).

Furthermore, Ariosto may be implicitly rejecting the canon of encomiastic poetry and separating himself from other court poets who could not even begin to think of such a move. Thus, the descriptions are anchored in ambiguity and irony from which they cannot escape. The encomiastic mode may be unsatisfactory to Ariosto but it is an essential part of court society. It can, however, allow poets access to those circles in which they are able to practise their art. The limitations imposed on the poet find some relief in the games he can play within the genre – in this case, the introduction of Alessandra Benucci.

The passage I have analyzed is really more about poetry and poets than women. It does, however, through stressing the importance of male writing, tend to subordinate women to the concerns and preoccupations of men. The *locus* where the statues have been put on display creates further ambiguity and emphasizes their transitional status. The palace of Rinaldo's host is "di gran fabrica e bella e bene intesa; / né a privato uom convenia tanta spesa" (73, ll. 7-8). Yet the palace is a private place only made public by invitation of the host to a few chosen men. Thus, the statues are on male territory and are viewed by men; the discourse which describes them inscribes them in the dominant value system. At the same time, Ariosto uses encomiastic poetry to demonstrate its limitations and perhaps to suggest other ways of describing women. But throughout the voice is male.

Works Cited

Alpers, Svetlana. "Ekphrasis and Aesthetic Attitude in Vasari's *Lives.*" *Journal of the Warburg and Courtauld Institutes* 23 (1960): 190-215.

Benson, Pamela. "A Defense of the Excellence of Bradamante." *Quaderni d'Italianistica* 3-4 (1982-83): 138-53.

DeSa Wiggins, Peter. *Figures in Ariosto's Tapestry: Character and Design in the "Orlando Furioso."* Baltimore: Johns Hopkins University Press, 1986. 17-40.

Feinstein, Wiley. "Bradamante in Love: Some Postfeminist Considerations on Ariosto." *Forum Italicum* 22 (1988): 48-59.

Günsberg, Maggie. "'Donna Liberata'? The Portrayal of Women in the Italian Renaissance Epic." *The Italianist* 7 (1987): 7-35.

Robinson, Lilian S. *Monstrous Regiment. The Lady Knight in Sixteenth-Century Epic.* New York and London: Garland, 1985. 114-90.

Santoro, Mario. *L'Anello di Angelica: Nuovi Saggi Ariosteschi.* Napoli: Federico & Ardia, 1983. 133-52.

Shapiro, Marianne. *The Poetics of Ariosto.* Detroit: Wayne State University Press, 1988. 192-239.

Shemek, Deanna. "Of Women, Knights, Arms and Love: The *Querelle des Femmes* in Ariosto's Poem." *Modern Language Notes* 104 (1989): 68-97.

Terpening, Ronnie H. "Poliziano's Treatment of a Classical Topos: *Ekphrasis,* Portal to the *Stanze.*" *Italian Quarterly* 17 (1973): 39-71.

XVI

Men Framing Women: *Sabadino degli Arienti's Gynevera de le clare donne* Reexamined

For men to write about women in the fifteenth and early sixteenth centuries involved a complex series of choices. At its most pragmatic level it meant evaluating the possibilities of advancement offered by a woman-oriented text. Writing for and about women presupposed that the female presence at court participated in and initiated patronage networks. Court women were perceived as alternative sources of patronage by writers, in particular by poets who performed their own work. Other intellectuals wrote theoretical "treatises" on women, usually with the express aim of winning patronage from a high-ranking lady. As shall be seen in Sabadino degli Arienti's case, a text of this type easily could have a dual function: both to encourage the more powerful female figures at court to act separately from their husbands and to pay indirect homage to the male partner for having so exemplary a wife. Most writers were not totally committed to the female patron; the treatise on women was often just one work among several on diverse subjects usually of more interest to the prince.

Another factor that needs to be taken into account is that the profemale treatise was relatively easy to write; preparation could be kept to a minimum.[1] This was because there already existed a model that fulfilled the requirements, providing an illustrious literary precedent: Boccaccio's *De mulieribus claris.*[2] It is perhaps

1. It is clear that many writers just borrowed numerous *exempla* from other writings without any clear intellectual structure. See Kolsky 1990 (especially 47–49).

2. *De mulieribus claris,* edited by Vittorio Zaccaria, is in vol. X of Boccaccio (1970). It has been translated into English by Guido A. Guarino (Boccaccio 1964). All the translations in this paper are my own. See also Torretta (1902–1903).

too tempting to consider the choice of this text rather cynically – as the manipulation of an archetype for purposes for which it was not originally intended. The composition of *De mulieribus claris* was partly an exercise in erudition, a learned compendium of famous women along humanist lines. It undoubtedly had an ideological aim, namely that of making possible a comparison between men (who already had their *De viris illustribus*) and women, to the disadvantage of the latter. It would seem that the idea of dedicating the work to a lady was an afterthought: "I realized that since the work spoke about women, it should not be dedicated to an important man but to a famous woman" [adverteremque satis non principi viro, sed potius, cum de mulieribus loqueretur, alicui insigni femine destinandum fore] (*De mulieribus*, 18). Accordingly, on completing *De mulieribus*, Boccaccio dedicated it to Andrea Acciaiuoli, after considering dedicating it to Giovanna I, Queen of Naples.[3] But the dedication is somewhat misleading, since the work does not lend itself very easily to the interpretation presented by Boccaccio in the pages to Andrea Acciaiuoli. Indeed, it has been argued that the treatise could be regarded as a virulent antifemale tract (Jordan 1987).

Later writers did not, in fact, follow Boccaccio's example mindlessly. *De mulieribus claris* offered, above all, a model for structuring a discourse on women that avoided extensive discursive writing. It left hardly any room for generalized comments or entry into the long-standing debate over women's position in society. It favored narrative discourse over more "committed" forms; often the entries under separate women are no more than novellas with an obvious moralistic point.[4]

3. Boccaccio states in the dedication that he originally intended offering the work to "Giovanna, most serene Queen of Jerusalem and Sicily" [Iohanna, serenissima Ierusalem et Sicilie regina] (18) but he changed his mind: "Fearing the lesser light might be completely eclipsed by the greater, I gradually changed my mind" [Timens ne a potiori lumine minor omnino fugaretur in tenebras, sensim retraxi consilium] (18).

4. Boccaccio is always more than ready to criticize the behavior of the women he describes, even if sometimes he is willing to acknowledge their more positive aspects. For example, his entry on Europa, Queen of Crete, contains the following comment after recounting how she was left alone tending her father's flock:

> Vagari licentia nimia virginibus et aures facile cuiuscunque verbis prebere, minime laudandum reor, cum contigisse sepe legerim his agentibus honestati non nunquam notas turpes imprimi, quas etiam perpetue demum castitatis decus abstersisse non potuit. (*De mulieribus*, 60)
>
> [I deplore the fact that young women are allowed to go as they please and listen to anyone's words because I have often read that precisely for these reasons their reputation is shamefully stained so that not even the honor of perpetual chastity can cancel the dishonor.]

Furthermore, the schema of individual biographies imposes a rigid formula on the enunciations. Women are not discussed as a group having specific social desires. They are instead represented as isolated social beings who have a personal story to tell; even if they have a historical dimension, women in *De mulieribus claris* seem to be fictitious.

The Boccaccian archetype expressly avoids, whenever possible, the problematic issue of women in Christianity. There are no saints or female martyrs and very few biblical figures of primary importance in *De muleribus claris.* It might be argued that Boccaccio wished to avoid difficulties with the religious authorities. Even so, he is asserting clearly, albeit indirectly, the power of the secular, perhaps creating a lay version of sacred hagiography, which would also explain why court writers were attracted to the text.

The court writer also would have perceived the possibilities for *encomium* inherent in the structure of the text. In the first place, contemporary (or near-contemporary) women might substitute the heroines of myth and early history and, in the process, they would be enhanced by implicit reference to the great women of the (mythical) past. Second, the composition of a court version of *De mulieribus claris* would demonstrate the power of male writing to structure female lives; male writing encoded the values by which a woman's existence was to be framed. What is more, these values implied a series of judgements about female behavior that inevitably were mediated by the male voice. Reputation and fame were dispensed with the aim of increasing the prestige of both writer and lady.

It is all too easy to dismiss such writings as examples of courtly adulation resulting in mediocre texts, or "copies." It will be argued here that, apart from implications regarding the way women are viewed in court society, the treatise to be examined represents an interesting case study in the substantial variations that can occur within a specific literary genre.

The work to be considered is *Gynevera de le clare donne* by Sabadino degli Arienti, written in 1490 (Arienti [1969]).[5] It is dedicated to Ginevra Sforza, wife of Giovanni II Bentivoglio, ruler of Bologna.[6] There seems nothing untoward in all this, given the courtly ethos of Sabadino. Nor is there anything

5. For Arienti's biography see the entry by Ghino Ghinassi (1962) in *Dizionario biografico degli italiani,* which also has a useful bibliography.
6. The standard history of Bentivoglio Bologna is Ady (1937).

exceptional in his reference to Ginevra's husband on the second page of the manuscript: "Tu sei ad contento del Bolognese populo copulata al più felice Cavaliero del mondo, Joanne Bentivoglio secundo, strenuo in arme [. . .] et Senatore perpetuo, primo de tanta illustre città" [To the joy of the Bolognese people you are joined in marriage to the happiest knight in the world, Giovanni II Bentivoglio, skilled in arms [. . .] and Senator for life, first citizen of such an illustrious city] (*Gynevera*, 2–3).

So courtly and conventional is the passage that it appears to require no further comment except that two years earlier Sabadino had compiled an anthology of poetry that can be seen to support a minor branch of the Bentivoglio and even persons indirectly associated with the Malvezzi conspiracy against Giovanni II (1488).[7] It seems that Sabadino was beginning to rethink his political choices in the two years between the conspiracy and his writing the *Gynevera*. Although he had not yet completely abandoned the line represented by his longtime employer Andrea Bentivoglio, a member of the senatorial branch of the family, he was expressing a political openness or awareness that eventually led him into the service of the Estensi at Ferrara. The *Gynevera* represents an attempt to come to terms with mainstream Bentivoglio politics in the aftermath of the Malvezzi conspiracy and, at the same time, to challenge them by offering a subtle revision of the dominant power ideology.[8]

The composition of the *Gynevera* also might be viewed as the work of someone wishing to demonstrate his credentials in the aftermath of the Malvezzi conspiracy while confirming his continuing allegiance to the principal branch of the Bentivoglio family. It may have been with some regret that Arienti felt compelled to submit more completely than before to the dictates of signorial power politics.

The senatorial branch of the Bentivoglio clan could no longer offer him the guarantee of a livelihood. Arienti looks at the possibilities of exploiting the network of ruling families in

7. For the Malvezzi conspiracy see Ady (1937: 103–10). The anthology is discussed by Vecchi Galli (1984).

8. Arienti was associated for twenty years with the senatorial branch of the Bentivoglio as Andrea Bentivoglio's secretary (1471 to 1491, the year of Andrea's death). He also composed a biography of his employer, *Vita del conte e senatore Andrea Bentivoglio* (Arienti 1840; see also Ambrosini 1909). A passing reference to the cultural divergences between the two branches is found in De Benedictis (1984: 28–29). It is, thus, not altogether surprising that Arienti began making overtures to Ercole I, Duke of Ferrara in the period immediately following Andrea Bentivoglio's death.

northern and central Italy, and the theme of dynastic alliances is associated here with Ginevra herself in the role of childbearer: "You have also had from such a husband, glorious Madam, angelic bearer of sixteen children" [Hai anchora havuto de tanto marito, gloriosa Madonna, angelica sobole de sexdeci figliuoli] (*Gynevera,* 4). Her children are then enumerated and usually the only detail given is whom they married:

> [C]um molta gloria et triumpho de tuta la cità nostra, matrimonialmente [ottavo figliuolo Hannibal secundo] se congiunse cum Lucretia, savia figliuola dell'alto Duca Hercule Estense, come difusamente habiamo scripto ne l'opera de lo *Hymeneo.* (*Gynevera,* 5)

> [To the great glory and triumph of all our city [Annibale II, the eighth son] was married to Lucrezia, the high-minded daughter of the noble Duke Ercole d'Este, as we have written at length in our work the *Hymeneo.*]

The reference to the marriage alliance and to his own work that celebrates it is politically expedient: the wedding marked Giovanni II's coming of age as the "ruler" of a state worthy to enter into matrimonial alliances with its neighbors and capable of putting on magnificent displays equal to those of other northern Italian courts. Arienti's recalling the *Hymeneo* serves to underline his loyalty to the signorial regime. In all this description of political alliances, Ginevra appears almost irrelevant; even the fact of childbirth is passed over in favor of her husband's capacity to produce politically useful children:

> La natività de quisti toi figlioli, certo non è manco presso noi iocunda per loro futura alteza, et augumento del felice nome Bentivoglio. (*Gynevera,* 6)

> [The birth of your children is indeed no less joyful for us because of their future greatness and of the increased prestige of the happy Bentivoglio name.]

The marriages are clearly part of Giovanni II's policy of finding allies in northern and central Italy. Thus, language becomes rhetoric used expediently to represent the Bentivoglio as part of a dynastic system, hence increasing its prestige.

It will be immediately apparent that the *Gynevera* has aims other than the praise of women. Indeed, it would not be hard to think that women are a secondary concern, given that the *Gynevera* gives priority to other discourses, principally the political discourse.

Yet Arienti's innovations with regard to the Boccaccian archetype should not be underestimated. First of all, Arienti's women are relatively recent and do not include any mythical or classical figures. Nor are there to be found many women of humble birth. Perhaps sensitive to such a radical change and the consequences it may have had for the status of his women, Arienti introduces parallels between the modern *exempla* and Boccaccio's women. For example, he quite often employs a formula of this type:

> [N]on haverebbe [Arienti's wife] perdonata a faticha nè a spesa, secundo le sue force, de honorare el mio terreo corpo di exequio et de sepulcro, et non cum manco amore che facesse Artamixia regina, moglie de Mausolo re de Caria. (*Gynevera*, 362)
>
> [She (Arienti's wife) would not have spared energy nor expense, as much as her resources would have allowed her, in honoring my earthly body with exequies and burial, with no less love than that displayed by Queen Artemisia, wife of Mausolus, King of Caria.]

The comparison clearly defines Arienti's ideological position. He insists on traditional virtues and structures within which he inscribes his discourse on women. Not surprisingly, the reference to Artemisia has its source in Boccaccio's *De mulieribus claris.* Thus, even in the case of his own wife Arienti was intent on creating a mythic dimension to lend her and other modern women a certain prestige, a literary pedigree and, by so doing, he sought to render Bolognese history more "universal" and in a particular sense, "grander." In *De mulieribus claris,* "Maria Puteolana bellatrice [the warrior]" is compared to Penthesilea, Queen of the Amazons (XXXII), Francesca Venusta to Busa [Paolina] (LXIX), Joan of Arc to Camilla (XXXIX), Isabella of Aragon to Veturia, mother of Coriolanus (LV) and so on.

Arienti's treatment of the biography of "Maria Puteolana" has considerable interest in the context of the *Gynevera.* Its ideological perspective would seem to place it in conflict with the dominant view of women as peacemakers. It may be that Arienti felt obliged to insert such figures for the sake of balance or through a sense of loyalty to his Boccaccian model. A collection of female lives may have seemed incomplete without the Amazons. Arienti specifies the fundamental notions that constitute the warrior-woman, at odds with those activities traditionally associated with women in contemporary society:

Non era data al tessere, a la rocha, all'aco, al fuso, nè al spechio, ma a l'arco, a la faretra, al dardo et tuta a l'arme. (*Gynevera*, 53)

[She was not interested in weaving, not in the bobbin, spindle or wheel nor in looking at herself in the mirror but her passion was weapons, the bow, quiver, arrow.]

The writer ensures that he "normalizes" her central activity in order to make other activities appear more grotesque:

Costei non era nobilitata de lascivi baci et de abraciamenti de gli homini, ma illustrata de cicatrice aquisite ne le bataglie. (*Gynevera*, 53)

[She did not seek nobility in lascivious kisses and embraces with men but was famous for the scars acquired in battle.]

She is represented as an asexual being, secure in her virginity. She is also the object of the male gaze as a kind of circus freak; for example, Arienti notes that "Robert, that most contented king of Sicily, renowned for his glorious virtue, did not refuse to go and see this brave woman" [Roberto felicissimo de Sicilia, come re de gloriosa virtute, non sdegnò andare ad vedere questa valorosa donna] (*Gynevera*, 55).

By contrast, the woman he next deals with (Francesca Venusta) is outstanding for her beauty: "[S]he was subjected to the stare of young men and had to fight other lascivious battles" [Fu molto combatuta da gli occhij de'giovani et da altre lascive battaglie] (*Gynevera*, 59). She does not take part in battles but spurs captains on to greater deeds in defense of Bologna, signing a letter to the captain of the Bolognese army "tua devota feminella" [your devoted little woman] (*Gynevera*, 62). The central narrative only indirectly involves the female "protagonist" who, indeed, becomes a pretext for Arienti to indulge in nostalgia for the lost civic virtues of Bologna:

[M]e doglio che li nostri primarij citadini de la republica patri circunscripti, che non sono curiosi conservare lo exemplo de le glorie de loro passati per reputatione de la nostra cità, et per acendere li posteri ad simile, overo a magior glorie. (*Gynevera*, 63–64)

[I am saddened by our leading citizens of the republic, shortsighted fathers, who are not interested in conserving the example of their ancestors' glorious deeds for the fame of our city and in order to inspire their descendants to similar or even greater glories.]

It is this declaration and the confirmation of an idealized past by Arienti that form the nucleus of the chapter. Perhaps because of the neglect of his female subject the writer institutes the parallel between Francesca Venusta and the Boccaccian Busa. The latter is treated positively in the *De mulieribus claris*, principally because she is represented exclusively in the well-defined role of mother: "She had the wounded treated with maternal love" [Vulneratos materna affectione curari fecit] (*De mulieribus*, 274). The implications are multiple for Arienti's text. Firstly, there is the connection between Republican Rome and Republican Bologna, and second, these political ideals inscribe women in a subordinate role. They constrain her to work for the state, matching male virtues with female ones (motherliness, chastity, virginity, and so on). Undoubtedly, the woman is involved in politics and in public events, but in no way does she set the political agenda. In fact, she becomes an image of a particular social regime preferred by the writer. Caterina Visconti, for example, has the courage and intelligence to save the Duchy of Milan – for her male progeny.[9]

Another way in which Arienti seeks to circumscribe his female subjects is to make them the object of male discourse on sexuality. He deals only with specific categories of women: virgins, wives, and widows. The latter play a particularly prominent role in the *Gynevera*, maybe as a result of the civil strife that is a backdrop to many of the narratives in the work; the husbands are frequently killed in factional disputes or in large-scale wars (Herlihy 1985). There are also demographic factors to take into account, such as the age at which men got married. It also has been suggested that "getting married empowered women in the princely courts of northern Italy" and the influential presence of married women is hence reflected in a text such as the *Gynevera* (see Ward Swain 1986: 194). The implications of this hypothesis become apparent on careful reading of some of the biographies in the text.

Arienti's narrative account of "Diana Saliceta di Bentivoglii" provides a convenient starting point. Diana Bentivoglio is "a woman made resplendent by noble lineage and virtue" [una donna fulvida de famoso sangue et de virtute] (*Gynevera*, 327), with nobility and virtue being interchangeable terms. The following analysis is not intended to be a discussion of the histori-

9. It is perhaps ironic that her eldest son for whom she made so many sacrifices turned out to be a terrible tyrant over whom the mother had no control. She could only reproach him with her tears and words, obviously to no avail (*Gynevera*, 78).

cal reality of this woman but is rather an examination of how she is inscribed ideologically in the text.

What seems to interest Arienti is the relationship between power and women, when the latter, that is, have the opportunity to influence society. In order to be acceptable to the male-constructed institutions of power, such women must be chaste and accept absolutely the constraints of marriage on female sexuality:

> Fu sempre honestissima ne le sue parole, le quale mai lasive se poterono existimare. Fu pudicissima et castissima et de l'honore et gratia del caro marito fu sopra tutte le cose del mondo observatrice. (*Gynevera,* 329)
>
> [Her speech was always honorable and nothing indecent was ever uttered by her. She was most modest and chaste and, above anything else in the world, she maintained the honor and favor of her dear husband.]

The conventionality of Arienti's position is indisputable, but perhaps it would be pertinent to add that Moderata Fonte, writing on *Il merito delle donne* toward the end of the sixteenth century, maintains that chastity is essential to a woman's sense of self since, by necessity, it is unique to women (Moderata Fonte 1988: 14, 52–55). It is not a coincidence that Arienti is himself the author of a tract, known as the *Trattato di pudicizia,* written for his late wife's sister some years before the *Gynevera.*[10] It is interesting to note that in the *Trattato* Arienti includes chastity among those "virtues of moral and political life" [virtute del morale e politico vivere] (f.3v) that have a positive influence on "this inconstant world, full of deceits, avarice, and betrayals" [questo mondo instabile pieno de inganni, avaricia e tradimenti] (f.4r).[11] Thus, Arienti stresses the political value of chastity as cementing social institutions. Failure to adhere to its dictates leads to social chaos and disorder:

> Di che molte volte ne segue incendii, morte, rapine et ruine de le famiglie e de le republiche et damnatione eterna de l'anime. (*Trattato,* f.5v)
>
> [From which many times there result burnings, deaths, pillaging and ruin of families and republics and eternal damnation of souls.]

10. See Chandler (1954), 110–13. The manuscript I have used is Bodleian Library, Oxford, Broxbourne ms. 85.7 (undated).

11. In this method of manuscript citation, f means folio (manuscript page), v means verso (back side of page), and r means recto (front side of page).

It is, however, understood that most women do not possess the qualities of a heroine and are overwhelmed by their own sexuality. Thus, it is only a political and moral elite who manage to overcome the inherent "defects" in female nature. The implication is that women have to struggle against their own nature in order to ensure that their behavior conforms to the norms imposed by men. It would no doubt be easy to criticize Arienti's stance for the way his key concepts control female behavior and relegate the majority of women to obscurity, only bringing to light a few carefully selected examples that do not have a great impact on social institutions. These presuppositions are behind the more important biographies of the *Gynevera de le clare donne*, the biography of Diana Bentivoglio being no exception.

She was, in all respects, a model wife: loving to her husband, producer of male offspring, "careful at all times and in all circumstances" [misurata in ogni tempo et fortuna] (*Gynevera*, 329). She also knew how to manage family affairs properly; she is indirectly praised for her skill in looking after her husband's property, guarding against "senseless profligacy" [disordinato consumamento] (330).

It becomes apparent that Arienti is gendering political ideologies. "Discreta misura" (330) – a feminine quality in this case – implies a particular social system based on civic values originating in an oligarchic view of city government. Magnificence, that is, conspicuous consumption, an increasing part of mainstream Bentivoglio politics, is implicitly criticized through Diana Bentivoglio's thrift:

> [Q]uesta prudentissima Diana gubernò la grande sua famiglia cum splendore, prudentia et misura, priva de cupidità et avaricia; et non solamente de le substantie de la casa fu salvatrice et dispensatrice, ma quelle augumentò cum le proprie mane et ingegno, de egregii ornamenti. (*Gynevera*, 330–31)

> [This most prudent Diana governed her great family with splendor, care and discretion, free from cupidity and avarice; and not only did she protect and distribute the wealth of the family but she greatly increased it with her own hands and intelligence.]

Her achievement lies in her ability to unify the extended family of which she is an integral part:

> [I]nfra marito, cognati, fratelli, figliuoli, nepoti, consobrini, nore, famigli, serve, et il concorso de la visitatione de' parenti et de li

amici, che per virtù de tanta donna dire pur possiamo, una minima parola discrepante de la pace et unione se sentisse già mai. (*Gynevera*, 331)

[From her husband, brothers-in-law, brothers, sons, nephews, cousins, daughters-in-law, familiars, servants, and the great rush of visiting relatives and friends, we can even say that, through the offices of such a woman, never was there heard a single word that contradicted the peace and union of the family.]

It is the description of a patronage network, with a woman at its center, extending outward from the nuclear family to include finally all supporters of the clan. Arienti goes much further than this. Diana Bentivoglio is metamorphosed into a Circe-like figure, having power over the domestic animals – "the dogs do not howl" [né li molti cani ululavano] (331) and so on – all because they are "happy at such a union" [lieti de tanta unione] (331).

The Bentivoglio even have at this time the approval of Pope Pius II who called the family "most holy" [sanctissima] (331). Although there may be an unintentional comic effect, the discourse is central to Arienti's vision of a tranquil Bologna and perhaps to his perception of the function of women in society:

Non è questa beata virtù in costei dignissima de memoria, casone de tanta unione et pace, che siano state le memorande opere in le grande fortune de l'alte donne? Certo sì. (*Gynevera*, 331)

[Is not this blessed virtue of hers most worthy to be remembered, the reason for such harmony and peace in the same way as those memorable deeds performed by noble women in moments of importance? Certainly they are.]

"Questa beata virtù" does not receive a full definition; it remains rather vague. Yet, it can be said to be an amalgam of the wifely virtues and, in addition, there is the unstated *dictum* that women, as homemakers, are biologically peaceful and tranquil. Arienti is suggesting that certain women have a specific political role to perform.

However, it is legitimate to ask at this point whether women are merely being used by Arienti to fulfill his own desired political ends; in other words, are they merely instruments for a higher political goal? Do women benefit at all? The most obvious answer would be that Arienti's female constructions are just that – constructions to fill a political need. The writer makes a point, however, of showing some of these women actively helping their less fortunate sisters (though charity was a traditional part of some women's duties). Discussing Ippolita Sforza, Arienti writes:

> Havea compassione a quelle misere donne che non se conservavano in pudica fama; le amoniva cum sancto modo Li rancori et le discordie che infra li suoi sentiva, levava via, reducendoli ad benivolentia et a pace. (*Gynevera*, 340)
>
> [She felt compassion for those poor women who had not preserved a reputation for modesty; she would religiously reprove them. [. . .] She settled grudges and disputes that occurred among members of her family, bringing about good will and peace among them.]

Ippolita Sforza was extremely generous to men and women alike, "she gave generously to charity" [era elemosinatrice molto] (341). Both Diana Bentivoglio and Ippolita Sforza can be seen as alternative responses to the dominant power politics that held sway over Bologna and, indeed, over the rest of the peninsula. It is paradoxical that the confirmation of traditional female values and roles can lead to a revision of [male] power politics perceived in a negative light. Thus, it is extremely hazardous to label such a text either reactionary or progressive, though undoubtedly it has elements of both in unequal measure.

Arienti in the *Gynevera* was looking back to a golden age where the "tranquil life" [quiete vivere] (260) was attainable through adherence to norms that had become "old-fashioned." The women he discussed are all exceptional. They have managed to overcome the deficiencies of their sex in contrast to most women who, according to Arienti, are in no position to leave their mark on society:

> La quale virtute et magnificentia tanto la dobiamo più lampegiante iudicare, *quanto rara in donne se vede*, perché la tenacità et avaritia non solo gli è famigliare, *ma innata e de propria natura cum el picolo animo.* (*Gynevera*, 162; emphasis added)
>
> [We have to judge her virtue and magnificence the more startling as it is rarely seen in a woman, because stinginess and avarice are not only common in them, but innate and part of their nature together with a small soul.]

Arienti believes implicitly in the natural weakness and shortcomings of women.[12] Hence he is able to separate the exceptional women from the unexceptional, held in low esteem by

12. The ultimate source is Aristotle; see Cline Horowitz (1976).

him. These relatively few heroic women are able to cast aside their "femaleness" and come closer to the ideal of men active in public life. Arienti is especially interested in that moment of crisis when certain women are able to extend their sphere of action: "At least you did not consume your years by the fire with the bobbin, wheel, reel and frame, speaking ill of your neighbor" [Che almeno non consumasti li tuoi anni [Cleofe di Lapi] intorno al fuoco cum la rocha, fuso, naspa et arcolaio dicendo male del proximo] (*Gynevera*, 138). They go beyond their female selves ("oltra misura del sexo muliebre," 265), but only in certain conditions.

The women, in fact, are often lost from sight in the narratives, as Arienti seems more interested in writing about general political issues. To participate in the political processes women have to observe certain rules. Most important, they have to demonstrate their total support for the institutions of marriage, virginity, chastity, and widowhood. In other words, such values are considered the backbone of civic society, without which political regimes go to ruin. One might interpret Arienti's insistence on these values as an attempt to return to a more traditional way of life, an indirect attack on the politics of *magnificentia* as practiced by northern Italian rulers in the late fifteenth century. This conservative vision of the city-state emphasizes the "honest pomp" [honesta pompa] (154), the "great frugality" [molta parsimonia] (159), and, in general, the Christian faith of the women discussed in the *Gynevera*. A Queen of Scotland provides Arienti with the opportunity to perorate on contemporary mores:

> Non fece lei, come molte fano, che postergandose l'honestate et il timore divino, per obtemperare a le loro disordinate lasivie, inquinano il sacro matrimonio; quale in summa reverentia se debbe havere, essendo da l'omnipotente Dio ordinato. (*Gynevera*, 315–16)
>
> [She did not, as many women do, poison holy matrimony by neglecting her chastity and fear of God in order to give rein to their disordered lust. Holy matrimony must be held in the greatest respect since it was commanded by the omnipotent God.]

It is implied that obedience to one's husband further strengthens the possibility of political power for women, in that matrimonial harmony can become an extended metaphor for social harmony. The woman, then, is regarded as the repository for values long since abandoned by men who often lack the virtue of *temperantia*, that is, "moderation and balance." They are dispensers of justice and clemency. It is perhaps precisely in the contradictions of the text, with its conservatism becoming a motivating force to change society, that Arienti's ambiguous female figure emerges.

BIBLIOGRAPHY

ADY, Cecilia M. (1937) *The Bentivoglio of Bologna. A study in Despotism.* Oxford: Oxford University Press.

AMBROSINI, R. (1909) *Un codice autografo di Giovanni Sabadino degli Arienti.* Bologna: Zanichelli.

ARIENTI, Joanne Sabadino de li (1840) *Vita del conte e senatore Andrea Bentivoglio*, ed. G. Giordani. Bologna: Tipi della Volpe.

___ (1969) *Gynevera de le clare donne*, ed. C. Ricci and A. Bacchi Della Lega. (*Scelta di curiosità letterarie inedite o rare*, vol. LXXXIV, dispensa CCXXIII.) Bologna: Commissione per i testi di lingua. Original edition, Bologna: Gaetano Romagnoli, 1887.

___ (undated) *Trattato di pudicizia.* Bodleian Library, Oxford: Broxbourne ms. 85.7.

BASILE, Bruno (ed.) (1984) *Bentivolorum Magnificentia.* Rome: Bulzoni.

BOCCACCIO, Giovanni (1970) *De mulieribus claris* in *Tutte le opere di Giovanni Boccaccio*, vol. X, ed. Vittorio Zaccaria. Milan: Mondadori.

CHANDLER, S. B. (1954) "Il *Trattato della pudicizia* di Sabadino degli Arienti." *La Bibliofilia* 56: 110–13.

CLINE HOROWITZ, Maryanne (1976) "Aristotle and Women." *Journal of the History of Biology* 9: 183–213.

DE BENEDICTIS, Angela (1984) "Quale 'corte' per quale 'signoria'?" In B. Basile (ed.) *Bentivolorum Magnificentia.* Rome: Bulzoni: 13–33.

FONTE, MODERATA (1988) *Il merito delle donne*, ed. Adriana Chemello. Venice: Eidos.

GHINASSI, Ghino (1962) "Arienti, Giovanni Sabadino degli." *Dizionario bibliografico degli italiani*, vol. 4. Rome: Istituto dell'Enciclopedia Italiana: 154–56.

GUARINO, Giudo A. (1964) *Concerning Famous Women.* (Translation of Giovanni Boccaccio's *De mulieribus claris*), London: Allen and Unwin.

HERLIHY, David (1985) "Did Women Have a Renaissance?: A Reconsideration." *Medievalia et Humanistica* (n.s.) 13: 1–22.

JORDAN, Constance (1987) "Boccaccio's In-famous Women: Gender and Civic Virtue in *De mulieribus claris.*" In C. Levin and J. Watson (eds.) *Ambiguous Realities.* Detroit: Wayne State University Press: 25–47.

KOLSKY, Stephen (1990) "Women through Men's Eyes: The Third Book of *Il Cortegiano.*" In Tom O'Neill (ed.) *Shared Horizons.* Dublin: Irish Academic Press: 41–91.

SWAIN WARD, Elisabeth (1986) " 'My Excellent and Most Singular Lord': Marriage in a Noble Family of Fifteenth-Century Italy." *Journal of Medieval and Renaissance Studies* 16: 171–95.

TORRETTA, Laura (1902–1903) "Il *Liber de claris mulieribus* di Giovanni Boccaccio." *Giornale Storica della Letteratura Italiana* 39 (1902): 252–92; 40 (1903): 35–65.

VECCHI GALLI, Paola (1984) " Il Ms. 165 della Biblioteca Universitaria di Bologna (con inediti di Sabadino degli Arienti)." In Bruno Basile (ed.) *Bentivolorum Magnificentia.* Rome: Bulzoni: 223–53.

BIBLIOGRAPHY

INDEX